READINGS IN APPLIED
TRANSFORMATIONAL
GRAMMAR

READINGS IN APPLIED TRANSFORMATIONAL GRAMMAR

Second Edition

Mark Lester

University of Hawaii

HOLT, RINEHART AND WINSTON, INC.
New York   Chicago   San Francisco   Atlanta
Dallas   Montreal   Toronto   London   Sydney

Copyright © 1970, 1973 by Holt, Rinehart and Winston, Inc.
All rights reserved
Library of Congress Catalog Card Number: 72–10306
ISBN: 0-03-091251-2
Printed in the United States of America
3456   090   987654321

PREFACE

The essays in this anthology deal with aspects of transformational grammar and the closely related field of psycholinguistics. They were written by leading scholars in their fields, and were intended for non-technical audiences. The anthology is divided into two parts: The essays in Part I cover psycholinguistic topics, while those in Part II deal with the applications of transformational grammar and psycholinguistics to the fields of literature, composition, second-language teaching, reading, and English language and education.

In the revision of an anthology, the great problem is not so much what articles to add, but what to eliminate. In this second edition, six essays have been dropped from the first edition. In general, I have deleted those that have been superseded by a more recent one in the same field by the same author (as is the case, for example, with Lenneberg's "On Explaining Language"), or when there has been a considerable advancement in the field (as, for example, in the section on reading).

Seven new articles by six new authors have been added in this edition: those by Krech and Lenneberg in Part I, by Spolsky and Carol Chomsky in the section on second-language teaching, both selections in the section on reading, and the article in the new section on English language and education.

With the exception of several essays that contain their own introduction and summary, each essay is preceded by an introduction that attempts to paraphrase the main ideas and arguments of the essay. Many of the essays in Part I are followed by notes explaining technical points. Most of the essays assume some prior knowledge of transformational grammar. If a reader is totally uninitiated into the mysteries of transformational grammar, he would be well advised to begin with Kellogg W. Hunt's article "How Little Sentences Grow into Big Ones" (p. 162), which contains a brief overview of how the syntactic component of a transformational grammar works.

I would like to thank Dr. Theodore Rodgers for calling several of the new articles to my attention.

M. L.

Honolulu, Hawaii
November 1972

CONTENTS

READINGS IN APPLIED
TRANSFORMATIONAL
GRAMMAR

PART I

The Psycholinguistic
Background

DAVID KRECH

Psychoneurobiochemeducation

INTRODUCTION

Professor Krech is interested in the chemistry of the brain, especially the physical and chemical basis of memory. That memory has a chemical basis is supported by such findings as (1) certain chemicals facilitate the conversion of short-term memory into long-term memory, (2) this conversion can be impeded by other chemicals, and (3) there is evidence for the transfer of the memories of one animal into a second animal by injecting the second animal with material extracted from the brain of the first. If the laying down of memories has a chemical basis, then

> one should find that an animal which has lived a life replete with opportunities for learning and memorizing would end with a brain chemically and morphologically different from an animal which has lived out an intellectually impoverished life.

David Krech: "Psychoneurobiochemeducation," *California Monthly*, Vol. LXXIX, No. 7 (June–July 1969), pp. 14–20. Reprinted by permission of the author and *California Monthly*.

Krech and his colleagues discovered that rats reared in a rich environment (toys, other rats, space to move in, music, even graduate assistants to play with) did indeed have brains chemically and morphologically different from the brains of deprived rats. The next question that Krech and his colleagues attacked was to discover just which element in the rat's enriched environment actually caused the enrichment of his brain. It turned out that a single element—the rat's freedom to explore space—was the critical factor. The other elements seemed to have little impact on the rat's brain. Krech concludes that this factor of space is species-specific to the rat.

> To generalize this hypothesis, I would suggest that *for each species there exists a set of species-specific experiences which are maximally enriching and which are maximally efficient in developing its brain.*

Krech then speculates about what it is that provides the species-specific experiences necessary for the development of the human brain. He states that language plays this role for humans, and gives two arguments to support this claim: (1) Human language is a species-specific ability. He supports this first point with evidence from brain research that the area responsible for speech in the human brain does not have analogues in the brains of any other animal. Thus, "Man's brain, and *man's brain alone,* is a language-supporting brain." (2) His second argument comes from the species-specific way in which children acquire language (see Lenneberg's article "On Explaining Language" for a greater development of this point).

I am a rat-brain psychologist with a weakness for speculations. During one of my speculative sprees I prepared a paper on some implications for education which seemed to me to derive from our rat-brain research. When a group of school administrators asked for an encore based upon my initial set of speculations, I acceded to the request. But I somehow had the uneasy feeling that they had something else in mind when they urged me to give the encore.

I keep recalling a story about a young man with a modest endowment as a singer who yearned, nevertheless, to become an operatic star. He bought the help of the best voice teachers in all of Italy, he worked prodigiously at his art, and in due time it was arranged for him to give a small solo during an operatic performance—and more than that—the performance was to take place at *La Scala.* On the appointed night, when his last long note drew to a close, a split-second of silence hung over the hall—then, as one, the entire audience rose from their seats and shouted Encore! Encore! The young man, overcome with indescribable joy, assumed the posture and again ran through his solo. And again the audience rose and shouted Encore! Encore! Again, and yet again this happened. Finally, the singer, exhausted by emotion as well as by his singing, went to the front of the stage and addressed the audience. He assured them of his undying gratitude for their reception, but, he pointed out, there were other artists to hear from, there was the rest of the performance to complete—he would simply have to resist their appeal for yet another encore. "NO," thundered the audience, "NO, you will sing that solo again and again until you get it right!"

You can see why I hesitated when the editors of *California Monthly* asked for yet another encore.

I have said that I was a rat psychologist. And so I am. Time was when rat research was a fairly harmless activity, pursued by underpaid, dedicated, well-meaning characters. The world took little note and cared even less about our researches on how rats learned to thread their way through mazes. Occasionally a misguided educator would take us seriously and try to fashion an educational psychology out of our rats-in-a-maze studies. But the classroom teachers, once removed from the School of Education, would quickly see through such nonsense, and forsaking all rats, would turn to the serious and difficult task of teaching children—unencumbered and unaided by our research and theory.

But that time no longer is. Our psychology, especially when combined with educational practice and theory, must now be listed among the Powerful and, even perhaps, the Dangerous sciences. I refer specifically to the recent research developments in brain biochemistry and behavior, and to the venerable mind-body problem beloved of philosophers and theologians. For brain biochemistry and behavior research seeks to find the *physical* basis for memory. In essence it asks the following question: In what corporal forms do we retain the remembrance of things past? What are the chemical or neurological or anatomical substrates of the evocative ghosts we call "memories"? Over the centuries of thought and decades of scientific research we have gained little on that question. Today, however, there is a feeling that we are on the verge of great discoveries. Indeed some researchers believe that we already know, in the rough, the form the final answer will take. And it is this: The physical basis of any memory, whatever else it may be, involves either the production of new proteins, the release of differentiated molecules of ribonucleic acids (RNA's) or the induction of higher enzymatic activity levels in the brain: In a word, for every separate memory in the mind we will eventually find a differentiated chemical in the brain—"chemical memory pellets," as it were.

What warrant do we have for such a prophecy? To begin with we have reason to believe that the storage of memory in the brain is a many-splendoured, multiphased actively changing affair. That is, any single memory is not merely "deposited" in a completed form in the brain. Rather, it goes through a complex developmental history in the brain in which it changes from a short-term into a long-term memory. And each stage in this consolidation process seems to be dependent upon different although interrelated chemical mechanisms. Let me indicate to you one set (of quite a number which are now available) of speculative hypotheses concerning this developmental transformation of memories.

First we can assume that immediately after every experience, a relatively short-lived reverberatory process is set up within the brain. This process continues for a time after the stimulus disappears and permits us to remember events which occurred moments or minutes ago. But this reverberatory process fairly quickly decays and disappears—and as it does, so does the related memory. However, under certain conditions, the short-term reverberatory process, before it disappears completely from the scene, triggers off a second and quite different series of events in the brain. This second series of events involves the release of new RNA's or the production of new proteins and other macromolecules. And these chemical changes are relatively long-lasting and serve as the physical bases of our long-term memories.

Now it can be supposed that if we increased the robustness or the survival time of the initial reverberatory process we might increase the probability of converting the short-term memory into a long-term memory. There are several ways one could do that. Through the repetition of the same stimulus one could presumably prolong or continually reinstate the reverberatory process and thus, perhaps, make it more effective in inducing permanent chemical changes in the brain. The old-fashioned term for this procedure is "drill" or "practice," and drill and practice are indeed effective techniques for helping the conversion of short-term memories into long-term ones.

But James McGaugh at U.C. Irvine got the bright idea that he could achieve much the same results chemically. His argument, very much simplified, went something like this: A drug which would increase neural and chemical activity within the brain might either increase the vigor of the reverberatory process, or the ease with which the long-term chemical processes would "take off," and thus facilitate the conversion of short-term memories into long-term ones. Apparently his idea was a sound one, for with the use of chemical compounds like strychnine and metrazol, which are central nervous system stimulants, McGaugh has been eminently successful in raising the intellectual level of hundreds of southern California mice.

In one of his experiments which is most pregnant with social implications, and promises, and forebodings for the future, McGaugh tested the maze-learning ability of two quite different strains of mice. One of the strains was, by heredity, particularly adept at maze learning; the other, particularly stupid at that task. Some animals from each strain were injected with different doses of metrazol after each daily learning trial to see whether there would be an improvement in their ability to retain what they had learned. Some were not. The findings pleased everyone—presumably even the mice. With the optimal dosage of metrazol, the chemically treated mice were 40 percent better in remembering their daily lessons than were their untreated brothers. Indeed, under metrazol treatment the hereditarily stupid mice were able to turn in better performances than their hereditarily superior but untreated colleagues. Here we have a "chemical memory pill" which not only improves memory and learning but can serve to make all mice equal whom God—or genetics—hath created unequal. May I suggest that some place in the back of your mind, you might begin to speculate on what it can mean—socially, educationally, politically—if and when we find drugs which will be similarly effective for human beings.

What chemistry can give, it can also take away. Bernard Agranoff of the University of Michigan argued that if we could prevent the brain from manufacturing the chemicals involved in the long-term memory process, then we would create an animal which might have normal short-term memories, but would be incapable of establishing enduring memories. Agranoff trained his goldfish to swim from one side of an aquarium to another, whenever a signal light was turned on, in order to avoid an electric shock. Goldfish can learn this task within a 40-minute period, and once learned, they remember it over many days. Now Agranoff varied his experiments. Immediately before, and in some experiments immediately after training, Agranoff injected puromycin or actinomycin-D (two antibiotics which prevent the formation of new proteins or nuclear RNA) into the brains of a new group of goldfish. His findings were most encouraging (to

Agranoff, that is, not necessarily to the goldfish). The injected gold-fish were not impaired in their *learning* of the shock-avoidance task since, presumably, the short-term reverberatory process which enables the fish to remember its lesson from one trial to another, a matter of a few seconds, does not involve the synthesis of new proteins or nuclear RNA. But when tested a day or two later the fish showed almost no retention for the task they had known so well the day before—indicating that the long-term process *is* dependent upon the synthesis of these compounds in the brain. Here, then, we find not only support for our general theory but we have a suggestion that there exist in antimetabolites whole families of chemical memory preventatives which seem not to interfere with the individual's immediate capacity to obey immediate orders, but which do prevent him from building up a permanent body of experiences, expectations, and skills. Conjure up, if you are of that mind, what evils such weapons can wreak in the hands of the Orwellian authorities of 1984.

A number of years ago, James McConnell at the University of Michigan threw all the brain researchers into a tizzy by reporting that he had succeeded in teaching planaria—a fairly primitive type of flatworm—to make a simple response to a light signal, that he then ground up his educated flatworms, fed the pieces to untrained fellow worms—and lo and behold, the uneducated flatworms wound up with the *memories* of the worms which they had just eaten, and without any training, could perform the response of the late-lamented and digested "donor" worms!

But then all hell broke loose when other workers in other laboratories and in other countries reported that they could train a *rat*, make an extract from its brain, inject this extract into an untrained rat, and that by so doing the recipient rat would acquire the memories of the now-dead donor rat. It is one thing to claim this for the primitive planaria which, after all, do not have very much in the way of a structurally differentiated and organized brain—but it is a very different thing to claim this for the rat which *is* a serious mammal, with a highly developed brain, not too different in complexity, in differentiation, and in organization from our own.

The dust raised by these reports has not yet settled. Indeed, most scientists are definitely on the side of the nonbelievers—but the work goes on, and we cannot predict the final outcome of these experiments, many of which have given negative results. However, as a result of this work, a number of brain researchers have been moved, over the last two or three years, from the position of stiff-necked disbelief to the position of "Well, maybe—I don't believe it, but well, maybe." And this is where *I* stand at the moment—fearless and foursquare proclaiming "Well, maybe. . . ." Now, if it should come to pass that McConnell and his fellow believers are right, then we will indeed have made a huge jump forward. For we would then have a most effective behavioral essay method which should enable us to "zero in" on this marvelous brain-goulash which can transfer information from one brain to another, and isolate and identify in detail all the "memory" proteins, enzymes, RNA's or other macromolecules. After that—the world of the mind is ours! But that day is not here yet.

Does the research I have reviewed mean that if and when we will have developed get-smart pills (à la McGaugh), or chemical erasures of wrong mental habits (à la Agranoff), or specific knowledge pills (à la McConnell), we will be able to do without head start programs, educational enrichment programs, school supervisors, educational research and, indeed, without most of our educational paraphernalia? The answer to this question is a most reassuring "No." I might even say "au contraire." Precisely because of the advances in brain biochemistry, the significance of the educator will be greatly increased—*and just as greatly changed.* Let me tell you why I think so by describing to you the results of some of our own work in the Berkeley laboratories.

Some time ago we set ourselves the following problem: If the laying down of memories involves the synthesis of chemical products in the brain, then one should find that an animal which has lived a life replete with opportunities for learning and memorizing would end with a brain chemically and morphologically different from an animal which has lived out an intellectually impoverished life. For almost two decades, now, E. L. Bennett, Marion Diamond, M. R. Rosenzweig, and I, together with technical assistants, graduate students and thousands of rats, have labored, and some of us have even sacrificed our lives, to find such evidence. Let me tell you some of what we found.

At weaning time we divide our experimental rats into two groups— half of the rats being placed in an "intellectually enriched" environment, the other half—their brothers—in the deprived environment. While both groups receive identical food and water, their psychological environments differ greatly. The animals in the first group live together in one large cage, are provided with many rat toys (tunnels to explore, ladders to climb, levers to press), and they are assigned to graduate students who are admonished to give these rats loving care and kindness, teach them to run mazes, and in general to provide them with the best and most expensive supervised higher education available to any young rat at the University of California. While these rats are thus being encouraged to store up many and varied memories, their brother rats, in the deprived group, live in isolated, barren cages, devoid of stimulation by either their environmental appurtenances, fellow rats, or graduate students. After about 80 days of this differential treatment, all the animals are sacrificed, their brains dissected out and various chemical and histological analyses performed. The results are convincing. The brain from a rat from the enriched environment—and presumably, therefore, with many more stored memories—has a heavier and thicker cortex, a better blood supply, larger brain cells, more glia cells, and increased activity of two brain enzymes, acetylcholinesterase and cholinesterase, than does the brain from an animal whose life has been less memorable.

We can draw several morals from these experiments. First, the growing animal's psychological environment is of crucial importance for the development of its brain. By manipulating the environment of the young, one can truly create a "lame brain"—with lighter cortex, shrunken brain cells, fewer glia cells, smaller blood vessels, and lower enzymatic activity levels—or one can create a more robust, a healthier, a more metabolically active brain. If it should turn out that what is true for the rat brain is also true for the human brain, and that by careful manipulation of this or that group's early environment we can develop among them bigger and better brains or smaller and meaner ones, the wondrous promises of a glorious future or the monstrous horrors of a Huxlian Brave New World are fairly self-evident.

The second conclusion I draw from our experiments is this: Since the effect of any chemical upon an organ is, in part, a function of the beginning chemical status of that organ, and since—as we have just seen—the chemical and anatomical status of the individual's brain is determined by his aducational experience, then the effectiveness of the biochemist's "get smart pill" will depend upon how the educator has prepared the brain in the first instance. Indeed, a review of all the data indicate that manipulating the educational and psychological environment is a more effective way of inducing long-lasting brain changes than direct administration of drugs. Another way of saying this is: The educator *can potentiate or undo the work of the brain biochemist.*

At Berkeley, we did not really know how to create a "psychologically enriched environment," so we threw everything into the environment including, almost, the kitchen sink. The cages were kept in brightly lighted, sound-filled rooms; the rats were given playmates to relate to, games to manipulate, maze problems to solve, new areas to explore. They were fondled and tamed and chucked under the chin at the drop of a site-visitor. We provided our happy rats with almost every kind of stimulation we could think of—or afford. And it seems to have worked. Of course, it is possible that in our "kitchen-sink design," many of the things we did were not at all necessary—indeed, some may have had an adverse effect. So we undertook a series of experiments to discover which elements of our environment were effective, and which were not. I shall not bore you with the details of the many experiments already run and many more which are now being run in the Berkeley laboratory. Let me list, however, some of the tentative conclusions which one can already make:

First: Sheer exercise or physical activity alone is not at all effective in developing the brain. A physical training director seems not to be an adequate substitute for a teacher.

Second: Varied visual stimulation, or indeed, any kind of visual stimulation is neither necessary nor sufficient to develop the brain— as we were able to demonstrate by using rats blinded at weaning age.

Third: Handling, or taming, or petting is also without effect in developing the growing rat's brain. Love is not enough.

Fourth: The presence of a brother rat in our intellectually-deprived rat's cage helps him not a whit. Bruderschaft is not enough.

Fifth: Teaching the rat to press levers for food—that and only that seems to help somewhat—but only minimally. Not every problem-set will do, either.

The only experience we have thus far found really effective is freedom to roam around in a large object-filled space. From a recent experiment in Diamond's laboratory there are some suggestions that if the young rat is given continuous and varied maze-problems to solve—that and little else—the rat will develop a number of the same brain changes (at least the morphological ones) which we had observed in our randomly "enriched" environment.

It is clear, then, that not *every* experience or variation in stimulation contributes equally to the development of the brain. But of even greater interest is the suggestion in the above data that the most effective way to develop the brain is through what I will call *species-specific enrichment experiences.* Here is what I mean: The ability of a rat to learn its way through tunnels and dark passages, to localize points in a three-dimensional space full of objects to be climbed upon, burrowed under and crawled through is, we can assume, of particular survival value for the rat as he is now constituted. Presumably, through the selective evolutionary process the rat has developed a brain which is peculiarly fitted to support and enhance these skills. The "effective rat brain" therefore, is one which is a good "space-brain"—not a lever-pressing brain or an arithmetic-reasoning brain. The effective stimulating environment, correspondingly, would be one which makes *spatial learning* demands on that brain—which "pushes" that particular kind of brain in that particular way. To generalize this hypothesis, I would suggest that *for each species there exists a set of species-specific experiences which are maximally enriching and which are maximally efficient in developing its brain.*

If there be any validity to my hypothesis, then the challenge to the human educator is clear. For the educator, too, you may have noticed, has been using the kitchen-sink approach when he seeks to design a psychologically or educationally enriched environment for the child. Some educators would bombard the child from infancy on, with every kind of stimulus change imaginable. His crib is festooned with jumping beads and dangling colored bits and pieces of wood (all sold very expensively to his affluent parents); he is given squishy, squeaking, squawking toys to play with, to fondle, to be frightened by, to choke on. He is jounced and bounced and picked up and put down. And when he goes to school—he finds the same blooming, buzzing confusion. He is stimulated with play activities, with opportunities for social interaction, with rhythmic movements, with music, with visual displays, with contact sports, with tactual experiences, and with anything and everything which the school system can think of—or afford. But it may be that a "stimulating environment" and an "enriched environment" are not one and the same thing. It is not true that a brain is a brain is a brain. The rat is a rat and he hath a rat's brain; the child is a child and he hath a child's brain—and each, according to my hypothesis, requires its own educational nutrient. What, then, are the species-specific enrichments for the human child?

Of course I do not know the answer to this question, but let me share with you my present enthusiastic guess that in the language arts you will find part of the answer.

I can start with no better text than a quotation from my teacher—Edward Chace Tolman, who was a completely devoted rat psychologist. "Speech," he wrote, ". . . is in any really developed and characteristic sense, the sole prerogative of the human being. . . . It is speech which first and foremost distinguishes man from the great apes," (1932). In my opinion, it is in the study of language, above anything else, that the psychologist will discover the psychology of man, and that the educator will discover how to educate man. In the first place, and we must be clear about this, human language, with its complex and *abstract structure*, has *nothing* in common with animal communication. Language is probably the clearest instance of a pure species-specific behavior. This is true whether you study language as a neurologist, or as a psychologist. Let us look at some brain research first.

Recently, Bryan Robinson, at the National Institute of Mental Health (1967), attempted to discover which areas of the monkey's brain controlled its vocalizations. Now the monkey most certainly uses vocalization for communication, but principally for communications with emotional tone such as threat, fear, pain, and pleasure. In Robinson's study 15 unanesthetized animals, with brains exposed by surgery, were used—5,880 different loci or spots in the brain were stimulated by electrodes to see whether such stimulation could bring forth vocalization. The loci explored included neocortical areas as well as areas in the limbic system—that older part of the mammalian brain which is most intimately involved with motivational and emotional responses.

Robinson's results were clear-cut: First, despite his exploration of several hundred different neocortical sites he was unable to raise a single sound from his animals by stimulating their *neocortex*; second: stimulation of the limbic system brought forth regular, consistent and identifiable vocalizations.

These results differ sharply from those found with the human brain. While there is some evidence that human cries and exclamations— uttered in moments of excitement—are also controlled by the limbic system, *speech and language clearly depend upon neocortical areas*— areas for which there simply are no analogues in the brain of any other animal. These areas are, of course, the well-known Broca and Wernicke areas in the left hemisphere of the human brain. It seems clear, as Robinson puts it, that "Human speech did not develop 'out of' primate vocalization, but arose from *new tissue* (italics my own) which" permitted it the necessary detachment from immediate, emotional situations." Man's brain, *and man's brain alone*, is a language-supporting brain.

Corresponding to the neurological picture, is the psycholinguist's view of language. Almost every psycholinguist is impressed not only with the unique nature of language itself, but with its unique mode of achievement by the child. Whatever value so-called reinforcement or stimulus-response theories of learning may have for describing acquisition of motor skills by people, maze-learning by rats, and bar-pressing by pigeons, these theories are assessed as completely trivial and utterly irrelevant when it comes to understanding that "stunning intellectual achievement," (McNeill, 1966), the acquisition of language by the child. Indeed, in reading the psycholinguist's work, one is left with the impression that we will have to develop a species-specific learning theory for this species-specific behavior of language. I must confess that I agree with them. And if we ever achieve an understanding of language development, and if we learn how to push the *human* brain with this *human* experience—then will we indeed be on our way.

Now I know that other people have proposed other ways with which to enrich the child's education. Some plug for what are referred to as "cognitive" experience or "productive thinking" experiences. Let me hasten to record that I quite agree with them. As a matter of fact, I am not at all certain that I am saying anything other than what my cognitive friends propose. For I hold with McNeill's judgment that ". . . the study of how language is acquired may provide insight into the very basis of mental life." And, I would go on, being human *means* having an effective mental, cognitive life.

Now, whether my guess merits this enthusiasm or not will perhaps eventually be determined by research. But here is the challenge and here is the promise for the educator: Drop your kitchen-sink approach, and specify and define for us the species-specific psychologically enriching experiences for the child—and we will be off and running!

And where will we run? It is perfectly reasonable to suppose that we will be able to find specific biochemical boosters and biochemical inhibitors for different kinds of memories and imagery, or for different kinds of abilities, or for different kinds of personality or temperament traits. With such chemical agents in hand, and with appropriate educational and training procedures, we may use them as supplementary therapy for those failing in this or that trait and thus will we be able to rectify and heal some of the mentally retarded and the senile. Of course we may use these agents for evil—to create docile, intellectually limited but efficient human beasts of burden, without memories beyond the order of the day (remember Agranoff's fish?).

But above all, there will be great changes made in the first and foremost and continuing business of society—the education and training of the young. The development of the mind of the child will come to rest in the knowledge and skills of the biochemist, and pharmacologist, and neurologist, and psychologist and educator. And there will be a new expert abroad in the land—the psychoneurobiochemeducator. And this multihybrid expert will have recourse—as I have suggested elsewhere—to protein memory consolidators, antimetabolite memory inhibitors, enzymatic learning stimulants, and many other potions and elixirs of the mind from our new psychoneurobiochemopharmacopia.

There is a grievous problem here, however. Experts—whatever else they may be—are notorious order-takers. *Who* will direct our psychoneurobiochemeducator where to work his expertise and *what* shall we tell him to do? Here we are talking about goals, and values, and aims. Shall our expert raise or lower docility, aggressiveness, musical ability, engineering ability, artistic sensitivity, effective intellectual functioning? Shall different ethnic or racial or national or social groups receive different treatments? In past centuries—and even today—this differential group treatment is precisely what our relatively primitive but quite effective medical and educational experts have been ordered by us to carry out. And they have done so! On one side of the town they have created enclaves of the sickly, the weak, the ignorant, the unskilled, in a word, the brutalized social vanquished; and on the other side, they have created the social victors—the healthy, the strong, the knowledgeable, the skilled. Will we continue to do this in the future with our much more sophisticated and effective psychoneurobiochemeducators? Who, in other words, will control the brain controllers—and to what ends?

I have thought and worried about these questions, and I must confess to you that I cannot avoid a dread feeling of unease about the future.

At the same time I keep whistling the following tune in an attempt to cheer myself up: If there be any validity at all to my speculations, they add up to this: The biochemist, neurologist, psychologist and educator will eventually add to the intellectual stature of man. And with this in mind, and clinging to a life-long faith in the virtues of knowledge and the intellect (for certainly, at this stage I can do no less) I find myself believing that man who, by taking thought, will have added cubits to his intellectual stature, will also acquire that added bit of wisdom and humaneness which will save us all.

GEORGE MILLER

The Psycholinguists

INTRODUCTION

Miller feels that the central task of psycholinguistics is "to describe the psychological processes that go on when people use sentences." In this essay he narrows the question to a consideration of the processes that we may suppose the listener performs on a spoken utterance. Miller recognizes six levels of activity: (1) hearing, (2) matching, (3) accepting, (4) interpreting, (5) understanding, and (6) believing. This is an ascending scale of abstraction ranging from "the superficial to the inscrutable."

The first level, hearing, is the simplest activity. Even an unknown language can be heard. However, the second level, matching, involves the hearer's ability to impose a *phonological* interpretation upon what is heard; that is, the hearer breaks the stream of sound into recognizable syllables and words. The third level, accepting, involves the ability to impose a *grammatical* interpretation upon the utterance; that is, the hearer can accept or reject the sentence as a grammatical sentence in his language and can also offer grammatical paraphrases of the sentence. The fourth level, interpreting, involves the hearer's ability to understand what the sentence means; that is, he can impose a *semantic* interpretation upon the sentence. The

Reprinted by permission of the author, from *Encounter*, Vol. 23, No. 1 (July 1964), pp. 29–37.

fifth level, understanding, involves the hearer's ability to grasp the contextual significance of the sentence, for example, the speaker's intention. The last level, believing, involves the hearer's ability to judge the truth of the sentence. Miller next explores the concept of "matching" in greater detail. He suggests that a hearer is able to recognize an utterance by virtue of his ability to generate an utterance of his own that has the same phonological properties as the utterance heard and that would also be appropriate to the occasion.

One difficulty with this theory of matching is that the number of possible sentences that the hearer might be called upon to match is unlimited. Obviously the capacity of the human brain is not so great that it can store all possible English sentences in its memory. Instead, Miller argues, the brain must have the capacity to generate and interpret (match) new sentences as it needs them. All human language (as opposed to nonhuman languages such as logical languages) are basically alike in that they are capable of being generated by man's unique linguistic capacity.

To demonstrate that man's linguistic capacity is innate and not learned, Miller compares the way a child acquires language with the difficulties that a computer would have if given the same data as the child. The child learns the language of his environment without instruction or motivation. The computer, however, cannot, even in theory, discover what kind of organization to look for. Miller concludes that children are born predisposed to learn language, or as Miller puts it, "Human language must be such that a child can acquire it."

The final part of the essay draws a distinction between the speaker's linguistic competence and his actual performance. There are many limitations on performance that have nothing to do with competence, and Miller illustrates this by presenting three versions of the same sentence. One of the three versions is almost completely beyond our ability to understand, even though it is basically the same as the other two versions. In this case the form of the sentence, even though it is grammatical, imposes an impossible burden on our memory.

Psychologists have long recognized that human minds feed on linguistic symbols. Linguists have always admitted that some kind of psycho-social motor must move the machinery of grammar and lexicon. Sooner or later they were certain to examine their intersection self-consciously. Perhaps it was also inevitable that the result would be called "psycholinguistics."

In fact, although the enterprise itself has slowly been gathering strength at least since the invention of the telephone, the name, in its unhyphenated form, is only about ten years old. Few seem pleased with the term, but the field has grown so rapidly and stirred so much interest in recent years that some way of referring to it is urgently needed. *Psycholinguistics* is as descriptive a term as any, and shorter than most.

Among psychologists it was principally the behaviourists who wished to take a closer look at language. Behaviourists generally try to replace anything subjective by its most tangible, physical manifestation, so they have had a long tradition of confusing thought with speech—or with "verbal behaviour," as many prefer to call it. Among linguists it was principally those with an anthropological sideline who were most willing to collaborate, perhaps because as anthropologists they were sensitive to all those social and psychological processes that support our linguistic practices. By working together they managed to call attention to an important field of scientific research and to integrate it, or at least to acquaint its various parts with one another, under this new rubric.*

Interest in psycholinguistics, however, is not confined to psychologists and linguists. Many people have been stirred by splendid visions of its practical possibilities. One thinks of medical applications to the diagnosis and treatment of a heterogeneous variety of language disorders ranging from simple stammering to the overwhelming complexities of aphasia.† One thinks too of pedagogical applications, of potential improvements in our methods for teaching reading and writing, or for teaching second languages. If psycholinguistic principles were made sufficiently explicit, they could be imparted to those technological miracles of the twentieth century, the computing machines, which would bring into view a whole spectrum of cybernetic possibilities.‡ We could exploit our electrical channels for voice communications more efficiently. We might improve and automate our dictionaries, using them for mechanical translation from one language to another. Perhaps computers could print what we say, or even say what we print, thus making speech visible for the deaf and printing

---

* A representative sample of research papers in this field can be found in *Psycholinguistics: A Book of Readings,* edited by S. Saporta (Holt, Rinehart and Winston, New York, 1962). R. Brown provides a readable survey from a psychologist's point of view in *Words and Things* (Free Press, Glencoe, Illinois, 1957).

† The CIBA Foundation Symposium, *Disorders of Language* (J. & A. Churchill, London, 1964), provides an excellent sample of the current status of medical psycholinguistics.

‡ *Natural Language and the Computer,* edited by P. L. Garvin (McGraw-Hill, New York, 1963).

audible for the blind. We might, in short, learn to adapt computers to dozens of our human purposes if only they could interpret our languages. Little wonder that assorted physicians, educators, philosophers, logicians, and engineers have been intrigued by this new adventure.

Of course, the realisation of practical benefits must await the success of the scientific effort; there is some danger that enthusiasm may colour our estimate of what can be accomplished. Not a few sceptics remain unconvinced; some can even be found who argue that success is impossible in principle. "Science," they say, "can go only so far. . . ."

The integration of psycholinguistic studies has occurred so recently that there is still some confusion concerning its scope and purpose; efforts to clarify it necessarily have something of the character of personal opinions.§ In my own version, the central task of this new science is to describe the psychological processes that go on when people use sentences. The real crux of the psycholinguistic problem does not appear until one tries to deal with sentences, for only then does the importance of productivity become completely obvious. It is true that productivity can also appear with individual words, but there it is not overwhelming. With sentences, productivity is literally unlimited.

Before considering this somewhat technical problem, however, it might be well to illustrate the variety of processes that psycholinguists hope to explain. This can best be done if we ask what a listener can do about a spoken utterance, and consider his alternatives in order from the superficial to the inscrutable.

The simplest thing one can do in the presence of a spoken utterance is to listen. Even if the language is incomprehensible, one can still *hear* an utterance as an auditory stimulus and respond to it in terms of some discriminative set: how loud, how fast, how long, from which direction, etc.

Given that an utterance is heard, the next level involves *matching* it as a phonemic pattern in terms of phonological skills acquired as a user of the language. The ability to match an input can be tested in psychological experiments by asking listeners to echo what they hear; a wide variety of experimental situations—experiments on the perception of speech and on the rote memorisation of verbal materials—can

§ My own opinions have been strongly influenced by Noam Chomsky. A rather technical exposition of this work can be found in Chapters 11–13 of the second volume of the *Handbook of Mathematical Psychology*, edited by R. D. Luce, R. R. Bush, and E. Galanter (Wiley, New York, 1963), from which many of the ideas discussed here have been drawn.

be summarised as tests of a person's ability to repeat the speech he hears under various conditions of audibility or delay.

If a listener can hear and match an utterance, the next question to ask is whether he will *accept* it as a sentence in terms of his knowledge of grammar. At this level we encounter processes difficult to study experimentally, and one is forced to rely most heavily on linguistic analyses of the structure of sentences. Some experiments are possible, however, for we can measure how much a listener's ability to accept the utterance as a sentence facilitates his ability to hear and match it; grammatical sentences are much easier to hear, utter or remember than are ungrammatical strings of words, and even nonsense (*pirot, karol, elat,* etc.) is easier to deal with if it looks grammatical (*pirots karolise elatically,* etc.).|| Needless to say, the grammatical knowledge we wish to study does not concern those explicit rules drilled into us by teachers of traditional grammar, but rather the implicit generative knowledge that we all must acquire in order to use a language appropriately.

Beyond grammatical acceptance comes semantic interpretation: we can ask how listeners *interpret* an utterance as meaningful in terms of their semantic system. Interpretation is not merely a matter of assigning meanings to individual words; we must also consider how these component meanings combine in grammatical sentences. Compare the sentences: *Healthy young babies sleep soundly* and *Colourless green ideas sleep furiously.* Although they are syntactically similar, the second is far harder to perceive and remember correctly—because it cannot be interpreted by the usual semantic rules for combining the senses of adjacent English words.# The interpretation of each word is affected by the company it keeps; a central problem is to systematise the interactions of words and phrases with their linguistic contexts. The lexicographer makes his major contribution at this point, but psychological studies of our ability to paraphrase an utterance also have their place.

At the next level it seems essential to make some distinction between interpreting an utterance and understanding it, for understanding frequently goes well beyond the linguistic context provided by the utterance itself. A husband greeted at the door by "I bought some electric light bulbs to-day" must do more than interpret its literal reference; he must understand that he should go to the kitchen and replace that

|| W. Epstein, "The Influence of Syntactical Structure on Learning," *American Journal of Psychology* (1961), vol. 74, pp. 80–85.

G. A. Miller and S. Isard, "Some Perceptual Consequences of Linguistic Rules," *Journal of Verbal Learning and Verbal Behavior* (1963), vol. 2, pp. 217–228. J. J. Katz and J. A. Fodor have recently contributed a thoughtful discussion of "The Structure of Semantic Theory," *Language* (1963), vol. 39, pp. 170–210.

burned-out lamp. Such contextual information lies well outside any grammar or lexicon. The listener can *understand* the function of an utterance in terms of contextual knowledge of the most diverse sort.

Finally, at a level now almost invisible through the clouds, a listener may *believe* that an utterance is valid in terms of its relevance to his own conduct. The child who says "I saw five lions in the garden" may be heard, matched, accepted, interpreted, and understood, but in few parts of the world will he be believed.

The boundaries between successive levels are not sharp and distinct. One shades off gradually into the next. Still the hierarchy is real enough and important to keep in mind. Simpler types of psycholinguistic processes can be studied rather intensively; already we know much about hearing and matching. Accepting and interpreting are just now coming into scientific focus. Understanding is still over the horizon, and pragmatic questions involving belief systems are presently so vague as to be hardly worth asking. But the whole range of processes must be included in any adequate definition of psycholinguistics.

I phrased the description of these various psycholinguistic processes in terms of a listener; the question inevitably arises as to whether a different hierarchy is required to describe the speaker. One problem a psycholinguist faces is to decide whether speaking and listening are two separate abilities, co-ordinate but distinct, or whether they are merely different manifestations of a single linguistic faculty.

The mouth and ear are different organs; at the simplest levels we must distinguish hearing and matching from vocalising and speaking. At more complex levels it is less easy to decide whether the two abilities are distinct. At some point they must converge, if only to explain why it is so difficult to speak and listen simultaneously. The question is where.

It is easy to demonstrate how important to a speaker is the sound of his own voice. If his speech is delayed a fifth of a second, amplified, and fed back into his own ears, the voice-ear asynchrony can be devastating to the motor skills of articulate speech. It is more difficult, however, to demonstrate that the same linguistic competence required for speaking is also involved in processing the speech of others.

Recently Morris Halle and Kenneth Stevens of the Massachusetts Institute of Technology revived a suggestion made by Wilhelm von Humboldt over a century ago.** Suppose we accept the notion that a listener recognises what he hears by comparing it with some internal

** M. Halle and K. N. Stevens, "Speech Recognition: A Model and a Program for Research," *IRE Transactions on Information Theory* (1962), vol. IT-8, pp. 155–159.

representation. To the extent that a match can be obtained, the input is accepted and interpreted. One trouble with this hypothesis, however, is that a listener must be ready to recognise any one of an enormous number of different sentences. It is inconceivable that a separate internal representation for each of them could be stored in his memory in advance. Halle and Stevens suggest that these internal representations must be generated as they are needed by following the same generative rules that are normally used in producing speech. In this way the rules of the language are incorporated into the theory only once, in a generative form; they need not be learned once by the ear and again by the tongue. This is a theory of a language-user, not of a speaker or a listener alone.

The listener begins with a guess about the input. On that basis he generates an internal matching signal. The first attempt will probably be in error; if so, the mismatch is reported and used as a basis for a next guess, which should be closer. This cycle repeats (unconsciously, almost certainly) until a satisfactory (not necessarily a correct) match is obtained, at which point the next segment of speech is scanned and matched, etc. The output is not a transformed version of the input; it is the programme that was followed to generate the matching representation.

The perceptual categories available to such a system are defined by the generative rules at its disposal. It is also reasonably obvious that its efficiency is critically dependent on the quality of the initial guess. If this guess is close, an iterative process can converge rapidly; if not, the listener will be unable to keep pace with the rapid flow of conversational speech.

A listener's first guess probably derives in part from syntactic markers in the form of intonation, inflection, suffixes, etc., and in part from his general knowledge of the semantic and situational context. Syntactic cues indicate how the input is to be grouped and which words function together; semantic and contextual contributions are more difficult to characterise, but must somehow enable him to limit the range of possible words that he can expect to hear.

How he is able to do this is an utter mystery, but the fact that he can do it is easily demonstrated.

The English psychologist David Bruce recorded a set of ordinary sentences and played them in the presence of noise so intense that the voice was just audible, but not intelligible.[tt] He told his listeners that these were sentences on some general topic—sports, say—and asked

---

[tt] "Effects of Context upon the Intelligibility of Heard Speech," in *Information Theory*, edited by Colin Cherry (Butterworths, London, 1956, pp. 245–252).

them to repeat what they heard. He then told them they would hear more sentences on a different topic, which they were also to repeat. This was done several times. Each time the listeners repeated sentences appropriate to the topic announced in advance. When at the end of the experiment Bruce told them they had heard the same recording every time—all he had changed was the topic they were given—most listeners were unable to believe it.

With an advance hypothesis about what the message will be we can tune our perceptual system to favour certain interpretations and reject others. This fact is no proof of a generative process in speech perception, but it does emphasise the important role of context. For most theories of speech perception the facilitation provided by context is merely a fortunate though rather complicated fact. For a generative theory it is essential.

Note that generative theories do not assume that a listener must be able to articulate the sounds he recognises, but merely that he be able to generate some internal representation to match the input. In this respect a generative theory differs from a motor theory (such as that of Sir Richard Paget) which assumes that we can identify only those utterances we are capable of producing ourselves. There is some rather compelling evidence against a motor theory. The American psychologist Eric Lenneberg has described the case of an eight-year-old boy with congenital anarthria; despite his complete inability to speak, the boy acquired an excellent ability to understand language.‡‡ Moreover, it is a common observation that utterances can be understood by young children before they are able to produce them. A motor theory of speech-perception draws too close a parallel between our two capacities as users of language. Even so, the two are more closely integrated than most people realise.

I have already offered the opinion that productivity sets the central problem for the psycholinguist and have even referred to it indirectly by arguing that we can produce too many different sentences to store them all in memory. The issue can be postponed no longer.

To make the problem plain, consider an example on the level of individual words. For several days I carried in my pocket a small white card on which was typed UNDERSTANDER. On suitable occasions I would hand it to someone. "How do you pronounce this?" I asked.

He pronounced it.

"Is it an English word?"

‡‡ "Understanding Language without Ability to Speak: A Case Report," *Journal of Abnormal and Social Psychology* (1962), vol. 65, pp. 419–425.

He hesitated. "I haven't seen it used very much. I'm not sure."
"Do you know what it means?"
"I suppose it means 'one who understands.' "
I thanked him and changed the subject.

Of course, understander *is* an English word, but to find it you must look in a large dictionary where you will probably read that it is "now rare." Rare enough, I think, for none of my respondents to have seen it before. Nevertheless, they all answered in the same way. Nobody seemed surprised. Nobody wondered how he could understand and pronounce a word without knowing whether it was a word. Everybody put the main stress on the third syllable and constructed a meaning from the verb "to understand" and the agentive suffix "*er*." Familiar morphological rules of English were applied as a matter of course, even though the combination was completely novel.

Probably no one but a psycholinguist captured by the ingenuous behaviouristic theory that words are vocal responses conditioned to occur in the presence of appropriate stimuli would find anything exceptional in this. Since none of my friends had seen the word before, and so could not have been "conditioned" to give the responses they did, how would this theory account for their "verbal behaviour"? Advocates of a conditioning theory of meaning—and there are several distinguished scientists among them—would probably explain linguistic productivity in terms of "conditioned generalisations."[§§] They could argue that my respondents had been conditioned to the word understand and to the suffix—*er*; responses to their union could conceivably be counted as instances of stimulus generalisation. In this way, novel responses could occur without special training.

Although a surprising amount of psychological ingenuity has been invested in this kind of argument, it is difficult to estimate its value. No one has carried the theory through for all the related combinations that must be explained simultaneously. One can speculate, however, that there would have to be many different kinds of generalisation, each with a carefully defined range of applicability. For example, it would be necessary to explain why "understander" is acceptable, whereas "erunderstand" is not. Worked out in detail, such a theory would become a sort of Pavlovian paraphrase of a linguistic description. Of course, if one believes there is some essential difference between behaviour governed by conditioned habits and behaviour

---

[§§] A dog conditioned to salivate at the sound of a tone will also salivate, though less copiously, at the sound of similar tones, the magnitude declining as the new tones become less similar to the original. This phenomenon is called "stimulus generalisation."

governed by rules, the paraphrase could never be more than a vast intellectual pun.

Original combinations of elements are the life blood of language. It is our ability to produce and comprehend such novelties that makes language so ubiquitously useful. As psychologists have become more seriously interested in the cognitive processes that language entails, they have been forced to recognise that the fundamental puzzle is not our ability to associate vocal noises with perceptual objects, but rather our combinatorial productivity—our ability to understand an unlimited diversity of utterances never heard before and to produce an equal variety of utterances similarly intelligible to other members of our speech community. Faced with this problem, concepts borrowed from conditioning theory seem not so much invalid as totally inadequate.

Some idea of the relative magnitudes of what we might call the productive as opposed to the reproductive components of any psycholinguistic theory is provided by statistical studies of language. A few numbers can reinforce the point. If you interrupt a speaker at some randomly chosen instant, there will be, on the average, about ten words that form grammatical and meaningful continuations. Often only one word is admissible and sometimes there are thousands, but on the average it works out to about ten. (If you think this estimate too low, I will not object; larger estimates strengthen the argument.) A simple English sentence can easily run to a length of twenty words, so elementary arithmetic tells us that there must be at least 10^{20} such sentences that a person who knows English must know how to deal with.[1] Compare this productive potential with the 10^4 or 10^5 individual words we know—the reproductive component of our theory—and the discrepancy is dramatically illustrated. Putting it differently, it would take 100,000,000,000 centuries (one thousand times the estimated age of the earth) to utter all the admissible twenty-word sentences of English. Thus, the probability that you might have heard any particular twenty-word sentence before is negligible. Unless it is a cliché, every sentence must come to you as a novel combination of morphemes. Yet you can interpret it at once if you know the English language.

With these facts in mind it is impossible to argue that we learn to understand sentences from teachers who have pronounced each one and explained what it meant. What we have learned are not particular strings of words, but *rules* for generating admissible strings of words.

Consider what it means to follow a rule; this consideration shifts the discussion of psycholinguistics into very difficult territory. The nature of rules has been a central concern of modern philosophy and perhaps no analysis has been more influential than Ludwig Wittgenstein's. Wittgenstein remarked that the most characteristic thing we can say about "rule-governed behavior" is that the person who knows the rules knows whether he is proceeding correctly or incorrectly. Although he may not be able to formulate the rules explicitly, he knows what it is to make a mistake. If this remark is accepted, we must ask ourselves whether an animal that has been conditioned is privy to any such knowledge about the correctness of what he is doing. Perhaps such a degree of insight could be achieved by the great apes, but surely not by all the various species that can acquire conditioned reflexes. On this basis alone it would seem necessary to preserve a distinction between conditioning and learning rules.

As psychologists have learned to appreciate the complexities of language, the prospect of reducing it to the laws of behaviour so carefully studied in lower animals has grown increasingly remote. We have been forced more and more into a position that non-psychologists probably take for granted, namely, that language is rule-governed behaviour characterised by enormous flexibility and freedom of choice.

Obvious as this conclusion may seem, it has important implications for any scientific theory of language. If rules involve the concepts of right and wrong, they introduce a normative aspect that has always been avoided in the natural sciences. One hears repeatedly that the scientist's ability to suppress normative judgments about his subject-matter enables him to see the world objectively, as it really is. To admit that language follows rules seems to put it outside the range of phenomena accessible to scientific investigation.[2]

At this point a psycholinguist who wishes to preserve his standing as a natural scientist faces an old but always difficult decision. Should he withdraw and leave the study of language to others? Or should he give up all pretence of being a "natural scientist," searching for causal explanations, and embrace a more phenomenological approach? Or should he push blindly ahead with his empirical methods, hoping to find a causal basis for normative practices, but running the risk that all his efforts will be wasted because rule-governed behaviour in principle lies beyond the scope of natural science?

To withdraw means to abandon hope of understanding scientifically all those human mental processes that involve language in any important degree. To persevere means to face the enormously difficult, if not actually impossible task of finding a place for normative rules in a descriptive science.

Difficult, yes. Still one wonders whether these alternatives are really as mutually exclusive as they seem.

The first thing we notice when we survey the languages of the world is how few we can understand and how diverse they all seem. Not until one looks for some time does an even more significant observation emerge concerning the pervasive similarities in the midst of all this diversity.

Every human group that anthropologists have studied has spoken a language. The language always has a lexicon and a grammar. The lexicon is not a haphazard collection of vocalisations, but is highly organised; it always has pronouns, means for dealing with time, space, and number, words to represent true and false, the basic concepts necessary for propositional logic. The grammar has distinguishable levels of structure, some phonological, some syntactic. The phonology always contains both vowels and consonants, and the phonemes can always be described in terms of distinctive features drawn from a limited set of possibilities. The syntax always specifies rules for grouping elements sequentially into phrases and sentences, rules governing normal intonation, rules for transforming some types of sentences into other types.

The nature and importance of these common properties, called "linguistic universals," are only beginning to emerge as our knowledge of the world's languages grows more systematic.‖ ‖ These universals appear even in languages that developed with a minimum of interaction. One is forced to assume, therefore, either that (*a*) no other kind of linguistic practices are conceivable, or that (*b*) something in the biological makeup of human beings favours languages having these similarities. Only a moment's reflection is needed to reject (*a*). When one considers the variety of artificial languages developed in mathematics, in the communication sciences, in the use of computers, in symbolic logic, and elsewhere, it soon becomes apparent that the universal features of natural languages are not the only ones possible. Natural languages are, in fact, rather special and often seem unnecessarily complicated.

A popular belief regards human language as a more or less free creation of the human intellect, as if its elements were chosen arbitrarily and could be combined into meaningful utterances by any rules that strike our collective fancy. The assumption is implicit, for example, in Wittgenstein's well-known conception of "the language game." This

‖ ‖ *Universals of Language,* edited by J. Greenberg (M.I.T. Technology Press, Cambridge, Mass., 1963).

metaphor, which casts valuable light on many aspects of language, can, if followed blindly, lead one to think that all linguistic rules are just as arbitrary as, say, the rules of chess or football. As Lenneberg has pointed out, however, it makes a great deal of sense to inquire into the biological basis for language, but very little to ask about the biological foundations of card games.##

Man is the only animal to have a combinatorially productive language. In the jargon of biology, language is "a species-specific form of behaviour." Other animals have signalling systems of various kinds and for various purposes—but only man has evolved this particular and highly improbable form of communication. Those who think of language as a free and spontaneous intellectual invention are also likely to believe that any animal with a brain sufficiently large to support a high level of intelligence can acquire a language. This assumption is demonstrably false. The human brain is not just an ape brain enlarged; its extra size is less important than its different structure. Moreover, Lenneberg has pointed out that nanocephalic dwarfs, with brains half the normal size but grown on the human blueprint, can use language reasonably well, and even mongoloids, not intelligent enough to perform the simplest functions for themselves, can acquire the rudiments.*** Talking and understanding language do not depend on being intelligent or having a large brain. They depend on "being human."

Serious attempts have been made to teach animals to speak. If words were conditioned responses, animals as intelligent as chimpanzees or porpoises should be able to learn them. These attempts have uniformly failed in the past and, if the argument here is correct, they will always fail in the future—for just the same reason that attempts to teach fish to walk or dogs to fly would fail. Such efforts misconstrue the basis for our linguistic competence: they fly in the face of biological facts.†††

E. Lenneberg, "Language, Evolution, and Purposive Behavior," in *Culture in History: Essays in Honor of Paul Radin* (Columbia University Press, New York, 1960).

*** E. Lenneberg, I. A. Nichols, and E. R. Rosenberger, "Primitive Stages of Language Development in Mongolism," in the *Proceedings* of the 42nd. Annual Meeting (1962) of the *Association for Research in Nervous and Mental Diseases*.

††† The belief that animals have, or could have, languages is as old as man's interest in the evolution of his special talent, but the truth of the matter has long been known. Listen, for example, to Max Müller (*Three Lectures on the Science of Language*) in 1889: "It is easy enough to show that animals communicate, but this is a fact which has never been doubted. Dogs who growl and bark leave no doubt in the minds of other dogs or cats, or even of man, of what they mean, but growling and barking are not language, nor do they even contain the elements of language."

Unfortunately, Müller's authority, great as it was, did not suffice, and in 1890 we hear Samuel Butler ("Thought and Language," in his *Collected Essays*) reply

Human language must be such that a child can acquire it. He acquires it, moreover, from parents who have no idea how to explain it to him. No careful schedule of rewards for correct or punishments for incorrect utterances is necessary. It is sufficient that the child be allowed to grow up naturally in an environment where language is used.

The child's achievement seems all the more remarkable when we recall the speed with which he accomplishes it and the limitations of his intelligence in other respects. It is difficult to avoid an impression that infants are little machines specially designed by nature to perform this particular learning task.

I believe this analogy with machines is worth pursuing. If we could imagine what a language-learning automaton would have to do, it would dramatise—and perhaps even clarify—what a child can do. The linguist and logician Noam Chomsky has argued that the description of such an automaton would comprise our hypothesis about the child's innate ability to learn languages or (to borrow a term from Ferdinand de Saussure) his innate *faculté de langage*.‡‡‡

Consider what information a language-learning automaton would be given to work with. Inputs to the machine would include a finite set of sentences, a finite set of non-sentences accompanied by some signal that they were incorrect, some way to indicate that one item is a repetition or elaboration or transformation of another, and some access to a universe of perceptual objects and events associated with the sentences. Inside the machine there would be a computer so programmed as to extract from these inputs the nature of the language, *i.e.*, the particular syntactic rules by which sentences are generated, and the rules that associate with each syntactic structure a particular phonetic representation and semantic interpretation. The important question, of course, is what programme of instructions would have to be given to the computer.

---

that although "growling and barking cannot be called very highly specialised language," still there is "a sayer, a sayee, and a covenanted symbol designedly applied. Our own speech is vertebrated and articulated by means of nouns, verbs, and the rules of grammar. A dog's speech is invertebrate, but I do not see how it is possible to deny that it possesses all the essential elements of language."

Müller and Butler did not argue about the facts of animal behaviour which Darwin had described. Their disagreement arose more directly from differences of opinion about the correct definition of the term "language." To-day our definitions of human language are more precise, so we can say with correspondingly more precision why Butler was wrong.

‡‡‡ N. Chomsky, "Explanatory Models in Linguistics," in *Logic, Methodology, and Philosophy of Science,* edited by E. Wagel, P. Suppes, and A. Tarski (Stanford University Press, Stanford, 1962, pp. 528–550).

We could instruct the computer to discover any imaginable set of rules that might, in some formal sense of the term, constitute a grammar. This approach—the natural one if we believe that human languages can be infinitely diverse and various—is doomed from the start. The computer would have to evaluate an infinitude of possible grammars; with only a finite corpus of evidence it would be impossible, even if sufficient time were available for computation, to arrive at any unique solution.[3]

A language-learning automaton could not possibly discover a suitable grammar unless some strong *a priori* assumptions were built into it from the start. These assumptions would limit the alternatives that the automaton considered—limit them presumably to the range defined by linguistic universals. The automaton would test various grammars of the appropriate form to see if they would generate all of the sentences and none of the non-sentences. Certain aspects would be tested before others; those found acceptable would be preserved for further evaluation. If we wished the automaton to replicate a child's performance, the order in which these aspects would be evaluated could only be decided after careful analysis of the successive stages of language acquisition in human children.

The actual construction of such an automaton is, of course, far beyond our reach at the present time. That is not the point. The lesson to learn from such speculations is that the whole project would be impossible unless the automaton—and so, presumably, a child—knew in advance to look for particular kinds of regularities and correspondences, to discover rules of a rather special kind uniquely characteristic of human language in general.

The features that human infants are prepared to notice sharply limit the structure of any human language. Even if one imagines creating by decree a Newspeak in which this generalisation were false, within one generation it would have become true again.[4]

Psycholinguistics does not deal with social practices determined arbitrarily either by caprice or intelligent design, but with practices that grow organically out of the biological nature of man and the linguistic capacities of human infants. To that extent, at least, it is possible to define an area of empirical fact well within the reach of our scientific methods.

Another line of scientific investigation is opened up by the observation that we do not always follow our own rules. If this were not so, of course, we would not speak of rules, but of the laws of language. The fact that we make mistakes, and that we can know we made mistakes, is central to the psycholinguistic problem. Before we can see the empirical issue this entails, however, we should first draw a crucial distinction between theories of language and theories of the users of language.

There is nothing in the linguistic description of a language to indicate what mistakes will occur. Mistakes result from the psychological limitations of people who use the language, not from the language itself. It would be meaningless to state rules for making mistakes.

A formal characterisation of a natural language in terms of a set of elements and rules for combining those elements must inevitably generate an infinitude of possible sentences that will never occur in actual use. Most of these sentences are too complicated for us. There is nothing mysterious about this. It is very similar to the situation in arithmetic where a student may understand perfectly the rules for multiplication, yet find that some multiplication problems are too difficult for him to do "in his head," *i.e.*, without extending his memory capacity by the use of pencil and paper.

There is no longest grammatical sentence. There is no limit to the number of different grammatical sentences. Moreover, since the number of elements and rules is finite, there must be some rules and elements that can recur any number of times in a grammatical sentence. Chomsky has even managed to pinpoint a kind of recursive operation in language that, in principle, lies beyond the power of any finite device to perform indefinitely often. Compare these sentences:

(R) Remarkable is the rapidity of the motion of the wing of the hummingbird.

(L) The hummingbird's wing's motion's rapidity is remarkable.

(E) The rapidity that the motion that the wing that the hummingbird has has has is remarkable.

When you parse these sentences you find that the phrase structure of (R) dangles off to the right; each prepositional phrase hangs to the noun in the prepositional phrase preceding it. In (R), therefore, we see a type of recurring construction that has been called right-branching. Sentence (L), on the other hand, is left-branching; each possessive modifies the possessive immediately following. Finally, (E) is an onion; it grows by embedding sentences within sentences.[5] Inside "The rapidity is remarkable" we first insert "the motion is rapid" by a syntactic transformation that permits us to construct relative clauses, and so we obtain "The rapidity that the motion has is remarkable." Then we repeat the transformation, this time inserting "the wing has motion" to obtain "The rapidity that the motion that the wing has has is remarkable." Repeating the transformation once more gives (E).

It is intuitively obvious that, of these three types of recursive operations, self-embedding (E) is psychologically the most difficult. Although they seem grammatical by any reasonable standard of grammar, such sentences never occur in ordinary usage because they exceed our cognitive capacities. Chomsky's achievement was to prove rigorously that any language that does *not* restrict this kind of recursive embedding contains sentences that cannot be spoken or understood by devices, human or mechanical, with finite memories. Any device that uses these rules must remember each left portion until it can be related to its corresponding right portion; if the memory of the user is limited, but the number of admissible left portions is not, it is inevitable that some admissible sentences will exceed the capacity of the user to process them correctly.§§§

It is necessary, therefore, to distinguish between a description of the language in terms of the rules that a person *knows* and uses and a description of that person's *performance* as a user of the rules. The distinction is sometimes criticised as "psycholatry" by strict adherents of behaviourism; "knowing" is considered too mentalistic and subjective, therefore unscientific. The objection cannot be taken seriously. Our conception of the rules that a language-user knows is indeed a hypothetical construct, not something observed directly in his behaviour. But if such hypotheses were to be forbidden, science in general would become an empty pursuit.

Given a reasonable hypothesis about the rules that a language-user knows, the exploration of his limitations in following those rules is proper work for an experimental psychologist. "Psychology should assist us," a great linguist once said, "in understanding what is going on in the mind of speakers, and more particularly how they are led to deviate from previously existing rules in consequence of conflicting tendencies." Otto Jespersen made this request of psychology in 1924; now at last the work is beginning.‖ ‖ ‖

One example. Stephen Isard and I asked Harvard undergraduates to memorise several sentences that differed in degree of self-embedding. For instance, the twenty-two words in the right-branching sentence, "We cheered the football squad that played the team that brought the mascot that chased the girls that were in the park," can be re-arranged to give one, two, three, or four self-embeddings; with four it becomes, "The girls (that the mascot (that the team (that the football squad (that we cheered) played) brought) chased) were in the park." One

§§§ N. Chomsky, *Syntactic Structures* (Mouton, The Hague, 1957).
‖ ‖ ‖ *The Philosophy of Grammar* (Allen and Unwin, London, 1924, p. 344).

self-embedding caused no difficulty; it was almost as easy to memorise as the sentence with none. Three or four embeddings were most difficult. When the sentence had two self-embeddings—"The team (that the football squad (that we cheered) played) brought the mascot that chased the girls that were in the park"—some subjects found it as easy to memorise as sentences with zero or one embedding, others found it as difficult as sentences with three or four. That is to say, everybody can manage one embedding, some people can manage two, but everybody has trouble with three or more.

Records of eye movements while people are reading such sentences show that the trouble begins with the long string of verbs, "cheered played brought," at which point all grasp of the sentence structure crumbles and they are left with a random list of verbs. This is just what would be expected from a computer executing a programme that did not make provision for a sub-routine to refer to itself, *i.e.*, that was not recursive. If our ability to handle this type of self-embedded recursion is really as limited as the experiment indicates, it places a strong limitation on the kinds of theories we can propose to explain our human capacities for processing information.

On the simpler levels of our psycholinguistic hierarchy the pessimists are wrong; much remains there to be explored and systematised by scientific methods. How far these methods can carry us remains an open question. Although syntax seems well within our grasp and techniques for studying semantic systems are now beginning to emerge, understanding and belief raise problems well beyond the scope of linguistics. Perhaps it is there that scientific progress will be forced to halt.

No psychological process is more important or difficult to understand than understanding, and nowhere has scientific psychology proved more disappointing to those who have turned to it for help. The complaint is as old as scientific psychology itself. It was probably first seen clearly by Wilhelm Dilthey, who called for a new kind of psychology— a kind to which Karl Jaspers later gave the name *"verstehende Psychologie"*—and in one form or another the division has plagued psychologists ever since. Obviously a tremendous gulf separates the interpretation of a sentence from the understanding of a personality, a society, historical epoch. But the gap is narrowing. Indeed, one can even pretend to see certain similarities between the generative theory of speech perception discussed above and the reconstructive intellectual processes that have been labelled *verstehende*. The analogy may some day prove helpful, but how optimistic one dares feel at the present time is not easily decided.

Meanwhile, the psycholinguists will undoubtedly continue to advance as far as they can. It should prove interesting to see how far that will be.

NOTES ON "THE PSYCHOLINGUISTS"

1. 10^{20} means 1 followed by 20 zeros (or 10 to the twentieth power). According to Miller, the average substitutability for a word in English is 10. That means if we take a two-word sentence, the number of possible combinations is 100; each of the 10 possible substitutes for the first word with each of the 10 substitutes for the second word (10×10). If we take a three-word sentence, the number of combinations is $10 \times 10 \times 10$, and so on.
2.   Miller is concerned that the introduction of *rules* into scientific investigation implies that the scientist is regulating behavior, not just observing it. Nothing could be farther from the case. A rule is a statement of a convention. For instance, a rule of written English is that a sentence begins with a capital letter. A linguist does not say that a writer should or should not follow the convention, he would merely observe that the convention exists. Furthermore, he can predict that any sentence that violates a convention will call attention to itself. Whether the violation was inadvertent (as in the case of a child) or intentional (as in the case of e. e. cummings) is another matter. Similarily, the grammar of English is the set of conventions that speakers of the language follow. If one of the conventions is violated, the sentence will sound "funny." For instance, the following two sentences violate the conventions governing the use of the progressive tense:

    a. *I am knowing what to do.*
    b. *He is thinking that this is the right answer.*

3.   In any limited corpus (no matter how big) there would be a large number of patterns that we would never notice because they are irrelevant to the way that we know human languages work. For instance, in a given corpus it might be the case that every sentence that begins with the letter *t* has an odd number of words, or that every seventh sentence has three prepositions in it. A computer would have no way of knowing that these patterns are accidental. Miller's point is that since the number of patterns in any given corpus is infinite, a human language learner must know what to look for in advance.
4.   Newspeak is the language employed by the government in George Orwell's novel *1984*. Miller's point is that even if it were possible to legislate

a made-up language, the next generation would learn it just as though it were a natural language.
5. The right branching version might be represented:
Remarkable is the rapidity
                    of the motion
                                of the wing
                                        of the hummingbird.
Left branching might be represented:
                        rapidity is remarkable.
                motion's
          wing's
The hummingbird's
Embedding might be represented:
The rapidity   is remarkable.
      that the motion   has
            that the wing   has
                  that the hummingbird has

NOAM CHOMSKY

Linguistic Theory

INTRODUCTION

Chomsky's essay is directed specifically to foreign language teachers, but virtually all of what he says is equally applicable to English teachers. Throughout the essay Chomsky cautions the teacher against over reliance on the "fundamental disciplines" of linguistics and psychology. Both fields are undergoing sweeping changes and have considerably retrenched their claims of pedagogical utility. Chomsky feels that this loss of confidence is "both healthy and realistic."

The main subject matter of the essay is an exploration cf the two main current theories of learning and the close connection between them and the two main current schools of linguistics. The two learning theories might be termed "empiricist" and "rule governed." Structural linguistics is closely associated with the "empiricist" school while transformational linguistics is associated with the "rule-governed" school.

From the empiricist point of view, a language is learned as a set of habits. These habits are acquired by reinforcement, association, and generalization. Chomsky argues that this theory is inadequate to account for

Reprinted by permission of the author from *Northeast Conference on the Teaching of Foreign Languages* (1966) Working Committee Reports, ed. by Robert C. Mead, Jr., pp. 43–49.

one of the most basic facts about language—its "creativity." That is, virtually every sentence a speaker of a language hears, says, reads, or writes is new to him. (A simple demonstration of the creativity of language is to open a book and select a sentence at random. Barring intentional quotation, the odds are almost incalculably remote that you will never see that exact sentence again.) Chomsky argues that if, for all practical purposes, each sentence we encounter is unique, the empiricist claim that language is learned as a set of habits seems inadequate.

From the rule-governed point of view, a language is learned through the formation of a set of rules of great generality that are used to generate and interpret new sentences. Chomsky terms this internal rule system the speaker's "linguistic competence." A linguist's rule system—a generative grammar—is a model of the speaker's linguistic competence.

Investigation of generative grammars has shown that in order for the rules to be sufficiently general they must be very abstract. By abstract, Chomsky means that they are often many steps removed from any kind of physical fact. Chomsky then poses the question as to whether rules of this abstraction are learned or inherent. His conclusion is that the human mind has an "intrinsic intellectual organization" which is inherently predisposed to make linguistic abstractions of great generality. Chomsky feels that the primary goal of both linguistic and psychological investigation of language is the determination and characterization of man's innate capacity for language.

I should like to make it clear from the outset that I am participating in this conference not as an expert on any aspect of the teaching of languages, but rather as someone whose primary concern is with the structure of language and, more generally, the nature of cognitive processes. Furthermore, I am, frankly, rather skeptical about the significance, for the teaching of languages, of such insights and understanding as have been attained in linguistics and psychology. Surely the teacher of language would do well to keep informed of progress and discussion in these fields, and the efforts of linguists and psychologists to approach the problems of language teaching from a principled point of view are extremely worthwhile, from an intellectual as well as a social point of view. Still, it is difficult to believe that either linguistics or psychology has achieved a level of theoretical understanding that might enable it to support a "technology" of language teaching. Both fields have made significant progress in recent decades, and, furthermore, both draw on centuries of careful thought and study. These disciplines are, at present, in a state of flux and agitation. What seemed to be well-established doctrine a few years ago may now be the subject of extensive debate. Although it would be difficult to document this generalization, it seems to me that there has been a significant decline, over the past ten or fifteen years, in the degree of confidence in the scope and security of foundations in both psychology and linguistics. I personally feel that this decline in confidence is both healthy and realistic. But it should serve as a warning to teachers that suggestions from the "fundamental disciplines" must be viewed with caution and skepticism.

Within psychology, there are now many who would question the view that the basic principles of learning are well understood. Long accepted principles of association and reinforcement, gestalt principles, the theory of concept formation as it has emerged in modern investigation, all of these have been sharply challenged in theoretical as well as experimental work. To me it seems that these principles are not merely inadequate but probably misconceived—that they deal with marginal aspects of acquisition of knowledge and leave the central core of the problem untouched.[1] In particular, it seems to me impossible to accept the view that linguistic behavior is a matter of habit, that it is slowly acquired by reinforcement, association, and generalization, or that linguistic concepts can be specified in terms of a space of elementary, physically defined "criterial attributes."[2] Language is not a "habit structure." Ordinary linguistic behavior characteristically involves innovation, formation of new sentences and new patterns in accordance with rules of great abstractness and intricacy. This is true both of the speaker, who constructs new utterances appropriate to the occasion, and of the hearer who must analyze and interpret these novel structures. There are no known principles of association or reinforcement, and no known sense of "generalization" that can begin to account for this characteristic "creative" aspect of normal language use. The new utterances that are produced and interpreted in the daily use of language are "similar" to those that constitute the past experience of speaker and hearer only in that they are determined, in their form and interpretation, by the same system of abstract underlying rules. There is no theory of association or generalization capable of accounting for this fact, and it would, I think, be a fundamental misunderstanding to seek such a theory, since the explanation very likely lies along different lines. The simple concepts of ordinary language (such concepts as "human being" or "knife" or "useful," etc., or, for that matter, the concept "grammatical sentence") cannot be specified in terms of a space of physical attributes, as in the concept formation paradigm. There is, correspondingly, no obvious analogy between the experimental results obtained in studies of concept formation and the actual processes that seem to underlie language learning.

Evidently, such an evaluation of the relevance of psychological theory to language acquisition requires justification, and it is far from uncontroversial. Nor will I attempt, within the framework of this paper, to supply any such justification. My point simply is that the relevance of psychological theory to acquisition of language is a highly dubious and questionable matter, subject to much controversy and plagued with uncertainties of all sorts. The applied psychologist and the teacher must certainly draw what suggestions and hints they can from psychological research, but they would be well-advised to do so with the constant realization of how fragile and tentative are the principles of the underlying discipline.

Turning to linguistics, we find much the same situation. Linguists have had their share in perpetuating the myth that linguistic behavior is "habitual" and that a fixed stock of "patterns" is acquired through practice and used as the basis for "analogy." These views could be maintained only as long as grammatical description was sufficiently vague and imprecise. As soon as an attempt is made to give a careful and precise account of the rules of sentence formation, the rules of phonetic organization, or the rules of sound-meaning correspondence in a language, the inadequacy of such an approach becomes apparent. What is more, the fundamental concepts of linguistic description have been subjected to serious critique. The principles of phonemic analysis, for example, have recently been called into question, and the status of the concept "phoneme" is very much in doubt. For that matter, there are basic unsolved problems concerning even the phonetic representations used as a basis for analysis of form in structural linguistics. Whereas a decade ago it would have been almost universally assumed that a phonetic representation is simply a record of physical fact, there is now considerable evidence that what the linguist takes to be a phonetic transcription is determined, in nontrivial ways, by the syntactic structure of the language, and that it is, to this extent, independent of the physical signal. I think there are by now very few linguists who believe that it is possible to arrive at the phonological or syntactic structure of a language by systematic application of "analytic procedures" of segmentation and classification, although fifteen or twenty years ago such a view was not only widely accepted but was also supported by significant results and quite plausible argument.

I would like to emphasize again that this questioning of fundamental principles is a very healthy phenomenon that has led to important advances and will undoubtedly continue to do so. It is, in fact, characteristic of any living subject. But it must be recognized that well-established theory, in fields like psychology and linguistics, is extremely limited in scope. The applications of physics to engineering may not be seriously affected by even the most deep-seated revolution in the foundations of physics, but the applications of psychology or linguistics to language teaching, such as they are, may be gravely affected by changing conceptions in these fields, since the body of theory that resists substantial modification is fairly small.

In general, the willingness to rely on "experts" is a frightening aspect of contemporary political and social life. Teachers, in particular, have a responsibility to make sure that ideas and proposals are evaluated on their merits, and not passively accepted on grounds of authority, real or presumed. The field of language teaching is no exception. It is possible—even likely—that principles of psychology and linguistics, and research in these disciplines, may supply insights useful to the language teacher. But this must be demonstrated, and cannot be presumed. It is the language teacher himself who must validate or refute any specific proposal. There is very little in psychology or linguistics that he can accept on faith.

I will not try to develop any specific proposals relating to the teaching of languages—as I mentioned before, because I am not competent to do so. But there are certain tendencies and developments within linguistics and psychology that may have some potential impact on the teaching of language. I think these can be usefully summarized under four main headings: the "creative" aspect of language use; the abstractness of linguistic representation; the universality of underlying linguistic structure; the role of intrinsic organization in cognitive processes. I would like to say just a few words about each of these topics.

The most obvious and characteristic property of normal linguistic behavior is that it is stimulus-free and innovative. Repetition of fixed phrases is a rarity; it is only under exceptional and quite uninteresting circumstances that one can seriously consider how "situational context" determines what is said, even in probabilistic terms. The notion that linguistic behavior consists of "responses" to "stimuli" is as much a myth as the idea that it is a matter of habit and generalization. To maintain such assumptions in the face of the actual facts, we must deprive the terms "stimulus" and "response" (similarly "habit" and "generalization") of any technical or precise meaning. This property of being innovative and stimulus-free is what I refer to by the term "creative aspect of language use." It is a property of language that was described in the seventeenth century and that serves as one cornerstone for classical linguistic theory, but that has gradually been forgotten in the development of modern linguistics, much to its detriment. Any theory of language must come to grips with this fundamental property of normal language use. A necessary but not sufficient step towards dealing with this problem is to recognize that the native speaker of a language has internalized a "generative grammar"—a system of rules that can be used in new and untried combinations to form new sentences and to assign semantic interpretations to new sentences. Once this fact has become clear, the immediate task of the linguist is likewise clarified. He must try to discover the rules of this generative grammar and the underlying principles on the basis of which it is organized.

The native speaker of a language has internalized a generative grammar in the sense just described, but he obviously has no awareness of this fact or of the properties of this grammar. The problem facing the linguist is to discover what constitutes unconscious, latent knowledge—to bring to light what is now sometimes called the speaker's intrinsic "linguistic competence." A generative grammar of a language is a theory of the speaker's competence. If correct, it expresses the principles that determine the intrinsic correlation of sound and meaning in the language in question. It thus serves as one component of a theory that can accommodate the characteristic creative aspect of language use.

When we try to construct explicit, generative grammars and investigate their properties, we discover at once many inadequacies in traditional and modern linguistic descriptions. It is often said that no complete generative grammar has ever been written for any language, the implication being that this "new-fangled" approach suffers in comparison with older and well-established approaches to language description, in this respect. The statement concerning generative grammar is quite accurate; the conclusion, if intended, reveals a serious misunderstanding. Even the small fragments of generative grammars that now exist are incomparably greater in explicit coverage than traditional or structuralist descriptions, and it is important to be aware of this fact. A generative grammar is simply one that gives explicit rules that determine the structure of sentences, their phonetic form, and their semantic interpretation. The limitations of generative grammar are the limitations of our knowledge, in these areas. Where traditional or structuralist descriptions are correct, they can immediately be incorporated into generative grammars. Insofar as these descriptions merely list examples of various kinds and make remarks (which may be interesting and suggestive) about them, then they cannot be directly incorporated into generative grammars. In other words, a traditional or structuralist description can be immediately incorporated into a generative grammar to the extent that it is correct and does not rely on the "intelligence of the reader" and his "linguistic intuition."[3] The limitations of generative grammar, then, are a direct reflection of the limitations of correctness and explicitness in earlier linguistic work.

A serious investigation of generative grammars quickly shows that the rules that determine the form of sentences and their interpretations are not only intricate but also quite abstract, in the sense that the structures they manipulate are related to physical fact only in a remote way, by a long chain of interpretative rules. This is as true on the level of phonology as it is on the level of syntax and semantics, and it is this fact that has led to the questioning both of structuralist principles and of the tacitly assumed psychological theory that underlies them. It is because of the abstractness of linguistic representations that one is forced, in my opinion, to reject not only the analytic procedures of modern linguistics, with their reliance on segmentation and classification, but also principles of association and generalization that have been discussed and studied in empiricist psychology. Although such phenomena as association and generalization, in the sense of psychological theory and philosophical speculation, may indeed exist, it is difficult to see how they have any bearing on the acquisition or use of language. If our current conceptions of generative grammar are at all accurate, then the structures manipulated and the principles operating in these grammars are not related to given sensory phenomena in any way describable in the terms that empiricist psychology offers, and what principles it suggests simply have no relation to the facts that demand explanation.[4]

If it is correct that the underlying principles of generative grammars cannot be acquired through experience and training, then they must be part of the intellectual organization which is a prerequisite for language acquisition. They must, therefore, be universal properties, properties of any generative grammar. These are, then, two distinct ways of approaching what is clearly the most fundamental question of linguistic science, namely, the question of linguistic universals. One way is by an investigation of a wide range of languages. Any hypothesis as to the nature of linguistic universals must meet the empirical condition that it is not falsified by any natural language, any language acquired and used by humans in the normal way. But there is also another and, for the time being, somewhat more promising way of studying the problem of universals. This is by deep investigation of a particular language, investigation directed towards establishing underlying principles of organization of great abstractness in this language. Where such principles can be established, we must account for their existence. One plausible hypothesis is that they are innate, therefore, universal. Another plausible hypothesis is that they are acquired through experience and training. Either hypothesis can be made precise; each will then be meaningful and worthy of attention. We can refute the former by showing that other aspects of this language or properties of other languages are inconsistent with it. We can refute the latter by showing that it does not yield the structures that we must presuppose to account for linguistic competence. In general, it seems to me quite impossible to account for many deep-seated aspects of language on the basis of training or experience, and that therefore one must search for an explanation for them in terms of intrinsic intellectual organization. An almost superstitious refusal to consider this proposal seriously has, in my opinion, enormously set back both linguistics and psychology. For the present, it seems to me that there is no more reason for assuming that the basic principles of grammar are learned than there is for making a comparable assumption about, let us say, visual perception. There is, in short, no more reason to suppose that a person learns that English has a generative grammar of a very special and quite explicitly definable sort than there is to suppose that the same person learns to analyze the visual field in terms of line, angle, motion, solidity, persons with faces, etc.[5]

Turning then to the last of the four topics mentioned above, I think that one of the most important current developments in psychology and neurophysiology is the investigation of intrinsic organization in cognition. In the particular case of language, there is good reason to believe that even the identification of the phonetic form of a sentence presupposes at least a partial syntactic analysis, so that the rules of the generative grammar may be brought into play even in identifying the signal. This view is opposed to the hypothesis that phonetic representation is determined by the signal completely, and that the perceptual analysis proceeds from formal signals to interpretation, a hypothesis which, I understand, has been widely quoted in discussion of language teaching. The role of the generative grammar in perception is paralleled by the role of the universal grammar—the system of invariant underlying principles of linguistic organization—in acquisition of language. In each case, it seems to me that the significance of the intrinsic organization is very great indeed, and that the primary goal of linguistic and psychological investigation of language must be to determine and characterize it.

I am not sure that this very brief discussion of some of the leading ideas of much current research has been sufficiently clear to be either informative or convincing. Once again, I would like to stress that the implications of these ideas for language teaching are far from clear to me. It is a rather dubious undertaking to try to predict the course of development of any field, but, for what it is worth, it seems to me likely that questions of this sort will dominate research in the coming years, and, to hazard a further guess, that this research will show that certain highly abstract structures and highly specific principles of organization are characteristic of all human languages, are intrinsic rather than acquired, play a central role in perception as well as in production of sentences, and provide the basis for the creative aspect of language use.

NOTES ON "LINGUISTIC THEORY"

1. Chomsky draws a distinction between "marginal" and "central" aspects of the acquisition of knowledge. By marginal Chomsky means the work of empiricist psychologists who have investigated learning theory in terms of measuring behavior that an organism is *not* inherently built to do, for instance, training pigeons to perform tricks on command. Chomsky complains that such investigation sheds little light on the central question of how an organism learns to perform behavior that it is built to do, for instance, how humans learn language. For a detailed discussion see Chomsky's "A Review of B. F. Skinner's *Verbal Behavior*" in *Language*, Vol. 35, pp. 26–58.
2. The term "criterial attributes" is used in Jerome Bruner, Jacqueline Goodnow, and George Austin's book *A Study of Thinking*. Criterial attributes are those attributes (or characteristics) of an object or concept that the individual takes for himself to be the defining attributes of that object or concept.
3. Chomsky says that the grammatical description of a language cannot *rely* on the "intelligence of the reader" of the grammar or upon his "linguistic intuition" to fill in the assumptions and implications of the description. The description is based completely on the speaker's intuition, but the description can only be *tested* to the degree that the claims of the description are made clear and precise.
4. To illustrate this point from the area of syntax, compare these two sentences (from Chomsky's *Syntactic Theory*):

> a. *I heard the shooting of the hunters.*
> b. *I heard the growling of the lions.*

Every speaker of English knows that (a) is ambiguous in a way that (b) is not. This is a fact that an adequate grammar must account for. However, there is no physically observable signal that marks the ambiguity of (a) or the lack of ambiguity of (b). Chomsky's point, of course, is that any theory of language that starts with only the information in the signal cannot possibly account for the difference between (a) and (b).

5. Put another way, our ability to use language is not dependent on the study of grammar any more than our ability to see is dependent on the study of visual perception. This distinction is sometimes termed the difference between "knowledge of" and "knowledge about." Every speaker of a language has a knowledge *of* that language which enables him to speak it, but unless he has been schooled on the subject, he has little knowledge *about* the language, for example, its history, and its phonological and grammatical structure.

ERIC H. LENNEBERG

The Capacity for Language Acquisition

INTRODUCTION

In this essay Lenneberg draws a distinction between biologically determined and culturally determined behavior. Biologically determined behavior is innate within the species, while culturally determined behavior is learned. Lenneberg argues that language and language acquisition, in certain key respects, are instances of biologically determined behavior.

Lenneberg proposes four criteria which distinguish biologically determined activity from culturally determined, and uses the activity of walking to illustrate the former and writing to illustrate the latter.

1. *Variation within species.* Where there is no significant variation within the species, the behavior is common to all members of the species and thus innate.

Reprinted by permission of the author, Prentice-Hall, Inc., and Columbia University Press from *The Structure of Language: Readings in the Philosophy of Language*, ed. by Jerry A. Fodor and Jerrold J. Katz, 1964. pp. 579–603.

An extended version of an article, written while its author was Career Investigator, National Institute of Mental Health, and published under the title "Language, Evolution, and Purposive Behavior" in S. Diamond, ed., *Culture in History: Essays in Honor of Paul Radin* (New York: Columbia University Press, 1960), pp. 869–893. Revised and reprinted by permission.

2. *History within species.* If an activity were innate, there could be no
record of a change in the activity from past to present. Consequently,
a biologically determined behavior has no history.

3. *Evidence for inherited predisposition.* A biologically determined
behavior is one that takes place spontaneously, that is, the behavior
is not dependent upon motivation or reward within the environment.

4. *Presumption of specific organic correlates.* Lenneberg divides this
criterion into two sections:

   a. *Onset and fixed developmental history.* An inherent activity appears in an individual member of the species at a predictable
   point of maturity and goes through a specific course of development.

   b. *Dependence upon environment.* All activity, innate or learned, is
   dependent upon the environment for some kind of stimulus. The
   difference between an innate activity and a learned activity is
   that the former activity may be said to be *programmed* into the
   organism—the environment serves only as a trigger of "innate
   releasing mechanism." A culturally determined activity, on the
   other hand, is nearly completely dependent upon the environment
   for its structure and sequence.

Lenneberg then examines language and language acquisition in light of
these four criteria in order to demonstrate that they are biologically determined activities.

1. *Variation with species.* While the amount of linguistic diversity in
the languages of the world is great, all languages share certain
fundamental properties: (1a) all have a phonology based on contrasting sounds, (2b) all languages string the individual units of
the language together into larger concatenated sequences called
phrases, sentences or discourses, and (3c) all languages have a grammar. Lenneberg concludes from these generalizations that all human
languages are the same in terms of their formal properties and
consequently these similarities must reflect some innate property of
man himself.

2. *History within species.* It is apparently natural for all languages to
change, but the change does not involve any kind of evolution: linguists are totally unable to trace the development of language back
to some primitive stage.

3. *Evidence for inherited predisposition.* Lenneberg points out that
while no man inherits a predisposition to learn a specific language,
he does inherit a propensity for language learning which is so powerful that it is manifested even in physically and mentally handicapped
children who are cut off from a normal linguistic environment.

4. *Presumption of specific organic correlates.*
   a. *Onset and fixed developmental history.* The development of speech

in children begins at a predictable age and seems to follow a specific maturational pattern.

b. *Dependence upon environment.* The question here is whether or not a child is "trained" to speak. Lenneberg argues that speech activity requires enormous creativity: children create linguistic forms that they have never heard before, that, in fact, do not exist in the adult model. Consequently, a child must possess some innate linguistic capability beyond what the mechanism of imitation could account for.

Lenneberg concludes the essay by sketching the model of language acquisition that is presented in behavioral psychology and then raises five problems that seem to be beyond the capacity of the model:

1. Even simple imitation of a sound requires the child to make generalizations and abstractions since no two sounds are ever acoustically identical.
2. Children "imitate" in a highly characteristic way: they do not appear to be striving to gain control over the motor skills of articulation, rather the goal seems to be the much more abstract skill of *naming*.
3. The noises that animals make seem related to some biological function such as courting, danger signals, anger, and the like. It is apparently impossible to train an animal to switch noises, that is, to use a noise in one situation that would normally be used in another. Humans, however, seem to be able to separate noise from emotion as part of their normal language development.
4. Children, without any special training, seem to automatically pay attention to language cues.
5. The great apes have the physical capacity to produce speech sounds, yet no primate has been able to learn to manipulate the vocal mechanism with anything approaching the level of skill that every child ordinarily displays.

There is a tendency among social scientists to regard language as a wholly learned and cultural phenomenon, an ingeniously devised instrument, purposefully introduced to subserve social functions, the artificial shaping of an amorphous, general capacity called *intelligence.* We scarcely entertain the notion that man may be equipped with highly specialized, biological propensities that favor and, indeed, shape the development of speech in the child and that roots of language may be as deeply grounded in our natural constitution as, for instance, our

predisposition to use our hands. To demonstrate the logical possibility
—if not probability—of such a situation is the purpose of this paper.
It is maintained that clarity on the problem of the biological foundation of language is of utmost importance in formulating both questions
and hypotheses regarding the function, mechanism, and history of
language.

The heuristic method to be employed here will be analogous to procedures employed in studying processes too slow and inert to be
amenable to laboratory experimentation, notably biological evolution.
The reasoning of our argument may gain by a few general statements
on this type of theory construction and by a review of the basic, modern principles evoked in current discussions of evolution.

In many scientific endeavors we are faced with the problem of
reconstructing a sequence of events from scattered, static evidence.
The writing of geological, phylogenetic, and cultural histories is alike
in this respect. But our treatment of geological and phylogenetic
history differs from cultural history when it comes to "explaining" the
causal relationships that hold between the events.

In geology we may trace cycles of elevation of the continent: subsequent leveling by erosion, followed by sedimentation at the bottom
of the sea, and then recurrent elevation of the once submerged land,
far above the level of the sea, resulting again in erosion and so forth.
We cannot *explain* these sequences in terms of purpose, for purpose
assumes a planned action, a pre-established end. Erosion, for instance,
serves no more the *purpose* of establishing a balance than the eruption
of a volcano serves the purpose of making erosion possible. It is
appropriate to speak about disturbed and re-established equilibria;
but the use of the word *purpose* has the common connotation of striving toward a goal, and, therefore, ought to be reserved for pieces of
behavior that do indeed aim at a pre-established end without, however, being bound by nature to reach such ends by pre-established
means.

In our discussions of phylogeny we must be as careful to avoid
teleological explanations as in the case of geological history. Yet, many
a time we seem to have no small difficulty in living up to this ideal.
It seems so reasonable to say that the *purpose* of man's increased
cranial vault is to house a large brain; and that the *purpose* of a large
brain is the perfection of intelligence. We must take exception to this
formulation because it implies finality in evolution or, at least, the
assumption of a pre-established direction and end.* The geneticist

---

* For a philosophical treatment of this point, see H. Feigl, "Notes on Causality"
in H. Feigl and M. Brodbeck, Eds., *Readings in the Philosophy of Science* (New

looks at evolution as the interplay between a *random* process and certain constraining factors. The random process is the blind generation of inheritable characteristics, i.e., mutations, while all the constraining factors have to do with viability of the individual or the species as a whole. Of the many new traits that may chance to appear, the great majority will have a lethal effect under given environmental conditions and are thus of no consequence for evolution. But occasionally there is one that *is* compatible with life and will thus result in perpetuation, at least over a limited period of time.

Attempts have been made to discover whether specific types of mutation could be regarded as adaptive responses of the germ plasm to environmental necessities, but I believe it is fair to say that so far results are not sufficient to conclude that there is a generally adaptive directionality in mutations. Dobzhansky states: "Genetics . . . asserts that the organism is not endowed with providential ability to respond to the requirements of the environment by producing mutations adapted to these requirements."[†]

If it is conceded that variability of inheritable traits due to mutation does not reflect direct responses to *needs*, it is quite conceivable that we may find characteristics that are compatible with life under prevailing conditions but that have no heightened adaptive value and can therefore not be explained in terms of utility to the organism.[‡] The differentiating characteristics of human races may be cases in point. The shape of skulls or the textures of hair cannot be rated by usefulness; nor can those mutations that have resulted in new species without extermination or limitation of the older forms.

The problem is more complicated when we observe a long and linear evolutionary trend, for instance the more or less steady increase in the body size of a species. When such a linear development occurs, we say that the evolved trait is *useful* to the species. I would like to stress, however, that the word *useful* (or reference to utility) must be employed with great care in this context and not without careful

---

York, Appleton-Century-Crofts, Inc. 1953), pp. 408–418, and E. Nagel, "Teleological Explanations and Teleological Systems," in S. Ratner, Ed., *Vision and Action: Essays in Honor of Horace Kallen* (New Brunswick, N.J.: Rutgers University Press, 1953). For a biotheoretical view see L. V. Bertalanffy, *Theoretische Biologie* (Berlin: Borntrager, 1932), vol. I. For the geneticist's position see J. B. S. Haldane, *Causes of Evolution* (New York: Harper & Row, Publishers, Inc., 1932).

† T. Dobzhansky, *Genetics and the Origin of Species* (3d ed.; New York: Columbia University Press, 1951) p. 51. See also the same author's broad survey of the entire field, *Evolution, Genetics, and Man* (New York: John Wiley and Sons, Inc., 1955).

‡ Cf. H. J. Muller, "Human Values in Relation to Evolution," *Science*, 127 (1958), 625f.

definition lest it be confused with purposiveness. In case of gradually increasing body size (take for instance the history of the horse), an individual animal stays alive if it is of a certain size, whereas an individual may perish if it falls short of the size that is critical at the time it is born. Since the individual cannot alter its inherited size, it also cannot change its fate of starving or being killed before maturation. Thus, no matter how *useful* it may be to be large, this state of affairs cannot be reached by purposeful striving of individual animals. Much less can we conceive of a super-individual entity (such as the species as a whole), making *use* of this or that trait in order to "insure the continuation" of the species. Something can become useful after it has come into being by a random process; but to make systematic use of a trait, such as size, seems to imply foresight and providence not usually accorded to the driving forces of genetics.

The situation is quite different when we come to a discussion of cultural history. Here, explanations in terms of long-range purpose and utility often are in order because man, indeed, does have final ends in view which he strives to achieve by this or that means. Frequently there are even explicit criteria for usefulness in reaching a goal, such as reduction of physical effort, maximizing gratification, or introducing order and manageability into a certain situation. In the development of coin money, for instance, there may have been some trial and error in the course of history, but many changes were introduced by fiat with the explicit purpose of facilitating economic intercourse. In other words, the development of coin money is the direct result of a certain property of human behavior, namely purposiveness. Or, more generally, it may be said that the phenomenon of *culture per se* is the outgrowth of this characteristic trait. But this should not obscure the fact that man and his abilities are also the product of biological evolution and that many of his traits are genetically determined and as such their existence must not be explained in terms of purpose. For instance the alternations between sleep and wakefulness, the shedding of tears, the closure of the epiglottis in swallowing, or any other unconditioned responses cannot be considered as the outcome of rational invention, as the end product of a purposeful striving just as any other genetic phenomena must not be accounted for in this way.

It is well to remember that purposiveness is a trait that is itself the result of evolutionary history, of phylogenetic development. Rudimentary forms of short-term purpose are observable as far back as the invertebrates. It is the ability to strive toward a goal (say nest building) by more than a single rigid action pattern. It is an ability to take advantage of specific environmental conditions in the accomplishment of certain tasks. For instance, birds are not confined to one specific type of material in the construction of their nests; the use of tiny shreds of newspaper incorporated in these structures is not an uncommon finding. Purposiveness requires anticipation or expectancy together with a flexibility in the choice of routes that lead to the goal.§

The purposiveness displayed in man's activities differs from that seen in lower animals not so much in quality as in degree. No other animal seems capable of performing actions with such long-range purpose as is seen in our socio-cultural activities. Not even such activities as nest building in birds which may last for days and weeks are the result of long-range purpose. This has been described by Tinbergen and commented on by Thorpe.‖ The nest is merely the end result of a very long series of individual tasks where each accomplishment seems to trigger off a striving for the fulfillment of the next task, and there is evidence that purposiveness, as defined above, does not actually extend over the entire plan; each task has its own characteristic, short-term purposiveness.

Our objective now is to examine language and to decide in which of its aspects we must assume it to be a genetically determined trait and in which of its aspects it might be the result of cultural activity. Insofar as it is revealed to be a biologically determined affair, we cannot explain it as the result of a purposefully devised system; we may not claim that *the reason* a child learns it is the inherent possibility of providing pleasure, security, or usefulness; or that language has this or that property because this was found in pre-historic times to serve best the purpose of communication. Any hedonistic or utilitarian explanation of language is tantamount to claim that speech as such is a cultural phenomenon or, at least, that it is the product of purposive behavior. Whereas, a demonstration that language is at least partly determined by innate predispositions would put serious constraints on utilitarian explanations of language and would instead focus our attention on physiological, anatomical, and genetic factors underlying verbal behavior.

Before embarking on the actual argument, a brief warning may be in place. The distinction between genetically determined and purposive behavior is *not* the same as the distinction between behavior that does or does not depend upon environmental conditions. The

§ W. H. Thorpe, *Learning and Instinct in Animals* (Cambridge, Mass.: Harvard University Press, 1956). This is the most scholarly source on the subject of innate and acquired behavior. My entire article has been thoroughly influenced by this book.

‖ Thorpe, *op. cit.*, Chap. 2; N. Tinbergen, "Specialists in Nest Building," *Country Life*, 30 (January 1953), 270–271.

following example based on work by B. F. Riess will illustrate this point; the quotation is due to Beach.

> The maternal behavior of primiparous female rats reared in isolation is indistinguishable from that of multiparous individuals. Animals with no maternal experience build nests before the first litter is born. However, pregnant rats that have been reared in cages containing nothing that can be picked up and transported do not build nests when material is made available. They simply heap their young in a pile in a corner of the cage. Other females that have been reared under conditions preventing them from licking and grooming their own bodies fail to clean their young at the time of parturition.#

From this example it is obvious that innate behavior may be intimately related to or dependent upon the organism's interaction with its environment, yet the action *sequence* as a whole (first carrying things in an unorganized way; then, when pregnant, carrying things in an organized way so that the end product is a nest) is innately given. In other words, it would not be reasonable to claim that the young female rat carries things around because she is planning to build a nest if she should be pregnant and that she is purposefully training herself in carrying around material to be better prepared for the eventualities in store for her.

On the other hand, *purposive* behavior may only be very indirectly related to environmental conditions and thus give the impression of completely spontaneous creation; the composition of the Jupiter Symphony is an example.

In our discussion of language, we shall proceed in the following way. We shall juxtapose two types of human activities, one of which we have good reasons to believe to be biologically given, i.e., walking, while the other one we can safely assume to be the result of cultural achievement and thus a product of purposiveness, namely, writing. By comparing these two types of activities, it will be shown that there are at least four good criteria which distinguish in man biologically determined from culturally determined behavior. When these criteria are applied to language, it will be seen that verbal behavior in many important respects resembles the biological type, while in other respects it bears the sign of cultural and purposive activity. Since the culturally determined features in language are widely noted, the discussion will emphasize innate factors more than cultural ones.

F. A. Beach, "The Descent of Instinct," *Psychological Review*, **62** (1955), 401–410. Since writing this article H. L. Teuber has drawn my attention to contrary evidence: I. Eibl-Eibesfeld, "Angeborenes und Erworbenes im Nestbauverhalten der Wanderratte," *Naturwissenschaft*, **42** (1955), 633:34.

| *Bipedal Gait* | *Writing* |

CRITERION 1

No intraspecies variations: The species has only one type of loco-motion; it is universal to all men. (This is a special case of the more general point that inherited traits have poor correlations—if any— with social groupings: cf. black hair or protruding zygoma.)

Intraspecies variations correlated with social organizations: A number of very different successful writing systems have co-existed. The geographical distribution of writing systems follows cultural and social lines of demarcation.

CRITERION 2

No history within species: We cannot trace the development of bipedal gait from a primitive to a complex stage throughout the history of human *cultures*. There are no geographical foci from which cultural diffusion of the trait seems to have emanated at earlier times. All human races have the same basic skeletal foot pattern. For significant variations in gait, we have to go back to fossil forms that represent a predecessor of modern man.

Only history within species: There are cultures where even the most primitive writing system is completely absent. We can follow the development of writing histori-cally just as we can study the distribution of writing geographi-cally. We can make good guesses as to the area of invention and development and trace the cultural diffusion over the surface of the globe and throughout the last few millenia of history. The emergence of writing is a rela-tively recent event.

CRITERION 3

Evidence for inherited predisposi-tion: Permanent and customary gait cannot be taught or learned by practice if the animal is not biologically constituted for this type of locomotion.

No evidence for inherited predis-position: Illiteracy in non-Western societies is not ordinarily a sign of mental deficiency but of defi-ciency in training. The condition can be quickly corrected by ap-propriate practice.

CRITERION 4

Presumption of specific organic correlates: In the case of gait, we do not have to *presume* organic correlates; we *know* them. However, behavioral traits that are regarded as the product of evolution (instincts) are also thought to be based on organic predispositions, in this case, on the grounds of circumstantial evidence and often in the absence of anatomical and physiological knowledge.

No assumption of specific organic correlates: We do, of course, assume a biological capacity for writing, but there is no evidence for innate predisposition for this activity.** A child's contact with written documents or with pencil and paper does not ordinarily result in automatic acquisition of the trait. Nor do we suppose that the people in a society that has evolved no writing system to be genetically different from those of a writing society. It is axiomatic in anthropology that any normal infant can acquire all cultural traits of any society given the specific cultural upbringing.

BIOLOGICAL AND SOCIO-CULTURAL FACTORS IN LANGUAGE

Let us now view language in the light of the four criteria discussed above in order to see to what extent language is part of our biological heritage.

1. **First Criterion: Variation within Species.** One of the major contributions of modern linguistics was the dispelling of the eighteenth-century notion of a *universal grammar* which, at that time, was based on the assumption of a universal logic. In America it was particularly the descriptivist school initiated by Franz Boas that has been most active during the last thirty years in demonstrating the truly amazing variety of phonological, grammatical, and semantic systems in the languages of the world. These workers have shown how the traditional method of describing languages in terms of logic must be abandoned for more objective, formal, and unprejudiced analyses; they have shown that lexicons of different languages are never strictly comparable; in fact, they have made us aware of the difficulty inherent in such notions as *word, tense,* or *parts of speech.* Thus, today anyone

** Cf. A. L. Drew, "A Neurological Appraisal of Familial Congenital Word-Blindness," *Brain,* 76 (1956), 440–460.

interested in language and speech is keenly aware of the great diversi-
fication of linguistic form in the languages of the world, and it is commonly acknowledged that their histories cannot be traced back to a
common "*ur-language*." In the light of this realization, it is very remarkable to note that in some respects all languages are alike and that this
similarity is by no means a *logical* necessity. Following are three points
in which languages are identical; they are, however, not the only
similarities.

1.1 *Phonology.* Speech is without exception a vocal affair, and,
more important, the vocalizations heard in the languages of the world
are always within fairly narrow limits of the total range of sounds that
man can produce. For instance, we can faithfully imitate the noises of
many mammals, the songs of a number of birds, the crying noises of
an infant; yet, these direct imitations never seem to be incorporated in
vocabularies. There is onomatopoeia, to be sure; but onomatopoetic
words are never faithful imitations but phonemicized expressions. This
is precisely the point: all languages have phonemic systems; that is,
the morphemes of all languages can be further segmented into smaller,
meaningless, components of functionally similar sounds. Words and
morphemes are constituted in all languages by a sequence of phonemes.
This is not a matter of definition or a methodological artifact. One can
visualize a very complex language in which the symbol for *cat* is a
perfect imitation of that animal's noise (and so on for other mammals),
for *baby* the infant's characteristic cries, for a *shrew* *s*colding yells; the
size of objects could be represented by sound intensity, *vertical direction* by pitch, *color* by vowel quality, *hunger* by roaring, *sex* by caress-
ing whimpers, and so on. In such a language we would have morphemes or words that could not be segmented into common, concatenated sound elements. Most words and perhaps all morphemes
would constitute a sound-Gestalt *sui generis* much the way pictograms
and idiograms cannot be analyzed into a small set of letters.

It would be interesting to see whether parrots speak in phonemes or
not; if they do not speak in phonemes (as I would assume), we would
have an empirical demonstration that the phonemic phenomenon is
neither a methodological artifact nor a logical necessity. One could,
for instance, take a parrot who was raised in Brazil and who has
acquired a good repertoire of Portuguese phrases and words, and
suddenly transplant him to an English-speaking environment where
he would add English bits to his stock of exclamations. If the first few
words are pronounced with a heavy Portuguese accent, we would have
evidence that the bird generalizes his Portuguese habits, that is, that
he has actually learned Portuguese phonemes which he now uses in

the production of English words. However, if his English acquisitions sound at once *native*, it would appear that the parrot merely has an ability for imitating sounds without deriving from it a generalized habit for the production of speech.

Whether this experiment is practically possible, I do not know. It is related here rather to highlight the problem at stake. It also suggests some empirical research on human subjects. If foreign accents are a proof for the existence of phonemes and if the child at three is said to speak phonemically (which every linguist would have to affirm), we would expect him to have an English accent if he is suddenly asked to pronounce say a simple German word—provided he has never heard German before. This is a project that could be done quite easily and objectively and which would be very revealing. (We are not speaking here of the young child's ability quickly to learn foreign languages, i.e., learn more than a single phonemic system. This is a different problem that will be discussed in greater detail.)

1.2 *Concatenation.* This term denotes the phenomenon of stringing up morphemes or words into a complex sequence called *phrases, sentences,* or *discourse.* No speech community has ever been described where communication is restricted to single-word discourse, where the customary utterance would be something like "water!" or "go," or "bird"; where it would be impossible, for example, to give geographical directions by means of concatenated, independent forms. Man everywhere talks in what appears to be a "blue streak."

1.3 *Syntactic structure.* We know of no language that concatenates randomly, that is, where any word may be followed by any other. There are contingencies between words (or, languages have typical statistical structures)†† but this in itself does not constitute grammars.‡‡ We can program stochastic processes into machines such that they generate symbols (e.g., words) with the same statistical properties as that noted for languages; yet these machines will not "speak grammatically," at least not insofar as they generate new sentences. It is generally assumed by linguists—and there are compelling reasons for this—that there must be a finite set of rules that defines all grammatical operations for any given language. Any native speaker will generate

---

†† G. A. Miller, *Language and Communication* (New York: McGraw-Hill Book Company, 1951), Chap. 10.
‡‡ N. A. Chomsky, *Syntactic Structures* (The Hague: Mouton, 1957), and N. A. Chomsky, "Three Models for the Description of Language," *IRE Transactions on Information Theory,* IT-2, 3 (no date), 113–124. I am also indebted to Chomsky for reading an earlier version of this article and for making valuable suggestions. See also G. A. Miller, E. Galanter, K. H. Pribram, *Plans and the Structure of Behavior* (New York: Holt, Rinehart and Winston, Inc., 1960), pp. 139–158.

sentences that conform to these grammatical rules, and any speaker of the speech community will recognize such sentences as grammatical. We are dealing here with an extremely complex mechanism and one that has never been fully described in purely formal terms for any language (if it had, we could program computers that can "speak" grammatically); and yet, we know that the mechanism must exist for the simple reason that every speaker knows and generally agrees with fellow speakers whether a sentence is grammatical or not. (This has nothing to do with familiarity or meaning of an utterance. One may easily demonstrate this by comparing Chomsky's two sentences, "colorless green ideas sleep furiously" and "furiously sleep ideas green colorless," where neither of the sentences are likely to have occurred prior to Chomsky's illustration, yet one is recognized as grammatical and the other not.) Note that types of sentence structures are as variable as speech sounds among languages of the world, but the phenomenon of grammar as such is absolutely universal.

1.4 *Conclusion.* The importance of the universality of phonematization (evidenced by the universality of small and finite phoneme stocks), of the universality of concatenation, and of the ubiquitous presence of grammar cannot be overestimated. Consider the vast differences in the forms and semantics of languages (making a common and focal origin of language most unlikely); consider the geographical separation of some human societies that must have persisted for thousands of years; consider the physical differentiation into a number of different stocks and races. Yet, everywhere man communicates in a strikingly similar pattern. There are only two kinds of conclusion that can be drawn from this situation. Either the similarities are due to the fact that, by happenstance, identical principles of communication have developed completely independently over and over, hundreds of times—an extremely improbable supposition, or the universal phenomena reflect some trait that is related to the genetic mutation that has constituted the speciation of *homo sapiens* and are, therefore, of a venerable age. I should like to take the latter view, and I feel strengthened in this position by the evidence that follows.

Perhaps someone would like to argue that a third explanation *is* possible, namely, that languages are alike because everywhere it was discovered that there is an "optimal way of oral communication" and that languages as we find them simply reflect optimization of conditions. This statement is either false or else it turns out to be simply a different formulation of my second alternative. It is objectively not true that languages are the most efficient communication systems possible. From an information-theoretical point of view, they are very redundant; as far as their grammars are concerned, they seem to be "unnecessarily complicated" (the simplicity of English grammar as against, say, Navaho is certain to be an illusion); in semantic efficiency they leave much to be desired. They can only be said to be ideally efficient if we add "given man's articulatory, perceptual, and intellectual capacity." But with this concession we have admitted that man's pattern of speech is determined by his biological equipment, a point that will be further expanded in connection with the fourth criterion.

2. **Second Criterion: History within Species.** Languages, like fashions, have histories, but nowhere does the historical evidence take us back to a stage where the phonemic mode of vocalization was in its infancy: we have no records testifying to an absence of grammar; we have no reason to believe that there are places or times where or when concatenation had not been developed. Perhaps this ought to be attributed to the rather recent development of written records. Yet, a lingering doubt remains: writing can be traced back some five thousand years, and, while the earliest written records give us few clues about the language they represent, some of our linguistic reconstructions reach back to about the same era. This is a time span that comprises about one tenth of the age of the earliest evidence of Levalloiso-Mousterian culture (some 50,000 years ago) and the appearance of fossil forms that may be considered to be the direct ancestors of modern man. Thus, the oldest documented history of languages may be short when compared with palaeontological history; but it would not be too short to demonstrate trends in the development of, for instance, phonematization if this phenomenon *did have a cultural history*. We might expect that historical phonemic changes follow a general pattern, namely, from a supposedly *primitive* stage to one that could be called *advanced*. But the phonemic changes that we actually find—and they occur rapidly (within periods of 10 to 15 generations), frequently, and continuously—seem to follow no universal line and have, by and large, a random directionality; we cannot make predictions as to the qualitative changes that will occur in English 300 years hence.

The concatenating phenomenon is, historically, completely static. Throughout the documented history there is evidence that concatenation must have existed in its present complex and universal form for at least some five thousand years and most likely considerably longer.

The history of syntax is the same as that of phonemes. Our oldest linguistic reconstructions are based on reliable evidence that there was *order* in the concatenation of forms, that there were rules and regularities governing the sequences of morphemes which from a formal

point of view cannot have been much different from grammatical
processes of modern languages. We are not speaking here of specific
grammars, but merely of the grammatical phenomenon as such. Syntax
changes as rapidly and widely as phonemic structures, but, again, we
cannot discern any constant and linear direction. At the most, there is
a certain cyclicity, one grammatical type perhaps alternating with
another. The so-called "analytical languages," such as Chinese and
English, were preceded by synthetic types; and there is reasonable
evidence, at least for Indo-European, that the grammatical *synthesis*
as seen in ancient Greek was preceded by a more analytic stage (inflectional endings having been derived from once independent words).
We cannot be sure, however, whether synthesis *generally* alternates
with analysis; indeed, the very polarity expressed by these two terms is
not very well defined in grammatical theory. It is widely agreed today
that no typology of modern grammars reflects stages of absolute, nonrecurring grammatical development. Nor do we have any means for
judging one grammatical system as more primitive than another.

Contrast to this situation the forms found in the animal kingdom.
Species *can* be ordered in terms of anatomical simplicity (which we
equate with primitivity) so that an arrangement from low to high
forms results; and since phylogenetic stages are assumed to be unique
and nonrecurring, we can construct phylogenetic history merely from
taxonomy. But this reasoning may not be extended to linguistics. No
classification of languages in terms of structural type (such as *synthetic, analytic* or *agglutinative*) provides us with a theory for a universal development of language.[1]

There can be no question today that we are unable to trace languages back to an ungrammatical, aphonemic, or simple imitative
stage; and there is, indeed, no cogent reason to believe that such a
stage has ever existed. This does not imply a nineteenth-century assumption of an instinct, particularly not an instinct for specific languages. Obviously, the child's acquisition of Chinese consists in the
acquisition of certain culturally evolved traits. But a phenomenon such
as phonematization *per se* need not be thought of as a cultural achievement, need not constitute the summation of inventions, need not have
resulted from a long series of trial and error learning in communication.

To put my point more bluntly: the absolutely unexceptional universality of phonemes, concatenation, and syntax and the absence of historical evidence for the slow cultural evolvement of these phenomena
lead me to suppose that we have here the reflection of a biological
matrix or Anlage which forces speech to be of one and no other basic
type.

3. Third Criterion: Evidence for Inherited Predisposition. The obvious experiments for testing the question, to what degree language is inherited, cannot be performed: we may not control the verbal stimulus input of the young child. However, pathology occasionally performs some quasi-experiments, and, while anomaly frequently introduces untoward nuisance variables, it gives us, nevertheless, some glimpses into the immensely intricate relation between man's nature and his verbal behavior.

Just as we can say with assurance that no man inherits a propensity for French, we can also and with equal confidence say that all men are endowed with an innate propensity for a type of behavior that develops automatically into language and that this propensity is so deeply ingrained that language-like behavior develops even under the most unfavorable conditions of peripheral and even central nervous system impairment.

Language development, or its substitute, is relatively independent of the infant's babbling, or of his ability to hear. The congenitally deaf who will usually fail to develop an intelligible vocal communication system, who either do not babble or to whom babbling is of no avail (the facts have not been reliably reported), will nevertheless learn the intricacies of language and learn to communicate efficiently through writing. Apparently, even under these reduced circumstances of stimulation the miracle of the development of a feeling for grammar takes place.

There is another important observation to be mentioned in connection with the deaf. Recently I had occasion to visit for half a year a public school for the congenitally deaf. At this school the children were not taught sign language on the theory that they must learn to make an adjustment to a speaking world and that absence of sign language would encourage the practice of lip-reading and attempts at vocalization. It was interesting to see that all children, without exception, communicated behind the teacher's back by means of "self-made" signs. I had the privilege of witnessing the admission of a new student, eight years old, who had recently been *discovered* by a social worker who was doing relief work in a slum area. This boy had never had any training and had, as far as I know, never met with other deaf children. This newcomer began to "talk" sign language with his contemporaries almost immediately upon arrival. The existence of an innate impulse for symbolic communication can hardly be questioned.

The case history of another handicapped child[§§] gives an illustration

[§§] See my article "Understanding Language Without Ability to Speak: A Case Report," *Journal of Abnormal and Social Psychology,* **65** (1962), 419–425.

that true organic muteness in the presence of good hearing is no hindrance for the development of a speech comprehension that is ever so much more detailed than, for instance, a dog's capacity to "understand" his master. This was a five-year-old boy who, as a consequence of fetal anoxia, had sustained moderate injury to the brain pre-natally, resulting in an inability to vocalize upon command. When completely relaxed and absorbed in play he was heard to make inarticulate sounds which at times appeared to express satisfaction, joy, or disappointment (when a tall tower of blocks would tumble to the floor). But the boy has never said a single word, nor has he ever used his voice to call someone's attention. I was once able, after considerable coaxing and promises of candy, to make him say "ah" into a microphone of a tape recorder. The tape recorder had a voltmeter with a large pointer that would make excursions with each sound picked up by the microphone. The child had been fascinated by this and had learned to make the pointer go through an excursion by clapping his hands. After his first production of the sound "ah" he was able to repeat the sound immediately afterwards, but when he came back the next day, he tried in vain to say "ah," despite the fact that he seemed to be giving himself all the prompting that he could think of, like holding the microphone in both hands and approaching it with his mouth as if to say "ah." A series of examinations revealed that this boy had a remarkable understanding of spoken English; he could execute such complex commands as "take a pencil and cross out all A's in this book," "look behind the tape-recorder and find a surprise" (this was a tape-recorded instruction delivered in the absence of the experimenter), "point at all pictures of things to eat." He was able to distinguish pronouns ("touch my nose; touch your nose"), to show one, two, three, four, or five fingers; he could distinguish between a question and a declarative statement by nodding a yes-or-no answer to the question but not to the declarative sentence. He would even nod yes or no correctly when asked about situations that were spatially and temporally removed. This is discrimination learning but on a plane that requires a much more intricate understanding and sensory organization than the simple association of an object and a sign.

These examples do not *prove* that language is an inherited phenomenon. But they do point to the degree of man's preparedness for speech, a preparedness which seems to be responsible for the universality of the speech phenomenon.

4. **Fourth Criterion: Presumption of Specific Organic Correlates.** From the title of this section it should not be inferred that we wish to draw a sharp line between behavior with and without organic basis.

Thought and emotion have no less an organic basis than breathing or the tonic neck reflex. Yet there is a difference between the former and the latter types which can be described in empirical terms. In drawing the distinction we must not forget that we are dealing with a difference of degree, not quality.

4.1 *Onset and fixed developmental history.* Any innate reflex activity and sensory irritability appears at a characteristic moment in an individual's pre- or post-natal maturational process and follows a typical natural history throughout life. For instance, rudiments of the tonic neck reflex have been observed in a 20-week-old embryo; during the second half of fetal life this reflex seems to be well established, and it is strongest during the first eight post-natal weeks, with a peak of activity during the fourth week. At 12 weeks the reflex is less conspicuous and it is normally absent by the twentieth week. If the tonic neck reflex is observed at a later period, it is usually a sign of neurological disorder or pathognomonic retardation. Another example is manual dexterity: our hands become increasingly skillful throughout infancy, greatest control being achieved during young adulthood after which time there is a steady decrease which is accelerated about the fifth decade. Also the acuity of sensory perception follows characteristic age curves. Sensitivity to a number of acoustic stimuli is very low at birth, rapidly reaches a peak during the second decade and then steadily declines throughout the rest of life.‖ ‖

In the case of human behavior it is not always easy to rid ourselves of our pervasive and often quite irrational belief that all of our activities are the result of training. For instance, in the case of walking on two feet it is popularly believed that this is the result of the social environment. People who hold this view earnestly propose that the healthy child learns to walk between its 12th and 18th month because this is the time during which the mother is expected to teach her child this accomplishment. Speculation is often carried to the extreme where it is assumed that children brought up in social isolation would probably be seen with different modes of locomotion than is actually observed. That this need not even be regarded seriously as a possible hypothesis may be seen from the developmental events alone. Gesell and associates write:

> Although incipient stepping movements occur during the first week [after delivery!], they are more marked and appear with greater

‖ ‖ Cf. A. Gesell "The Ontogenesis of Infant Behavior" in L. Carmichael, Ed., *Manual of Child Psychology* (New York: John Wiley and Sons, Inc., 1946). For data on hearing see J. Sataloff, *Industrial Deafness, Hearing Testing, and Noise Measurement* (New York: McGraw-Hill, 1957), pp. 248 ff.

frequency at about 16 weeks. At this time also the infant pushes against pressure applied to the soles of the feet. At 28 weeks he makes dancing and bouncing reactions when held in the upright [N.B.] position. Flexion and extension of the legs are accompanied by raising the arms. At 48 weeks the infant cruises or walks, using support.##

We get a flavor here of how deeply walking is based on reflexes that must, under all circumstances, be called *innate*. Also, walking is not an isolated event in the child's developmental history. It is merely one aspect of his total development of motor activity and posture. Compare the same authors' description of the development of the upright position:

> [Stiffening of] the knees occurs before full extension of the legs at the hips. At 40 weeks the infant can pull himself to his knees. He can also stand, holding onto support. At 48 weeks he can lift one foot while he supports his weight on the other, an immature anticipation of a three-year-old ability to stand on one foot with momentary balance. At this age he can also pull himself to standing by holding onto the side rails of the crib. In standing he supports his weight on the entire sole surface.***

Anyone who has observed a child during the second half of his first year knows that there is continuous activity and exercise, so to speak, and that most accomplishments occur spontaneously and not as a response to specific training (for instance, climbing out of the playpen).

The most suggestive (even though not conclusive) evidence for this point comes from animal experiments. Thorpe††† reports on an experiment by Grohmann in which young pigeons were reared in narrow tubes which prevented them from moving their wings. He writes:

> Thus they could not carry out the incipient flights which would naturally be regarded as in the nature of practice. When Grohmann's control birds, which were allowed free practice flights every day, had progressed to a certain point, both groups were tested for flying ability, but no difference was found between them. In other words, the instinctive behavior pattern of flight had been maturing at a steady rate, quite irrespective of the birds' opportunity of exercising it. Those that had been kept in tubes had reached just the same stage of development as those that had what appeared to be the advantage

A. Gesell, *The First Five Years of Life; A Guide to the Study of the Pre-school Child* (New York: Harper & Row, Inc., 1940). p. 70.
*** Gesell, *op. cit.*, p. 68.
††† Thorpe, *op. cit.*, p. 51.

of practice. There is little reasonable doubt that at a later stage further skill in the fine adjustment of flight is acquired as a result of practice . . . ; [Grohmann's] work . . . suffices to show how cautious one must be in interpreting what appears to be the learning behavior of young birds.

Coghill[‡‡‡] has shown how the primary neural mechanism of swimming and walking in Amblystoma is laid down before the animal can at all respond to its environment. Also, it is common knowledge that neonate colts or calves can stand immediately after birth and that most quadrupeds can either take a few steps or at least go through walking motions within the first few hours of life. If locomotion is innate in such a great variety of vertebrates, why should man be an exception?

The developmental history is not always perfectly synchronized with the advance of chronological age so that we often have the impression that individual maturational phenomena, such as control over equilibrium in stance or the onset of menstruation, occur more or less randomly within a given period. This is probably an erroneous notion arising from our lack of information on other concomitant developmental aspects. If we had complete and accurate longitudinal case histories (instead of dealing with data gathered in cross-sectional surveys), developmental histories would probably reveal fairly constant sequences of events.

Contrast now the appearance and history of acquired behavior. A child waves goodbye when he is taught to do so. Some children may learn it before they can speak; some may learn it only in school; and in some cultures, it may never be practiced at all. Another characteristic of acquired habits or skills is that they may be lost at any time during the individual's life so that neither onset nor disappearance of the phenomenon fits into an established place of the life cycle.

When the development of speech is considered in this light, it appears to follow *maturational* development. Cultural differences seem to have no effect on the age of onset and mastery of speech. Unfortunately, completely reliable data on cross-cultural comparison of language development are still a desideratum, but a check through pertinent literature in anthropology and child development have revealed no contradictory evidence. Nor have the author's personal experience with two North American Indian tribes (Zuni and Navaho) or his inquiries from natives of non-English speaking countries cast the slightest doubt on perfect chronological commensurability of language

‡‡‡ G. E. Coghill, *Anatomy and the Problem of Behavior* (Cambridge, England: Cambridge University Press, 1929).

development throughout the world. This is also congruent with our present belief that a normal child will learn any language with the same degree of ease, whereas a child who has failed to learn the language of his native land by the time he is six, also could not learn a foreign *simpler* language without trouble. We have to conclude from this that natural languages differ little in terms of complexity when regarded from a developmental point of view.

Compare this situation with writing. Writing does not develop automatically at a specific age and it also seems that various cultures have developed writing systems of varying degrees of difficulty. For instance, the *petroglyphs* left behind by the North American Indians of the South West can be roughly interpreted even today by the naïve observer. The picture of a woman, an infant, and two feet in a certain direction is most likely a message involving a mother, child, and walking. Narrowing down the meaning of this inscription is easier than one written in Runes. Knowledge of Chinese characters requires greater study than that of the Roman alphabet. I have also made some clinical observations that deserve mention in this connection.

Neuro-psychiatrists are familiar with a condition that is referred to in the American medical literature as *specific reading disability*. It consists of a marked congenital difficulty in learning to write. Intensive drill will sometimes correct this deficit but cases have been reported (see reference in 7n for bibliography) where writing was never acquired despite a normal IQ as measured by the usual tests. I have examined eight such cases (who were seen in a neuro-medical outpatient department) in order to find out whether these patients had learned some more primitive type of graphic representation. It appeared that none of them had the slightest difficulty in understanding such symbols as arrows pointing in certain directions, simple representations of stars, hearts, or crosses; nor was there any difficulty in interpreting simple action sequences represented by three very schematic stick-men designs:

("man walking   he enters a house   he is sitting down")

Each of these three pictures was understood when presented individually as well as in conjunction.

Presumably, these subjects have difficulty with some aspects of English orthography but not with visual pattern recognition or the interpretation of graphic symbols. The condition, therefore, is not actually a general *reading difficulty* but merely a difficulty with certain, at present unidentified, associative processes involved in *our* type of writing system. It would be interesting to know whether other countries have the same incidence and types of "specific reading disability" as encountered in England and the United States.

Let us now take a closer look at the longitudinal development of language acquisition. Unfortunately, we only have data gathered within our own culture; but even this much will be instructive, and there is, indeed, very little reason to believe that the main phenomena should differ significantly in nonEnglish speaking communities.

All children go through identical phases in the process of acquiring speech. First, they have a few words or phrases, never longer than three syllables, that refer to objects, persons, or complex situations. At this stage they may have a repertoire of fifty short utterances that are somewhat stereotyped and are never combined one with the other. All attempts to make the child string up the words that he is known to use singly will fail until he reaches a certain stage of maturation. When this is attained, the combining of words seems to be quite automatic, that is, he will surprise the parents by suddenly putting two words together that may not have been given him for repetition, in fact, that may often sound queer enough to make it quite unlikely that anyone in the child's environment has ever spoken these words in just that sequence. "Eat cup" may mean "the dog is eating out of the cup" or "is the dog eating the cup?" and so on. Whatever was meant by this utterance (which was actually heard), it is a sequence of words that nobody had used in the particular situation in which the words were spoken. As the child grows older, longer phrases are composed of individual vocabulary items which had been in the child's repertoire for many months, sometimes years.

Other aspects of language exhibit a similar developmental constancy. There are certain sentence structures that are virtually never heard during the first three years of life (for instance, conditionals or subjunctives). The frequency of occurrence of words shows certain characteristic constancies for child language, which, interestingly enough, are somewhat different from the frequency of occurrences of adult speech. In English, the most frequently occurring words are the articles *a* and *the*; yet, the child's first words never include these. (There is an active process of selection going on that must not be confused with mechanical parroting.) There is also a fairly constant semantic development. Children seem to begin speech with very characteristic semantic generalizations. The word *car* may be extended at first to all vehicles (a child of my acquaintance once pointed to a plane and said *car*); *dog* to all animals; *daddy* to all people or all men. But there is already an ordering activity apparent that is characteristic of speech as a whole.

Also, the usage of words have a characteristic history. All observers of longitudinal child-language development have reported a difficulty in naming colors correctly at an early stage.§§§ The curriculum of many public Kindergartens includes special training in color naming. This characteristic difficulty for the child at 2½ to 3½ years of age is the more interesting as color words are among the most frequently occurring words in English, and it is hard to see that their correct use should have smaller reinforcement value than words such as *big* and *small*, *hot* and *cold*, or *heavy* and *light*, *wet* and *dry*, all of which are words used correctly before color words. Of course, we do not take this observation to mean that something like a special structure has to mature which is particularly involved in color naming. The point here is that naming is a complex process which presents varying degrees of difficulty or, in other words, which depends upon a number of skills that develop at a slow rate. All we can say at our present state of knowledge is that on his second birthday the child does not ordinarily have the capacity to learn to name four basic colors consistently and correctly, whereas he develops this capacity within the next two or three years. (To make a distinction between *concrete* and *abstract* names is of little help since we only have *post hoc* definitions of these terms.)

Another line of evidence that would support the thesis that language-learning follows a maturational course is the phenomenon of foreign accents; it seems as if the degree of accent correlates fairly well with the age during which a second language is acquired. The following case will illustrate the point: Mr. R. W., whose major interest is the study of language, is a middle-aged graduate of one of this country's universities. He was born and lived in Germany until he was twelve years old when his family emigrated from Germany to a Portuguese-speaking country where he spent the next ten years. Within two years after his arrival in the new country he had such a perfect command over the second language that his foreign background was never suspected when he spoke to natives. At the age of 22 he came to the United States where he was at once obliged to speak English exclusively. From then on he had no further opportunity to speak Portuguese, and only occasionally (never more than a few hours at a time)

§§§ For theory and experimental work on this problem, see my paper: "A Probabilistic Approach to Language Learning" *Behavioral Science,* 2 (1957), 1–13.

has he spoken German since his arrival in this country. The result is interesting. His ability to speak English has completely displaced his facility in Portuguese and even the availability of his German vocabulary seems to have suffered in the course of the years. Yet, his pronunciation of English is marked by a gross and virtually insuperable foreign accent while his German continues to sound like that of a native and his Portuguese, as evidenced in the pronunciation of isolated words, continues to have the phonological characteristics of perfect Portuguese. (Yet, this person has heard and spoken more English during his life than either German or Portuguese.)

Here again it would be important to verify empirically the plasticity for the acquisition of languages throughout an individual's life history. Systematic research on immigrant families and their progress in learning English as a function of the age of the learner would seem to be a quite feasible and interesting study.

Before leaving the subject of fixed developmental histories in language learning, we must briefly consider those cases where language does not develop normally. Speech disturbances are among the most common complaints of the pediatric patient with neurologic disorders. It is precisely the area of speech disorders in childhood, which can shed the most light on the nature of language development; yet, despite a very prolific literature, the most elementary observations have either not yet been made or the reports cannot be used reliably. This is primarily due to the imprecise terminology common in these studies, to a predilection for subjective interpretation, to the complete absence of complete and accurate case reports of longitudinal descriptions (instead of the now fashionable cross-sectional studies of many hundreds of subjects), poor categories for classification, and similar other shortcomings. The only aspect in which little or no further spade-work needs to be done in this respect is the establishment of norms for speech development. We have little trouble today in deciding whether or not a patient's speech is normal for his age.

If speech disturbances were viewed as nature's own experiments on the development of speech, a wide variety of observational research projects could be formulated details of which need not be gone into here. Suffice it to point out that research could easily be conducted that would constitute direct verification of (or means for refining) the view that language development follows a characteristic, natural history. It would be very revealing, for instance, to know exactly under what circumstances the present practice of speech "therapy" (which is strictly speaking a training procedure) is successful. This would include detailed description of the patient's condition before and after treatment, perfectly objective evaluation of his improvement, and an accurate assessment of the role that specific speech therapy played in the course of the condition. In reporting on the patient's condition, it is not enough to mention one or another type of speech defect, but a complete inventory of the subject's speech facility ought to be given in addition to a complete and accurate report of his clinical and developmental status. Speech is so complicated a matter that we must not be surprised that a full case report is meaningful only after collecting most meticulous data on hours of patient testing and observations. A few scattered clinical notes, a random collection of psychological test results and a global statement of "improvement" is meaningless in this field. Among the most important objectives of a "log" of a long course of speech therapy is the determination whether language must be taught and learned in terms of a hierarchy of levels of complexity, whether it is essential that one set of skills precedes another, or whether almost anything can be taught and learned in a wide variety of orders. If there *is* a hierarchy of complexity, what are the linguistic correlates, what are the factors that make some linguistic aspects "easy," and what makes them "difficult"? Answers to these questions would be major contributions to our present state of knowledge.

In conclusion, I would like to suggest (subject to further verification) that the development of speech does not proceed randomly; there are certain regularities that characterize speech at certain stages of development, but empirical work still needs to be done on the individual differences that may also be observed. Moreover, we know that language development, viewed cross-culturally, has never been said to deviate essentially from development in Western cultures, and if we accept temporarily and subject to further work this indirect evidence, it would be more reasonable to assume that the acquisition of language is controlled by a biologically determined set of factors and not by intentional training, considering that cultures differ radically in their educational procedures.

4.2 *Dependence upon Environment*. Thorpe[1] describes the behavior of a hand-reared Tawny Owl "which, after being fed, would act as if pouncing upon living prey although it had never had the experience of dealing with a living mouse." This is not an isolated instance. Ethologists are familiar with this and similar types of action patterns that are usually triggered by so-called "innate releasing

---

[1] W. H. Thorpe, "The Modern Concept of Instinctive Behavior" *Bulletin Animal Behavior,* 1, 7, (1948), 12f.

mechanisms." Thorpe### notes that for every action pattern there is an ideal training stimulus such that every time it acts upon the animal, the latter will go through the entire action pattern. However, it is said that if the animal has not encountered the ideal stimulus in his environment for some time, the threshold for the release of the action pattern is lowered so that a stimulus that ordinarily does not evoke the patterned response is now capable of so doing. In the complete and continuing absence of suitable stimuli for the release of the mechanical action pattern, the threshold is lowered to a zero point, that is, the action pattern will go off in the complete absence of any environmental stimulus. This is the significance of the behavior of Thorpe's hand-reared Tawny Owl. But the absence of environmental stimuli does not imply absence of stimulation. Just as there is no effect without a cause, so there is no biological activity without a stimulus. In the owl's case, the stimuli must be assumed to be within the organism, i.e., be reducible to chemico-physical events. Again, this is nothing that is peculiar to innate action patterns because the behavior of pigeons that learn to pick at certain spots is also the direct result of chemico-physical reactions that take place within the bird's body. But differences there are. Compare the owl's pouncing behavior with Skinner's rat that learned to "purchase" a token which it would drop into a food-dispensing machine.**** In the case of the rat, various bits of spontaneous rat behavior have been artificially (from the rat's point of view, *randomly*) chained so that the *sequence* of rat-behavior-bits has a *perfect* correspondence to a sequence of environmental events. Or, in other words, every individual bit of behavior making up the food-purchasing sequence was at one time preceded by a distinct environmental stimulus or at least linked to a reinforcing event. The only reason the total food-purchasing behavior appears in the sequence that it does, is that environmental stimuli and reinforcements have been arbitrarily arranged in a particular order. But the owl's pouncing behavior, which may not be as complex an affair as the purchase of food but still is elaborate enough and may last for as long a time as it takes the rat to purchase food, cannot be decomposed into bits of individual behavior components that can be rearranged into any combination and sequence. The sequence is completely fixed. This is a very important point. These days of electronic computers have made it fashionable to use electronic metaphors. We may say that innate behavior, such as the owl's pouncing is *programmed* into the organism. Environmental conditions may trigger the sequence (or perhaps forcefully prevent it),

---

Thorpe, *Learning and Instinct in Animals, op. cit.,* introductory chapters.
**** B. F. Skinner, *The Behavior of Organisms: An Experimental Analysis* (New York: Appleton-Century-Crofts, Inc., 1938).

but once it goes off it follows a prescribed course. It hardly needs to be pointed out that food purchasing is different.

If we were asked whether instinctive behavior, such as the predisposition for nest-building, or the pouncing of the owl, is primarily based on organic factors, we could hardly fail to answer in the affirmative. Since the environment alone is either insufficient for producing the behavior (dogs are not stimulated to build nests), or in some cases quite unnecessary, the action pattern must have an internal cause. This statement must be true even if we shall never discover the neuroanatomical basis of the behavior.

Let us now consider how language development fits into this scheme. The purpose of the following discussion will be to show that the rat who learns to press a lever or to purchase food gives us no more insight into the process of language acquisition than, for instance, thorough observations on the nest building habit of the rat or the acquisition of flight in the bird.

The constancy in language developmental histories is merely an indirect cue for the deep-seated nature of language predispositions in the child. Much stronger arguments can be marshalled.

First of all, in the case of the food purchasing rat, the sequence of behavior is pre-planned by the trainer and in that sense it has a rational aim. But language "training" and acquisition cannot possibly be the result of rational pre-planning because no adult "knows" how he generates new grammatical sentences. This fact cannot be appreciated except by sophisticated analysis of the principles of language. In the current explanations of language-learning we hear a good deal of how the supposedly random babbling of the infant is gradually shaped into words by the trainer's waiting for the accidental appearance of certain sounds which can then be reinforced, and thereby elicited with greater frequency, and how from this procedure the infant learns to imitate in general. This conception of speech acquisition is unsatisfactory from many viewpoints; for the time being, we merely point out that *imitation* (whatever psychological processes this term might cover) may be part of language-learning but by no means its most important aspects. Speech activity is virtually never a mechanical play-back device. This is most readily seen on the morphological level, where children will automatically extend inflexional suffixes both to nonsense words[††††] and to words that have irregular forms such as *good-gooder, go-goed, foot-foots*. Not quite so obvious, but in a sense

[††††] J. Berko, "The Child's Learning of English Morphology," *Word*, 14 (1958) 150–177. Compare also D. L. Wolfle, "The Relation between Linguistic Structure and Associative Interference in Artificial Linguistic Material," *Language Monograph*, 11 (1932) 1–55.

much more striking, is the generalization that takes place in syntactic matters. Here it becomes quite clear that there must be a second process in addition to imitation, for the language of children is not confined to stereotyped sentences. Children ask questions that have never been asked before ("What does blue look like from in back?"), make statements that have never been stated before (" I buyed a fire dog for a grillion dollars!"), and in general apply grammatical rules that only few adults could make explicit ("I didn't hit Billy; Billy hit me!").

The phenomenon of morphological generalization puts great strains on a simple referent-symbol association theory of language. The -*s* suffix of the third person singular ("he go[e]*s*") has no demonstrable referent taking this word in its literal meaning; nor the *s* of plurality, the *ed* of the past tense, the -*er* of the comparative. The referent of the "small" words such as *the, is, will* is completely nebulous, and neither training nor learning can possibly be the result of any kind of referent-symbol contiguity, that is, the proximity of the words *the* and *man* welds them into a unit. As long as ten years ago, Lashley[‡‡‡‡] thoroughly demonstrated the impossibility of explaining syntax on the grounds of temporal contiguity association, and he has pointed to the generality of his observations on language with respect to other motor behavior. Lashley's argument is so compelling that little can be added to it. More recently, Chomsky[§§§§] has demonstrated from a purely formal approach that grammatical sentences cannot be the product of stochastic processes in which the probability of occurrence of an element (morpheme or word) is entirely determined by preceding elements, and Miller[‖‖‖‖] and Chomsky[####] have discussed the psychological implications of this observation. We have neither a good theoretical model nor any practical insights into how we could teach an organism to respond to plurality, third-person-ness, past-ness, let alone how we could train him to use these responses in the correct order and verbal contexts within original sentence constructions. Con-

---

[‡‡‡‡] K. S. Lashley, "The Problem of Serial Order in Behavior" in L. A. Jeffress, Ed., *Cerebral Mechanisms in Behavior, The Hixon Symposium* (New York: John Wiley and Sons, Inc., 1951).

[§§§§] Chomsky, "Three Models for the Description of Language," *op. cit.*

[‖‖‖‖] N. Chomsky, G. A. Miller, "Introduction to the Formal Analysis of Natural Languages" in R. D. Luce, R. R. Bush, E. Galanter, Eds., *Handbook of Mathematical Psychology* (New York: John Wiley and Sons, Inc., 1963). N. Chomsky, G. A. Miller, "Finitary Models of Language Users," in R. D. Luce, R. R. Bush, E. Galanter, *op. cit.*

[####] J. S. Bruner, "Mechanisms Riding High," *Contemporary Psychology*, 2 (1957) 155–157.

sequently, both the teaching and learning of language cannot simply be explained by extrapolating from rat and pigeon experiments where all learning follows an explicit program.

All that we have said about production of speech is equally valid for the understanding of speech. The baby can repeat new words with great ease and be satisfied with his own baby-talk replica of the adult prototype, because he seems to perceive adult words not like a tape recorder but like a "phoneme-analyzer." He recognizes the functional similarity between phones and between his own reproduction of the adult speech sounds, and this enables him to disregard the very marked, objective, physical differences between a baby's voice and a middle-aged man's voice. Chomsky and Miller regard the child at three as a machine that can make syntactic analysis of the input speech. Obviously, children are not given rules which they can apply. They are merely exposed to a great number of examples of how the syntax works, and from these examples they completely automatically acquire principles with which new sentences can be formed that will conform to the universally recognized rules of the game. (We must not be disturbed by the fact that a transcription of a child's speech— or adult's speech for that matter—would be quite unpolished stylistically. There might be incomplete sentences and every now and then ungrammatical constructions resulting primarily from beginning a sentence one way and finishing it another. The important point here is that words are neither randomly arranged nor confined to unchangeable, stereotyped sequences. At every stage there is a characteristic structure.)

A word on the problem of motivation is in place. Animals are not passive objects upon which the environment acts. Their peripheral sensitivities are centrally controlled to the extent that, for instance, a certain odor may at one time have an arousing effect upon an individual animal but at another time (say after consuming a satiating meal) leave it inert. Moreover, *ability to stimulate* is not an objective physical property such as weight or temperature. It can only be defined with reference to a given animal species. A tree might stimulate a monkey to do some acrobatics, a beaver to start gnawing, and a grandmother to rest in its shade (where the latter is merely a subspecies). Motivation for action resides in the physiological state of the organism and in some instances can be immediately correlated with clear-cut states of deprivation, say of food or sex. Ordinarily it is false to assume that the environment *produces* a given type of behavior; it merely triggers it. There are many ways of chasing and eating a rabbit, and even though all of its predators may be motivated by the same physiological drive, hunger, the mode of catching and consuming the rabbit will bear the characteristic stamp of the predator's species.

In view of this, it seems reasonable to assert that there are certain propensities built into animals and man to utilize the environment in a fairly species-specific way. Sometimes this is obscured (a) because of individual differences in behavior traits and (b) because behavior is also affected, within limits, by environmental variations (such as availability *either* of little sticks, *or* of leaves, *or* of rags for the building of nests; analogously, because a child may grow up *either* in a Chinese, *or* in a German, *or* in a Navaho speaking environment).

The appearance of language may be thought to be due to an innately mapped-in *program* for behavior, the exact realization of the program being dependent upon the peculiarities of the (speech) environment. As long as the child is surrounded at all by a speaking environment, speech will develop in an automatic way, with a rigid developmental history, a highly specific mode for generalization behavior, and a relative dependence upon the maturational history of the child.

It may seem as if we were begging the question here: If speech develops automatically provided a speech environment is given, how did the speech environment come about originally? Actually, we are in no greater logical trouble than is encountered by explanations of any social phenomenon in biology, for instance, communal life as the evolution of herds, flocks, or schools. Compare also the colonial life of ants, the family formation of badgers, the social stratification of chickens. Nor is human language the only form of communication that has evolved in the animal kingdom. Bees and many species of birds have communication systems, and in none of these cases do we find ourselves forced to argue either that these communication systems (or the social phenomena) are the result of purposeful invention or that an individual of the species undergoes a purposeful training program to acquire the trait. If in the case of lower animals we assume without compunction that the communicating trait is the result of an *innate predisposition elicited by environmental circumstances*, we have no reason to assume *a priori* that the language trait of man is purely acquired behavior (not pre-determined by innate predispositions). We are making no stronger a claim here than what is expressed by Dobzhansky's words:

> The genetic equipment of our species was molded by natural selection; it conferred upon our ancestors the capacity to develop language and culture. This capacity was decisive in the biological success of

man as a species; . . . man . . . has become specialized to live in a
man-made environment.*****

CONSEQUENCES FOR THEORY AND
RESEARCH

The great achievement of contemporary psychology was the replacement of mentalistic explanations by mechanistic ones and the simul-
taneous insistence upon empirical testability of hypothesized laws.
In the search for laws of behavior it seemed at once desirable to discover the most universal laws since this alone, it was thought, could
give our theoretical edifice insurance against *ad hoc* explanations.
Many behaviorists have explicitly renounced interest in those aspects
of behavior that are specific to one species and consequently, confine
themselves, by program, to what is universal to the behavior of *all*
organisms. This attitude has cost the science of behavior a price: it has
made it difficult to recognize the very intimate connection between the
behavior repertoire of a species and its biologically defined constitution, that is, its anatomy and physiology.

The treatment of language by behaviorists is an excellent example
of this situation. The literature, including experimental reports, in the
area of verbal behavior is very voluminous and cannot be reviewed
here. In general it may be characterized as a gigantic attempt to prove
that general principles of association, reinforcement, and generalization are at work also in this type of behavior. The basic process of language acquisition is roughly pictured as follows: The child associates
the sounds of the human voice with need-satisfying circumstances;
when he hears his own random babbling, these sounds are recognized
to be similar to those uttered by the adults so that the pleasure or
anticipation of pleasure associated with mother's voice is now transferred to his own vocalizations. Thus, hearing his own sounds becomes
a pleasurable experience in itself, the more so as mother tends to reinforce these sounds, particularly if they by chance resemble a word such
as *Dada*. This induces a quantitative increase in the infant's vocal output. Soon he will learn that approximating adult speech patterns, i.e.,
imitating, is generally reinforced, and this is thought to put him on his
way toward adult forms of language. Admittedly, this account is a
gross simplification of what has been published on the subject, but
the basic mechanisms postulated are not violated. Many psychologists
have noted that the concept of imitation is not satisfactory in an ex-

***** T. Dobzhansky, "Evolution at Work" *Science,* **122** (1958) 1091–1098.

planation because it is precisely the process that needs to be accounted for. I am in agreement with this objection but would add to the current views on the problem of language acquisition that there is a host of other questions that have not even been recognized, let alone *answered.* A few illustrations follow.

1. The perception of similarities is a general psychological problem closely related to the problem of generalization which, however, in the perception of speech sounds plays a particularly prominent role. Acoustically, the sounds of a two-month-old infant are totally different from those of the mother; how then can it become aware of similarities between his and his mother's voices? There is also great random variation in the acoustic nature of phonemes. The identical physical sound is in one context assignable to one phoneme and in another context to another phoneme. This is even true for the speech of one individual. Thus, phoneme identification is dependent upon analysis of larger language units thus calling for a sound-Gestalt perception which may well be based on highly specialized sensory skills. We cannot be sure, for instance, whether a dog that has learned to respond to some twenty spoken commands responds to these words phonemically or whether he responds to secondary extralinguistic cues such as its master's movements. (This is an empirical question and the evidence so far is in favor of the latter.)

2. Even if we agree that we do not know how the process of imitation works, everyone has to admit that in some way the child learns to behave like those around him, that is, to imitate. Bracketing the problem of imitation *per se*, there is a still more primitive problem: why does the child begin to "imitate" in as highly characteristic a way as he does? His first goal does not appear to be a replication of the motor skill—he does not at first simply parrot—but his first accomplishment is to *name* objects; in fact, the motor skill lags significantly behind the naming. There is nothing necessary or obvious about this. Talking birds do the exact opposite—if they learn to name at all, for which there is, again, no good evidence. Reinforcement theory does not explain this; to the contrary, from the common psychological accounts of the beginning of verbal behavior the perfection of the motor skill intuitively ought to have preference over the more abstract naming skill in the infant's learning agenda. The naming of objects, that is, to learn that there is a general class of objects called *cup* is notoriously difficult for animals.

3. Most terrestial vertebrates make noises, and in mammals these are produced through the larynx and oro-pharyngeal cavity. Without exception these acoustic signals serve some biological function which,

in their homologous form in man, would relate to emotions. Examples are courting, territoriality, warnings and danger signals, anger, care for the young. It is extremely difficult and, for many species, reportedly impossible to train animals to use these vocal signals for instrumental conditioning. It is not possible, to my knowledge, to teach a dog to howl in order to obtain a morsel of food; a tomcat to make courting noises to avoid shock; a rat to squeal in order to have doors opened in a maze. There are many indications that human vocalization is phylogenetically also related to the expression of emotions; yet, in the course of normal development a child begins to make use of his vocal apparatus independently from his emotions. Why is this so?

4. The general problem of attention has haunted practically every research in psychology, and so we are not surprised to encounter it also in connection with language acquisition. The apes that were raised in human homes failed to develop speech partly, it was thought, because they could not be induced to pay attention to the relevant cues in their environment. But why do all children without any special training automatically attend to these cues?

5. It is well known that there is a nearly perfect homology of muscles and bones in the head and neck of mammals and the geometry of the oral cavity of the great apes is sufficiently similar to that of man to make it potentially and physically possible to produce speech sounds. Except for a report on a single chimpanzee, who could whisper a few "words" in heavy and, to the outside, incomprehensible chimpanzee accent,[†††††] no chimpanzee or other primate has been able to learn to coordinate respiration, laryngeal, and oral mechanism with the speed, precision, and endurance that every child displays. What is the extraordinary skill due to? Does it merely depend on practice, or are there physiological predispositions?

Many more questions of this kind could be asked. They are all essential to our understanding of language and speech yet we have no answers to any one of them. Present-day psychology tends to brush these problems aside by simply admitting that it is in the biological nature of man to behave in this way and not in that and that biological aspects of behavior may be disregarded in the psychological treatment of it. But such a position endangers the discovery value which a psychological description of behavior may have. It threatens many a conclusion to boil down to the triviality that children learn to speak

---

[†††††] K. J. Hayes and C. Hayes, "A Home-Raised Chimpanzee" in R. G. Kuhlen and G. G. Thompson, eds., *Psychological Studies of Human Development* (New York: Appleton-Century-Crofts, Inc., 1952), p. 117.

because they are children and that all children learn to speak provided they are healthy and live in a normal environment.

If, on the other hand, the study of speech and language is from the outset seen as a study in biology (including the study of the interaction between heredity and environment), we can hope to combine research on questions such as those posed above with those that are customarily asked in psychology and thus to obtain new insights into the nature of man. It is true that this approach will not allow us to generalize our findings to all species or to speak about "the organism" in general. But I see no reason why the difference between species and their behavior should be less interesting or pertinent to a general science than the similarities.

SUMMARY AND CONCLUSION

The behavior repertoire of many animals depends upon certain biological predispositions. On the one hand, the animal may be constitutionally pre-destined or have an Anlage for the exercise of given behavior patterns, or, on the other hand, it is innately tuned to react to specific environmental stimuli in a species-characteristic fashion. In a sense, all of man's activities are a consequence of his inherited endowments including his capacity for culture and social structure. But some of his behavior patterns, for instance, bipedal gait, are based upon very specific anatomical and physiological predispositions, whereas other patterns, such as writing, are based on more general capacities of motor coordination, perception, and cognitive processes. In the present article, criteria were developed to distinguish behavior patterns based on specific predispositions from those based on general ones. When these criteria are applied to language, one discovers that it falls between these two poles, though considerably closer to the side of special predispositions than to its opposite.

Since it is proper to speak of language as species-specific behavior, we are implicitly postulating a biological matrix for the development of speech and language. This is tantamount to an assumption that the general morphology characteristic of the order *primates* and/or universal physiological processes such as *respiration* and *motor-coordination* have undergone specialized adaptations, making the exercise of this behavior possible. At present, there is scanty evidence for this because proper questions that might lead to decisive answers—either for or against the hypothesis—have not been asked. Let us hope that the present formulations help us to ask such novel questions.

NOTES ON "THE CAPACITY FOR LANGUAGE ACQUISITION"

1. The terms *analytical, synthetic,* and *agglutinative* were used by historical linguists to describe the morphology of different language types. Leonard Bloomfield, in his book *Language,* cites several examples of schemes for classifying the morphological structure of world languages:

> *One such scheme distinguishes* analytic *languages, which use few bound forms, from* synthetic, *which use many. At one extreme is a completely analytic language, like modern Chinese, where each word is a one-syllable morpheme or a compound word or phrase-word; at the other, a highly synthetic language like Eskimo, which unites long strings of bound forms into single words, such as* [a:wlisa-ut-iss? ar-si-niarpu-ŋa] *"I am looking for something suitable for a fish-line."* . . . *Another scheme of this sort divided languages into four morphologic types, isolating, agglutinative, polysynthetic, and inflecting. Isolating languages were those which, like Chinese, used no bound forms; in agglutinative languages the bound forms were supposed merely to follow one another, Turkish being the stock example; polysynthetic languages expressed semantically important elements, such as verbal goals, by means of bound forms, as does Eskimo; inflectional languages showed a merging of semantically distinct features either in a single bound form or in closely united bound forms. (Holt, Rinehart and Winston, Inc., New York, 1933, 207–208)*

ERIC H. LENNEBERG

On Explaining Language

The article begins with the author's summary of why language can be
viewed as a biological phenomenon. The article itself is broken down into
eleven sections, plus a conclusion, each with its own title. We will discuss
these sections in order. The first, "Predictability of language development," gives evidence that language development is highly correlated
with motor development and brain maturation.

The second section, "Effect of certain variations in social environment,"
deals with the effect of the environment on language development. The
author distinguishes between language use and language capacity. Unfavorable environmental circumstances may effect language use, but the
underlying capacity for language "is not easily arrested." He presents
detailed evidence from a study of the language of the children of deaf
parents which leads him to conclude that

Eric H. Lenneberg, "On Explaining Language," *Science*, Vol. 164 (9 May 1969),
pp. 635–643. Copyright 1969 by the American Association for the Advancement
of Science. Reprinted by permission of the author and *Science*.

the earliest development of human sounds appears to be relatively independent of the amount, nature, or timing of the sounds made by parents.

The third section, "Effect of variations in genetic background," gives further evidence of the biological nature of language development through a study of the language development of twins.

The fourth section, "Attempts to modify language development," examines the attempt to teach English to (1) congenitally deaf children, and (2) children suffering from mongolism. Congenitally deaf children failed to learn from formal instruction, but at the same time seemed to know some of the subleties of English syntax beyond what they had been schooled in. The work with mongoloid children showed that they were incapable of being taught to use or even repeat sentences that involved syntactic rules that they did not already have. Since normal children also have great difficulty in repeating sentences that involve new rules, Lenneberg feels

that language does not come about by simple imitation, but that the child abstracts regularities or relations from the language he hears, which he then applies to building up language for himself as an apparatus of principles.

The fifth section, "What sets the pace of language development?," argues that the pace of language development is most closely associated with the level of physical and mental development. Lenneberg believes that language development is not tied to development of the motor skills of articulating organs or to a growing knowledge of associations between visual and auditory patterns.

In the sixth section, "Brain correlates," Lenneberg shows that language functions are closely related to specialized areas of the brain. Evidence from injuries suggests that the brains of young children can reestablish a language-specialized area in the right hemisphere if the original one in the left hemisphere has been destroyed. However, by the time of the early teens, this ability has been lost. Thus damage to language-specialized areas in adults tends to be permanent.

The seventh section, "Critical age for language acquisition," connects the information about the brain in the section above with the normal history of language development in children. Lenneberg argues that the brain has a biological propensity toward language learning in the early years that is lost when the brain reaches its final state of maturity in the teens. This argument is supported by evidence from the development of language in retarded children.

In the eighth section, "Biological approach: Defining language further," Lenneberg argues against the view that language is a tool that "man has shaped for himself to serve a purpose." He states that human language, like human cognition, does not exist apart from the human brain. This in turn suggests that all human languages, being products of the same kind of brain, must be alike in some general sense. The shared features of all human languages are called *language universals*. One type of evidence to support the existence of language universals is the uniform way in which children from very different cultures and languages acquire their first language. Another type of evidence is drawn from the study of language itself.

The ninth section, "Environment and maturation," defines maturation as a sequence of states. At each state of development, the organism is sensitive to a certain range of inputs. If these inputs are received, the organism is capable of transforming itself into a more advanced state, which in turn is sensitive to another range of inputs, and so on. Lenneberg argues that the brain provides the internal states necessary for language development and the environment provides the necessary external inputs. As Lenneberg puts it, "Every stage of maturation is unstable. It is prone to change into specific directions, but requires a trigger from the environment."

In the tenth section, "Pseudo homologies and naive 'Evolutionizing'," Lenneberg discusses possible analogues (homologies) of human language in other species. In a biological sense a homology is a trait that appears in two different but related species. Lenneberg argues that all known systems of animal communication fail to meet rigorous definitions of homology. Furthermore, it is pointless to speculate about the origins of human language because we know nothing about the ecological and social conditions of early man that shaped the evolution of language.

In the eleventh section, "Species specificities and cognitive specialization," Lenneberg argues for the uniqueness of human language. Every mammalian species has an anatomically distinct brain. Man's brain is similar in certain respects to that of other primates, but it also has dramatic differences. Since a brain is an integrated organ, we would expect species-specific traits to be produced by a species-specific brain. Lenneberg argues that human language and human cognition are two such species-specific traits.

Many explanations have been offered for many aspects of language; there is little agreement, however, on how to explain various problems or even on what there is to be explained. Of course, explanations differ with the personal inclinations and interests of the investigator. My interests are in man as a biological species, and I believe that the study of language is relevant to these interests because language has the following six characteristics. (i) It is a form of behavior present in all cultures of the world. (ii) In all cultures its onset is age correlated. (iii) There is only one acquisition strategy—it is the same for all babies everywhere in the world. (iv) It is based intrinsically upon the same formal operating characteristics whatever its outward form.[1] (v) Throughout man's recorded history these operating characteristics have been constant. (vi) It is a form of behavior that may be impaired specifically by circumscribed brain lesions which may leave other mental and motor skills relatively unaffected.

Any form of human behavior that has all of these six characteristics may likewise be assumed to have a rather specific biological foundation. This, of course, does not mean that language cannot be studied from different points of view; it can, for example, be investigated for its cultural or social variations, its capacity to reflect individual differences, or its applications. The purpose of this article, however, is to discuss the aspects of language to which biological concepts are applied most appropriately.[2] Further, my concern is with the development of language in children—not with its origin in the species.

PREDICTABILITY OF LANGUAGE DEVELOPMENT

A little boy starts washing his hands before dinner no sooner than when his parents decide that training in cleanliness should begin. However, children begin to speak no sooner and no later than when they reach a given stage of physical maturation (Table 1). There are individual variations in development, particularly with respect to age correlation. It is interesting that language development correlates better with motor development than it does with chronological age. If we take these two variables (motor and language development) and make ordinal scales out of the stages shown in Table 1 and then use them for a correlation matrix, the result is a remarkably small degree of scatter. Since motor development is one of the most important indices of maturation, it is not unreasonable to propose that language development, too, is related to physical growth and development. This impression is further corroborated by examination of retarded children. Here the age correlation is very poor, whereas the correlation between motor and language development continues to

---

[1] E. H. Lenneberg, in *The Structure of Language, Readings in the Philosophy of Language*, J. A. Fodor and J. J. Katz, Eds. (Prentice-Hall, Englewood Cliffs, N. J., 1964).

[2] For complete treatment, see E. H. Lenneberg, *Biological Foundations of Language* (Wiley, New York, 1967).

Table 1. Correlation of motor and language development

Age (years)	Motor milestones	Language milestones
0.5	Sits using hands for support; unilateral reaching	Cooing sounds change to babbling by introduction of consonantal sounds
1	Stands; walks when held by one hand	Syllabic reduplication; signs of understanding some words; applies some sounds regularly to signify persons or objects, that is, the first words
1.5	Prehension and release fully developed; gait propulsive; creeps downstairs backward	Repertoire of 3 to 50 words not joined in phrases; trains of sounds and intonation patterns resembling discourse; good progress in understanding
2	Runs (with falls); walks stairs with one foot forward only	More than 50 words; two-word phrases most common; more interest in verbal communication; no more babbling
2.5	Jumps with both feet; stands on one foot for 1 second; builds tower of six cubes	Every day new words; utterances of three and more words; seems to understand almost everything said to him; still many grammatical deviations
3	Tiptoes 3 yards (2.7 meters); walks stairs with alternating feet; jumps 0.9 meter	Vocabulary of some 1000 words; about 80 percent intelligibility; grammar of utterances close approximation to colloquial adult; syntactic mistakes fewer in variety, systematic, predictable
4.5	Jumps over rope; hops on one foot; walks on line	Language well established; grammatical anomalies restricted either to unusual constructions or to the more literate aspects of discourse

be high.[3] Nevertheless, there is evidence that the statistical relation between motor and language development is not due to any immediate, causal relation; peripheral motor disabilities can occur that do not delay language acquisition.

Just as it is possible to correlate the variable language development with the variables chronological age or motor development, it is possible to relate it to the physical indications of brain maturation, such as the gross weight of the brain, neurodensity in the cerebral cortex, or the changing weight proportions of given substances in either gray or white matter. On almost all counts, language begins when such maturational indices have attained at least 65 percent of

[3] E. H. Lenneberg, I. A. Nichols, E. F. Rosenberger, in *Disorders of Communication* D. Rioch, Ed. (Research Publications of Association for Research in Nervous and Mental Disorders, New York, 1964), vol. 42.

their mature values. (Inversely, language acquisition becomes more difficult when the physical maturation of the brain is complete.) These correlations do not prove causal connections, although they suggest some interesting questions for further research.

EFFECT OF CERTAIN VARIATIONS IN SOCIAL ENVIRONMENT

In most of the studies on this topic the language development of children in orphanages or socially deprived households has been compared with that of children in so-called normal, middle-class environments. Statistically significant differences are usually reported, which is sometimes taken as a demonstration that language development is contingent on specific language training. That certain aspects of the environment are absolutely essential for language development is undeniable, but it is important to distinguish between what the children actually do, and what they can do.

There is nothing particularly surprising or revealing in the demonstration that language deficits occur in children who hear no language, very little language, or only the discourse of uneducated persons. But what interests us is the underlying capacity for language. This is not a spurious question; for instance, some children have the capacity for language but do not use it, either because of peripheral handicaps such as congenital deafness or because of psychiatric disturbances such as childhood schizophrenia; other children may not speak because they do not have a sufficient capacity for language, on account of certain severely retarding diseases.

There is a simple technique for ascertaining the degree of development of the capacity for speech and language. Instead of assessing it by means of an inventory of the vocabulary, the grammatical complexity of the utterances, the clarity of pronunciation, and the like, and computing a score derived from several subjects of this kind, it is preferable to describe the children's ability in terms of a few broad and general developmental stages, such as those shown in Table 1. Tests which are essentially inventories of vocabulary and syntactic constructions are likely to reflect simply the deficiencies of the environment; they obscure the child's potentialities and capabilities.

I have used the schema described to compare the speech development of children in many different societies, some of them much more primitive than our own. In none of these studies could I find evidence of variation in developmental rate, despite the enormous differences in social environment.

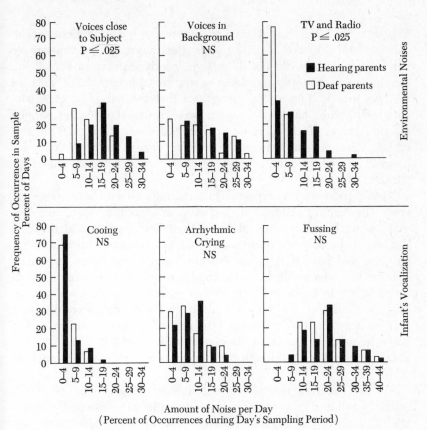

Fig. 1. Frequency distributions of various noises. The basic counting unit is individual recording days.

I have also had an opportunity to study the effect of a dramatically different speech environment upon the development of vocalizations during the first 3 months of life.[4] It is very common in our culture for congenitally deaf individuals to marry one another, creating households in which all vocal sounds are decidedly different from those normally heard and in which the sounds of babies cannot be attended to directly. Six deaf mothers and ten hearing mothers were asked, during their last month of pregnancy, to participate in our study. The babies were visited at home when they were no more than 10 days old and were seen biweekly thereafter for at least 3 months. Each visit consisted of 3 hours of observation and 24 hours of mechanical recording of all sounds made and heard by the baby. Data were analyzed quantitatively and qualitatively. Figure 1 shows that

[4] E. H. Lenneberg, F. G. Rebelsky, I. A. Nichols, *Hum. Develop.* 8, 23 (1965).

although the environment was quantitatively quite different in the experimental and the control groups, the frequency distributions of various baby noises did not differ significantly; as seen in Fig. 2, the developmental histories of cooing noises are also remarkably alike in the two groups. Figure 3 demonstrates that the babies of deaf parents tend to fuss an equal amount, even though the hearing parents are much more likely to come to the child when it fusses. Thus the earliest development of human sounds appears to be relatively independent of the amount, nature, or timing of the sounds made by parents.

I have observed this type of child-rearing through later stages, as well. The hearing children of deaf parents eventually learn two languages and sound systems: those of their deaf parents and those of the rest of the community. In some instances, communication between children and parents is predominantly by gestures. In no case have I found any adverse effects upon the language development of standard English in these children. Although the mothers made sounds different from the children's, and although the children's vocalizations had no significant effect upon attaining what they wanted during early infancy, language in these children invariably began at the usual time and went through the same stages as is normally encountered.

Also of interest may be the following observations on fairly retarded children growing up in state institutions that are badly understaffed. During the day the children play in large, bare rooms, attended by only one person, often an older retardate who herself lacks a perfect command of language. The children's only entertainment is provided by a large television set, playing all day at full strength. Although most of these retarded children have only primitive beginnings of language, there are always some among them who manage, even under these extremely deprived circumstances, to pick up an amazing degree of language skill. Apparently they learn language partly through the television programs, whose level is often quite adequate for them!

From these instances we see that language capacity follows its own natural history. The child can avail himself of this capacity if the environment provides a minimum of stimulation and opportunity. His engagement in language activity can be limited by his environmental circumstances, but the underlying capacity is not easily arrested. Impoverished environments are not conducive to good language development, but good language development is not contingent

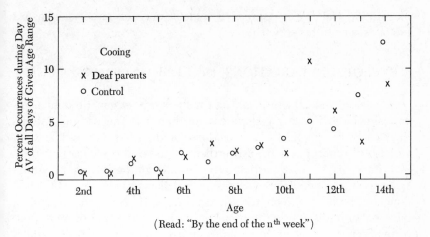

Fig. 2. Each baby's day was divided into 6-minute periods; the presence or absence of cooing was noted for each period; this yielded a percentage for each baby's day; days of all babies were ordered by their ages, and the average was taken for all days of identical age. Nonaveraged data were published in (4).

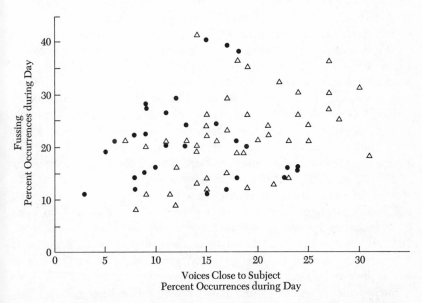

Fig. 3. Relation between the amount of parents' noises heard by the baby and the amount of fussing noises made by the baby. Each symbol is one baby's day; (solid circles) deaf parents; (triangles) hearing parents.

on specific training measures;[5] a wide variety of rather haphazard factors seems to be sufficient.

EFFECT OF VARIATIONS IN GENETIC BACKGROUND

Man is an unsatisfactory subject for the study of genetic influences; we cannot do breeding experiments on him and can use only statistical controls. Practically any evidence adduced is susceptible to a variety of interpretations. Nevertheless, there are indications that inheritance is at least partially responsible for deviations in verbal skills, as in the familial occurrence of a deficit termed congenital language disability (2, chapter 6). Studies, with complete pedigrees, have been published on the occurrence and distribution of stuttering, of hyperfluencies, of voice qualities, and of many other traits, which constitute supporting though not conclusive evidence that inheritance plays a role in language acquisition. In addition to such family studies, much research has been carried out on twins. Particularly notable are the studies of Luchsinger, who reported on the concordance of developmental histories and of many aspects of speech and language. Zygosity was established in these cases by serology (Fig. 4). Developmental data of this kind are, in my opinion, of greater relevance to our speculations on genetic background than are pedigrees.

The nonbiologist frequently and mistakenly thinks of genes as being directly responsible for one property or another; this leads him to the fallacy, especially when behavior is concerned, of dichotomizing everything as being dependent on either genes or environment. Genes act merely on intracellular biochemical processes, although these processes have indirect effects on events in the individual's developmental history. Many alterations in structure and function indirectly attributable to genes are more immediately the consequence of alterations in the schedule of developmental events. Therefore, the studies on twins are important in that they show that homozygotes reach milestones in language development at the same age, in contrast to heterozygotes, in whom divergences are relatively common. It is also interesting that the nature of the deviations—the symptoms, if you wish—are, in the vast majority, identical in homozygotes but not in heterozygotes.

Such evidence indicates that man's biological heritage endows him with sensitivities and propensities that lead to language development

[5] R. Brown, C. Cazden, U. Bellugi, in *The 1967 Minnesota Symposium on Child Psychology*, J. P. Hill, Ed. (Univ. of Minnesota Press, Minneapolis, in press).

in children, who are spoken to (in contrast to chimpanzee infants, who do not automatically develop language—either receptive or productive—under identical treatment). The endowment has a genetic foundation, but this is not to say that there are "genes for language," or that the environment is of no importance.

ATTEMPTS TO MODIFY LANGUAGE DEVELOPMENT

Let us now consider children who have the capacity for language acquisition but fail to develop it for lack of exposure. This is the case with the congenitally deaf, who are allowed to grow up without either language or speech until school age, when suddenly language is brought to them in very unnatural ways. Before this time they may have half a dozen words they can utter, read, write, or finger–spell, but I have known of no profoundly deaf child (in New England, where my investigations were conducted) with whom one could communicate by use of the English language before school age.

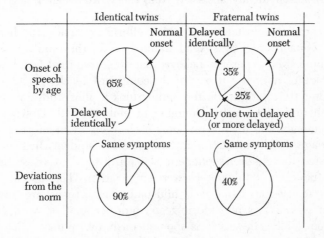

Fig. 4. The onset of speech and its subsequent development tend to be more uniform among identical twins than fraternal twins.

When deaf children enter an oralist school, lipreading and speech become the major preoccupation of training. However, in most children these activities remain poor for many more years, and in some, throughout life. Their knowledge of language comes through learning to read and write. However, teachers in the oral tradition restrict expression in the graphic medium on the hypothesis that it interferes with lipreading and speech skills. Thus, exposure to language (i) comes much later in these children's lives than is normal, (ii) is dramatically reduced in quantity, (iii) is presented through a different medium and sensory modality, and (iv) is taught to the children rather as a second language is taught, instead of through the simple immersion into a sea of language that most children experience. The deaf children are immediately required to use grammatically correct sentences, and every mistake is discussed and explained to them.

The results of this procedure are interesting but not very encouraging from the educational point of view. During the early years of schooling, the children's spontaneous writings have a very unusual pattern; there is little evidence that the teachers' instruction in "how to compose correct sentences" is of any avail. Yet, careful analysis of their compositions shows that some subleties of English syntax that are usually not part of the grammar taught in the school do make their appearance, sometimes quite early. There can be no question that the children do not simply imitate what they see; some of the teachings fall by the wayside, whereas a number of aspects of language are automatically absorbed from the written material given to the children.

There are other instances in which efforts are made to change a child's language skills by special training, as in the mildly retarded, for example. Many parents believe that their retarded child would function quite normally if somebody could just teach him to speak. At Children's Hospital in Boston I undertook a pilot study in which a speech therapist saw a small number of children with Downe's syndrome (mongolism) for several hours each week, in an effort to speed up language development. Later, two graduate students in linguistics investigated the children's phonetic skills and tried to assess the capacities of each child for clearer enunciation. Throughout these attempts, it was found that if a child had a small repertoire of single words, it was always possible to teach him yet another word, but if he was not joining these words spontaneously into phrases, there was nothing that could be done to induce him to do so. The articulatory skills were somewhat different. It was often possible to make a child who had always had slurred speech say a specific word more clearly. However, the moment the child returned to spontaneous utterances, he would fall back to the style that was usual for him. The most interesting results were obtained when the retarded children were required simply to repeat well-formed sentences. A child who had not developed to a stage in which he used certain grammatical rules spontaneously, who was still missing the syntactic foundations and prerequisites, could not be taught to repeat a sentence that was formed by such higher rules. This was true even in sentences of very few words. Similar observations have since been made on normal children,[6] with uniformly similar results; normal children, too, can repeat correctly only that which is formed by rules they have already mastered. This is the best indication that language does not come about by simple imitation, but that the child abstracts regularities or relations from the language he hears, which he then applies to building up language for himself as an apparatus of principles.

WHAT SETS THE PACE OF LANGUAGE DEVELOPMENT?

There is a widespread belief that the development of language is dependent on the motor skills of the articulating organs. Some psychologists believe that species other than man fail to develop language only because of anatomical differences in their oral structures. However, we have evidence that this is not so.

It is important that we are clear about the essential nature of language. Since my interests are in language capacities, I am concerned with the development of the child's knowledge of how language works. This is not the same as the acquisition of "the first word." The best test for the presence and development of this knowledge is the manner in which discourse is understood. In most instances, it is true that there is a relation between speech and understanding, but this relation is not a necessary one.[7]

By understanding, I mean something quite specific. In the realm of phonology, understanding involves a process that roughly corresponds to the linguists' phonematization (in contrast, for example, to a "pictographic" understanding: phonematization results in seeing similarities between speech sounds, whereas pictographic understanding would treat a word as an indivisible sound pattern). In the realm of semantics, understanding involves seeing the basis on which objects are categorized, thus enabling a child to name an object correctly that he has never seen before. (The child does not start out with a hypothesis that "table" is the proper name of a unique object or that it refers to all things that have four appendages.) In the realm of grammar, understanding involves the extraction of relations between word classes; an example is the understanding of predication. By application of these tests, it can be shown empirically that Aunt

[6] D. Slobin, personal communication.
[7] E. H. Lenneberg, *J. Abnorm. Soc. Psychol.* 65, 419 (1962).

Pauline's favorite lapdog does not have a little language knowledge, but, in fact, fails the test of understanding on all counts.

A survey of children with a variety of handicaps shows that their grasp of how language works is intimately related to their general cognitive growth, which, in turn, is partly dependent on physical maturation and partly on opportunities to interact with a stimulus-rich environment. In many retarding diseases, for example, language development is predicted best by the rate of advancement in mental age (using tests of nonverbal intelligence). In an investigation of congenitally blind children,[8] we are again finding that major milestones for language development are highly correlated with physical development. A naive conception of language development as an accumulation of associations between visual and auditory patterns would be hard put to explain this.

BRAIN CORRELATES

In adults, language functions take place predominantly in the left hemisphere. A number of cortical fields have been related to specific aspects of language. The details are still somewhat controversial and need not concern us here. It is certain, however, that precentral areas of the frontal lobe are principally involved in the production of language, whereas the postcentral parietal and superior temporal fields are involved in sensory functions. These cortical specializations are not present at birth, but become only gradually established during childhood, in a process very similar to that of embryological history; there is evidence of differentiation and regulation of function. In the adult, traumata causing large left-sided central cortical lesions carry a highly predictable prognosis; in 70 percent of all cases, aphasia occurs, and in about half of these, the condition is irreversible (I am basing these figures on our experience with penetrating head injuries incurred in war).

Comparable traumatic lesions in childhood have quite different consequences, the prognosis being directly related to the age at which the insult is incurred. Lesions of the left hemisphere in children under age 2 are no more injurious to future language development than are lesions of the right hemisphere. Children whose brain is traumatized after the onset of language but before the age of 4 usually have transient aphasias; language is quickly reestablished, however, if the right hemisphere remains intact. Often these children regain language

[8] E. H. Lenneberg, S. Fraiberg, N. Stein, research in progress.

by going through stages of language development similar to those of the 2-year-old, but they traverse each stage at greater speed. Lesions incurred before the very early teens also carry an excellent prognosis, permanent residues of symptoms being extremely rare.

The prognosis becomes rapidly worse for lesions that occur after this period; the young men who become casualties of war have symptoms virtually identical with those of stroke patients of advanced age. Experience with the surgical removal of an entire cerebral hemisphere closely parallels this picture. The basis for prognosticating operative success is, again, the age at which the disease has been contracted for which the operation is performed.

If a disturbance in the left hemisphere occurs early enough in life, the right hemisphere remains competent for language throughout life. Apparently this process is comparable to regulation, as we know it from morphogenesis. If the disease occurs after a certain critical period of life, namely, the early teens, this regulative capacity is lost and language is interfered with permanently. Thus the time at which the hemispherectomy is performed is less important than the time of the lesion.

CRITICAL AGE FOR LANGUAGE ACQUISITON

The most reasonable interpretation of this picture of recovery from aphasia in childhood is not that there is vicarious functioning, or taking over, by the right hemisphere because of need, but rather that language functions are not yet confined to the left hemisphere during early life. Apparently both hemispheres are involved at the beginning, and a specialization takes place later (which is the characteristic of differentiation), resulting in a kind of left-right polarization of functions. Therefore, the recovery from aphasia during preteen years may partly be regarded as a reinstatment of activities that had never been lost. There is evidence that children at this age are capable of developing language in the same natural way as do very young children. Not only do symptoms subside, but active language development continues to occur. Similarly, we see that healthy children have a quite different propensity for acquiring foreign languages before the early teens than after the late teens, the period in between being transitional. For the young adult, second-language learning is an academic exercise, and there is a vast variety in degree of proficiency. It rapidly becomes more and more difficult to overcome the accent and interfering influences of the mother tongue.

Neurological material strongly suggests that something happens in the brain during the early teens that changes the propensity for language acquisition. We do not know the factors involved, but it is interesting that the critical period coincides with the time at which the human brain attains its final state of maturity in terms of structure, function, and biochemistry (electroencephalographic patterns slightly lag behind, but become stabilized by about 16 years). Apparently the maturation of the brain marks the end of regulation and locks certain functions into place.

There is further evidence that corroborates the notion of a critical period for primary language acquisition, most importantly, the developmental histories of retarded children. It is dangerous to make sweeping generalizations about all retarded children, because so much depends on the specific disease that causes the retardation. But if we concentrate on diseases in which the pathological condition is essentially stationary, such as microcephaly vera or mongolism, it is possible to make fairly general predictions about language development. If the child's mental developmental age is 2 when he is 4 years old (that is, his I.Q. is 50), one may safely predict that some small progress will be made in language development. He will slowly move through the usual stages of infant language, although the rate of development will gradually slow down. In virtually all of these cases, language development comes to a complete standstill in the early teens, so that these individuals are arrested in primitive stages of language development that are perpetuated for the rest of their lives. Training and motivation are of little help.

Development in the congenitally deaf is also revealing. When they first enter school, their language acquisition is usually quite spectacular, considering the enormous odds against them. However, children who by their early teens have still not mastered all of the principles that underlie the production of sentences appear to encounter almost unsurmountable difficulties in perfecting verbal skills.

There is also evidence of the converse. Children who suddenly lose their hearing (usually a consequence of meningitis) show very different degrees of language skill, depending on whether the disease strikes before the onset of language or after. If it occurs before they are 18 months old, such children encounter difficulties with language development that are very much the same as those encountered by the congenitally deaf. Children who lose their hearing after they have acquired language, however, at age 3 to 4, have a different prospect. Their speech deteriorates rapidly; usually within weeks they stop using language, and so far it has proved impossible to maintain the skill by educational procedures [although new techniques developed in England and described by Fry[9] give promise of great improvement]. Many such children then live without language for a relatively long time, often 2 to 3 years, and when they enter the schools for the deaf, must be trained in the same way that other deaf children are trained. However, training is much more successful, and their language habits stand out dramatically against those of their less fortunate colleagues. There appears to be a direct relation between the length of time during which a child has been exposed to language and the proficiency seen at the time of retraining.

BIOLOGICAL APPROACH:
DEFINING LANGUAGE FURTHER

Some investigators propose that language is an artifact—a tool that man has shaped for himself to serve a purpose. This assumption induces the view that language consists of many individual traits, each independent of the other. However, the panorama of observations presented above suggests a biological predisposition for the development of language that is anchored in the operating characteristics of the human brain.[10] Man's cognitive apparatus apparently becomes a language receiver and transmitter, provided the growing organism is exposed to minimum and haphazard environmental events.

However, this assumption leads to a view different from that suggested by the artifact assumption. Instead of thinking of language as a collection of separate and mutually independent traits, one comes to see it as a profoundly integrated activity. Language is to be understood as an operation rather than a static product of the mind. Its modus operandi reflects that of human cognition, because language is an intimate part of cognition. Thus the biological view denies that language is the cause of cognition, or even its effect, since language is not an object (like a tool) that exists apart from a living human brain.

As biologists, we are interested in the operating principles of language because we hope that this will give us some clues about the operating principles of the human brain. We know there is just one species *Homo sapiens*, and it is therefore reasonable to assume that individuals who speak Turkish, English, or Basque (or who spoke

---

[9] D. B. Fry, in *The Genesis of Language: A Psycholinguistic Approach*, F. Smith and G. A. Miller, Eds. (MIT Press, Cambridge, 1966).
[10] For details, see E. H. Lenneberg, *Perception and Language*, in preparation.

Sanskrit some millennia ago) all have (or had) the same kind of brain, that is, a computer with the same operating principles and the same sensorium. Therefore, in a biological investigation one must try to disregard the differences between the languages of the world and to discover the general principles of operation that are common to all of them. This is not an easy matter; in fact there are social scientists who doubt the existence of language universals. As students of language we cannot fail to be impressed with the enormous differences among languages. Yet every normal child learns the language to which he is exposed. Perhaps we are simply claiming that common denominators must exist; can we prove their existence? If we discovered a totally isolated tribe with a language unknown to any outsider, how could we find out whether this language is generated by a computer that has the same biological characteristics as do our brains, and how could we prove that it shares the universal features of all languages?

As a start, we could exchange children between our two cultures to discover whether the same language developmental history would occur in those exchanged. Our data would be gross developmental stages, correlated with the emergence of motor milestones. A bioassay of this kind (already performed many times, always with positive results) gives only part of the answer.

In theory, one may also adduce more rigorous proof of similarity among languages. The conception of language universals is difficult to grasp intuitively, because we find it so hard to translate from one language to another and because the grammars appear, on the surface, to be so different. But it is entirely possible that underneath the structural difference that makes it so difficult for the adult speaker to learn a second language (particularly one that is not a cognate of his own) there are significant formal identities.

Virtually every aspect of language is the expression of relations. This is true of phonology (as stressed by Roman Jakobson and his school), semantics, and syntax. For instance, in all languages of the world words label a set of relational principles instead of being labels of specific objects. Knowing a word is never a simple association between an object and an acoustic pattern, but the successful operation of those principles, or application of those rules, that lead to using the word "table" or "house" for objects never before encountered. The language universal in this instance is not the type of object that comes to have a world, nor the particular relations involved; the universal is the generality that words stand for relations instead of being unique names for one object.

Further, no language has ever been described that does not have a second order of relational principles, namely, principles in which relations are being related, that is, syntax in which relations between words are being specified. Once again, the universal is not a particular relation that occurs in all languages (though there are several such relations) but that all languages have relations of relations.

Mathematics may be used as a highly abstract form of description, not of scattered facts but of the dynamic interrelations—the operating principles—found in nature. Chomsky and his students have done this. Their aim has been to develop algorithms for specific languages, primarily English, that make explicit the series of computations that may account for the structure of sentences. The fact that these attempts have only been partially successful is irrelevant to the argument here. (Since every native speaker of English *can* tell a well-formed sentence from an ill-formed one, it is evident that some principles must exist; the question is merely whether the Chomskyites have discovered the correct ones.) The development of algorithms is only one province of mathematics, and in the eyes of many mathematicians a relatively limited one. There is a more exciting prospect; once we know something about the basic relational operating principles underlying a few languages, it should be possible to characterize formally the abstract system *language* as a whole. If our assumption of the existence of basic, structural language universals is correct, one ought to be able to adduce rigorous proof for the existence of homeomorphisms between any natural languages, that is, any of the systems characterized formally. If a category calculus were developed for this sort of thing, there would be one level of generality on which a common denominator could be found; this may be done trivially (for instance by using the product of all systems). However, our present knowledge of the relations, and the relations of relations, found in the languages so far investigated in depth encourages us to expect a significant solution.

ENVIRONMENT AND MATURATION

Everything in life, including behavior and language, is interaction of the individual with its milieu. But the milieu is not constant. The organism itself helps to shape it (this is true of cells and organs as much as of animals and man). Thus, the organism and its environment is a dynamic system and, phylogenetically, developed as such.

The development of language in the child may be elucidated by applying to it the conceptual framework of developmental biology. Maturation may be characterized as a sequence of states. At each state, the growing organism is capable of accepting some specific input; this it breaks down and resynthesizes in such a way that it makes itself develop into a new state. This new state makes the organism sensitive to new and different types of input, whose acceptance transforms it to yet a further state, which opens the way to still different input, and so on. This is called epigenesis. It is the story of embryological development observable in the formation of the body, as well as in certain aspects of behavior.

At various epigenetic states, the organism may be susceptible to more than one sort of input—it may be susceptible to two or more distinct kinds or even to an infinite variety of inputs, as long as they are within determined limits—and the developmental history varies with the nature of the input accepted. In other words, the organism, during development, comes to crossroads; if condition A is present, it goes one way; if condition B is present, it goes another. We speak of states here, but this is, of course, an abstraction. Every stage of maturation is unstable. It is prone to change into specific directions, but requires a trigger from the environment.

When language acquisition in the child is studied from the point of view of developmental biology, one makes an effort to describe developmental stages together with their tendencies for change and the conditions that bring about that change. I believe that the schema of physical maturation is applicable to the study of language development because children appear to be sensitive to successively different aspects of the language environment. The child first reacts only to intonation patterns. With continued exposure to these patterns as they occur in a given language, mechanisms develop that allow him to process the patterns, and in most instances to reproduce them (although the latter is not a necessary condition for further development). This changes him so that he reaches a new state, a new potential or language development. Now he becomes aware of certain articulatory aspects, can process them and possibly also reproduce them, and so on. A similar sequence of acceptance, synthesis, and state of new acceptance can be demonstrated on the level of semantics and syntax.

That the embryological concepts of differentiation, as well as of determination and regulation, are applicable to the brain processes associated with language development is best illustrated by the material discussed above under the headings "brain correlates" and "critical age for language acquisition." Furthermore, the correlation between language development and other maturational indices suggests that there are anatomical and physiological processes whose maturation sets the pace for both cognitive and language development; it is to these maturational processes that the concept differentiation refers. We often transfer the meaning of the word to the verbal behavior itself, which is not unreasonable, although, strictly speaking, it is the physical correlates only that differentiate.

PSEUDO HOMOLOGIES
AND NAIVE "EVOLUTIONIZING"

The relation between species is established on the basis of structural, physiological, biochemical, and often behavioral correspondences, called homologies. The identification of homologies frequently poses heuristic problems. Common sense may be very misleading in this matter. Unless there is cogent evidence that the correspondences noted are due to a common phylogenetic origin, one must entertain the possibility that resemblances are spurious (though perhaps due to convergence). In other words, not all criteria are equally reliable for the discovery of true homologies. The criteria must pass the following two tests if they are to reveal common biological origins. (i) They must be applicable to traits that have a demonstrable (or at least conceivable) genetic basis; and (ii) the traits to which they apply must not have a sporadic and seemingly random distribution over the taxa of the entire animal kingdom. Homologies cannot be established by relying on similarity that rests on superficial inspection (a whale is not a fish); on logical rather than biological aspects (animals that move at 14 miles per hour are not necessarily related to one another); and on anthropocentric imputation of motives (a squirrel's hoarding of nuts may have nothing in common with man's provisions for his future).

Comparisons of language with animal communication that purport to throw light on the problem of its phylogenetic origins infringe on every one of these guidelines. Attempts to write generative grammars for the language of the bees in order to discover in what respect that language is similar to and different from man's language fail to pass test (i). Syntax does not have a genetic basis any more than do arithmetic or algebra; these are calculi used to describe relations. It may be that the activities or circumstances to which the calculi are applied are in some way related to genetically determined capacities. However, merely the fact that the calculus may or may not be applied obviously does not settle that issue.

The common practice of searching the entire animal kingdom for communication behavior that resembles man's in one aspect or another fails test (ii). The fact that some bird species and perhaps two or three cetaceans can make noises that sound like words, that some insects use discrete signals when they communicate, or that recombination of signals has been observed to occur in communication systems of a dozen totally unrelated species are not signs of a common phylogeny or genetically based relationship to language. Furthermore, the similarities noted between human language and animal communication all rest on superficial intuition. The resemblances that exist between human language and the language of the bees and the birds are spurious. The comparative criteria are usually logical[12] instead of biological; and the very idea that there must be a common denominator underlying all communication systems of animals and man is based on an anthropocentric imputation.

Everything in biology has a history, and so every communication system is the result of evolution. But traits or skills do not have an evolutionary history of their own, that is, a history that is independent of the history of the species. Contemporary species are discontinuous groups (except for those in the process of branching) with discontinuous communication behavior. Therefore, historical continuity need not lead to continuity between contemporary communication systems, many of which (including man's) constitute unique developments.

Another recent practice is to give speculative accounts of just how, why, and when human language developed. This is a somewhat futile undertaking. The knowledge that we have gained about the mechanisms of evolution does not enable us to give specific accounts of every event of the past. Paleontological evidence points to the nature of its fauna, flora, and climate. The precursors of modern man have left for us their bones, teeth, and primitive tools. None of these bears any necessary or assured relation to any type of communication system. Most speculations on the nature of the most primitive sounds, on the first discovery of their usefulness, on the reasons for the hypertrophy of the brain, or the consequences of a narrow pelvis are in vain. We can no longer reconstruct what the selection pressures were or in what order they came, because we know too little that is securely established by hard evidence about the ecological and social conditions of fossil man. Moreover, we do not even know what the targets of actual selection were. This is particularly troublesome because every genetic alteration brings about several changes at once, some of which must be quite incidental to the selective process.

---

[12] See, for instance, C. F. Hockett, in *Animal Communication*, W. E. Lanyon and W. N. Tavelga, Eds. (American Institute of Biological Sciences, Washington, D. C., 1960); and in *Sci. Amer.* 203, 89 (1960).

SPECIES SPECIFICITIES
AND COGNITIVE SPECIALIZATION

In the 19th century it was demonstrated that man is not in a category apart from that of animals. Today it seems to be necessary to defend the view (before many psychologists) that man is not identical with all other animals—in fact, that every animal species is unique, and that most of the commonalities that exist are, at best, homologies. It is frequently claimed that the principles of behavioral function are identical—in all vertebrates, for example—and that the differences between species are differences of magnitude, rather than quality. At other times, it is assumed that cognitive functions are alike in two species except that one of the two may have additionally acquired a capacity for a specific activity. I find fault with both views.

Since behavioral capacities (I prefer the term cognition) are the product of brain function, my point can well be illustrated by considering some aspects of brain evolution. Every mammalian species has an anatomically distinct brain. Homologies are common, but innovations can also be demonstrated. When man's brain is compared with the brain of other primates, extensive correspondences can be found, but there are major problems when it comes to the identification of homologies. Dramatic differences exist not only in size but also in details of the developmental histories; together with differences in cerebrocortical histology, topography, and extent, there are differences in subcortical fiber-connections, as pointed out by Geschwind[13] most recently and by others before him. The problem is, what do we make of the innovations? Is it possible that each innovation (usually an innovation is not a clear-cut anatomical entity) is like an independent component that is simply added to the components common to all the more old-fashioned brains? And if so, is it likely that the new component is simply adding a routine to the computational facilities already available? Both presumptions are naive. A brain is an integrated organ, and cognition results from the integrated operation of all its tissues and suborgans. Man's brain is not a chimpanzee's brain plus added "association facilities." Its functions have undergone reintegration at the same pace as its evolutionary developments.

The identical argument applies to cognitive functions. Cognition is not made up of isolated processes such as perception, storing, and retrieval. Animals do not all have an identical memory mechanism

[13] N. Geschwind, *Brain* 88, 237, 585 (1965).
[14] I thank H. Levin and M. Seligman for comments and criticisms.

except that some have a larger storage capacity. As the structure of most proteins, the morphology of most cells, and the gross anatomy of most animals show certain species specificities (as do details of behavioral repertoires), so we may expect that cognition, too, in all of its aspects, has its species specificities. My assumption, therefore, is that man's cognition is not essentially that of every other primate with merely the addition of the capacity for language; instead, I propose that his entire cognitive function, of which his capacity for language is an integral part, is species-specific. I repeat once more that I make this assumption not because I think man is in a category all of his own, but because every animal species must be assumed to have cognitive specificities.

CONCLUSION

The human brain is a biochemical machine; it computes the relations expressed in sentences and their components. It has a print-out consisting of acoustic patterns that are capable of similar relational computation by machines of the same constitution using the same program. Linguists, biologists, and psychologists have all discussed certain aspects of the machine.

Linguists, particularly those developing generative grammar, aim at a formal description of the machine's behavior; they search mathematics for a calculus to describe it adequately. Different calculations are matched against the behavior to test their descriptive adequacy. This is an empirical procedure. The raw data are the way a speaker of a language understands collections of words or the relationships he sees. A totally adequate calculus has not yet been discovered. Once available, it will merely describe, in formal terms, the process of relational interpretation in the realm of verbal behavior. It will describe a set of operations; however, it will not make any claims of isomorphism between the formal operations and the biological operations they describe.

Biologists try to understand the nature, growth, and function of the machine (the human brain) itself. They make little inroads here and there, and generally play catch-as-catch-can; everything about the machine interests them (including the descriptions furnished by linguists).

Traditionally, learning theory has been involved neither in a specific description of this particular machine's behavior nor in its physical constitution. Its concern has been with the use of the machine:

What makes it go? Can one make it operate more or less often? What purposes does it serve?

Answers provided by each of these inquiries into language are not intrinsically antagonistic, as has often been claimed. It is only certain overgeneralizations that come into conflict. This is especially so when claims are made that any one of these approaches provides answers to all the questions that matter.

PART II

*The Application of
Transformational Grammar
to English Teaching*

RICHARD OHMANN

Generative Grammars and the Concept of Literary Style

INTRODUCTION

For Ohmann, an author's style is his characteristic way of writing. The task of the student of style is to identify in some precise way what it is that distinguishes one way of writing from another. Ohmann lists a dozen ways that this task has been approached, and concludes that, in spite of partial successes, these approaches have failed "to yield a full and convincing explication of the notion of style."

Ohmann argues that the study of style (stylistics) is dependent on a theory of linguistics and a theory of semantics because these two latter theories describe the system of language. A style is a characteristic *use* of the options within the system. As Ohmann puts it, "it is difficult to see how the *uses* of a system can be understood unless the system itself has been mapped out." The relative failure of the various approaches to stylistic analysis resulted from not having as a base an adequate theory of language.

Ohmann then makes two claims: (1) that transformational grammar provides such an adequate theory of language, and (2) that it is now possible to make significant advances "in the practice of stylistic analysis." He

Reprinted by permission of the author from *Word*, Vol. XX (December), 1964, pp. 423–439.

then adds, "I hope to state a case for the first of these claims, and to make a very modest initial thrust toward documenting the second." The argument for the first claim begins by clarifying what is meant by a *way* of doing something. In human actions, there are areas of restriction and areas of freedom. Ohmann illustrates this by considering the actions of a pianist and a tennis player; each has to follow certain conventions, but each has a number of options within the conventions. Style, in this sense, is the habitual or recurrent use of those options.

Ohmann then raises the question of whether such a distinction between restriction and freedom exists in literature. Some literary critics believe that form (the way in which it is written) is inseparable from the work's meaning. To change a word is to change the meaning, or to say it another way, to get exactly *this* meaning, exactly *these* words had to have been used. Thus, it follows that style does not exist since there are no options that the writer could have used in creating this particular work, that is, if a single word were changed, it would be a different work with a different meaning. Ohmann rejects this conclusion as being counterintuitive.

Ohmann argues that the very concept of style implies that the words on the page could be changed without changing the basic meaning. Thus, a writer's style is his characteristic way of exercising the options available within the system of the language. Another writer, with a different style, could convey the same meaning, but he would choose his own way of expressing it. Style, then, involves the notion that there are alternative ways of saying the same thing.

The transformational component of a generative grammar has three characteristics which afford promising insights into the notion of alternativeness: (1) optional transformational rules will produce alternative sets of sentences that mean the same thing. Ohmann illustrates this by the set, "Dickens wrote *Bleak House*; *Bleak House* was written by Dickens; and Dickens was the writer of *Bleak House*." The second and third sentences result from the applications of optional rules to the first sentence. (2) Transformational rules, even though they alter the form of the sentence to which they are applied, preserve some of the features of the original (kernel) sentence. Thus, "transformational alternatives seem to be different renderings of the same proposition." (3) Transformational rules also govern the way kernel sentences are combined to make complex sentences. This is important because the complexity of sentence structure seems to be closely related to what the reader perceives as the writer's style. Ohmann concludes the first part of his paper by saying, "there is at least some reason, then, to hold that a style is in part a characteristic way of deploying the transformational apparatus of a language, and to expect that transformational analysis will be a valuable aid to the description of actual styles."

The second of the two claims was to show that, with transformational grammar providing a theoretical base, a more refined stylistic analysis is now possible. Ohmann does this by contrasting four modern writers:

Faulkner, Hemingway, James, and D. H. Lawrence. He selects a brief passage from each author and reduces the passage to strings of kernel sentences. One of Ohmann's main points is that writers who have a distinctive style often have a characteristic way of combining kernel sentences, that is, they have a favorite group of transformational rules. Ohmann illustrates this by contrasting the transformational rules employed in the passages from Faulkner and Hemingway. Faulkner favors the relative clause transformation, the conjunction transformation and the comparative transformation, all of which are *additive*, that is, they add "information about a 'thing' with a minimum of repetition." Hemingway, on the other hand, relies on the transformations that produce indirect discourse. Ohmann argues that the author's habitual use of certain types of transformations implies that these writers have "a certain conceptual orientation, a preferred way of organizing experience."

Ohmann discusses two other ways in which transformational grammar gives insight into style. Some writers have a characteristic way of *ordering* the elementary sentences. Sentences may be developed to the right or left of the main clause (termed right and left branching), or the main clause can be split by adding additional material in the middle (termed self-embedding). Self-embedding is usually avoided because it puts such a strain on the memory. One of the things that characterizes Henry James' idiosyncratic style is his fondness for self-embedded constructions at the expense of the more normal right- and left-branching ones.

Finally, a style may be characterized by a preference for a certain type of *operation* (as opposed to rule). There are many transformational rules, but all of them can be subsumed under one of four basic operations. Rules either add, delete, reorder, or combine. We have seen above that writers can favor individual rules. Ohmann points out that writers can favor certain operations as well. He shows that while D. H. Lawrence uses a variety of transformational rules, they tend to have the same effect—the operation of deletion, a fact which Ohmann connects with the "driving insistence" one feels in reading Lawrence's style.

A style is a way of writing—that is what the word means. And that is almost as much as one can say with assurance on the subject, which has been remarkably unencumbered by theoretical insights. Yet we know a good deal more than that, in a way: the same way, roughly in which a native speaker "knows" the grammar of English, although no existing grammatical analysis gives a full and adequate account of his linguistic intuition. Readers familiar with literature have what might sensibly be called a *stylistic* intuition, a rather loosely structured, but often reliable, feeling for the quiddity of a writer's linguistic method, a sense of differences between stretches of literary discourse which are not differences in content. In fact many readers can tell, by skimming a batch of unfamiliar passages, not only that the differences are there, but who the authors are. Read the first few paragraphs of a *New Yorker* story and you can often (without a surreptitious glance at the end) identify it as a Cheever, an O'Hara, an Updike, or a Salinger, even if the subject matter is uncharacteristic. Further evidence, if any is needed, of the reliability of stylistic intuitions is the ability of some to write convincing parodies, and of others to recognize them as such. Thus the theorist of style is confronted by a kind of task that is commonplace enough in most fields: the task of explicating and toughening up for rigorous use a notion already familiar to the layman.

But in stylistics the scholar has always had to make do with a theoretical apparatus not far removed from that of the layman. And although many practitioners have plied their craft with great subtlety, a survey of their work leaves one far from certain what that craft *is*. For the attempt to isolate the cues one attends to in identifying styles and in writing stylistic parody has sprawled out into an almost embarrassing profusion of critical methods. And most of these methods, I believe, are interesting in inverse proportion to their emphasis on what we sense as style. The following list will suggest, but not exhaust, the multiplicity of approaches:

1. What might be called "diachronic stylistics," the study of changes in national literary style from one period to the next. Clearly this approach presupposes a mastery of what might be called

2. "Synchronic stylistics," or the study of this or that period style. Since the style of a period can only be the sum of linguistic habits shared by most writers of that period, synchronic stylistics presupposes in turn the ability to describe the style of a single writer. But there is little agreement upon how such description is to be managed; many methods compete for critical attention.

3. Impressionism: the application of metaphorical labels to styles ("masculine," "limber," "staccato," "flowing," "involuted," etc.), and the attempt to evaluate (Swift's style is the best, or the most natural to English). This sort of criticism makes agreeable parlor conversation, records something of the critic's emotional response, and gives intuition its due, but little else can be said in its favor.

4. The study of sound, especially of rhythm. This approach is capable of some rigor, but the more rigor (that is, the more strictly the critic attends to physical or to phonemic features), the less relevance to what we sense as style. For—let me state this dogmatically—

in prose, at least, rhythm as perceived is largely dependent upon syntax, and even upon content, not upon stress, intonation, and juncture alone.

5. The study of tropes. Attention to metaphor, antithesis, synecdoche, zeugma, and the other figures of classical rhetoric often proceeds from a desire to see the writer's style in terms of what he thought he was doing, and to this extent points away from a descriptive analysis of style, and toward the history or philosophy of rhetorical theory. Even when the studies of figurative language maintain a descriptive focus, they embrace only a small, though important, part of style, and liberally mixed with content, at that.

6. The study of imagery. The fact that a writer favors images of disease, money, battle, or the like, is frequently of great interest, but imagery divorced from its syntactic embodiment is surely more a matter of content than of style.

7. The study of what is variously called "tone," "stance," "role," and so on: roughly, the writer's attitude toward what he is saying, toward his reader, and toward himself, as suggested by his language. The critic in this vein infers, from the locutions on the printed page, a hypothetical live situation in which such language would be appropriate, and discusses the social and emotional features of that situation. This approach has unquestionably been fruitful. Its success depends on a highly developed sense of connotative meaning, both of words and of constructions, and this sense is something that many critics possess in abundance. Tone, however, like figurative language, is only a part of style, and the question remains in what measure tone itself is a product of formal linguistic features.

8. The study of literary structure, which, like the study of tropes and tone, has flourished among the new critics. And to be sure, patterns of organization in a literary work are *related* to style (the way a novel is put together may have an analogue in the way a sentence is put together), but to consider structure a *component* of style, except perhaps in a short poem, stretches the meaning of the term "style" to its limits.

9. The analysis of particular and local effects—a change of verb tense, or the placement of an interrogative, for instance, in a certain passage. Clearly, individual strategies of this sort fit more comfortably under the heading of *technique* than of style, for style has to do primarily with the habitual, the recurrent.

10. The study of special idiosyncrasies, such as the omission of causal connectives from contexts where they usually appear. Such quirks are doubtless stylistic elements, and they can richly reward analysis, as a number of studies by Leo Spitzer have shown. But a few

idiosyncrasies do not add up to a style, by any method of calculation.

11. The study of a writer's lexicon, as pursued, for example, by Josephine Miles. Lexical preferences, unless seen in the context of a ramified system of word classes, are like imagery patterns, in that they reveal more about content than about style.

12. The statistical study of grammatical features—abstract nouns, adjectives, subordinate clauses, questions, and the like. This method is without doubt pertinent, but significant results have been highly elusive. One reason is the crudeness of the categories which traditional grammar has made available to critics, whose knowledge of linguistics generally seems to lag by a few decades. (Linguists, by and large, have not busied themselves with stylistics.) Another reason, equally important, is the overwhelming inefficiency of the procedure, given the very large number of grammatical categories, and the lack of any grammatical system that relates them in meaningful, formally motivated ways. Without such a theory, a collection of counts is simply a collection of counts.

And indeed, the inability of these and other methods, in spite of many partial successes, to yield a full and convincing explication of the notion of style seems in general to follow from the absence of an appropriate underlying linguistic and semantic theory. A style is a characteristic use of language, and it is difficult to see how the *uses* of a system can be understood unless the system itself has been mapped out. It is no surprise, in other words, to find stylistics in a state of disorganization when syntax and semantics, upon which stylistics clearly depends, have themselves been hampered by the lack of a theory that is inclusive, unified, and plausible.

The situation in stylistics is understandably analogous to that in the philosophy of language,* though more muddled still. Just as philosophers have tended to concentrate on this or that discrete feature of language—words, or groups of words, or grammatical predication, or the relation of reference, or logical structure—in isolation from the rest, so analysts of style have talked about sound, tropes, images, diction, devices of conjunction, parallel structure, and so on, without any apparent sense of priority or centrality among these concerns. Thus, in a time when linguistic theory and practice have passed through at least one renaissance, the most serviceable studies of style† continue to pro-

---

* See Jerrold Katz and Jerry Fodor, "What's Wrong with the Philosophy of Language?," *Inquiry* V (1962), pp. 197–237.

† William K. Wimsatt, *The Prose Style of Samuel Johnson* (New Haven, 1941), and Jonas Barish, *Ben Johnson and the Language of Prose Comedy* (Cambridge, Mass., 1960), to name just two of the best.

ceed from the critic's naked intuition, fortified against the winds of ignorance only by literary sophistication and the tattered garments of traditional grammar. Especially damaging is the critic's inability, for lack of a theory, to take into account the deeper structural features of language, precisely those which should enter most revealingly into a stylistic description.

It is my contention that recent developments in generative grammar, particularly on the transformational model, promise, first, to clear away a good deal of the mist from stylistic theory, and, second, to make possible a corresponding refinement in the practice of stylistic analysis. In the remainder of this paper I hope to state a case for the first of these claims, and to make a very modest initial thrust toward documenting the second.

That Chomsky's formulation of grammatical theory is potentially useful should become apparent from an examination of the common sense notion of style. In general that notion applies to human action that is partly invariant and partly variable. A style is a *way* of doing *it*. Now this picture leads to few complications if the action is playing the piano or playing tennis. The pianist performing a Mozart concerto must strike certain notes in a certain order, under certain restrictions of tempo, in a certain relation to the orchestra, and so on. These limitations define the part of his behavior that is fixed. Likewise, the tennis player must hit the ball over the net with the racket in a way partly determined by the rules of the game (errors and cheating are not style). But each has a significant amount of freedom, beyond these established regularities: the tennis player, for instance, chooses from a repertory of strokes, shots, and possible placements (analogous, perhaps, to the linguistic resources of the writer or speaker), and he also has freedom of intensity, smoothness, flamboyance, etc. (as the writer or speaker has freedom in the use of paralinguistic resources like loudness and emphatic punctuation). The tennis player's use of these options, in so far as it is habitual or recurrent, constitutes his style. But the relevant division between fixed and variable components in literature is by no means so obvious. What *is* content, and what is form, or style? The attack on a dichotomy of form and content has been persistent in modern criticism; to change so much as a word, the argument runs, is to change the meaning as well. This austere doctrine has a certain theoretical appeal, given the supposed impossibility of finding exact synonyms, and the ontological queerness of disembodied content—propositions, for instance—divorced from any verbal expression. Yet at the same time this doctrine leads to the altogether counterintuitive conclusion that there can be no such thing as style, or that style is simply a part of content.‡

To put the problem more concretely, the idea of style implies that words on a page might have been different, or differently arranged, without a corresponding difference in substance. Another writer would have said *it* another *way*. For the idea of style to apply, in short, writing must involve choices of verbal formulation. Yet suppose we try to list the alternatives to a given segment of prose: "After dinner, the senator made a speech." A dozen close approximations may suggest themselves ("When dinner was over, the senator made a speech," "The senator made a speech after dinner," "A speech was made by the senator after dinner," etc.), as well as a very large number of more distant renderings ("The senator made a post-prandial oration," "The termination of dinner brought a speech from the senator," etc.). Which ones represent stylistic variations on the original, and which ones say different things? We may have intuitions, but to support them is no trivial undertaking. Clearly it would help to have a grammar that provided certain relationships, formally statable, of alternativeness among constructions. One such relationship, for example, might be that which holds between two different constructions that are derived from the same starting point. And, of course, a generative grammar allows the formulation of precisely this sort of relationship.

In the phrase structure component, to begin with, there are alternate ways of proceeding from identically labeled nodes, alternate ways of expanding (or rewriting) a symbol. A verb phrase may be expanded§ into a transitive verb plus a noun phrase, a copula plus an adjective, a copula plus a noun phrase, or any one of several other combinations.‖ The various possibilities for rewriting at this stage of the grammar account for some of the major sentence types in English, and since the structural meaning of, say, V_t + NP differs considerably from that of Be + Adj, a writer's preference for one or another of these forms may be a stylistic choice of some interest.

---

‡ For an earlier attempt by the present author to deal with this problem, see "Prolegomena to the Analysis of Prose Style," in *Style in Prose Fiction; English Institute Essays*, 1958, Harold C. Martin, Ed. (New York, 1959), pp. 1–24.

§ I do not mean to suggest that a speaker or writer actually performs these operations. But the different possibilities of expansion in the grammar do offer an analogue to the choices open to the writer.

‖ Possibly some other order of expansion is preferable, such as the one Lees uses: VP→(Prev) Aux+MV. See Robert B. Lees, *The Grammar of English Nominalizations*, Part II, *International Journal of American Linguistics* XXVI 3 (1960), 5. If the grammar takes this form, then the choice I am speaking of enters only with the expansion of the main verb. Such questions are immaterial, however, to my point.

But notice that the possibility of alternative routings in the phrase structure component does not really solve the problem of style in a satisfactory way. I have been looking for linguistically constant features that may be expressed in different ways. The difficulty with taking a unit like the verb phrase for such a constant is its abstractness, its lack of structure. The symbol VP merely stands for a *position* in a string at one level of description. Two different expansions of VP will both occupy the same position, but will not necessarily retain any structural feature in common. Nor will the sentences that ultimately result from the two derivations necessarily share any morphemes or even morphemes from the same classes. Thus, the rewriting of VP as $V_t + NP$ is part of a derivation that leads eventually to the sentence "Columbus discovered America," among others. But there is no kernel sentence corresponding (semantically) to this one which results from a derivation in which NP is rewritten $Be + Adj$. Sentences like "Columbus was brave," or possibly "Columbus was nautical" are about as close as one can come. And certainly they are not stylistically different expressions of the same thing, in the sense required for stylistics—not in the way that "America was discovered by Columbus" is. The phrase structure part of the grammar does not account for intuitively felt relationships of sameness and difference between sentences, for the possibility of saying one "thing" in two different ways. Perhaps this is one reason why almost no important work in stylistic criticism has evolved from the grammatical analyses of American linguists.

To be of genuine interest for stylistics, a grammar must do more than simply provide for alternate derivations from the same point of origin. There are at least three important characteristics of transformational rules which make them more promising as a source of insight into style than phrase structure rules. In the first place, a large number of transformations are optional, and in quite a different sense from the sense in which it is optional how VP is expanded. VP must *be* expanded by one of the various rules, or of course no sentence will result from the derivation. But an optional transformation need not be applied at all. Given a string or pair of strings so structured that a certain optional transformation can apply, failure to apply it will not keep the derivation from terminating in a sentence.# Thus "Dickens wrote *Bleak House*" is a sentence, as well as "*Bleak House* was written by Dickens," which has undergone the passive transformation. Likewise, "Dickens was the writer of *Bleak House*" is a sentence, one that comes from the same kernel string as the other two, via a different optional transforma-

---

This is simply to rephrase the definition of an optional transformation; see Noam Chomsky, *Syntactic Structures* ('s-Gravenhage, 1957), p. 45.

tion: agentive nominalization.** Technically, transformations apply to underlying strings with certain structures, but for the purposes of this paper they may be thought of as manipulations—reordering, combination, addition, deletion—performed on fully formed sentences, rather than as ways of *getting* to parts of fully formed sentences from incomplete, abstract symbols such as NP. Each application of a different optional transformation to a sentence results in a new sentence, similar in some ways to the original one. Thus a grammar with transformational rules will generate many pairs and limited sets of sentences, like the set of three sentences about Dickens, which belong together in an intimate structural way—not simply by virtue of being sentences. Many such sets of sentences will strike a speaker as saying "the same thing"—as being alternatives, that is, in precisely the sense required for stylistics.

A second and related reason why transformational happenings are relevant to style is the very fact that a transformation applies to one or more *strings*, or elements with structure, not to single symbols like VP, and that it applies to those strings by virtue of their structure. A transformation works changes on structure, but normally leaves *part* of the structure unchanged. And in any case, the new structure bears a precisely specifiable relationship to the old one, a relationship, incidentally, that speakers of the language will intuitively feel. Moreover, the transform retains at least some morphemes from the original string; that is, transformations are specified in such a way that "Columbus discovered America" cannot become, under the passive transformation, "*Bleak House* was written by Dickens," although this sentence has the same structure as the proper transform "America was discovered by Columbus." This property of transformations—their preserving some features from the original string—accounts for the fact that sets of sentences which are transformational alternatives seem to be different renderings of the same proposition.†† Again, this is the sort of relationship which seems intuitively to underlie the notion of style, and for which only a transformational grammar offers a formal analogue.

The third value of a transformational grammar to the analyst of style is its power to explain how complex sentences are generated, and how they are related to simple sentences. Writers differ noticeably in the amounts and kinds of syntactic complexity they habitually allow themselves, but these matters have been hard to approach through conventional methods of analysis. Since the complexity of a sentence is the

** Lees, *op. cit.*, p. 70 (transformation T47).
†† Notice that many such sets, including the three sentences about Dickens, will share the same *truth conditions*, to use the philosopher's term. This fact gives further encouragement to anyone who would treat transformational alernatives as different expressions of the same proposition.

product of the generalized transformations it has gone through, a breakdown of the sentence into its component simple sentences and the generalized transformations applied (in the order of application) will be an account of its complexity.‡‡ And since the same set of simple sentences may usually be combined in different ways, a set of complex sentences may be generated from them, each of which differs from the others only in transformational history, while embodying the same simple "propositions." Such differences should be interestingly approachable through transformational analysis. So should major variations in type of compounding: self-embedding as against left- and right-branching, for example, or the formation of endocentric as against the formation of exocentric constructions. These deep grammatical possibilities in a language may well be exploited differently from writer to writer, and if so, the differences will certainly be of stylistic interest.

Let me summarize. A generative grammar with a transformational component provides apparatus for breaking down a sentence in a stretch of discourse into underlying kernel sentences (or strings, strictly speaking) and for specifying the grammatical operations that have been performed upon them. It also permits the analyst to construct, from the same set of kernel sentences, other non-kernel sentences. These may reasonably be thought of as *alternatives* to the original sentence, in that they are simply different constructs out of the identical elementary grammatical units.§§ Thus the idea of alternative phrasings, which is crucial to the notion of style, has a clear analogue within the framework of a transformational grammar.

But is it the *right* analogue? What I have called "transformational alternatives" are different derivatives from the same kernel sentences. The notion of style calls for different ways of expressing the same content. Kernel sentences are not "content," to be sure. Yet they *have* content, and much of that content is preserved through transformational operations. "Dickens was the writer of *Bleak House* and America was discovered by Columbus" says much the same thing, if not exactly the same thing, as "Dickens wrote *Bleak House*; Columbus discovered

‡‡ Since deletions and additions will probably have taken place in the course of the derivation, the complex sentence will naturally not contain all and only all of the linguistic elements contained in the component sentences. These must be reconstructed and supplied with appropriate hypothetical elements, but there is generally a strong formal motivation for reconstructing the component sentences in one way rather than another.

§§ Of course the alternative forms need not be complete sentences, or single sentences. That is, the alternatives to sentence A may include (1) sentence B, (2) part of sentence C, and (3) the group of sentences, D, E, and F. The most interesting alternatives to a given sentence often arrange the kernel material in units of different lengths.

America." Of course some transformations import new content, others eliminate features of content, and no transformation leaves content absolutely unaltered. The analogue is not perfect. But it is worth remembering that other kinds of tampering with sentences (e.g., substitution of synonyms) also change content. And, to look at it another way, the most useful sense of "content"—*cognitive* content—may be such that transformations do generally leave it unaltered (and such that synonyms do exist).‖ ‖ In any case, transformational alternatives come as close to "different expressions of the same content" as other sorts of alternatives; moreover, they have the practical advantage of being accessible to formal, rather than to impressionistic, analysis. There is at least some reason, then, to hold that a style is in part a characteristic way of deploying the transformational apparatus of a language, and to expect that transformational analysis will be a valuable aid to the description of actual styles.

So much for theory and prophecy. The final proof must come, if it comes at all, from a fairly extensive attempt to study literary styles in the way I am suggesting. For a transformational analysis, however appealing theoretically, will not be worth much unless it can implement better stylistic descriptions than have been achieved by other methods—"better" in that they isolate more fully, economically, and demonstrably the linguistic features to which a perceptive reader responds in sensing one style to be different from another. The space available here will not suffice for a full scale demonstration, nor do I now have at my disposal nearly enough stylistic description to prove my case. Besides, the necessary grammatical machinery is by no means available yet (in fact, it is too early to say with certainty that Chomsky's plan for grammars is the right one—there are many dissenters). I shall use the rest of this paper merely to outline, by example, a simple analytic procedure that draws on the concept of grammatical transformations, and to suggest some virtues of this procedure.

My first specimen passage comes from Faulkner's story, "The Bear." It is part of a sentence nearly two pages long, and its style is complex, highly individual, and difficult—if it is read aloud, most hearers will not grasp it on first hearing. It is also, I believe, quite typically Faulknerian:

> the desk and the shelf above it on which rested the letters in which
> McCaslin recorded the slow outward trickle of food and supplies and
> equipment which returned each fall as cotton made and ginned and

‖ ‖ I owe this point and several others to correspondence and conversation with Noam Chomsky.

sold (two threads frail as truth and impalpable as equators yet cable-strong to bind for life them who made the cotton to the land their sweat fell on), and the older ledgers clumsy and archaic in size and shape, on the yellowed pages of which were recorded in the faded hand of his father Theophilus and his uncle Amodeus during the two decades before the Civil War, the manumission in title at least of Carothers McCaslin's slaves: . . .##

I propose to reduce the complexity of the passage by reversing the effects of three generalized transformations, plus a few related singulary transformations:

1. The relative clause transformation (GT 19 in Lees' *The Grammar of English Nominalizations*, p. 89), along with the wh-transformations (Lees, T5 and T6, p. 39), the transformation which later deletes "which" and "be" to leave post-nominal modifiers (Lees, T58, p. 94), and the transformation which shifts these modifiers to prenominal position (Lees, T64, p. 98).***

2. The conjunction transformation (Chomsky, *Syntactic Structures*, p. 36).

3. The comparative transformation, which, along with several reduction transformations and one order change,††† is responsible for sentences like "George is as tall as John."‡‡‡

Without this grammatical apparatus, the passage reads as follows:

the desk. The shelf was above it. The ledgers₁ rested on the shelf. The ledgers₁ were old. McCaslin recorded the trickle of food in the ledgers₁. McCaslin recorded the trickle of supplies in the ledgers₁. McCaslin recorded the trickle of equipment in the ledgers₁. The trickle was slow. The trickle was outward. The trickle returned each fall as cotton. The cotton was made. The cotton was ginned. The cotton was sold. The trickle was a thread. The cotton was a thread. The threads were frail. Truth is frail. The threads were impalpable. Equators are impalpable. The threads were strong to bind them for life to the land. They made the cotton. Their sweat fell on the land. Cables are strong. The ledgers₂ were old. The ledgers₂ rested on the shelf. The ledgers₂

William Faulkner, "The Bear," in *Go Down Moses* (New York: Modern Library, 1942), pp. 255–256.

*** For another version of these transformations, see Carlota S. Smith, "A Class of Complex Modifiers in English," *Language* XXXVII (1961), pp. 347–348, 361–362.

††† Strong as cables→cable-strong.

‡‡‡ Lees, "Grammatical Analysis of the English Comparative Construction," *Word* XVII (1961), pp. 182–183. Carlota S. Smith, in "A Class of Complex Modifiers in English," offers a fuller treatment of such constructions, but Lees' simpler analysis is adequate for my present purposes.

were clumsy in size. The ledgers$_2$ were clumsy in shape. The ledgers$_2$ were archaic in size. The ledgers$_2$ were archaic in shape. On the pages of the ledgers$_2$ were recorded in the hand of his father during the two decades the manumission in title at least of Carothers McCaslin's slaves. On the pages of the ledgers$_2$ were recorded in the hand of his uncle during the two decades the manumission in title at least of Carothers McCaslin slaves. The pages were yellowed. The hand was faded. The decades were before the Civil War. His father was Theophilus. His uncle was Amodeus.§§§

There is some artificiality in this process, of course. The order of the reduced sentences is in part arbitrary. More important, the transformations I have reversed are not the last ones applied in the generation of the original construction; hence precisely the set of sentences (strings) above would not have occurred at any point in the derivation. Nonetheless, this drastic reduction of the original passage reveals several important things:

1. The content of the passage remains roughly the same: aside from the loss of distinctions between "and" and "yet," "as ―― as" and "more ____ than," relative clauses and conjoined sentences, and the like, changes in content are minor. But the style, obviously, has undergone a revolution. In the reduced form of the passage there are virtually no traces of what we recognize as Faulkner's style.

2. This denaturing has been accomplished by reversing the effects of only three generalized transformations, as well as a few related singulary transformations. The total number of optional transformations involved is negligible as against the total number that apparently exist in the grammar as a whole. In other words, the style of the original passage leans heavily upon a very small amount of grammatical apparatus.

3. Most of the sentences in the reduced version of the passage are kernel sentences. Most of the rest are only one transformation away from kernel sentences. Further reduction, by undoing any number of other transformations, would not change the passage or its style nearly so much as has already been done.‖ ‖ ‖

4. The three major transformations I have deleted have an important feature in common. Each of them combines two sentences that share at least one morpheme.### and in such a way that the transform

---

§§§ Subscripts mark differences in referent.

‖ ‖ ‖ Passives and pronouns are also fairly prominent here, but not enough to make them striking as stylistic features.

Except that conjunction may also operate on two sentences with no common morphemes.

may contain only one occurrence of that morpheme (or those morphemes), while preserving the unshared parts of the original sentences. That is to say, these transformations are all what might be called "additive." To put the matter semantically, they offer methods of adding information about a single "thing" with a minimum of repetition. Thus the two sentences "The threads were impalpable" and "The threads were frail" might be combined through any one of the three generalized transformations at issue here: "The threads which were impalpable were frail" (relative); "The threads were frail and impalpable" (conjunction); and "The threads were more frail than impalpable" (comparison). The three transforms are somewhat similar, both formally and semantically; and it seems reasonable to suppose that a writer whose style is so largely based on just these three semantically related transformations demonstrates in that style a certain conceptual orientation, a preferred way of organizing experience.**** If that orientation could be specified, it would almost certainly provide insight into other, non-stylistic features of Faulkner's thought and artistry. The possibility of such insight is one of the main justifications for studying style.

The move from formal description of styles to critical and semantic interpretation should be the ultimate goal of stylistics, but in this article I am concerned only with the first step: description. My first example shows that the style of at least one short passage can be rather efficiently and informatively described in terms of a few grammatical operations. It might be objected, however, that the transformations I have concentrated on in destroying the style of the Faulkner passage are of such prominence in the grammar, and in the use of English, that *any* writer must depend heavily upon them. To show that this is not universally the case, it is sufficient to perform the same reductions on a characteristic passage from the work of another writer with a quite different style. Consider, therefore, the conclusion of Hemingway's story, "Soldier's Home":

> So his mother prayed for him and then they stood up and Krebs kissed his mother and went out of the house. He had tried so to keep his life from being complicated. Still, none of it had touched him. He had felt sorry for his mother and she had made him lie. He would go to Kansas City and get a job and she would feel all right about it. There would be one more scene maybe before he got away. He would

---

**** It is apparently common for stylistic features to cluster like this in the work of an author. See my study, *Shaw; The Style and the Man* (Middletown, Conn., 1962), for numerous examples, and for an attempt to link style with cognitive orientation.

not go down to his father's office. He would miss that one. He wanted
his life to go smoothly. It had just gotten going that way. Well, that
was all over now, anyway. He would go over to the schoolyard and
watch Helen play indoor baseball.††††

Reversing the effects of the relative and comparative transformations barely alters the passage: only the prenominal modifier "indoor"
is affected. Removing the conjunctions does result in some changes:

> So his mother prayed for him. Then they stood up. Krebs kissed his
> mother. Krebs went out of the house. He had tried so to keep his life
> from being complicated. Still, none of it had touched him. He had felt
> sorry for his mother. She had made him lie. He would go to Kansas
> City. He would get a job. She would feel all right about it. There
> would be one more scene maybe before he got away. He would not
> go down to his father's office. He would miss that one. He wanted his
> life to go smoothly. It had just gotten going that way. Well, that was
> all over now, anyway. He would go over to the schoolyard. He would
> watch Helen play indoor baseball.

Notice that the reduced passage still sounds very much like Hemingway. Nothing has been changed that seems crucial to his style. Note
too that although the revised passage is quite simple, none of the
sentences is from the kernel. Hemingway is not innocent of transformations: he is relying on pronominalization, on a group of nominalizations, and, most notably, on a sequence of transformations responsible
for what critics call the "*style indirect libre.*" These transformations
work this way:

1. GT; quotation, or reported thought:

$$
\text{He} \left\{\begin{array}{l} \text{thought} \\ \text{said} \\ \text{felt} \\ \text{etc.} \end{array}\right\} \text{NPabst} \atop \text{She has made me lie} \left.\begin{array}{l} \\ \\ \\ \\ \\ \end{array}\right\} \rightarrow \text{He thought, "She has made me lie"}
$$

2. Indirect discourse (change of pronouns and of verb tense):

> He thought, "She has made me lie" → He thought that she had made
> him lie

†††† *The Short Stories of Ernest Hemingway* (New York, 1953), pp. 152–153.

3. Deletion:

He thought that she had made him lie → She had made him lie[‡‡‡‡]

The original passage, stripped of the effects of these transformations, reads as follows:

> So his mother prayed for him and they stood up and Krebs kissed his mother and went out of the house. He thought this: I have tried so to keep my life from being complicated. Still, none of it has touched me. I have felt sorry for my mother and she has made me lie. I will go to Kansas City and get a job and she will feel all right about it. There will be one more scene maybe before I get away. I will not go down to my father's office. I will miss that one. I want my life to go smoothly. It has just gotten going that way. Well, that is all over now, anyway. I will go over to the schoolyard and watch Helen play indoor baseball.

The peculiar double vision of the style, the sense of the narrator peering into the character's mind and scrupulously reporting its contents, the possibility of distance and gentle irony—all these are gone with the transformational wind.

To be sure, these transformations do not in themselves distinguish Hemingway's style from the styles of many other writers (Virginia Woolf, Ford Madox Ford, James Joyce, etc.). But it is interesting, and promising, that a stylistic difference so huge as that between the Faulkner and Hemingway passages can be largely explained on the basis of so little grammatical apparatus.

Up to this point, I have been exploring some effects on style of particular transformations and groups of transformations, and arguing that this method of description has, potentially, considerable value for literary critics. But there are at least two other ways in which transformational machinery will aid the analyst of style.

First, it has often been pointed out that constructions may be left-branching ("Once George had left, the host and hostess gossiped briskly"), right-branching ("The host and hostess gossiped briskly, once George had left"), or self-embedding ("The host and hostess, once George had left, gossiped briskly"). Neither left- nor right-

[‡‡‡‡] Morris Halle (Massachusetts Institute of Technology) explained these transformations to me. He is treating them in a forthcoming article on Virginia Woolf's style, and I make no attempt here to put the rules in proper and complete form. It should be noted though, that there is at present no justification for the grammar to contain rule number three as a transformation, since the transform is already generated by other rules.

branching constructions tax the hearer's understanding, even when compounded at some length ("a very few not at all well liked union officials"; "the dog that worried the cat that chased the rat that ate the cheese that lay in the house that Jack built"). But layers of self-embedding quickly put too great a strain on the unaided memory ("the house in which the cheese that the rat that the cat that the dog worried chased ate lay was built by Jack"). Even a relatively small amount of self-embedding in a written passage can slow a reader down considerably.

With these preliminaries, consider the following sentence, which begins a short story:

> She had practically, he believed, conveyed the intimation, the horrid, brutal, vulgar menace, in the course of their last dreadful conversation, when, for whatever was left him of pluck or confidence—confidence in what he would fain have called a little more aggressively the strength of his position—he had judged best not to take it up.§§§§

The style is idiosyncratic in the highest degree, and the writer is, of course, Henry James. His special brand of complexity is impossible to unravel through the method I pursued with Faulkner. A number of *different* transformations are involved. But notice that most of this complexity results from self-embedding. With the embedded elements removed the sentence is still far from simple, but the Jamesian intricacy is gone:

> She had practically conveyed the intimation in the course of their last dreadful conversation, when he had judged best not to take it up.

The following are the deleted sentences, with their full structure restored:

> He believed [it].
> [The intimation was a] horrid, brutal, vulgar menace.
> [Something] was left him of pluck or confidence.
> [It was] confidence in the strength of his position.
> He would fain have called [it that], a little more aggressively.

The embedded elements, in short, significantly outweigh the main sentence itself, and needless to say, the strain on attention and memory required to follow the progress of the main sentence over and

§§§§ "The Bench of Desolation," *Ten Short Stories of Henry James*, Michael Swan, Ed. (London, 1948), p. 284.

around so many obstacles is considerable. The difficulty, as well as the Jamesian flavor, is considerably lessened merely by substituting left- and right-branching constructions for self-embedding, even though all the kernel sentences are retained:

> He believed that in the course of their last dreadful conversation she had practically conveyed the intimation, a horrid, brutal, vulgar menace, which he had then judged best not to take up, for whatever was left him of pluck or confidence—confidence in the strength of his position, as he would fain have called it, a little more aggressively.

It seems likely that much of James's later style can be laid to this syntactic device—a matter of *positioning* various constructions, rather than of favoring a few particular constructions. The relevance of positioning to style is, to be sure, no news. But again, transformational analysis should clarify the subject, both by providing descriptive rigor and by making available a set of alternatives to each complex sentence.

Finally, styles may also contrast in the kinds of transformational operations on which they are built. There are four possibilities: addition, deletion, reordering, and combination. Of these, my final sample depends heavily on deletion. The passage is from D. H. Lawrence's *Studies in Classic American Literature,* a book with an especially brusque, emphatic style, which results partly from Lawrence's affection for kernel sentences. But his main idiosyncrasy is the use of truncated sentences, which have gone through a variety of deletion transformations. Here is the excerpt:

> The renegade hates life itself. He wants the death of life. So these many "reformers" and "idealists" who glorify the savages in America. They are death-birds, life-haters. Renegades.
>
> We can't go back. And Melville couldn't. Much as he hated the civilized humanity he knew. He couldn't go back to the savages. He wanted to. He tried to. And he couldn't.
>
> Because in the first place, it made him sick.‖ ‖ ‖ ‖

With the deleted segments replaced, the passage reads, somewhat absurdly, like this:

> The renegade hates life itself. He wants the death of life. So these many "reformers" and "idealists" who glorify the savages in America [want the death of life]. They are death-birds. [They are] life-haters. [They are] renegades.
>
> We can't go back. And Melville couldn't [go back]. [Melville

‖ ‖ ‖ ‖ D. H. Lawrence, *Studies in Classic American Literature* (New York: Anchor Books, 1955), p. 149.

couldn't go back, as] much as he hated the civilized humanity he
knew. He couldn't go back to the savages. He wanted to [go back
to the savages]. He tried to [go back to the savages]. And he couldn't
[go back to the savages].
   [He couldn't go back to the savages] because, in the first place, it
made him sick [to go back to the savages].

One does not need grammatical theory to see that Lawrence is
deleting. But the restoration of the full form which is allowed by the
grammar does reveal two interesting things. First, there is a large
amount of repetition in the original passage, much more than actually
shows. Perhaps this fact accounts for the driving insistence one feels
in reading it. Second, Lawrentian deletion is a stylistic alternative to
conjunction, which can also take place whenever there are two sentences partly alike in their constituents. The reasons for Lawrence's
preferring deletion to conjunction might well be worth some study.
   And in general, study of that sort should be the goal of stylistic
analysis. All I have done here is outline, briefly and in part informally,
a fruitful method of stylistic *description*. But no *analysis* of a style, in
the fuller sense, can get off the ground until there are adequate
methods for the humble task of description. Such methods, I think, are
provided by transformational grammar. Furthermore, I have argued,
such a grammar is especially useful for this purpose in that it alone
is powerful enough to set forth, formally and accurately, stylistic
alternatives to a given passage or a given set of linguistic habits.
   Now there is no reason to generalize from four passages to infinity,
and in fact full stylistic descriptions of the work of even the four
writers I have discussed would need to be far more elaborate than the
sketches I have offered here. Moreover, many styles that readers perceive as distinctive are more complex in their syntactic patterns than
these four. Finally, though syntax seems to be a central determinant
of style, it is admittedly not the whole of style. Imagery, figures of
speech, and the rest are often quite important. But to perform on
various styles the kind of analysis I have attempted in this paper is to
be convinced that transformational patterns constitute a significant
part of what the sensitive reader perceives as style. Transformational
analysis of literary discourse promises to the critic stylistic descriptions
which are at once simpler and deeper than any hitherto available, and
therefore more adequate foundations for critical interpretation. Not
only that: if, as seems likely to happen, generative grammars with
transformational rules help the linguist or critic to explicate convincingly the elusive but persistent notion of style, that achievement
will stand as one more piece of evidence in favor of such grammars.

RICHARD OHMANN

Literature as Sentences

INTRODUCTION

The essay begins with a distinction between surface structure and deep structure, "typically, a surface structure overlays a deep structure which it may resemble but little, and which determines the 'content' of the sentence." Notice that Ohmann has connected "content" with the deep structure. Throughout the essay Ohmann draws a distinction between "form" and the surface structure on the one hand and "content" and the deep structure on the other. At the close of the essay Ohmann makes the distinction explicit:

> I have indicated some areas where a rich exchange between linguistics and critical theory might eventually take place. To wit, the elusive intuition we have of *form* and *content* may turn out to be anchored in a distinction between the surface structures and the deep structures of sentences.

To illustrate how the theory of transformational grammar can assist the literary critic in his task of relating form and meaning, Ohmann gives two

Reprinted by permission of the author, the National Council of Teachers of English, from *College English*, Vol. 27, No. 4 (January), 1966 pp. 261–267.

samples, the final sentence of Joseph Conrad's "The Secret Sharer" and the
first sentence of Dylan Thomas' "A Winter's Tale."

In his comments on "The Secret Sharer" Ohmann makes these points:
1. The surface structure feeds information to the reader at a certain rate
and in a certain way. The surface structure gives the writer control over
the way the reader comes to understand the meaning of the passage. Stated
in slightly different terms, the author's control of the surface structure
determines the progression of the reader's understanding of the deep structure. In the passage he cites from Conrad, Ohmann says,

> This progression in the deep structure rather precisely mirrors both
> the rhetorical movement of the sentence from the narrator to Leggatt
> via the hat that links them, and the thematic effect of the sentence,
> which is to transfer Leggatt's experience to the narrator via the nar-
> rator's vicarious and actual participation in it.

2. A word can be heavily emphasized in the deep structure without
being repeated in the surface structure. In this case, the word *share* is of
key thematic importance in understanding the whole work, yet it appears
in the surface structure of the last sentence only once. However, in the deep
structure, Ohmann points out that thirteen sentences "go to the semantic
development of 'sharer.'" *Share* thus plays a complex syntactic role in the
deep structure. Ohmann argues that the very act of understanding the
sentence concentrates the reader's attention on the word *share*. Words that
have many separate functions in the deep structure are said to have a high
degree of "syntactic density."

3. By a greater conscious understanding of the deep structure, the reader
may better understand the structuring ("the build") of the thematic
meaning of the whole work.

4. Finally, a point which Ohmann develops at length in his article "Generative Grammars and the Concept of Literary Style." Each writer tends to
exercise the options in the grammar in a characteristic way:

> his style, in other words, rests on syntactic options within sentences . . .
> these syntactic preferences correlate with habits of meaning that tell
> us something about his mode of conceiving experience.

In the case of Conrad, Ohmann claims that "Conrad draws heavily on
operations that link one thing with another associatively."

Dylan Thomas' "A Winter's Tale" raises a different kind of critical question: the ungrammatical or deviant use of language which is common in
modern poetry. Ohmann begins by rejecting the notion that such deviance
is simply a reflection of the irrational nature of the world. Quite the opposite:

> And if he (the poet) strays from grammatical patterns he does not
> thereby leave language or reason behind: if anything, he draws the

more deeply on linguistic structure and on the processes of human understanding that are implicit in our use of well-formed sentences.

Ohmann's main point is that the reader interprets the surface deviance in terms of "the base sentences that lie beneath ungrammatical constructions." The surface deviance is corrected by analogy to similar grammatical constructions. For instance, when the word *twilight* is used as the subject of *ferry* we can resolve the surface ungrammaticality by interpreting *twilight* as an animate noun. Another example is the interpretation of the phrase *river wended vales*. Ohmann's own interpretation is that the normally intransitive verb *wend* is interpreted as being analogous to the class of verbs that can be either transitive or intransitive, such as *paint* or *rub*. *Wend* is then interpreted by Ohmann to mean "make a mark on the surface of, by traversing." The key point here is that *wend* is doing double duty. In addition to its own ordinary intransitive meaning, it has picked up additional meanings from the class that it is analogized with. As Ohmann explains it:

> I have been leading up to the point that every syntactically deviant construction has more than one possible interpretation, and that readers resolve the conflict by a process that involves deep and intricately motivated decisions and thus puts to work considerable linguistic knowledge, syntactic as well as semantic.

Ohmann's final major point is that a poet's use of deviance is not random: the deviancy has a kind of consistency in it which springs from "particular semantic impulses, particular ways of looking at experience." Ohmann shows that Thomas' deviancy

> converts juxtaposition into action, inanimate into human, abstract into physical, static into active. Now, much of Thomas' poetry displays the world as process, as interacting forces and repeating cycles, in which human beings and human thought are indifferently caught up. I suggest that Thomas' syntactical irregularities often serve this vision of things.

Critics permit themselves, for this or that purpose, to identify literature with great books, with imaginative writing, with expressiveness in writing, with the non-referential and non-pragmatic, with beauty in language, with order, with myth, with structured and formed discourse—the list of definitions is nearly endless—with verbal play, with uses of language that stress the medium itself, with the expression of an age, with dogma, with the *cri de coeur*, with neurosis. Now of course literature is itself and not another thing, to paraphrase Bishop Butler; yet analogies and classifications have merit. For a short space let us think of literature as sentences.

To do so will not tax the imagination, because the work of literature indubitably *is* composed of sentences, most of them well-ordered, many of them deviant (no pejorative meant), some of them incomplete. But since much the same holds for dust-jacket copy, the Congressional Record, and transcripts of board meetings, the small effort required to think of literature as sentences may be repaid by a correspondingly small insight into literature as such. Although I do not believe this to be so, for the moment I shall hold the question in abeyance, and stay mainly within the territory held in common by all forms of discourse. In other words, I am not asking what is special about the sentences *of literature*, but what is special about *sentences* that they should interest the student of literature. Although I employ the framework of generative grammar and scraps of its terminology,* what I have to say should not ring in the traditionally educated grammatical ear with outlandish discord.

First, then, the sentence is the primary unit of understanding. Linguists have so trenchantly discredited the old definition—"a sentence is a complete thought"—that the truth therein has fallen into neglect. To be sure, we delimit the class of sentences by formal criteria, but each of the structures that qualifies will express a semantic unity not characteristic of greater or lesser structures. The meanings borne by morphemes, phrases, and clauses hook together to express a meaning that can stand more or less by itself. This point, far from denying the structuralist's definition of a sentence as a single free utterance, or *form*, seems the inevitable corollary of such definitions: forms carry meanings, and it is natural that an independent form should carry an independent meaning. Or, to come at the thing another way, consider that one task of a grammar is to supply structural descriptions, and that the sentence is the unit so described. A structural description specifies the way each part of a sentence is tied to each other part, and the semantic rules of a grammar use the structural description as starting point in interpreting the whole. A reader or hearer does something analogous when he resolves the structures and meanings of sentences, and thereby understands them. Still another way to approach the primacy of the sentence is to notice that the initial symbol for all

* I draw especially on Noam Chomsky, *Aspects of the Theory of Syntax* (Cambridge, Mass., 1965) and Jerrold J. Katz and Paul Postal, *An Integrated Theory of Linguistic Descriptions* (Cambridge, Mass., 1964).

derivations in a generative grammar is "S" for sentence: the sentence is the domain of grammatical structure—rather like the equation in algebra—and hence the domain of meaning.

These remarks, which will seem truisms to some and heresy to others, cannot be elaborated here. Instead, I want to register an obvious comment on their relevance to literary theory and literary criticism. Criticism, whatever else it does, must interpret works of literature. Theory concerns itself in part with the question, "what things legitimately bear on critical interpretation?" But beyond a doubt, interpretation begins with sentences. Whatever complex apprehension the critic develops of the whole work, that understanding arrives mundanely, sentence by sentence. For this reason, and because the form of a sentence dictates a rudimentary mode of understanding, sentences have a good deal to do with the subliminal meaning (and form) of a literary work. They prepare and direct the reader's attention in particular ways.

My second point about sentences should dispel some of the abstractness of the first. Most sentences directly and obliquely put more linguistic apparatus into operation than is readily apparent, and call on more of the reader's linguistic competence. Typically, a surface structure overlays a deep structure which it may resemble but little, and which determines the "content" of the sentence. For concreteness, take this rather ordinary example, an independent clause from Joyce's "Araby": "Gazing up into the darkness I saw myself as a creature driven and derided by vanity." The surface structure may be represented as follows, using the convention of labeled brackets:†

$$^S[^{Adv}[V + Part\ ^{PP}[P\ ^{NP}[D + N]]]\ ^{Nuc}[N\ ^{VP}[V + N\ ^{PP}[P\ ^{NP}[D + N\ ^{Adj}[V + and + V\ ^{PP}[P + N]]]]]]]$$

The nucleus has a transitive verb with a direct object. In the deep structure, by contrast, the matrix sentence is of the form $^S[NP\ ^{VP}[V + Complement + NP]]$: "I + saw + as a creature + me." It has embedded in it one sentence with an intransitive verb and an adverb of location—"I gazed up into the darkness"—and two additional sentences with transitive verbs and direct objects—"Vanity drove the creature," and "Vanity derided the creature." Since "darkness" and "vanity" are derived nouns, the embedded sentences must in turn contain embeddings, of, say "(Something) is dark" and "(Someone) is vain." Thus the word "vanity," object of a preposition in the surface

---

† Each set of brackets encloses the constituent indicated by its superscript label. The notation is equivalent to a tree diagram. Symbols: S = Sentence, Adv = Adverbial, V = Verb, Part = Particle, PP = Prepositional Phrase, P = Preposition, NP = Noun Phrase, D = Determiner, N = Noun, Nuc = Nucleus, VP = Verb Phrase, Adj = Adjectival.

structure, is subject of two verbs in the deep, and its root is a predicate adjective. The word "creature," object of a preposition in the surface structure, also has a triple function in the deep structure: verbal complement, direct object of "drive," and direct object of "deride." Several transformations (including the passive) deform the six basic sentences, and several others relate them to each other. The complexity goes much farther, but this is enough to suggest that a number of grammatical processes are required to generate the initial sentence and that its structure is moderately involved. Moreover, a reader will not understand the sentence unless he grasps the relations marked in the deep structure. As it draws on a variety of syntactic resources, the sentence also activates a variety of semantic processes and modes of comprehension, yet in brief compass and in a surface *form* that radically permutes *content*.

I choose these terms wilfully: that there are interesting grounds here for a form-content division seems to me quite certain. Joyce might have written, "I gazed up into the darkness. I saw myself as a creature. The creature was driven by vanity. The creature was derided by vanity." Or, "Vanity drove and derided the creature I saw myself as, gazer up, gazer into the darkness." Content remains roughly the same, for the basic sentences are unchanged. But the style is different. And each revision structures and screens the content differently. The original sentence acquires part of its meaning and part of its unique character by resonating against these unwritten alternatives. It is at the level of sentences, I would argue, that the distinction between form and content comes clear, and that the intuition of style has its formal equivalent.[‡]

Sentences play on structure in still another way, more shadowy, but of considerable interest for criticism. It is a commonplace that not every noun can serve as object of every verb, that a given noun can be modified only by adjectives of certain classes, and so on. For instance, a well-defined group of verbs, including "exasperate," "delight," "please," and "astound," require animate objects; another group, including "exert," "behave," and "pride," need reflexive objects. Such interdependencies abound in a grammar, which must account for them by subcategorizing nouns, adjectives, and the other major classes.[§] The importance of categorical restrictions is clearest in sentences that disregard them—deviant sentences. It happens that the example from

---

[‡] I have argued the point at length in "Generative Grammars and the Concept of Literary Style," *Word*, 20 (Dec. 1964), 423–439.

[§] Chomsky discusses ways of doing this in *Aspects of the Theory of Syntax*, Chapter 2.

Joyce is slightly deviant in this way: in one of the underlying sentences
—"Vanity derided the creature"—a verb that requires a human subject in fact has as its subject the abstract noun "vanity." The dislocation forces the reader to use a supplementary method of interpretation:
here, presumably he aligns "vanity" (the word) with the class of
human nouns and sees vanity (the thing) as a distinct, active power in
the narrator's psyche. Such deviance is so common in metaphor and
elsewhere that one scarcely notices it, yet it helps to specify the way
things happen in the writer's special world, and the modes of thought
appropriate to that world.

I have meant to suggest that sentences normally comprise intricacies
of form and meaning whose effects are not the less substantial for their
subtlety. From this point, what sorts of critical description follow?
Perhaps I can direct attention toward a few tentative answers, out of
the many that warrant study, and come finally to a word on critical
theory. Two samples must carry the discussion; one is the final sentence of "The Secret Sharer":

> Walking to the taffrail, I was in time to make out, on the very edge
> of a darkness thrown by a towering black mass like the very gateway
> of Erebus—yes, I was in time to catch an evanescent glimpse of my
> white hat left behind to mark the spot where the secret sharer of my
> cabin and of my thoughts, as though he were my second self, had
> lowered himself into the water to take his punishment: a free man,
> a proud swimmer striking out for a new destiny.

I hope others will agree that the sentence justly represents its
author: that it portrays a mind energetically stretching to subdue a
dazzling experience *outside* the self, in a way that has innumerable
counterparts elsewhere in Conrad. How does scrutiny of the deep
structure support this intuition? First, notice a matter of emphasis, of
rhetoric. The matrix sentence, which lends a surface form to the whole,
is "# S # I was in time # S #" (repeated twice). The embedded
sentences that complete it are "I walked to the taffrail," "I made out +
NP," and "I caught + NP." The point of departure, then, is the narrator himself: where he was, what he did, what he saw. But a glance
at the deep structure will explain why one feels a quite different
emphasis in the sentence as a whole: seven of the embedded sentences
have "sharer" as grammatical subject; in another three the subject is a
noun linked to "sharer" by the copula; in two "sharer" is direct object;
and in two more "share" is the verb. Thus thirteen sentences go to the
semantic development of "sharer," as follows:

1. The secret sharer had lowered the secret sharer into the water.
2. The secret sharer took his punishment.
3. The secret sharer swam.
4. The secret sharer was a swimmer.
5. The swimmer was proud.
6. The swimmer struck out for a new destiny.
7. The secret sharer was a man.
8. The man was free.
9. The secret sharer was my second self.
10. The secret sharer had (it).
11. (Someone) punished the secret sharer.
12. (Someone) shared my cabin.
13. (Someone) shared my thoughts.

In a fundamental way, the sentence is mainly *about* Leggatt, although the surface structure indicates otherwise.

Yet the surface structure does not simply throw a false scent, and the way the sentence comes to focus on the secret sharer is also instructive. It begins with the narrator, as we have seen, and "I" is the subject of five basic sentences early on. Then "hat" takes over as the syntactic focus, receiving development in seven base sentences. Finally, the sentence arrives at "sharer." This progression in the deep structure rather precisely mirrors both the rhetorical movement of the sentence from the narrator to Leggatt via the hat that links them, and the thematic effect of the sentence, which is to transfer Leggatt's experience to the narrator via the narrator's vicarious and actual participation in it. Here I shall leave this abbreviated rhetorical analysis, with a cautionary word: I do not mean to suggest that only an examination of deep structure reveals Conrad's skillful emphasis—on the contrary, such an examination supports and in a sense explains what any careful reader of the story notices.

A second critical point adjoins the first. The morpheme "share" appears once in the sentence, but it performs at least twelve separate functions, as the deep structure shows. "I," "hat," and "mass" also play complex roles. Thus at certain points the sentence has extraordinary "density," as I shall call it. Since a reader must register these multiple functions in order to understand the sentence, it is reasonable to suppose that the very process of understanding concentrates his attention on centers of density. Syntactic density, I am suggesting, exercises an important influence on literary comprehension.

Third, by tuning in on deep structures, the critic may often apprehend more fully the build of a literary work. I have already mentioned how the syntax of Conrad's final sentence develops his theme. Consider two related points. First, "The Secret Sharer" is an initiation story in which the hero, through moral and mental effort, locates himself vis à vis society and the natural world, and thus passes into full manhood. The syntax of the last sentence schematizes the relationships he has achieved, in identifying with Leggatt's heroic defection, and in fixing on a point of reference—the hat—that connects him to the darker powers of nature. Second, the syntax and meaning of the last sentence bring to completion the pattern initiated by the syntax and meaning of the first few sentences, which present human beings and natural objects in thought-bewildering disarray. I can do no more than mention these structural connections here, but I am convinced that they supplement and help explain an ordinary critical reading of the story.

Another kind of critical point concerns habits of meaning revealed by sentence structure. One example must suffice. We have already marked how the sentence shifts its focus from "I" to "hat" to "sharer." A similar process goes on in the first part of the sentence: "I" is the initial subject, with "hat" as object. "Hat" is subject of another base sentence that ends with "edge," the object of a preposition in a locative phrase. "Edge" in turn becomes object of a sentence that has "darkness" as subject. "Darkness" is object in one with "mass" as subject, and in much the same way the emphasis passes to "gateway" and "Erebus." The syntax executes a chaining effect here which cuts across various kinds of construction. Chaining is far from the only type of syntactic expansion, but it is one Conrad favors. I would suggest this hypothesis: that syntactically and in other ways Conrad draws heavily on operations that link one thing with another associatively. This may be untrue, or if true it may be unrevealing; certainly it needs clearer expression. But I think it comes close to something that we all notice in Conrad, and in any case the general critical point exemplified here deserves exploration: that each writer tends to exploit deep linguistic resources in characteristic ways—that his style, in other words, rests on syntactic options within sentences (see fn. ‡)—and that these syntactic preferences correlate with habits of meaning that tell us something about his mode of conceiving experience.

My other sample passage is the first sentence of Dylan Thomas' "A Winter's Tale":‖

It is a winter's tale
That the snow blind twilight ferries over the lakes
And floating fields from the farm in the cup of the vales,
Gliding windless through the hand folded flakes,
The pale breath of cattle at the stealthy sail,

And the stars falling cold,
And the smell of hay in the snow, and the far owl
Warning among the folds, and the frozen hold
Flocked with the sheep white smoke of the farm house cowl
In the river wended vales where the tale was told.

Some of the language here raises a large and familiar critical question, that of unorthodox grammar in modern poetry, which has traditionally received a somewhat facile answer. We say that loss of confidence in order and reason leads to dislocation of syntax, as if errant grammar were an appeal to the irrational. A cursory examination of deep structure in verse like Thomas', or even in wildly deviant verse like some of Cummings', will show the matter to be more complex than that.

How can deviance be most penetratingly analyzed? Normally, I think, in terms of the base sentences that lie beneath ungrammatical constructions. Surface structure alone does not show "the river wended vales" (line 10) to be deviant, since we have many well-formed constructions of the same word-class sequence: "machine made toys," "sun dried earth," and so on. The particular deviance of "the river wended vales" becomes apparent when we try to refer it to an appropriate underlying structure. A natural one to consider is "the river wends the vales" (cf. "the sun dries the earth"), but of course this makes "wend" a transitive verb, which it is not, except in the idiomatic "wend its way." So does another possibility, "NP + wends the vales with rivers" (cf. "NP + makes the toys by machine"). This reading adds still other kinds of deviance, in that the Noun Phrase will have to be animate, and in that rivers are too cumbersome to be used instrumentally in the way implied. Let us assume that the reader rejects the more flagrant deviance in favor of the less, and we are back to "the river wends the vales." Suppose now that "the vales" is not after all a direct object, but a locative construction, as in "the wolf prowls the forest"; this preserves the intransitivity of "wend," and thereby avoids a serious form of deviance. But notice that there is *no* transformation in English that converts "the wolf prowls the forest" into "the wolf prowled forest," and so this path is blocked as well. Assume, finally, that given a choice between shifting a word like "wend" from one subclass to another and adding a transformational rule to the grammar, a reader will choose the former course; hence he selects the first interpretation mentioned: "the river wends the vales."

If so, how does he understand the anomalous transitive use of "wend"? Perhaps by assimilating the verb to a certain class that may be either transitive or intransitive: "paint," "rub," and the like. Then he will take "wend" to mean something like "make a mark on the surface of, by traversing"; in fact, this is roughly how I read Thomas' phrase. But I may be wrong, and in any case my goal is not to solve the riddle. Rather, I have been leading up to the point that every syntactically deviant construction has more than one possible interpretation, and that readers resolve the conflict by a process that involves deep and intricately motivated decisions and thus puts to work considerable linguistic knowledge, syntactic as well as semantic.[#] The decisions nearly always go on implicitly, but aside from that I see no reason to think that deviance of this sort is an appeal to, or an expression of, irrationality.

Moreover, when a poet deviates from normal syntax he is not doing what comes most habitually, but is making a special sort of choice. And since there are innumerable kinds of deviance, we should expect that the ones elected by a poem or poet spring from particular semantic impulses, particular ways of looking at experience. For instance, I think such a tendency displays itself in Thomas' lines. The construction just noted conceives the passing of rivers through vales as an agent acting upon an object. Likewise, "flocked" in line 9 becomes a transitive verb, and the spatial connection Thomas refers to—flocks in a hold—is reshaped into an action—flocking—performed by an unnamed agent upon the hold. There are many other examples in the poem of deviance that projects unaccustomed activity and process upon nature. Next, notice that beneath line 2 is the sentence "the twilight is blind," in which an inanimate noun takes an animate adjective, and that in line 5 "sail" takes the animate adjective "stealthy." This type of deviance also runs throughout the poem: Thomas sees nature as personal. Again, "twilight" is subject of "ferries," and should thus be a concrete noun, as should the object, "tale." Here and elsewhere in the poem the division between substance and abstraction tends to disappear. Again and again syntactic deviance breaks down

---

[#] See Jerrold J. Katz, "Semi-sentences," in Jerry A. Fodor and Jerrold J. Katz, Eds., *The Structure of Language* (1964), pp. 400–416. The same volume includes two other relevant papers, Chomsky, "Degrees of Grammaticalness," pp. 384–389, and Paul Ziff, "On Understanding 'Understanding Utterances,'" pp. 390–399. Samuel R. Levin has briefly discussed ungrammatical poetry within a similar framework in *Linguistic Structures in Poetry* (The Hague, 1962), Chapters 2 and 3.

categorical boundaries and converts juxtaposition into action, inanimate into human, abstract into physical, static into active. Now, much of Thomas' poetry displays the world as process, as interacting forces and repeating cycles, in which human beings and human thought are indifferently caught up.** I suggest that Thomas' syntactical irregularities often serve this vision of things. To say so, of course, is only to extend the natural critical premise that a good poet sets linguistic forms to work for him in the cause of artistic and thematic form. And if he strays from grammatical patterns he does not thereby leave language or reason behind: if anything, he draws the more deeply on linguistic structure and on the processes of human understanding that are implicit in our use of well-formed sentences.

Most of what I have said falls short of adequate precision, and much of the detail rests on conjecture about English grammar, which at this point is by no means fully understood. But I hope that in loosely stringing together several hypotheses about the fundamental role of the sentence I have indicated some areas where a rich exchange between linguistics and critical theory might eventually take place. To wit, the elusive intuition we have of *form* and *content* may turn out to be anchored in a distinction between the surface structures and the deep structures of sentences. If so, syntactic theory will also feed into the theory of *style*. Still more evidently, the proper *analysis* of styles waits on a satisfactory analysis of sentences. Matters of *rhetoric,* such as emphasis and order, also promise to come clearer as we better understand internal relations in sentences. More generally, we may be able to enlarge and deepen our concept of literary *structure* as we are increasingly able to make it subsume linguistic structure—including especially the structure of deviant sentences. And most important, since critical understanding follows and builds on understanding of sentences, generative grammar should eventually be a reliable assistant in the effort of seeing just how a given literary work sifts through a reader's mind, what cognitive and emotional processes it sets in motion, and what organization of experience it encourages. In so far as critical theory concerns itself with meaning, it cannot afford to bypass the complex and elegant structures that lie at the inception of all verbal meaning.

** Ralph Maud's fine study, *Entrances to Dylan Thomas' Poetry* (Pittsburgh, 1963), describes the phenomenon well in a chapter called "Process Poems."

JOSEPH C. BEAVER

A Grammar of Prosody

INTRODUCTION

The starting point for Beaver's article is a paraphrase of the main thesis of Morris Halle and Samuel J. Keyser's article "Chaucer and the Study of Prosody" in the December 1966 issue of *College English.* In their article, Halle and Keyser develop a set of rules which, according to Beaver, provides "a grammar of meter, comparable to the generative grammarian's 'rules of competence,' which will determine (that is, provide a metrical description of) what are metrical and what are unmetrical lines."

Beaver reprints the set of three rules (called "principles" by Halle and Keyser) and extends them to cover different kinds of meter other than iambic pentameter. The first principle is that a line of verse consists of a fixed number of positions. The second principle states that a position is normally occupied by a single syllable, but gives certain conditions under which the position may be occupied by two syllables or by none. The third principle (as extended by Beaver) states that in order for a line to be metrical, a *stress maximum* may occupy only even positions in iambic verse and odd positions in trochaic verse. Halle and Keyser explicitly define a stress maximum as "a syllable bearing linguistically determined stress that is greater

Reprinted by permission of the author and the National Council of Teachers of English, from *College English,* Vol. 29, No. 4 (January), 1968, pp. 310–321.

than that of the two syllables adjacent to it in the same verse." A stress
maximum is thus a valley-peak-valley stress pattern.

It is important to realize that a stress maximum does not correspond to a
"foot" in traditional metrics. In a line of iambic pentameter, for instance,
there are by definition, five feet, each foot with two syllables, the first
syllable bearing a lighter stress than the second. From the view-point of the
Halle-Keyser metrics, however, a line of iambic pentameter is regular if the
stress maximums in the line (if there are any) fall on the even syllables.
The line would be unmetrical only if a stress maximum fell on an odd-
numbered syllable. Beaver points out that,

> These metrical rules, or principles, may be regarded as claims about
> the metrical competence of the poet. It could be said that it is claimed
> the poet internalizes, not a poetic foot (some recurring pattern of stress
> and unstress), but a sequence of positions to be occupied by syllables;
> it is claimed that he is aware somehow of whether a given syllable Y
> occurs in an arithmetically even or arithmetically odd position; it
> is claimed further that the poet is metrically conscious only of stress
> maxima (linguistically determined lexical stress sandwiched by un-
> stressed syllables, without intervening major syntactic boundary); it is
> claimed that he allows these to occur, or accepts their occurrence, only
> in even positions for iambic meter and only in odd positions for
> trochaic meter.

The advantage of the Halle-Keyser metrics over the traditional foot
metrics is the explanatory power of the former. For example, Beaver points
out that in Shakespeare's pentameter sonnets, more lines actually begin with
trochaic feet than with iambic. Beaver comments on such a line from
Sonnet II:

> "Proving his beauty by succession thine."

Traditional prosody finds itself in the uncomfortable position, here, of
saying that the most common occurrence is the allowable exception. In
our view, an initial "trochee" is entirely regular—all that matters is
that stress maxima occur, when they occur at all, in even positions.

The remainder of the article is devoted to further illustrating the explanatory power of the Halle-Keyser metrical theory. Beaver here summarizes
his main points:

> The principles, together with the stress rules here suggested, offer a
> unified explanation for the fact that the majority of iambic lines begin
> with trochaic feet; for the absence of regular feet at various other
> positions in the line; for our acceptance of strong stress before or
> after juncture, even in odd-numbered positions; for the fact that spe-
> cial intonation features do not appear to violate the acceptability of
> metrical lines; for the rejection of iambs in trochaic verse; for the fact

that poetry in duple meter in verse lines shorter than decasyllabic appears to be more irresistably metrical. Finally, they offer a well-defined procedure for basic metrical-stylistic analysis.

∗

In their recent study of Chaucerian meter, Morris Halle and Samuel Jay Keyser propose a theory of prosody which they hope may serve as a framework for the study of "a major portion of English poets."[*] The rules of stress assignment and meter they have discovered for Chaucer's iambic pentameter appear to me quite convincing (with some minor reservations to be discussed later), and metrical rules of this sort should be of considerable help in stylistic analysis, whether for individual poets or for different periods of poetry. But I think the major role of the Halle-Keyser rules (or, ultimately, more refined rules of this kind) will be to constitute essentially a grammar of meter, comparable to the generative grammarian's "rules of competence," which will determine (i.e., provide a metrical description of) what are metrical and what are unmetrical lines. And in this role, in addition to providing a basic framework for stylistic analysis, which may have to be supplemented with something comparable to "rules of performance,"[†] such rules should be useful in providing explanations for metrical phenomena, and in determining various prosodic questions, some of major importance. For example, why has the decasyllabic line (iambic pentameter) been the overwhelmingly predominant vehicle for English verse? Or, alternatively, in what way does it provide the freedom and flexibility the poet obviously finds there? Why do shorter line lengths (tetrameter, trimeter) in duple meter appear to be so much more "rhythmic" than pentameter, exhibiting always a more insistent beat or accent? Why does trochaic meter appear more inflexible than iambic (i.e., why does it seem peculiarly beat-insistent, or, why does it show such a low tolerance for "irregular feet")? The purpose of the present article is to explore, in a preliminary way, some of these questions, to examine possible extensions of the rules Halle and Keyser have proposed, to suggest a different set of stress rules to use in con-

[*] Morris Halle and Samuel J. Keyser, "Chaucer and the Study of Prosody," *College English*, Vol. 28 (Dec. 1966), pp. 187–219.

[†] For those unfamiliar with generative terminology, Chomsky has distinguished between rules of competence (in effect, these are the grammar of the language; they are the rules which will generate grammatical sentences), and rules of performance (stylistic rules, which will allow grammatically deviant sentences, or place certain restrictions upon the use of what would be, technically, grammatical sentences). See Noam Chomsky, *Aspects of the Theory of Syntax* (Cambridge, Mass., 1965), pp. 8–15, and *passim*.

junction with the Halle-Keyser principles of meter (for purposes of analysis of English poetry of the past three centuries), and to provide a critical commentary on the new prosodic system.

Two sets of rules are essential to the system: rules of stress, and rules (Halle and Keyser use the word "principles") of meter. It is the rules of meter Halle and Keyser think may have provided the system of prosody for a major portion of English poets, and I reproduce them here.

Principle 1

The iambic pentameter verse consists of ten positions to which may be appended one or two extra-metrical syllables.

Principle 2

A position is normally occupied by a single syllable, but under certain conditions it may be occupied by more than one syllable, or by none.

Condition 1

Two vowels may constitute a single position provided that they adjoin, or are separated by a liquid or nasal or by a word boundary which may be followed by *h-*, and provided that one of them is a weakly stressed or unstressed vowel.

Condition 2

An unstressed or weakly stressed mono-syllabic word may constitute a single metrical position with a preceding stressed or unstressed syllable.

Principle 3

A stress maximum may only occupy even positions within a verse, but not every even position need be so occupied.

Definition

A stress maximum is constituted by a syllable bearing linguistically determined stress that is greater than that of the two syllables adjacent to it in the same verse.‡

‡ Halle and Keyser, p. 197. The *stress maximum* is reminiscent of Jespersen, who, in "Notes on Meter," points out that the initial syllable of a verse can not be judged to bear ictus until the second syllable occurs—because there is nothing

For purposes of this article, I assume that these three principles are in fact the principles of all English regular-metered verse, and extend them, as Halle and Keyser suggest, to embrace different kinds of meter in obvious ways:

    1A. a tetrameter iambic or trochaic line consists of 8 positions, a trimeter line of 6, etc.

    3A. for trochaic verse, stress maxima may occupy only odd positions, though not every odd position need be occupied.

Turning now to rules of stress (which are needed to determine stress maxima—see "Definition" under 3), it could be argued that a different set would be needed for every period of verse (and every dialect). But I think that a set can be constructed—perhaps somewhat primitive, but adequate to our purpose—sufficient to provide a working tool for most English verse of the last three centuries. We adopt Seymour Chatman's distinction of five types of syllables for purposes of arriving at linguistically determined "lexical stress," and we identify stress maxima from certain configurations of these syllable types.[§] The five kinds of syllables are:

---

preceding the first syllable for purposes of comparison. For this reason, an initial trochee in iambic verse disappoints only in the second syllable, not in the first. If this is the only disappointment in a decasyllabic line, and if the third syllable carries even less stress than the second (Jespersen uses four degrees of stress), the line will show only 10% disappointment, as compared to a 20% occasioned by an initial iamb in a trochaic line. The recognition of stress relationship to adjacent syllables and the concomitant notion that stress next to nothing can not be optimum stress are key elements of the Halle-Keyser rules. See Otto Jespersen, "Notes on Metre," in *Essays in the Language of Literature,* ed. Seymour Chatman and Samuel R. Levin (New York 1967), pp. 71–90.

    § Seymour Chatman, *A Theory of Meter,* (The Hague. 1965), pp. 123 ff. Note that one could also evolve a theory of phrase and clause accent to supplement lexical stress. One could for example postulate that in prepositional phrases the head word bears phrase accent, that in determiner-adjective-noun phrases the noun bears phrase accent (in American English, if not in British English), that in NV-terminal juncture clauses, the V bears clausal accent, that in NV-adverb clauses, the adverb bears clausal accent, and so forth.

    The supplementing of rules of lexical stress with accent rules of this kind would yield some additional stress maxima, specifically where two back to back lexically stressed syllables would otherwise cancel each other out. Halle and Keyser do propose to include rules of this kind in their theory on the grounds that one should make as strong a hypothesis as the facts will support (personal communication). I do not employ such rules in the present exploratory article. Like lexical secondary stress (which I also do not use in the present article), it is not at present clear to me that such rules need be a part of the metrical rules determining stress maxima, even though they are clearly a part of the phonological rules of the language.

a. full-voweled monosyllabic words with non-reducible vowels (*e.g.*, "straight," "bright," etc.)

b. reducible full-voweled monosyllabic words ("a," "to," "shall," "you," "it," "can," etc. In general, most non-lexical monosyllabic words can reduce the vowel coloring to /i/

c. stressed syllables of polysyllabic words

d. full-vowelled unstressed syllables in polysyllabic words

e. unstressed syllables in polysyllabic words with reduced vowels

We now assume that a syllable of type a or c, preceded and followed by syllables of types b, d, or e will constitute a *stress maximum*, unless a syntactic juncture intervenes—for, following Halle-Keyser, we will maintain that if a major syntactic boundary intervenes between two metrical positions, neutralization occurs, which is to say, the adjacent positions cannot carry stress maxima.||

The center syllable, then, of any sequence of three syllables which meets this description is a stress maximum:

$$\text{Syll.} \qquad\qquad \text{Syll.} \qquad\qquad \text{Syll.}$$

$$\begin{bmatrix}\begin{Bmatrix} b \\ d \\ e \end{Bmatrix}\end{bmatrix} \qquad \begin{bmatrix}\begin{Bmatrix} a \\ c \end{Bmatrix}\end{bmatrix} \qquad \begin{bmatrix}\begin{Bmatrix} b \\ d \\ e \end{Bmatrix}\end{bmatrix}$$

In essence, what is proposed for the determination of stress maxima is a rule which is *lexically* based, but which operates as a determinant of *underlying* stress in any phrase segment of three sequential syllables.

Since it is *capacity* for reduction that determines the membership of "b," rather than whether the monosyllable is in fact reduced in a given instance, and since the rule deals with only two stresses (stress and unstress), the system proposed here will find a somewhat different set of stress maxima than any alternative system that assigns four (or even three) degrees of stress, or that assigns phrasal and clausal stress on a basis of syntactic order.

To briefly illustrate the use of the Halle-Keyser rules of prosody in combination with the rules of stress I propose consider the familiar lines from Hamlet:

1 2   3   4   5 6   7   8   9   10
Oh that this too too solid flesh would melt,

1   2   3   4   5 6   7 8 9   10
Thaw, and resolve itself into a dew.

|| Halle and Keyser, pp. 203, 204. Notice that for the same reason (incapacity for stress subordination) a syllable at the beginning of a line cannot bear stress maximum, no matter what the meter; nor can the syllable at the end of a line, unless there is appended an extra-metrical syllable.

Both lines have ten positions occupied with syllables, and there are
no problems of extra-metrical syllables. The lines are iambic pentameter, and our rules call for stress maxima, if there are any, to fall
only on even-numbered positions.

The syllables that could, by virtue of their linguistically determined
stress, conceivably carry stress maxima are: "Oh," the first syllable of
"solid," "flesh," "melt," "thaw," the second syllables of "resolve" and
"itself," and "dew." These are either the accented syllables of polysyllabic words (*solid*), or else they are non-reducible full-vowelled
monosyllables (*melt*):

> 1   2   3   4   5   6   7   8   9   10
> *Oh* that this too too *solid* *flesh* would *melt*,

> 1   2   3   4   5   6   7 8 9   10
> *Thaw*, and re*solve* it*self* *in*to a *dew*.

The unitalicized syllables are of types b, d, or e. Most of them are type
b, reducible full-voweled monosyllables. For example, "too" is a full
voweled syllable (/tuw/) but it frequently reduces to a neutralized
vowel (/tɨ/), as in "too much" said rapidly, with stress on "much." It
is important to note that it is this capacity for reduction, rather than
how the word may actually be said in a particular instance, which
determines its classification.

Let us now examine the italicized syllables, those with linguistically
determined stress. The first syllables in both lines carry linguistic stress
(they are type a: non-reducible full-vowelled monosyllables). However, neither "Oh" nor "Thaw" is a stress maximum, and for two
reasons. First, no syllable precedes them in their respective lines, and
they thus cannot be thrown into relief by unaccented syllables on
each side. For this reason, neither the first, nor the last syllable of a
line (unless an extra-metrical syllable follows) may be a stress maximum. So "melt" and "dew," though both are linguistically stressed
(they are non-reducible full-vowelled monosyllables), also do not constitute stress maxima.

But there is a second reason why neither "Oh" nor "thaw" can be a
stress maximum, namely, that these syllables are followed by major
syntactic junctures, which have the effect of neutralization: neither
the syllable before, nor the syllable after major syntactic juncture, may
carry stress maxima.

This leaves five candidates for stress maxima, positions 6 and 8 in
line one (*solid* *flesh*) and positions 4, 6, and 7 in line two (re*solve*
it*self* *in*to). The second syllable of "itself" and the first of "into" have
linguistically determined stress (they are type c—accented syllables
of polysyllabic words), but they are back to back. Thus each keeps

the other from being a stress maximum: neither can be bordered on both sides by non-stressed syllables.

This leaves then only three linguistically stressed syllables to consider: "flesh," the first of "solid," and the second of "resolve." In each of these cases, unstressed syllables are to be found on both sides, without intervening juncture. These three syllables, then, do constitute stress maxima. Further, they fall on even positions, so the two lines are metrical by our rules, the first showing positions 6 and 8 occupied, and the second showing only position 4 occupied (not every even position need be occupied):

<pre>
 1   2   3   4   5   6   7   8   9   10
Oh that this too too solid flesh would melt,

 1   2   3   4   5 6   7 8 9   10
Thaw and resolve itself into a dew.
</pre>

* * * * * *

These metrical rules, or principles, may be regarded as claims about the metrical competence of the poet.[#] It could be said that it is claimed the poet internalizes, not a poetic foot (some recurring pattern of stress and unstress), but a sequence of positions to be occupied by syllables; it is claimed that he is aware somehow of whether a given syllable Y occurs in an arithmetically even or arithmetically odd position; it is claimed further that the poet is metrically conscious only of stress maxima (linguistically determined lexical stress sandwiched by unstressed syllables, without intervening major syntactic boundary); it is claimed that he allows these to occur, or accepts their occurrence, only in even positions for iambic meter and only in odd positions for trochaic meter.[**] His grammar, *per se,* is not concerned with mere "accent" (though possibly his rules of performance might register cognition of these and other refinements).

* * * * * *

[#] It would be useful to have a word comparable, in this metrical context, to "native speaker" in the more general linguistic situation. The claims in any event are of the competence of the poet and of those attuned to poetry in some metrical sense, but I shall use the word "poet," in this situation, to refer to both. By "competence" is meant what the poet and the attuned reader know (though not necessarily what they can articulate) about the rules of meter.

[**] Or, obviously, some other pattern of position occupancy in the cases of dactyllic or anapestic verse.

By way of comparison, it could be said that traditional "school-room" prosody also may be reduced to a set of claims: namely that the poet internalizes a recurring group of stressed and unstressed syllables in a certain sequence—this is essentially the claim of the "foot" concept.

Let us turn now to such matters as the greater rhythmic regularity of short-line verse (tetrameter and trimeter), and the long noted and frequently debated difference in character between iambic and trochaic verse. Otto Jespersen, for example, contends that trochaic meter is characterized by a "falling" rhythm, and iambic meter by a "rising" rhythm; in the former, there is a tendency to "linger" on the stressed syllable.†† This suggests that the trochaic "foot" might be quantitatively longer than the iambic. No measurements of performance that I know of have established this,‡‡ but even those who do not accept the foot (Chatman, and Jespersen himself, in part—p. 74) unite in finding a more regular and insistent beat to trochaic verse.

If we assume, however, that the difference attributed to trochaic verse is in fact a difference to be found generally in *all* short-lined verse whether trochaic *or* iambic, there can be found an explanation for the assumed difference. Since most trochaic verse in English is in short-lines, and since our impressions of iambic verse are derived almost entirely from pentameter, it would seem entirely possible that the issue has been falsely formulated—that the differences of rhythm encountered are attributed not to the type of foot, but to the length of line in which the foot characteristically appears. And it will be argued below that the more regular beat of short-lined verse is accounted for by the fact that a much higher percentage of positions available for stress maxima are occupied than is the case in decasyllabic verse.

In English, most trochaic poems are in tetrameter, or trimeter.§§

†† Otto Jespersen, "Notes on Metre," in *Essays in the Language of Literature,* ed. Seymour Chatman and Samuel R. Levin (New York, 1967), pp. 86–88.

‡‡ One, in fact, shows the iambic foot as longer: Ada Snell, "An Objective Study of Syllabic Quantity in English Verse," *PMLA* XXXIII (1918), 396–408; XXXIV (1919), 416–435. Though this was not her principle objective, her measurements did show the average iambic foot to be of .69 seconds duration, and the average trochaic foot to be .55 (XXXIV, p. 433).

However, her tabulations on p. 432 show the average short syllable (unstressed) of the trochaic foot to be .35 seconds, and the average long syllable (stressed) as .20! Obviously, from an examination of the other figures, the two columns were accidentally reversed in the printing, a fact which may possibly have contributed to what seems to me Chatman's misleading conclusion that her figures "demonstrated clearly that syllable length was not necessarily an indication of metrical ictus, that indeed unstressed syllables could last longer than adjacent stressed syllables" (Chatman, p. 80). On the contrary, Snell's figures, to me, suggest that there is a clear general correspondence between the classical prosodist's length and ictus, so far as performance is concerned.

§§ Poe claimed that he wrote "The Raven" in trochaic "octameter acatalectic" alternating with "heptametre catalectic" but the heavy internal junctures after the fourth foot in most lines, and the internal rhyme, clearly suggest that the poem is in fact tetrameter.

> Once up*on* a *mid*night *dreary*
> While I *pon*de*red weak* and *weary*

Here, for example are two 10 line passages from Longfellow's "The Song of Hiawatha," the syllables carrying stress maxima, in accordance with rules here adopted, printed in italics.

> Till at *length* a small green *feather*
> From the earth shot slowly *up*ward,
> Then *an*other and *an*other,
> And be*fore* the *Sum*mer *end*ed
> Stood the *maize* in *all* its *beau*ty,
> With its *shin*ing *robes* a*bout* it,
> And its long, soft, yellow *tress*es:
> And in *rap*ture Hia*wa*tha
> Cried aloud, "It is Mon*dam*in!
> Yes, the *friend* of man, Mon*dam*in!"

"The Song of Hiawatha,"
Section V.

> Straight be*tween* them *ran* the *path*way.
> Never *grew* the *grass* upon it;
> Singing birds, that *ut*ter *false*hoods,
> Story-*tell*ers, mischief-*mak*ers,
> Found no *eag*er *ear* to *lis*ten,
> Could not breed ill-will be*tween* them,
> For they *kept* each *oth*er's *coun*sel,
> Spake with *nak*ed *hearts* together,
> Pondering *much* and *much* con*triv*ing
> How the *tribes* of *men* might *pros*per.

"The Song of Hiawatha,"
Section VI.

A tetrameter line has available only three positions (2, 4, and 6 for iambic, 3, 5, and 7 for trochaic) for occupancy by stress maxima—a trimeter line only two. Pentameter has four. In the lines quoted from "The Song of Hiawatha," 46 of 60 available positions are occupied by stress maxima, for a 77% occupancy. Various randomly selected pas-

---

> Over *many* a *quaint* and *cur*ious
> Volume (of) for*got*ten lore

Note in the four lines (as I have rearranged them) that ten of the eleven available positions carry stress maxima, which are indicated by italics. The position not occupied is enclosed in parentheses.

sages in "Hiawatha" show an average 75% occupancy.‖ ‖ By contrast, an analysis of 10 of Shakespeare's sonnets (where there are four available positions per line, or 56 per sonnet) show an average of only 27.7 stress maxima per sonnet, or 49% occupancy.##

But the high occupancy ratio in Longfellow's trochaic verse is matched by that in various randomly sampled short-lined *iambic* poems. A. E. Housman's ballad stanzas show about 75% occupancy; even so varied a poem, metrically, as "Loveliest of trees, the *cherry* now" (the first line with only one stress maximum) shows 27 out of 35 positions occupied, or 77%.

Nor does the type of poet, or the type of verse (e.g., sonnet, or blank verse) seem ordinarily to affect the density of stress maxima. Edwin Arlington Robinson's blank verse dramatic monologues show about the same occupancy as Shakespeare's sonnets, and so do Robert Frost's blank verse and e. e. cummings' sonnets and other pentameter poems.*** (The condition indeed appears so general that when we find poetry departing significantly from the pattern, the occupancy ratio and distribution provide a basic tool for initial stylistic analysis, as we shall see a little later.)

It appears then that the often noticed difference between trochaic and iambic verse, if understood as actually a perceived difference between poems of different line length, may be correlated with the much greater density of stress maxima in short-lined verse: about 75% occupancy for short-lined verse, contrasted to 50% occupancy for decasyllabic verse. Put another way, there is 50% greater density of occupancy in short line verse.

Such an explanation follows naturally upon the concepts of positions and stress maxima. But the concept of feet does not explain it, for in fact just as high a percentage of iambs is found in pentameter as in shorter lines (or troches in trochaic lines). Shakespeare's sonnet LXXXIX, for example, which shows only 27 stress maxima in 56 available positions, shows 66 iambic feet out of a possible 70 (defining an iambic foot for this purpose as one which can be read, by any reasonable stretch of performance rules, as a lesser stressed syllable followed by a more greatly stressed syllable). For purposes of direct compari-

---

‖ ‖ The lowest percentage of occupancy I found in Hiawatha was 64%, in a thirteen line passage, also from section V. Four of the thirteen lines contain only one stress maximum each: "Sorrowing for her Hia*wa*tha," "He meanwhile sat weary *wai*ting," "Till the sun dropped from the *hea*ven," and "As a red leaf in the *au*tumn."

The following sonnets were analyzed; I, II, XXIX, LV, LVIII, LXXIII, LXXXIX, XC, XCI, CVII.

*** I am indebted to Helen Tulsky for work with e. e. cummings' poetry.

son, here is Sonnet LXXXIX, with stress maxima italicized, and with only those "feet" which do *not* seem, to me, susceptible to an iambic reading printed in capital letters:

> SAY THAT thou didst for*sake* me for some fault,
> And I will com*MENT UPon* that offense.
> SPEAK OF my *lame*ness, and I *straight* will halt,
> A*gainst* thy *reasons making* no defence.
> Thou canst not, love, dis*grace* me *half* so ill,
> To *set* a *form* up*on* de*sired* change,
> As I'll my*self* disgrace, KNOWING thy will.
> I will ac*quain*tance *strang*le, and look strange,
> Be *abs*ent from thy walks, and in thy tongue
> Thy *sweet* be*lov*ed *name* no more shall dwell,
> Lest I, too much profane, should *do* it wrong
> And *hap*ly of our *old* ac*quaint*ance tell.
> For thee, *against* my*self* I'll *vow* debate,
> For I must ne'er love him whom thou dost hate.

I have designated 28 stress maxima here, but count only 27 that fall in an even position, since the stress on the second syllable of "upon" in line 2 falls on position 7, thus making that line unmetrical. The point is that there are 66 syllables in even position capable of some kind of stress, but only 27 of these are stress maxima.

❖   ❖   ❖   ❖   ❖   ❖

Glancing now at English triple meters, anapestic and dactyllic, it might at first appear that the insistent beat in these meters is at odds with our assumption that the phenomenon is associated with "short line verse," for most triple meters are in lines longer than decasyllabic. Indeed, the percentage of occupancy of available positions by stress maxima in anapestic verse appears to run higher than for the short line verse examined earlier. Byron's "Destruction of Sennacherib" and "On the Day of the Destruction of Jerusalem by Titus" show 96 stress maxima out of a possible 117 positions, for somewhat over 80% occupancy.

But in this case I think we must look for a different explanation of the rhythmic insistency. If the phenomenon in short line duple meters is to be accounted for—as I think it must—by a relative numerical scarcity of available positions as these relate to the syntactic units that normally comprise a line, in triple meter verse I think it is to be

explained by the fact that the poet has to rely excessively on preposi-
tion-determiner-noun sequences, and other set syntactic patterns of
English, to throw the stress always on the third syllable. It is worth
noting, however, that complete lines without any stress maxima are
possible in triple meter, as witness Byron's "When the blue wave rolls
nightly on deep Galilee," where each potential stress maximum is
cancelled by an adjacent non-reducible full-vowelled monosyllabic or
accented syllable of a polysyllabic.†††

* * * * * *

Certain aspects of the Halle-Keyser principles of meter may provoke attack, and there remain some formal problems to be solved.
For one thing, there is the claim—if I am right in postulating that
their first principle in effect makes a claim—having to do with internal-
izing in some manner a sequence of positions (up to 10, in the case of
decasyllabic verse) and identifying within this chain those positions
which may be legitimately occupied with stress maxima. At first consideration, this might appear counter-intuitive. The claim asks nothing
of rhythmic or temporal considerations. It is quasi-arithmetic, and on
the face of it seems harder to believe than what amounts to the traditional claim that what is internalized is a recurring rhythmic pattern
consisting of stronger and weaker pulses (which claim, of course, has
support from psychological research).

To this objection, it might be answered that counting is the basis of
all rhythm, musical as well as poetic. But how much counting (up to
what number, without assistance of metrical grouping) is another
question. In music, for example, one does not "count" higher than four
in most cases—indeed, it can be argued that one does not have to
internalize a count higher than three, since the various quadruple
meters lend themselves to subdivision so easily. Herein lies the strength
of the foot concept, since it hypothesizes only a recurring pattern of
stress and unstress that never exceeds three (in English). The stress
maximum concept on the other hand (at least in its unsupported
version) implies that we can internalize 10 positions and be satisfied—
to use Jespersen's word—by an event in the 8th position (which may

---

††† These comments on triple meter are based on the assumption of a set of
rules that would provide, in anapestic tetrameter, for a 12 position verse, with
stress maxima allowed to occupy only positions 3, 6, or 9, and with provisions for
empty initial positions, and for extra-metrical syllables. In actuality, I think the
framing of rules for triple meters in English poses difficulties not encountered in
duple meters. Conditions for empty medial positions where there are terminal
junctures would have to be set, for most poets who employ the medium.

not have occurred in 2, 4, or 6); or dissatisfied by an event in the 7th, even though we have no other occurrences anywhere in the line to use as an interval or distance estimate. Such observations suggest that rules for stress maxima should be supplemented by rules perhaps of another sort.

A quite minor detail is the fact that the rules of meter indicate that a position may under certain conditions be unoccupied, though the conditions are not specified in the rules. In fact, the only position which may be unoccupied appears to be the first position in iambic pentameter, though as I have suggested (footnote †††) provision for other empty positions would probably have to be made in other meters.

On this point, note that if we postulate a set of rules governing trochaic verse exactly parallel to those generating iambic verse (including the conditions of position occupancy by more than one syllable, and the possibility of zero occupancy), we have no way to distinguish consistently beheaded iambic verse (zero initial position) from consistently catalectic trochaic verse (zero final position). Thus, Tennyson's "Locksley Hall" and many others of this form:

> Cómrădes, léave mĕ hére ă líttlĕ, while ăs yét 'tĭs éarlў mórn;
>
> Léave mĕ hére, ănd whén yŏu wánt mĕ, sóund ŭpón thĕ búglĕ hórn.

Tennyson's poem continues in a precisely similar metrical manner for 194 lines, with stress on the first and last syllables of each line. An obvious solution to this problem is to view such poems or portions of poems as metrically ambiguous in their surface structure, and postulate that they are, in their deep structure, either iambic with initial position always unoccupied, or trochaic, with final position always unoccupied.††† As a matter of fact, many poets have capitalized on this ambiguity. In "To a Skylark," Shelley chooses a stanza form which maintains the ambiguity through the first four lines of each stanza, resolving it in the iambic hexameter fifth line. And much of the charm of John Donne's "Go and catch a falling star," consists in precisely this ambiguity, which he maintains unresolved throughout the three stanzas.

Finally, it might be argued that the principles appear to offer no way of dealing with the reality of run-on lines—that is, if a line is in fact run on (proceeds without major juncture into the next), why then

---

††† "Locksley Hall," like "The Raven," seems to me misleadingly arranged with respect to line length. A major syntactic break occurs in the middle of each line; instead of rhyming octameter couplets (as Tennyson arranged it), these seem to me to be tetrameter quatrains, with lines 2 and 4 rhyming, and—as Poe would have put it—tetrameter trochaic acatalectic alternating with tetrameter trochaic catalectic.

can not the tenth syllable of the first line (or the first syllable of the second line, in trochaic verse) be considered occupied by stress maximum? The major difficulty is that if this be admitted, we will be forced in some cases to find stress maxima in initial position in iambic verse, thus losing the strength of our position (see next paragraph) that an initial stress does not make an irregular or unmetrical line. However, it must be remembered that our principles postulate a verse line as *a sequence of positions only*: the verse line is taken as a primitive, so to speak, and in this light, the foregoing objection loses some of its force.

Far more than offsetting these present possible inadequacies is the explanatory power of the principles. Initial "trochees" in iambic verse pose no problem at all: to say a line begins with a trochee is to say that the first position contains a stress greater than the second position, but no more: in our view, the first position cannot contain a stress maximum. And in fact, more of the lines in Shakespeare's sonnets begin on accented than on unaccented syllables: in the ten sonnets studied, only 52 of 140 lines had stress maxima in position 2. More common are lines like this one from Sonnet II:

"Proving his beauty by succession thine."

Traditional prosody finds itself in the uncomfortable position, here, of saying that the most common occurrence is the allowable exception. In our view, an initial "trochee" is entirely regular—all that matters is that stress maxima occur, when they occur at all, in even positions.

In a similar vein, the absence of bona fide iambs in various feet other than the first poses no problem. The fact that "by" in "Proving his beauty by succession thine" is unstressed does not embarrass the metrical theory. Traditional prosody, on the other hand, must say that in some sense "bý succéssion thine" occurs.

Our acceptance of strong accent after internal juncture also demonstrates the explanatory power of the rules. The following line shows an accented syllable in the wrong position, but it is not a stress maximum (because it is neutralized by juncture), and we intuitively feel that its occurrence does no violence to the meter.

"As I'll myself disgrace, *know*ing thy will"—Sonnet LXXXIX

We readily accept also special intonations which might appear to violate the meter, if meter is taken to be based on performance. But our principles and our stress rules say nothing at all about how lines may happen to be read. Stress maxima are defined in terms of linguistically determined stress (*i.e.*, not performance determined). In the present study, a syllable is one of the five kinds§§§ distinguished by Chatman, and it belongs in that class *regardless of how it is performed.* The following lines may be performed with unusual stress on the italicized syllables in odd positions, but it does not make the lines unmetrical:

1. Say that thou didst forsake *me*⁷ for some fault—Sonnet LXXXIX

2. As he would add a shilling to *more*⁹ shillings—Robinson, "Ben Jonson Entertains a Visitor from Stratford."

3. Oh, that this too *too*⁵ solid flesh would melt—Hamlet

In 1, "sake" is the stressed syllable of a polysyllabic word, and "me" is a reducible full-vowelled monosyllabic (as are most pronouns). The fact that "me" may be said louder (perhaps to indicate that in the past the reverse had been true) or higher than "-sake" does not alter the linguistic fact. In 2, which has an extra-metrical syllable after the 10th position, "more" is a prenominal adjective and subject to reduction (even though it may not be so performed in this instance), and therefore is not a stress maximum. In each case, the performance can not alter what as native speakers we know, and our knowledge of inherent linguistic stress overrides performance. Ictus in our sense is not synonymous with what is phonetically higher or louder or with what is more carefully enunciated. Therefore we need no performance records to determine the meter of the poem—though we need a knowledge of "performance" i.e., a corpus) from which to derive our rules of stress in the first place.

And, as Halle and Keyser have demonstrated, our principles explain the otherwise unexplainable phenomenon that while iambic lines can accept initial trochees, trochaic lines frequently cannot accept initial iambs. In "Proving his beauty by succession thine," the initial accent on "*Proving*" cannot be a stress maximum, and thus its occurrence on an odd position in iambic verse does not alter the meter. But if, to parallel Jesperson's illustration, we change Longfellow's trochaic line

---

§§§ In fact four kinds, for in this analysis I do not distinguish between his types d and e: between full-vowelled unstressed syllables in polysyllabic words and unstressed syllables in polysyllabic words with neutralized vowels.

"Straight between them ran the pathway"

to read

"Be*tween* them straight ran the pathway"

we have created a stress maximum in an even position, thus violating the rule of trochaic meter.

So the Halle-Keyser prosodic system is first of all a grammar of verse: it is a set of rules which enables us to say that certain lines are metrical, and certain lines are not metrical. Beyond this lies the question of whether the rules can be used significantly for stylistic analysis. This article has not for the most part concerned itself with this question. The distinction drawn between short-line and long-line verse (75% density of stress maxima in the former, 50% in the latter) is not fundamentally a stylistic distinction. Rather, it would appear that the language mechanics of verse lines shorter than decasyllabic linguistically requires the higher percentage of occupancy because of the relatively fewer available positions for stress maxima in each line to correlate with normal syntactic units.

Perhaps we should look for stylistic devices to emanate from something corresponding to rules of performance, rather than to metrical competence. In effect performance—but in an oral production sense— is what earlier structuralist analyses of metrical stress dealt with.‖ ‖ ‖ If efforts are made to supplement rules for determination of stress maxima with rules showing how phrase accent and clause accent, etc., may be appended, these might have more to do with metrical performance (not oral-production) than with metrical competence.###

‖ ‖ ‖ Though Seymour Chatman has now shifted his position substantially, *A Theory of Meter* is still performance-oriented in this sense.

See footnote §. For a full "grammar of prosody," further refinement might be needed, but I think their necessity would have to be demonstrated. For example, I have not used secondary stress in polysyllabic words as stress maxima. Thus, Poe's line

1 2 3 4 5 6 7 8 9 10 11 12 13 14 15
To the tintinnabu*la*tion that so *mu*sically wells would show stress maxima in positions 7 and 11, but not in 3 or 5 or 13, all of which are occupied by syllables that possibly have secondary stress of some kind. A glance at several dictionaries will show how divided opinion is on the question of secondary stress. And the fact that secondary stress can be subordinated to primary stress seems to me to eliminate it from stress maximum status. Observe the behavior of the third syllable of "refuge" in the following triple meter:

Thĕ réfŭgeé cáme tŏ thĕ víllăge hĕ knéw.

Additional conditions for occupancy of a position by more than one syllable might be needed, though I have so far encountered few situations that are not encompassed by those in the Halle-Keyser principles.

However, certain basic stylistic determinations may be derived from the rules. Relative density of stress maxima occupancy comes first to mind as a stylistic determinant. I have said that most of the decasyllabic verse examined shows about 50% occupancy, and have suggested that this ordinarily obtains, irrespective of poet or period. But individual poems may show significant variance; and individual efforts in different verse forms may exhibit differences. An analysis of the first ten of John Donne's "Holy Sonnets" shows 236 of 560 positions occupied, for 42% density of occupancy, as compared to the 49% found for ten of Shakespeare's sonnets.

Predilection for placing stress maxima in certain positions would appear to be, potentially, a more telling stylistic determinant. My study of the sonnets of Shakespeare and Donne shows distribution of stress maxima in the four available positions (140 possibilities for each position) as follows:

POSITION	Number Stress Maxima		Percentage Stress Maxima	
	S.	D.	S.	D.
2	52	65	37%	46%
4	76	50	54%	36%
6	65	47	46%	33%
8	83	74	59%	53%

Shakespeare uses position 8 most, followed by 4, then 6, then 2. Donne also uses 8 most, but favors next position 2 (last with Shakespeare), then 4, then 6. This suggests, in Donne, a metrical structure tending to support stability at the extremities of the lines, somewhat like a suspension bridge, perhaps at the expense of medial stability. Shakespeare, on the other hand, tends to provide anchors at half way points. This possibly subjective interpretation might be represented in this manner:

John Donne

William Shakespeare

Distribution of the stress maxima does appear to provide the richest source for stylistic analysis. Many more possibilities suggest themselves. For example, if a poet has employed positions 6 and 8 in one or two lines, how long will it be till he balances by placing maxima in 2 and 4? What overall distributional patterns of occupancy present

themselves, and what is their significance? What lines show total
occupancy? What show none? In the ten sonnets of Shakespeare,
there were 10 lines with no stress maxima; in the sonnets of Donne,
there were 11. The following are typical:

> "Some glory in their birth, some in their skill"
> > Shakespeare, Sonnet XCI.
> "My worlds both parts, and (oh) both parts must die"
> > Donne, Holy Sonnet 5.

The particular uses—and the frequency—of *un*metrical lines is another potential stylistic consideration. There is always the possibility
of a lapse on the part of the poet, and occasionally a poet may be
a poor metrist (see footnote †††), but some lines unmetrical by the
rules seem calculated for effect. In the ten sonnets of Shakespeare I
found only one clearly unmetrical line (which, incidentally, is about
⅔ of 1%, as compared to the 1% of unmetrical lines Halle and Keyser
found in Chaucer), but four in Donne. The unmetrical line of Shakespeare's occurs in Sonnet LXXXIX:

> "And I will comment up*on* that offense."

As pointed out earlier, a stress maximum falls on position 7, rendering
the line unmetrical. This would seem to be merely a lapse.
     John Donne's unmetrical lines, however, occur with sufficient fre-
quency to suggest deliberation. He appears to seek the device which
will capture attention, by departing from the usual (note that he does
not attempt to achieve novelty—which would not have been novelty—
by low frequency use of position 2, and the attendant stress in initial
position). One of the ways of doing this is by deliberately placing
stress maxima in off positions. In Sonnet I, we find:

> "Thou hast *made* me, and shall thy *worke* decay?"

where the very first stress maximum occurs in position 3, perhaps
underscoring the conflict, the contradiction in the two thoughts Donne
contemplates. An unmetrical line in a passage that interests because
of its use of double position occupancy occurs in Sonnet IV:

> line 5 Or like a thiefe, which till deaths doome be read,
>
> 6 Wisheth him*selfe* deliverĕd from prison;

7 But *damn'd* and *hal'd* to execŭtiŏn,

8 Wisheth that *still* he might be imprisonĕd.

Here "wisheth" is used in positions 1 and 2 of line 6, and the line is metrical (but the extra-metrical syllable at the end, the second of "prison," is made to carry the rhyme). Then in line 8, the two syllables of "wisheth" both occupy position one, which places the stress maximum in position 3 for an unmetrical line. Alternatively, if "wisheth" occupies two positions, "still" carries stress maximum in position 4, but now the stress maximum in "imprisoned" falls in position 9, for an unmetrical line. One could assign "be" and "im-" to the same position by condition one of the rules, and, with other adjustments, argue that the line is metrical. The other two unmetrical lines are printed without comment:

7
To where they're bred, and would *presse* me, to hell—
Sonnet VI.

9
Make sinnes, else equall, in mee more *hein*ous?
Sonnet IX.

It may be noted in passing that Donne's experiments in position occupancy by more than one syllable are most interesting, and is another aspect which lends his verse its rough-hewn effect.

❋   ❋   ❋   ❋   ❋   ❋

In summary, the Halle-Keyser principles of prosody appear to bear a relationship to traditional prosody somewhat akin to that which transformational grammar bears to traditional grammar. Their approach represents an attempt to make explicit what had been only implicit. Pursuing the analogy, the principles appear also to represent certain claims about the nature of metrical competence, and though the claims may at first pose something of a credibility gap, in fact they stretch the credulity no more than the failure of implicit claims in traditional prosody to account for what would otherwise be an intolerable percentage of unmetrical lines. The principles, together with the stress rules here suggested, offer a unified explanation for the fact that the majority of iambic lines begin with trochaic feet; for the absence of regular feet at various other positions in the line; for our acceptance of strong stress before or after juncture, even in odd-numbered positions; for the fact that special intonation features do not appear to violate the acceptability of metrical lines, for the rejection of iambs in trochaic verse; for the fact that poetry in duple meter in verse lines shorter than decasyllabic appears to be more irresistably metrical. Finally, they offer a well-defined procedure for basic metrical-stylistic analysis.****

**** I would like to acknowledge the valuable assistance of Don Seigel, who read two versions of this paper and whose criticism has been most helpful.

I am indebted also to Morris Halle and Samuel Keyser for a detailed commentary. I have adopted some of their suggestions, but responsibility for the entire paper is my own.

George Hansen, Elsa Atkins, and Leonard Stenson have helped in various ways.

COMPOSITION

KELLOGG W. HUNT

How Little Sentences
Grow into Big Ones

INTRODUCTION

The article begins with a sketch of the main syntactic components of a transformational grammar: the phrase structure rules, the simple transformational rules, and the sentence combining rules. The part of the grammar that is of particular interest to Hunt is the last mentioned set of rules: the sentence combining transformations. These rules are cyclical, that is, they can be applied over and over, each time producing a longer and more complex sentence. Hunt's main point is that

> the ability to combine more and more kernel sentences is a mark of maturity. The older a child becomes, the more he can combine. Apparently, too, the higher the IQ, the faster children learn to do this.

Hunt breaks the sentence combining transformations into two large families: (1) noun modification and (2) nominalization, that is, the reduction of a whole sentence into a clause or phrase that functions like a unitary noun. The strength of this article is that Hunt takes the reader through the operation of the sentence combining transformations in "slow-motion."

Reprinted by permission of the author and the National Council of Teachers of English, from *New Directions in Elementary English*, ed. by Alexander Frazier.

*

We are all aware of the planned obsolescence in automobiles. When I was a boy, cars were streamlined to reduce wind resistance. The ideal shape was the teardrop. Now instead, the outlines of cars are sharp and crisp, and no one talks of wind resistance, only of sales resistance. One year the ads proclaim the transcendent beauty of tail fins that shoot straight up like the tails on airplanes. But at the same moment, on the drawing boards of the car designers is the plan for the next year's model. Next year tail fins will shoot straight out like horizontal stabilizers instead.

In language arts teaching we have our obsolescence too, but it is never planned. No one advocates functional grammar or structural grammar because he knows it will not wear well. He advocates it instead because he thinks it is better than last year's model. It isn't always. Sometimes it wears badly.

The newest model in grammar is called generative-transformational.* It is called generative because it aims to be as explicit as the mathematical formulae that generate a circle or a straight line on a sheet of graph paper. An explicit formula is capable of being proved true or false. A vague statement is not capable of being proved either true or false. So generative grammar aims to say explicitly many of the things that traditional grammars have said only vaguely. It tries to generate the same sentences that people generate, and it tries to generate none of the nonsentences. This grammar is by no means complete, but no other grammar is complete either, as any experienced grammarian knows. (The second half of the generative-transformational label will be touched on later in this paper.)

NATURE OF GENERATIVE-TRANSFORMATIONAL GRAMMAR

So far, generative-transformational grammar appears only in the learned journals which most English teachers never read. There are only about three books on the subject which most English teachers can hope to wade through if they are diligent: Robert's *English Syntax*,[†] Rogovin's *Modern English Sentence Structure*,[‡] and Thomas's

* For further information on the subject see Kellogg W. Hunt, "Recent Measures in Syntactic Development," *Elementary English*, 43 (November 1966), 732–739.
  † Paul Roberts, *English Syntax* (New York: Harcourt, Brace, and World, Inc., 1964).
  ‡ Syrell Rogovin, *Modern English Sentence Structure* (New York: Random House, Inc., 1965).

Transformational Grammar and the Teacher of English.§ So when I try to survey the subject from beginning to end so quickly, you can expect that I will sweep past many points where you would like to challenge me, if you do not first lose interest.

I will call the grammar by its initials, g-t. Ordinarily, g-t grammar is presented as a series of formulae that to many people look horribly scientific. Sample formulae look like this:

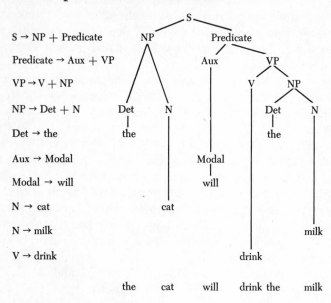

S → NP + Predicate

Predicate → Aux + VP

VP → V + NP

NP → Det + N

Det → the

Aux → Modal

Modal → will

N → cat

N → milk

V → drink

But what these formulae mean is not at all strange and forbidding. In fact it is so familiar to language arts teachers that I am afraid I will be dull and commonplace for the next several pages. I am going to talk about some things you know so well that you may never have noticed them. First, I will talk about little sentences. These formulae would produce or generate the one little sentence *The cat will drink the milk*. They also ascribe a structural description to that sentence. A structural description is somewhat like a sentence diagram, though it is also different in some respects. The structural description says that the sentence can be broken first of all into two parts: *The cat* is one part and *will drink the milk* is the second. It also says that the second part is composed of two subparts, *will* and *drink the milk*. It

§ Owen Thomas, *Transformational Grammar and the Teacher of English* (New York: Holt, Rinehart, and Winston, Inc., 1965).

breaks the second subpart into two sub-subparts *drink* and *the milk*. It breaks *the milk* down into its two parts, *the* and *milk*.

Who cares what the structural description of a sentence is? Why have we been analyzing sentences all these years? Have we known why? Actually there are several reasons. First, the meaning of the whole sentence is made from the meaning of exactly those components, not other components. That is, one *the* forms a meaningful unit with *milk*, but not with any other one word in the sentence: *drink the* is not a meaningful unit, nor is *will drink the*. Furthermore, *the milk* next forms a meaningful unit with drink: *drink the milk*. But *the cat the milk* is not a meaningful unit. This larger unit *drink the milk* forms a meaningful unit with *will* to produce the next unit, and finally *will drink the milk* joins with *the cat* to give the meaning of the whole sentence. Here we happen to have worked from the small units to the large unit, but we could have worked from large to small as we did in the formula. When you listen you work from large to small, but when you speak or write you work from small to large.

REASONS FOR STRUCTURAL DESCRIPTION OF SENTENCES

One reason to give the structural description of the sentence, then, is to show which are the meaningful parts and what is the order in which those parts are joined together one after another to give the whole meaning of the sentence.

When I used to assemble model airplanes with my son, we had to learn about subassemblies and sub-subassemblies. We had to glue the parts together in the proper order or some part would be left over and we would have to tear the whole thing apart to get it in. Sentences too have their subassemblies, and the order of assembly is no chance matter.

There are two other reasons to show the structural description of a sentence. Some words are called nouns in this description and some are called verbs and some are called modals. Which names we use for these sets of words would not matter, except that these names have been used for two thousand years. We could call them class 1, class 2, class 3 words instead if we gained anything by the change. One reason we group words into those various classes or sets is to show that thousands of English sentences can be made simply by substituting one noun in the same place as another noun and some new modal in place of another modal. But we never can substitute a noun for a modal or a modal for a noun. For instance if it is English to say

The cat will drink the milk.

we know it will also be English to say

> John will drink the milk.
> The dog will drink the milk.
> Mary will drink the milk.

One animate noun substitutes here for another animate noun. Similarly one modal substitutes for another.

> The cat   can   drink the milk.
> The cat should drink the milk.
> The cat   may   drink the milk.
> The cat might drink the milk.

But we know too that a modal cannot be substituted for a noun. It is not English to say

> Could will drink the milk.
> The cat John the milk.

Regularities such as these make a language easy enough that people can learn it. When we learn a new word we unconsciously learn whether it is a noun or a verb, and so we unconsciously learn countless thousands of new sentences in which it can be used. So this is a second reason why the structural description of a sentence helps to show what we know when we know our language.

A third reason to show the structural description is to show what can be conjoined. For instance we said earlier that *the cat* is a grammatical unit, but that *drink the* is not. That tells us that·it will not be English to conjoin *drink the* and *taste a* as in the sentence.

> The cat will drink the and taste a milk.

However, it will be English to say

> The cat will taste and drink the milk.

for *taste* and *drink* are both V's. But words are not all that can be conjoined. Larger structures can be too.
Here two VP's are conjoined though there is only one NP and one modal:

> The cat will drink the milk and go to sleep.

But only the components generated by the rules can be conjoined. Words cannot be conjoined at random.

Just as one noun phrase can be substituted for another noun phrase but for nothing else, so one noun phrase can be conjoined with another noun phrase, but not with anything else. Just as a VP can be replaced by another VP but not by a modal or an NP, so one can be conjoined to another bearing the same label in the formulae.

So when we give the structural description of a sentence, we are simply pointing out explicitly some of the things we know unconsciously when we know our language.

That is not all that a g-t grammar shows about little sentences. It also assigns certain functional relations to certain components. What are here called functional relations are not the same as the grammatical categories. For instance, *the cat* is an NP and *the milk* is another NP. But one is subject and the other is object. And the subject NP does not mean the same as an object NP. In the following sentences both *John* and *Mary* are NP's, but in one sentence *John* is the subject, and in the other *Mary* is the subject. Any youngster knows the difference between the two.

> John hit Mary first.
> Mary hit John first.

One NP is often substitutable grammatically for another NP, whether subject or object, but an NP which is subject does not mean the same as it does when it is object.

Take another simple example.

> The boy is easy to please.
> The boy is eager to please.

In one sentence, the boy pleases other people and is eager to do so. In the other sentence, other people please the boy and to do so is easy. In one sentence, *the boy* has the subject meaning relationship to *please*. In the other sentence, *the boy* has the object meaning relationship to *please*. But in both sentences, *boy* is the formal subject of the verb *is*.

The g-t grammarian makes further distinctions between the formal subject and the formal object and the semantic subject and the semantic object. For instance, the two following sentences mean the same thing (that is, if one is true the other is true, and if one is false the other is false).

The boy pleases other people.
Other people are pleased by the boy.

The semantic subject in both sentences is *the boy*: the boy does the pleasing. But one verb agrees with the formal subject *the boy* which is singular, *the boy pleases*. The other verb agrees with the formal subject *other people* which is plural: *other people are pleased*. So in this sentence the semantic subject is not the same as the formal subject. The verb agrees with the formal subject and that may not be the semantic subject.

FORMULAE FOR MAKING BIGGER SENTENCES

The sentence we started out with was extremely simple. A g-t grammar gives formulae to produce all these different simplest sentences: sentences with direct objects, predicate nominals (John is a hero), predicate adjectives (John is heroic), indirect objects (John gave Mary a book), and many constituents which are not named in school book grammars. These simplest sentences used to be called kernel sentences by the g-t grammarian. That term is not being used in recent publications, but I shall continue to use it here.

A g-t grammar also gives you explicit directions on how to make big sentences out of little ones. Of course, being a native English speaker you know that, but you know it unconsciously without even knowing how you learned it. The grammar merely tries to describe what you know and what you do. But before I talk about how we make big sentences out of little sentences, I want to take a couple of minutes to give you a sample of how we make question sentences and imperative sentences and passive sentences out of statement or declarative sentences.

If you have a statement sentence with a modal, all you have to do to make it into a yes-no question sentence is to put the modal before the subject:

The cat will drink the milk.
Will the cat drink the milk?

The cat with the tiger markings and the ragged ears will drink the milk.
Will the cat with the tiger markings and the ragged ears drink the milk?

The formulae for other questions are almost as simple.

The inversion of modal and subject signals that a yes-no question is being asked. What is the meaning there signaled? It is simply "The speaker requests the listener to affirm or deny the following sentence." All yes-no questions bear that same relation to the statements from which they are formed. *Will the cat drink the milk?* means "The speaker requests the listener to affirm or deny the sentence, *The cat will drink the milk.*"

To produce an imperative sentence you must begin with a sentence that has *you*, meaning the listener, as the subject, and *will* (the volitional *will*, not the future tense *will*) as its modal: *You will be here on time tomorrow.* The verb following *will* is always in the uninflected form, and that is just the form we always want. We say *You are here, You will be here,* and consequently we say in the imperative *Be here,* not *Are here.* To form an imperative sentence from such a declarative sentence, all you have to do is delete the *you will*: *Be here on time tomorrow.* The absence of the subject and the uninflected form of the verb are the formal signals that an imperative has been uttered. We say that *you will* has been deleted, because if we add a tag question at the end of the imperative, we put the *you* and the *will* back in, though in negative form.

Be here on time tomorrow, won't you?

The meaning signaled by the interrogative is "The speaker requests that you will: Be here on time tomorrow."

Passive sentences are formed from kernel sentences by as simple a formula. Take this example: *The cat will drink the milk: The milk will be drunk by the cat.* (1) Whatever expression functioned as semantic direct object now becomes formal subject. (2) Whatever expression functioned as semantic subject now follows *by* (or is deleted along with *by*) at the end of the sentence. (3) The proper form of *be* is inserted before the main verb and the main verb takes the past participle form. Thus:

(1) The cat will (2) drink (3) the milk.
(3) The milk will (2) be drunk by (1) the cat.

These are the formal signals of the passive. The meaning of the passive does not differ from that of the active, but in a passive sentence the semantic subject does not need to be mentioned. Instead of saying "Someone hurt him" we can say "He was hurt."

VARIETY OF TRANSFORMATIONS

These changes which we English speakers make on active declarative sentences to turn them into questions and imperatives and passives are called singulary transformations, because they change a single sentence of one sort into a single sentence of another sort. Children before they ever get to school can form questions and imperatives in an endless stream, though they have no conscious notion of the general rules which they have learned to follow.

Which comes first, the question or the statement? Which comes first, "He will come" or "Will he come?" It depends on what you mean by "comes first." If you mean, "Which does the child learn first?" then we have no certain answer. Having watched my own infants when they were angry and demanding, I feel certain that infants speak imperatives long before they speak any words at all. I remember too that four-year-olds generate questions much faster than their parents want to generate answers.

But the statement comes before the question in a thoroughly different sense. It is simpler to write a grammar which generates first the form and meaning of statements than to write one which generates questions first and then transforms them into statements.

In many elementary grammar books, I see questions and statements mixed together indiscriminately, though the relation of one to the other is never explained.

Far more useful for the language arts program, however, are the transformations which have been called sentence-combining. They take one sentence of a certain sort and another of a certain sort and combine them to produce one new sentence. The g-t grammar tries to tell exactly what changes are made in the process. The process of combining little sentences into bigger ones can be repeated an indefinite number of times so that two, three, four, five, and even ten or twenty can be combined into one complicated sentence. Below we will combine seventeen into one. Furthermore, the meaning of the complicated sentence is the meaning of all the simple sentences put together.

This process is particularly interesting because apparently the ability to combine more and more kernel sentences is a mark of maturity. The older a child becomes, the more he can combine. Apparently, too, the higher the IQ, the faster children learn to do this, so that by the time they are in the twelfth grade, the students with superior IQ's tend to be well ahead of students with average IQ's.

THE PROCESS OF COMBINING SENTENCES

I want to sketch for you that process of combining sentences.

Very young children combine two sentences into one by putting *and's* between. We can call this sentence coordination. Children in the earlier grades do this far more often than adults. In writing, fourth graders do so four or five times as often as twelfth graders in the same number of words. As they get older, they learn not to use sentence coordination so much. Also children use sentence coordination more often in speech than in writing. In fact, Dr. Griffin and his associates at Peabody have found that fifth graders use two or three times as much sentence coordination in their speech as they do in their writing for the same number of words.||

So we may think of sentence coordination as a relatively immature device for joining little sentences into bigger ones. It is a device which they will outgrow, or, better yet, which they will replace with the other devices I will now describe. Sentence coordination is the only transformation that we know to be used *less* frequently by older students.

Often two adjoining sentences have a certain relation between them such that the event recorded in one sentence happened at the same time as that in the other. When such is the case, *when* can be put in front of one sentence, making it an adverbial clause with the other as the main or independent clause:

My mother came home and I got spanked. (*When* my mother, etc.)
We climbed out on the end of the limb and it broke. (*When* we climbed out, etc.)

There are many subordinators besides *when* which introduce movable adverbial clauses, and, in writing, students use a few more of them as they get older. Dr. Griffin finds that in the speech of students from kindergarten to seventh grade, there is a general increase in their number. I find that in writing there is also a slight increase from the fourth grade up to the twelfth.|| ||

So-called adjective relative clauses are also produced by sentence-combining transformations. They can be formed when one sentence contains the same noun or the same adverb of time or place as another

|| Roy C. O'Donnell, William J. Griffin & R. C. Norris, *Syntax of Kindergarten and Elementary School Children: A Transformational Analysis* (Champaign, Illinois: National Council of Teachers of English, 1967).
|| || Kellogg W. Hunt, *Grammatical Structures Written at Three Grade Levels* (Champaign, Illinois: National Council of Teachers of English, 1965).

sentence contains. Let me take as my main clause *The man did something* and then combine with it a number of different sentences in the form of adjective clauses. At the same time, we will notice that in all the examples I happen to have chosen, the. adjective clause can be reduced by deletion to a single word modifier of a noun or to a phrasal modifier of a noun.

> The man did something.
>
> The man was big.
> The man (who was big) did something.
> The (big) man did something.
>
> The man was at the door.
> The man (who was at the door) did something.
> The man (at the door) did something.
>
> The man had a derby.
> The man (who had a derby) did something.
> The man (with a derby) did something.
>
> The man was swinging a cane.
> The man (who was swinging a cane) did something.
> The man (swinging a cane) did something.

We find that as students mature they use more and more adjective clauses in their writing. Furthermore, as students mature they use more and more of these single-word or phrasal modifiers of nouns. So we see that the ability to combine sentences into adjective clauses and to delete parts of the clause to produce single word or single phrase modifiers is indeed a mark of maturity.

Now let us see how a twelfth grader can combine five sentences into one. You will see that the twelfth grader is telling about a sailor. In fact the word *sailor* is subject of each of the sentences which he has consolidated into one.

> The sailor was tall.
> The sailor was rather ugly.
> The sailor had a limp.
> The sailor had offered them the prize.
> The sailor finally came on deck.

There are lots of bad ways to combine these sentences. One is with sentence coordinators:

> The sailor was tall and he was rather ugly and he had a limp and he had offered them the prize and he finally came on deck.

I have seen fourth graders who wrote almost that way.

Another bad way to combine the sentences is to produce a great number of relative adjective clauses all modifying the word *sailor*. No one would ever write like this:

> The sailor who was tall and who was rather ugly and who had offered them the prize finally came on deck.

Rarely do we let more than one full adjective clause modify a single noun. Instead we reduce the potential clauses to single word modifiers or phrasal modifiers.

I fancy most of you are way ahead of me already. You have been so uncomfortable with these bad sentences that you have already rewritten them as the twelfth grader did. But even so I am going to ask you to combine these sentences with me, one by one, slow motion, so we can study the process.

Below, I have numbered the minimal sentences S1, S2, etc. The procedure will be as follows. First, I will state a general transformational rule for English sentences. Then we will apply that rule to two of the sentences and see what we come out with. Next I will state another transformational rule, or the same one again, and we will apply that rule in the third sentence plus what we produced the previous time. Or instead I may state a rule which changes what we produced though it does not incorporate a new sentence.

The rules read like this: If you have a sentence of one particular pattern and a second of another particular pattern, it will be good English if you rewrite them into one according to the formula. Instead of using abstract but more exact symbols like NP for noun phrase or VP for predicate, I have used the words *someone* or *something* for noun phrases, and the words *did something* for predicates in general. *A twelfth grader consolidates 5 sentences into 1, using noun modifiers.*

S1 The sailor finally came on deck.
S2 The sailor was tall.
S3 The sailor was rather ugly.
S4 The sailor had a limp.
S5 The sailor had offered them a prize.

Transformation #1

> Someone did something + Someone did something else → The someone (who did something else) did something.

Application to S1 and S2:

> The sailor who was tall finally came on deck.

Transformation #2

> Someone (who was X) did something → Someone X did something (or some X person did something).

Application to what we produced last time:

> The tall sailor finally came on deck.

Transformation #1 again

> Someone did something + Someone did something else → The someone (who did something else) did something.

Application to S3 plus what we produced last time:

> The tall sailor (who was rather ugly) finally came on deck.

Transformation #2 again

> Someone (who was X) did something → Someone X did something (or some X person did something).

Application to what we produced last time:

> The tall, rather ugly sailor finally came on deck.

Transformation #3

> Someone had something → someone with something.

Application to S4 plus what we produced before:

> The tall, rather ugly sailor with a limp finally came on deck.

Transformation #1 again

> Someone did something + Someone did something else → The someone (who did something else) did something.

Application to S5 plus what we produced before:

> The tall, rather ugly sailor with a limp, who had offered them a prize, finally came on deck.

An average fourth grader does not write four modifiers to a single noun. He will write only two or at most three at a time. He would be likely to resort to *and's* and produce about three sentences.

> The sailor was tall and rather ugly and had a limp. He had offered them the prize. Finally he came on deck.

I have just finished talking about noun modifiers, attempting to show that syntactic maturity is the ability to consolidate several sentences by reducing some sentences to modifiers of a single noun.

THE NOMINALIZING TENDENCY IN CONSOLIDATION

The second tendency I will talk about today is called the nominalizing tendency. What the writer does is to take a whole sentence, or at least a whole predicate, and make it into a structure which can function like a noun. That is, the whole transformed sentence can now be subject in some other sentence, or object of a verb, or object of a preposition. This whole new sentence can then be nominalized in turn, and so on and so on. The best way to illustrate this process is to show you a number of kernel sentences and let you put them together.

A twelfth grader consolidates 6 sentences into 1, nominalizing some.

S1 Macbeth breaks up the feast with something.
S2 Macbeth remarks something.
S3 Macbeth displays fear.
S4 Macbeth fears a ghost.
S5 Banquo is the ghost.
S6 Only Macbeth sees the ghost.

Transformation #1

Someone remarks about something → someone's remark about something.
Someone displays something → someone's display of something.
Someone fears something → someone's fear of something.

Application to S1 and S2:

Macbeth breaks up the feast with his remarks (about something).

Transformation #1 again, plus coordination plus deletion

(The coordination transformation is too complex to explain here.)

Application to S3 plus what we produced before:

Macbeth breaks up the feast with his remarks and his display of fear.

Transformation #1 again

Application to S4 plus what we produced before:

Macbeth breaks up the feast with his remarks and his display of fear of a ghost.

Transformation #2

Someone has something → the something of someone.

Application to S5 plus what we produced before:

Macbeth breaks up the feast with his remarks and his display of fear of a ghost of Banquo.

Transformation #3

Someone sees something → something is seeable (visible) to someone. (*Visible* replaces seeable somewhat as *edible* replaces *eatable*. *Understandable, divisible* are regular forms.)

Application to S6 plus what we produced before:

Macbeth breaks up the feast with his remarks and his display of fear of a ghost of Banquo visible only to him.

Here is still another sequence of transformations, this time showing the way in which a superior adult incorporates a great variety of kernel sentences as nominalizations, modifiers, etc., into a single sentence with highly complex relationships expressed between or among its constituent ideas.

*A superior adult consolidates 17 sentences into 1, using modifiers,
nominalizations, etc.*

S1 He also noted S2.
S2 S3 would apply only to S4.
S3 Someone cuts back something.
   (Someone's cutback of something)
S4 Someone stockpiles weapons.
   (Someone's stockpiling of weapons)
   (He also noted that [someone's] cutback [of something] would
   apply only to [someone's stockpiling] of weapons.)
S5 The weapons are for an arsenal.
   (He also noted that the cutback would apply only to the stock-
   piling of weapons for an arsenal.)
S6 The arsenal is for atomic weapons (?)
   (. . . an atomic [weapon] arsenal)
S7 The arsenal already bulges.
   (. . . an already bulging atomic arsenal)
S8 S3 would not affect the strength.
   (He also noted that the cutback would apply only to the stock-
   piling of weapons for an already bulging atomic arsenal and
   would have no effect on the strength.)
S9 The strength overwhelms someone.
   (. . . the overwhelming strength)
S10 The strength retaliates.
   (. . . the overwhelming retaliatory strength)
S11 The SAC has the strength.
   (. . . the overwhelming retaliatory strength of the SAC)
S12 The force has the strength.
   (. . . strength of the SAC and of the force)
S13 The force carries missiles.
   (. . . the missile force)
S14 The missiles are intercontinental.
   (. . . the intercontinental missile force)
S15 The fleet has the strength.
   (. . . strength of the SAC, of the intercontinental missile force, or
   the fleet)
S16 The fleet carries missiles.
   (. . . the missile fleet)
S17 The missiles are Polaris.
   (. . . the Polaris missile fleet)
   He also noted that the cutback would apply only to the stockpiling of weapons for an already bulging atomic arsenal and
   would have no effect on the overwhelming retaliatory strength of
   the SAC, of the intercontinental missile force, or the Polaris
   missile fleet.

SUMMARY AND CONCLUSION

This has been an exceedingly rough sketch of g-t grammar. We started out with fairly explicit rules that generated an exceedingly simple sentence and also its structural description. Then we saw that questions, imperatives, and passives bear a certain explicit relationship to those simple active statement sentences, both in form and in meaning.

Then we saw that quite complicated sentences can be consolidated out of a number of exceedingly simple sentences. As children get older, they can consolidate larger and larger numbers of them. Average twelfth graders consolidate half a dozen with moderate frequency. But to find as many as seventeen consolidated into one, one must look to the highbrow magazines such as *Harper's* and *Atlantic*. Only superior adults can keep that many in mind at once and keep them all straight, too.

No one yet knows whether elementary school children can be hurried along this path.

KELLOGG W. HUNT

Recent Measures in Syntactic Development

INTRODUCTION

According to Hunt, there are three well-established generalizations about the way in which the sentences of children change with the children's increasing maturity: (1) there are more of them, that is, children write more on a given topic as they get older; (2) the sentences become longer; and (3) the children use subordinate clauses more frequently. Hunt's investigation has led him to reformulate observations (2) and (3).

Hunt establishes a unit for measuring the frequencies of subordinate clauses and finds that, as expected, they increase as children mature. Next, he subclassifies the types of subordinate clauses to see if the various types all increase at the same rate. The result is that of the three main types—noun clauses, adverb clauses, and adjective clauses—the first two do not greatly increase with maturity. Consequently, point (3) above can be considerably refined: as children mature, they use more and more adjective clauses. As Hunt puts it, "we see, then, that the subordinate clause index is a team which moves ahead, but it moves ahead because one member does almost all the work."

Reprinted with permission of the author and the National Council of Teachers of English from *Elementary English,* Vol. XLIII (November), 1966, pp. 732–739.

Hunt points out that young children write strings of independent clauses whereas older children and adults reduce many of the independent clauses to subordinate clauses, particularly adjective clauses, which in turn are often reduced to adjectival phrases or even single words, for example, modifying adjectives and appositives. This process of reduction increases the total number of words per clause by decreasing the number of clauses. In effect, the older writers pack more information into fewer clauses by the grammatical processes known as embedding and deletion. As Hunt explains it,

> older students reduce more of their clauses to subordinate clause status, attaching them to other main clauses; and secondly . . . the clauses they do write, whether subordinate or main, happen to have more words in them.

In order to measure the amount of "packing" within the boundaries of the independent clause, Hunt proposes the "minimal terminable unit" or "T-unit" for short. Hunt defines the T-unit as "the shortest units into which a piece of discourse can be cut without leaving any sentence fragments as residue." Thus a T-unit always contains just one independent clause plus however many subordinate clauses there are attached to the independent clause. The T-unit can be used in several differer : ways. One way is to count the average *number* of T-units per sentence. Another way is to count the average *length* of T-units per sentence.

Hunt points out that fourth graders have more T-units on the average per sentence than superior adults do. This is a reflection of the comment made earlier that young children tend to make up sentences out of strings of independent clauses. The observation, incidentally, suggests that pure sentence length in itself is not a very revealing measure of syntactic sophistication.

On the other hand, the length of the average T-unit appears to be closely correlated with maturity of the writer. This, in turn, is a reflection of the earlier observation that older writers pack more into the T-unit by reducing independent clauses to subordinate clauses, and subordinate clauses to phrases and words. Hunt suggests that there are two possible ways to increasing the length of the T-unit: (1) add more dependent clauses and (2) lengthen the existing clauses by adding phrases and words (derived from reduced clauses). According to Hunt, both ways are important in increasing the size of the T-unit during the school years. In the writing of superior adults and superior twelfth graders, the length of the T-unit jumps significantly. Here the increased length seems to be solely the result of adding more words to the clauses without increasing their number. As Hunt puts it,

> to advance beyond the level of the average twelfth grader, the writer must learn to reduce and consolidate clauses much more often. Supe-

rior twelfth graders do not write more subordinate clauses than average twelfth graders. Instead they write much longer clauses, just as superior adults do.

Hunt closes the essay by turning the investigation to what makes a sentence hard to read. Longer sentences are harder to read than short ones. However, it is not sentence length that is the important factor, it is the fact that "the clauses are longer. And the clauses are longer, it can be inferred, only because more have been consolidated into a single one."

Any teacher of English can tell a fourth-grade theme from a twelfth-grade theme. Probably anyone in this room could make still finer distinctions: he could tell the average fourth-grade theme from the average eighth-grade theme. Just how would he detect the difference? For one thing he would rely on word choice. The vocabulary of the average eighth grader is measurably different from that of the average fourth grader. But also the teacher would feel that some of the sentence structures used by the eighth grader were too mature to be used by a fourth grader. Sentence structure, not vocabulary, is my subject for this paper.

The educational researcher respects the teacher's intuitive sense of maturity, but he wishes he knew how to measure it quantitatively, by counting something—if only he knew what to count. He knows of course that it takes centuries to build up a science. All during the Middle Ages the alchemists were poking away at the information which eventually led to modern scientific chemistry. It took centuries to establish the science. The science of measuring syntactic maturity is barely emerging from the stages of alchemy. It scarcely deserves to be called a science at all. But we do know a few things.

For the last thirty years we have known at least three things about the development of language structure. First, as children mature they tend to produce more words on any given subject. They have more to say. Second, as children mature, the sentences they use tend to be longer. Third, as children mature a larger proportion of their clauses are subordinate clauses.[*]

In the last two years it has been possible to add a few more measures, and I will come to them later. But first let me turn back to the statement about subordinate clauses and try to make clear its significance

[*] Dorothea McCarthy, "Language Development in Children." *Manual of Child Psychology*, ed. Leonard Carmichael. New York: John Wiley & Sons, Inc., 1954.

for the teaching program. It would be worse than useless for a fourth-grade teacher to say to her students, "Now if you will go back to your last paper and add more subordinate clauses to the main clauses, you will be writing like Miss Hill's wonderful sixth graders or Miss Summit's wonderful eighth graders instead of my own miserable fourth graders." Such an approach would be worse than useless. But the facts behind so useless a statement are not useless; they are useful if we know how to use them. Let us look at some fourth-grade writings. We find pairs of main clauses like this:

There was a lady next door and the lady was a singer.

Now an older student would not be likely to repeat the noun *lady*. He might rewrite the two clauses in any of several ways: one way would be to reduce the second main clause to a relative adjective clause.

There was a lady next door who was a singer.

Now instead of two main clauses and no subordinate clauses, we have one main clause and one subordinate clause.

Let me give you a few more examples of pairs of fourth-grade main clauses. In every instance one of the main clauses could have been reduced to a relative adjective clause.

Moby Dick was a very big whale. He lived in the sea. (who lived in the sea.)

His owner was a milkman. The milkman was very strict to the mother and babies. (who was very strict . . .)

Once upon a time I had a cat. This cat was a beautiful cat. It was also mean. (who was a beautiful cat.)

One day Nancy got a letter from her Uncle Joe. It was her great uncle. (who was her great uncle.)

I have a new bicycle. I like to ride it. (which I like to ride.)

We have a lot on Lake Talquin. This lot has a dock on it. (On Lake Talquin we have a lot which has a dock on it.)

Today we went to see a film. The film was about a white-headed whale. (which was about a white-headed whale.)

The jewel was in the drawer. It was red. (The jewel which was red . . .)

Beautiful Joe was a dog, he was born on a farm. (that was born on a farm.)

One colt was trembling. It was lying down on the hay. (One colt which was lying down . . .)

A convenient way to measure the frequency of subordinate clauses is to divide the total number of clauses, both subordinate and main, by the number of main clauses. I will call this the "subordinate clause index."[†] It is expressed as a decimal fraction. The index will always be 1 (for the main clause) plus whatever number of subordinate clauses are attached to it.

I find that average fourth-grade writers have a subordinate clause index of about 1.3; that is, they write a subordinate clause three-tenths as often as they write a main clause. Average eighth graders have an index of 1.4; they write a subordinate clause four-tenths as often as a main clause. Average twelfth graders have an index of 1.68. They write a subordinate clause about six-tenths as often as a main clause. If you jump now to the superior adult writers who produce articles for *Harper's* and *Atlantic* you find that they have an index of 1.78: they write about seven-tenths as many subordinate clauses as main clauses. However, some mature article writers have much higher indexes. One had a score of 2.36, indicating that his average main clause had one and a third subordinate clauses related to it.

The general trend of development is fairly clear: for fourth grade the score was 1.3, for eighth 1.4, for twelfth 1.6, and for superior adults 1.7.

It would be interesting to go back to the grades earlier than the fourth to see if the number of subordinate clauses is smaller back there. Fortunately Professors O'Donnell, Griffin, and Norris at Peabody have provided us with data within the last year.[‡] Reporting on their results for speech alone, they find a general increase in number of subordinate clauses from kindergarten to the seventh grade where the study ended. These kindergarten students have an index of 1.16. Putting their figures and mine together, we see that the trend is clear. From the first public school grade to the last the number of subordinate clauses increases steadily for every grade.

This tendency has implications for teaching language. Without ever using the words "main clause" and "subordinate clause," the language arts teacher who sees pairs of main clauses like those I have mentioned can show her students another way of saying the same thing.

† The "subordination ratio" which has been used for thirty years has usually been figured in another way.

‡ Published as an NCTE research monograph entitled *A Transformational Analysis of the Language of Kindergarten and Elementary School Children,* NCTE Research Report #8. Champaign, Illinois, 1967.

One further refining statement can be made about subordinate clauses and the index of their frequency. There are three common kinds of such clauses: noun, movable adverb, and adjective. The other kinds, such as clauses of comparison, are uncommon. Though the total of all three increases with maturity, not all three increase equally. Noun clauses in general are no index of maturity: the number of them is determined instead by the mode of discourse, the subject matter, all the way from the early grades to maturity. Movable adverb clauses do seem to increase with maturity in the very early grades, but the ceiling is reached early, and after the middle grades the frequency of them tells more about mode of discourse and subject matter than about maturity. But adjective clauses are different. From the earliest grades to the latest the number of them increases steadily, and among skilled adults the adjective clause is still more frequent than it is with students finishing high school. We see, then, that the subordinate clause index is a team which moves ahead, but it moves ahead because one member does almost all the work. The other two sometimes pull ahead but sometimes pull back too, depending on factors other than mental maturity.

But of course subordinating clauses is not all there is to syntactic development. In every pair of examples I have given so far, it would have been possible to reduce one of the clauses still further so that it is no longer a clause at all, but merely a word or phrase consolidated inside the other clause. In this fashion two clauses will become one clause. The one clause will now be one word or one phrase longer than it was before, but it will be shorter than the two clauses were together. By throwing away some of one clause we will gain in succinctness. The final expression will be tighter, less diffuse, more mature.

Let me illustrate now with the same examples, and then back up the examples with figures to indicate that older students do indeed more often make one longer clause out of two shorter ones.

A clause with a predicate adjective can all be thrown away except for the adjective.

> Once upon a time I had a *beautiful, mean* cat.
> The *red* jewel was in the drawer.

Eighth graders write more than 150 percent as many single-word adjectives before nouns as fourth graders do.

If a clause contains a prepositional phrase after a form of *be* you can throw away all but that prepositional phrase.

The jewel *in the drawer* was red.
Today we saw a film *about Moby Dick*.

Eighth graders use such prepositional phrases to modify nouns 170 percent as often, and twelfth graders 240 percent as often, as fourth graders do.

If the clause contains a *have* you can often put what follows the *have* into a genitive form and throw away the rest.

I like to ride *my* new bicycle.
Our lot on Lake Talquin has a dock on it.

Twelfth graders used 130 percent as many genitives as fourth graders do.

If a clause contains a predicate nominal, it can become an appositive, and the rest can be thrown away.

There was a lady next door, *a singer*.
His owner, *a milkman*, was very strict to the mother and babies.
One day Nancy got a letter from her *great uncle* Joe.

Eighth graders wrote a third more appositives than fourth graders.

Often clauses with non-finite verbs can all be thrown away except for the verbs, which now become modifiers of nouns.

Beautiful Joe was a dog *born on a farm*.
One *trembling* colt was lying down on the hay.
One colt, *lying down on the hay*, was trembling.

Eighth graders wrote 160 percent and twelfth graders wrote 190 percent as many non-finite verb modifiers of nouns as fourth graders did.

I have used this set of examples twice now, to show two different things: first, how it is that older students reduce more of their clauses to subordinate clause status, attaching them to other main clauses; and secondly, how it is that the clauses they do write, whether subordinate or main, happen to have more words in them.§ Those extra added

---

§ A clause is here defined as one subject or one set of coordinate subjects with one finite verb or one finite set of coordinated verbs. Thus *I went home* is one clause, and so is *Jim and I went home and rode our bikes*.

The average clause length for any body of writing, however long or short, is simply the total number of words divided by the total number of clauses. For a sentence such as *She said he ought to try harder*, there are 7 words and 2 clauses, so the average clause length is 3.5 words for that body of writing.

words are not padding. They are all that is left out of useless whole clauses when the padding has been thrown away. From a six-word clause five words may be thrown away, with only one word salvaged. So adding that one more word to some other clause indicates a substantial gain. Though an increase of one word in clause length may not sound very impressive, a gain of five words or so in succinctness is indeed impressive. What was said in two clauses totalling twelve words is now said in one clause of seven words.

It is not as if some fourth-grade teacher had said "Add one word to each clause you have written." Instead it is as if she had said, "In this sentence you can throw away all but one word or one phrase. You can consolidate that word or phrase with this other expression into a larger, more comprehensively organized, unit of thought."

Substantial evidence is accumulating that as school children mature they do indeed learn to put their thoughts into longer and longer clauses. My own first research dealt with children of strictly average IQ, that is, with children having scores between 90 and 110. I worked first with three grades, fairly widely spaced: fourth grade, when students are just beginning to write with some degree of comfortableness; twelfth grade when the student of average IQ writes about as well as he ever will, perhaps; eighth grade, half way between the beginning and end of that public school period. The clauses written by these fourth graders were 6.6 words long. Clauses by eighth graders were 20 percent longer and clauses by twelfth graders were 30 percent longer. But development does not stop there. The writers of articles for *Harper's* and *Atlantic* write clauses about 175 percent as long as those written by fourth graders of average IQ. In fact, in clause length, the superior adult is farther ahead of the average twelfth grader than the average twelfth grader is ahead of his little brother back in the fourth grade.

If the evidence is as sound as it seems to be, then one ought to be able to predict on the basis of it. If this tendency to lengthen clauses is a general characteristic of linguistic development, then one might predict in several directions. He might predict that if growth is fairly steady after the fourth grade, then it probably is perceptible before the fourth grade too. And if growth occurs in writing, then it probably occurs in speech too. If one is going to measure the development which occurs earlier than the fourth grade, of course, it is speech, not writing, he must study.

Fortunately the Peabody study has provided us with some confirming evidence within the last few months. Notice the slight but steady increase as I read these figures. The clauses spoken by the kinder-garten children are 6.1 words long. For first graders, 6.7 words. For second graders 7.1 words. Third graders 7.2. Fifth graders 7.5. Seventh graders 7.8. At every grade level there is an increase in the clause length of their speech. Clause length plots as a smooth rising curve, all the way to the maturity of *Harper's* and *Atlantic* articles.

One might predict in yet another direction. He might predict that children with superior IQ's will have matured more in language struc-ture at even an early age. Since my results are not conclusive at this time, I am not sure whether, as early as the fourth grade, children with IQ scores above 130 write, on the average, slightly longer clauses and write a larger proportion of subordinate clauses than fourth graders with average IQ. By the time children of superior IQ reach the twelfth grade, however, their superiority in clause-length is unmistakable. They are almost as far ahead of average twelfth graders as average twelfth graders are ahead of fourth graders. In fact, in clause length, twelfth graders with IQ above 130 are closer to writers of *Harper's* and *Atlantic* articles than they are to twelfth graders of average IQ.

These longer clauses written by older students are not produced by combining just two clauses, but by combining four or six or eight. Superior adults can combine a dozen clauses into one, by the process already briefly suggested.

So, for a third time, I suggest that teachers who understand the find-ings of language development research may be able to apply those findings in the classroom. For years teachers have occasionally com-bined pairs of clauses as we were doing here a few minutes ago. But so far as I know it has never occurred to anyone to show that six or eight or a dozen are often consolidated into one mature clause. It is by this process that little sentences grow into big ones.‖

Here is a clause written by an average eighth grader. "He was a rare white whale with a crooked jaw." That consolidates five clauses. (1) He was a whale. (2) The whale was white. (3) The whale was rare. (4) The whale had a jaw. (5) The jaw was crooked. Average fourth graders do not ordinarily write like that. In fact, in five thousand clauses written by fourth graders we found a single nominal that resulted from as many as five of these consolidations only three times. Five is simply too many for a fourth grader, but he often consolidates three.

‖ See "How Little Sentences Grow into Big Ones," a paper by Kellogg W. Hunt read at the NCTE's Spring Institute on New Directions in Elementary English, Chicago, March 7, 1966, to be published with the proceedings of that institute.

Despite this eighth grader's relative maturity, even he failed to consolidate clauses where he might have. He missed opportunities. He wrote:

> Moby Dick was a dangerous whale. People had never been able to catch him. He was a rare white whale with a crooked jaw. He was a killer too. He was long and strong.

There are many ways to consolidate this further and I won't rewrite the whole passage. The first two clauses could well be consolidated and so could the last two:

> Moby Dick was a dangerous whale that people had never been able to catch. He was a killer too, long and strong.

I am recommending, then, that throughout the elementary and secondary grades the process of clause-consolidation is one of the things which the language arts program should study. Transformational grammarians speak of this process as the result of embedding and deletion transformations.

Finally I want to describe to you a new unit of measurement which is very convenient for syntactic development research. It is certainly more significant than sentence length which is still reported to be the most widely used measure of language maturity.# To introduce this unit let me read a theme as written by one of our fourth graders. The theme is one sentence long.

> I like the movie we saw about Moby Dick the white whale the captain said if you can kill the white whale Moby Dick I will give this gold to the one that can do it and it is worth sixteen dollars they tried and tried but while they were trying they killed a whale and used the oil for the lamps they almost caught the white whale.

In sentence length this fourth grader is superior to the average writer in *Harper's* and *Atlantic*. Now let me cut that sentence up into the new units. Each unit will consist of exactly one main clause plus whatever subordinate clauses happen to be attached to or embedded within it.

1. I like the movie we saw about Moby Dick, the white whale.
2. The captain said if you can kill the white whale, Moby Dick, I will give this gold to the one that can do it.

For instance, see the article on "Language Development" in the 1960 edition of the *Encyclopaedia of Educational Research*.

3. And it is worth sixteen dollars.
4. They tried and tried.
5. But while they were trying they killed a whale and used the oil for the lamps.
6. They almost caught the white whale.

For lack of a better name I call these units "minimal terminable units." They are "terminable" in the sense that it is grammatically acceptable to terminate each one with a capital letter at the beginning and a period or question mark at the end. They are "minimal" in the sense that they are the shortest units into which a piece of discourse can be cut without leaving any sentence fragments as residue. They are thus "minimal terminable units." I wish I could call these units "the shortest allowable sentences" but instead I call them "T-units," for short. To repeat, each is exactly one main clause plus whatever subordinate clauses are attached to that main clause.

In ordinary prose about half the sentences consist of just one such T-unit. The other half of the sentences consist of two or more T-units, often joined with *and's*. Such sentences are "compound," or "compound-complex." Cutting a passage into T-units cuts each compound sentence or compound-complex sentence into two or more T-units. Now if it were true that as writers mature they put more and more T-units into their sentences, then sentence length would be a better measure of maturity than T-unit length. But such is not the case. Occasionally a very young student will string one T-unit after another after another, with *ands* between or nothing between. The passage I read a moment ago combined six T-units into one sentence. The result of this tendency is that my fourth graders average more T-units per sentence than superior adults do. That fact upsets sentence length as an index of maturity. That same fact explains why T-unit length is a better index of maturity than sentence length.

A useful name for the average number of T-units per sentence might be "main clause coordination index." It probably should not be called "sentence coordination index."

Now let us pull all these various indexes together into a single piece of arithmetic. "Average clause length" is the number of words per clause. "Subordinate clause index" is the number of clauses per T-unit. "Average T-unit length" is the number of words per T-unit. "Main clause coordination index" is the number of T-units per sentence. "Average sentence length" is the number of words per sentence.

These five measures are very useful analytically and are all related arithmetically. The number of words per clause times the number of clauses per T-unit equals the number of words per T-unit. That times the number of T-units per sentence gives the number of words per sentence. The first index times the second equals the third. The third times the fourth equals the fifth. Clause length times subordinate clause index equals T-unit length. That figure times main clause co-ordination index equals sentence length.**

Finally, as a review, let me mention again the tendencies that have been known for thirty years concerning the development of language structure. First, as students mature they tend to have more to say about any subject. Second, as students mature their sentences tend to get longer. Third, as students mature they tend to write more subordinate clauses per main clause.

In the last few years a few more statements about syntactic development have been added. First, as students mature they tend to produce longer clauses. From kindergarten to at least the seventh grade, and probably beyond that time, this appears to be true of speech. And from the beginning to at least the twelfth grade this appears to be true of writing. Clause length is a better index of language maturity than sentence length. You will recall that clauses can be lengthened by a process that is here described as reduction and consolidation. That same process is described by generative-transformational grammarians as embedding transformations. Second, a convenient unit, intervening in size between the clause and the compound sentence is the "minimal terminable unit," defined as one main clause plus whatever subordinate clauses are attached to it or embedded within. This too is a better index of language maturity than sentence length. You will recall that "T-units" can be lengthened either by lengthening clauses or by increasing the number of subordinate clauses per T-unit. In the writing of average students throughout the public school grades, the one factor is about as influential as the other in effecting longer T-units. But the equality of influence stops there. The average twelfth grader has approached the ceiling in number of subordinate clauses. To advance beyond the level of the average twelfth grader, the writer must learn to reduce and consolidate clauses much more often. Superior twelfth graders do not write more subordinate clauses than average twelfth graders. Instead they write much longer clauses, just as superior adults do.

But making one clause out of two is child's play. Long before the

** Kellogg W. Hunt, "A Synopsis of Clause-to-Sentence Factors," *English Journal*, 54 (April 1965) 300–309. Also Kellogg W. Hunt, *Grammatical Structures Written at Three Grade Levels*, Research Report #3, NCTE, Champaign, Ill., 1965.

average child gets to the fourth grade he can consolidate two, though he does not do so very often. Some average fourth graders consolidate three into one. Some average eight graders consolidate four into one. Some average twelfth graders consolidate five into one. Superior twelfth graders consolidate six and seven. Superior adults consolidate more than that.[††] For a teacher to stretch a youngster, to push against the limits of his present accomplishment, two is nowhere near enough.

So far I have talked only about building up little sentences into bigger ones. Before I close I want to mention the other side of the coin, breaking big sentences down into little ones, as the mature reader or listener does with such lightning speed.

In recent months we have compared the syntactic traits that make a sentence hard to write and the syntactic traits that make it hard to read. We have compared the sentences written by children with those read by them but written by adults. For our reading samples we have used the *McCall-Crabbs Reading Lessons,* since the readability of each passage therein is supposedly already established. The passages cover roughly grades four to nine.

We find that sentences more difficult to read do not have more T-units per sentence. The number is about the same whether the sentences are easy or difficult. Listen to this sameness for grades 4 to 9: 1.13, 1.12, 1.13, 1.10, 1.13, 1.10.

You will remember that as children mature they tend to write subordinate clauses more often. But as sentences written by adults get easier or harder to read there seems to be no change. Listen to this sameness for passages that are 80 percent comprehensible to children in grades 4 through 9: 1.4, 1.4, 1.4, 1.4, 1.4, 1.4. (It sounds as if the record player were stuck in the same groove.)

But the clause length of passages, for 80 percent comprehension, increases steadily for grades 4 through 9 just as it increases as children write. Here are our figures so far: 8.45, 9.13, 9.59, 10.19, 11.01, 10.83.

In other words, the difficulty in reading sentences usually lies down inside the clause. Longer clauses tend to be more difficult. On the basis of previous research on what constitutes these clauses, it seems clear what it is that makes longer clauses harder to read and harder to write. On the whole, longer clauses have a larger number of sentences or clauses reduced and consolidated into one. It is by that process that little clauses grow into big ones.

[††] Kellogg W. Hunt, *Sentence Structures Used by Superior Students in Grades Four and Twelve, and by Superior Adults.* USOE Research Project No. 5-0313. Available from ERIC Document Reproducing Service, Bell and Howell, 1700 Shaw Boulevard, Cleveland, Ohio 44112.

Little by little the evidence piles up that the reduction and consolidation of many clauses into one is intimately related to syntactic growth both in writing and reading. If writers must build up clauses, then readers must break them down. A whole new range of applications is opened up for approaching reading difficulty.

For many years we have known that longer sentences tend to be harder to read. But in the last few months we have learned more about why that is true. It is not because longer sentences have more T-units coordinated into them, for they do not. It is not because they have more subordinate clauses attached to main clauses, for they do not. Instead it is because the clauses are longer. And the clauses are longer, it can be inferred, only because more have been consolidated into a single one.

All this has implications for the teaching of reading in the early grades. Teachers need to be trained in clause-consolidation so that children can be taught what otherwise they must discover unaided. They will discover it. That we know. But at present they must do so unaided.

Here is another place where the results of research should crawl out of the learned journals and into the classroom.

MARK LESTER

The Value of Transformational
Grammar in Teaching Composition

INTRODUCTION

The essay begins with the assertion that "there simply appears to be no correlation between a writer's conscious study of grammar and his ability to write." If we accept this view, will the study of transformational grammar succeed in improving writing where earlier theories of grammar have failed? Lester answers that it will not for several reasons: (1) the entry price for transformational grammar is high. In order to apply transformational grammar to the problems of style, the student must first learn the grammar. On the college level, at least, there is simply not enough time to teach both the fundamental theory of transformational grammar and also its application to writing within the compass of the usual freshman English course. (2) The theory of transformational grammar itself suggests that the conscious study of language may have only a remote connection with language behavior.

Lester argues that a transformational grammar is a deductive approach to language, as opposed to structural linguistics which used an inductive approach. In crude terms, a deductive approach begins with abstract rules

Reprinted with permission of the author and the National Council of Teachers of English from *College Composition and Communication*, Vol. XVIII, No. 5 (December), 1967, pp. 227–231.

and moves to tangible data to show the operation of these rules, whereas an inductive theory begins with data and works toward abstract generalizations about the data. In the transformational view, a child approaches the data of his language deductively, that is, he deduces a grammar for his own language from the innate general principles that must underlie all human languages. These abstract general principles are completely beyond his conscious awareness. The structural view is that the child discovers the patterns of his language in an inductive way. The transformational grammarians draw a distinction between competence and performance. Competence is the amazing linguistic capacity every speaker of a language possesses for his language. Performance is the tangible produce of competence. Lester claims that performance is the proper subject matter of the composition class because it can be discussed and compared with other performances. Competence is simply too abstract to grapple with. Lester's main point is that

> the complexity of human language competence is so vast that we can hardly expect our petty tinkering with the surface of performance to produce lasting results.

The balance of the essay is devoted to a slightly different topic. Lester notes that a student's level of verbal performance often seems to outstrip his level of written performance. If we assume that the same linguistic competence underlies both, the fact that the two levels of performance are not the same seems counter to the theory. Lester argues that the faults we find with student composition, "abrupt transitions, vague pronoun references, poor organization, unintended ambiguity" and the like, are characteristic of spoken communication, even by the most careful speakers. The point is that in conversation the speaker receives a feedback from the hearer which enables him to make the necessary corrections and explanations. Obviously, in written communication the writer seldom receives any immediate and continuous feedback from the reader. However, the writer does have the advantage of being able to rewrite at his leisure. Unless the writer is able to seize this advantage and comes to see his performance as the reader will see it, he will have great difficulty in communicating clearly. Lester claims that

> the writer's inability to project himself into the role of a reader is the single most important cause for the difference in levels of verbal and written performances.

Lester argues that there is a quite specific reason from the transformational point of view why it is so difficult for the writer to play the role of a reader. The structural linguist's view of the "chain of speech" was that the speaker encoded his message into language and transmitted the language through some physical vehicle—sound waves or marks on paper, as the case may be. The hearer/reader decoded the language from the vehicle in some inductive way and then discovered the message from the language.

The transformationalists, however, offer a completely different view of operations that the hearer/reader go through. Lester argues that

> the vehicle does not contain enough information to allow the receiver to abstract the language from the vehicle inductively.

Instead, they argue that the hearer/reader must impose an interpretation on the vehicle by some kind of matching process, that is, the hearer/reader matches his expectations, both linguistic and nonlinguistic, against the sound or marks he perceives. When his interpretation coincides with his preception of the vehicle, the resulting match is taken as the speaker's intended message. The key point here is that the role of the hearer/reader is not passive, but quite active. He is continually unconsciously testing and adjusting his own understanding. As a consequence of this view,

> when the sender and receiver are one and the same, the matching process is completely short-circuited; he does not need to perceive the words because he already knows the meaning. This is why it is almost impossible for a writer to see his essay the same way any other reader will. For the writer, the transitions are not abrupt, the pronoun references are perfectly clear, the organization is transparent, and there is no unintended ambiguity because he knows perfectly well what the sender's exact message is.

Lester closes the essay with a suggestion for a classroom trick to get across to students the magnitude of the problem of seeing their own writing as the reader will see it.

$$*$$

The value of transformational grammar as a theory of language is great and consequently it is a legitimate field of study in its own right. However, it is a moot question as to whether it has any direct value per se in the teaching of composition. We would all agree that the goal of composition teaching is to enable the student to write better. The value of transformational grammar must be measured in terms of that goal.

The fact that a goal is universally applauded does not, unfortunately, mean that it is universally understood. In fact, I see two quite different meanings of "better writing." One is better grammatically, that is, a paper that has fewer grammatical errors than a second paper is better written than the second. The other meaning is better stylistically, that is, if two papers are equally free from grammatical error, the one that is better organized and more fluent is better written than the other.

Composition classes often separate these two goals completely. Unfortunately, the first tends to drive out the second by a kind corollary to Gresham's Law: the tangible is preferred to the intangible. We have all had students in our freshman classes who got straight A's in their high school composition courses solely through the negative virtue of being able to write a sentence free of mechanical error. The fact that the students' papers were banal in content and incoherent in organization was never noticed by the harassed teacher who considered the assignment a success if the bulk of the essays were written on one side of the page.

Most teachers would justify teaching grammar on the grounds that its study would improve the student's ability to write a grammatical sentence. Unlike its predecessors, transformational grammar has been very wary about making any such claim. Eighteenth-century Latin grammars, nineteenth-century historical grammars, and twentieth-century structural grammars all claimed salutary benefits. These claims, however, when put to the test, have all proven false. There simply appears to be no correlation between a writer's conscious study of grammar and his ability to write. The claim is obviously false, for, if it were true, then all linguists would be great writers.

It could be argued, as each of the above grammars did about its predecessor, that because the newest form of grammar is so superior to the bad old grammars it will succeed where the others have failed. Having been led down the garden path three times before by linguists, I think composition teachers have the right to be suspicious of claims of utility until the usefulness has actually been demonstrated. Frank Zidonis at Ohio State University has been studying the effect of transformational grammar on the writing of junior high school children. His findings are encouraging, but far from conclusive.

On the college level, "better writing" generally means better stylistically. In the area of stylistic analysis, transformational grammar promises exciting things. Richard Ohmann's article in the December 1964 issue of *Word*, "Generative Grammars and the Concept of Literary Style," is impressive. In this article, Ohmann differentiates the style of several modern writers in terms of the characteristic way each combines kernel sentences. Henry James, for instance, relies on a self-embedding process, while D. H. Lawrence relies on deletion and

Faulkner on a piling up of kernel and near kernel sentences. In the following excerpt, Ohmann summarizes the basic idea of his approach.

A generative grammar with a transformational component provides apparatus for breaking down a sentence in a stretch of discourse into underlying kernel sentences (or strings, strictly speaking) and for specifying the grammatical operations that have been performed upon them. It also permits the analyst to construct, from the same set of kernel sentences, other non-kernel sentences. These may reasonably be thought of as *alternatives* to the original sentence, in that they are simply different constructs out of the identical elementary grammatical units. Thus the idea of alternative phrasings, which is crucial to the notion of style, has a clear analogue within the framework of a transformational grammar.

Does the application of transformational grammar to stylistic analysis justify the study of grammar in the composition class? I think that the answer must be No. Last year I was allowed to conduct an experimental class of first semester Freshman English using transformational grammar. At the end of the semester, I reluctantly reported that the experiment should not be repeated because, while in some ways the operation was a success, the patient had died.

The main difficulty with the course was a mechanical one: I was forced to use two-thirds of the semester teaching grammar. This did not leave much time to explore the applications of transformational grammar to grammatical and stylistic problems. By the ordinary measure, my students could not organize and write a theme as well as students in a rhetorically oriented section because we were left with almost no time to deal with rhetorical problems. The course was a success in that the students seemed to enjoy it, and they felt that they had gained a great deal from it in terms of their understanding of language. The fact remains that, however pleasant the side effects, the study of transformational grammar as an aid in teaching composition could not justify itself in terms of the time expended on the grammar.

Mechanical problems are amenable to mechanical solutions. The applications of transformational grammar could be studied in Freshman English if the responsibility for teaching it were pushed off onto the high school, the universal cure for all our problems. The high schools are, of course, totally unprepared to assume such a burden, and are so naive as to look to the colleges and universities for guidance.

Before committing ourselves to a massive retraining program of all English teachers, I think it is important to examine more carefully (1) what the basic concepts of transformational grammar are and

(2) what implication these concepts have for the pedagogical application of transformational grammar in general.

For the transformational grammarian, the study of language falls under the model of scientific explanation that has been called the "covering law model" by its originator, Rudolf Carnap. The essence of the covering law model is that an assertion can be proved only by its ability to predict data. Einstein verified his general theory of relativity by predicting that when a solar eclipse took place, the stars next to the sun, normally invisible because of the sun's light, would appear to shift over a few seconds of a degree.

The covering law model is essentially a deductive theory. Einstein deduced that, if his theory was correct, light would have mass and, as a further consequence, light would bend in the gravitational field of the sun. The covering law model says nothing about methods of data collection, nor does it inquire how the scientist got his idea in the first place. It may seem pointless to labor the definition of a deductive theory, but linguistics up to the publication of Chomsky's *Syntactic Structures* was dominated by a rigorously inductive model of scientific explanation. The profound differences between these two approaches to scientific theory are discussed brilliantly in Michael Polanyi's *Personal Knowledge*.

What a grammatical theory of a language must predict is the totality of all the grammatical sentences in the language, along with an analysis of each that can account for a native speaker's ability to recognize ambiguity and paraphrase. To do this, the transformational grammarian predicates the existence of a small number of element-like units, such as noun phrase, verb phrase, and transitive verb, which can combine in a large number of ways to form molecular units, or sentences.

The implications of this theory of grammar bear directly on the teaching of composition. For a child to learn to speak, he must have the innate capacity of building a theory of his own language that enables him to generate and understand an infinite number of new sentences. This theory is built without conscious effort, without external rewards or punishments, and without any necessary instruction from the adult community. This amazing linguistic capacity or competence is apparently the birthright of every normal child.

Miller, Galanter and Pribram in their highly respected book, *Plans and the Structure of Behavior*, argue that our conscious minds are almost totally ignorant of how or by what steps or processes we perform any complex process or skill. In other words, the performance of a skill involves innate competencies beyond our conscious knowledge and control. A poet can no more describe how he actually writes a poem than Willie Mays can tell how he actually hits a curve ball. This strongly suggests that there is little hope that by teaching a student conscious grammatical rules we can affect his unconscious grammatical processes.

Transformational grammar has thus clearly separated innate language competence from actual language performance. Only the performance is tangible. In composition classes we can discuss it, evaluate its success or failure, and compare it with similar performances. This seems to me the proper study of composition. Competence, on the other hand, like the part of the iceberg below the surface, is always there, but is never visible.

All too often, however, composition classes try to deal with competence. Students are assigned books of logic in order that they may learn to think straight. They are given rhetorical forms in which to channel their thoughts (which have assumedly already been properly straightened by the study of logic). They are given methods of composing, such as outlining their essays before they begin writing. The fallacy here, of course, is that logic and rhetoric are conscious processes of analysis that can be applied only to the performance *ex post facto*.

Assuming that the logical and rhetorical faults in the student's performance have been called to his conscious attention, we cannot thereby guarantee that this conscious instruction will in any way affect the student's basic competence. And unless the level of competence is altered, the student's performance next week will be about the same as it was this week. It may seem the counsel of despair to say that, if we cannot improve the student's writing, at least we do it no harm, but even this sorry consolation may not be true. Albert Kitzhaber reported in his book *Themes, Theories, and Therapy: The Teaching of Writing in College* that college sophomores at Dartmouth, on the average, wrote slightly worse than they did as entering freshmen, but by the time they had become seniors their writing had noticeably deteriorated from its pre-college peak. The point, stated more seriously, is that the complexity of human language competence is so vast that we can hardly expect our petty tinkering with the surface of performance to produce lasting results.

There is at least one area, nevertheless, where I think transformational grammar can be very helpful to the composition teacher. We have all noticed that the level of some students' verbal performance is much higher than the level of their written performance. This seems all the more puzzling since we have assumed that the same basic language competence underlies both.

From the standpoint of the communications engineer, however, the two situations are quite different. In conversation the speaker's language is riddled with abrupt transitions, vague pronoun references, poor organization, unintended ambiguity and all the other faults we find in his written work. Unless the speaker is grossly inept, this verbal stumbling does not block communication; in fact, the hearer usually notices very little of it. What makes communication possible in this situation is the ability of the speaker to gauge the reaction of the hearer. He can tell when the hearer is puzzled and can make further explanations. He continually readjusts the rate of information. In short, he relies on the phenomenon called feedback.

In writing, the situation is reversed. The writer has the opportunity to pick and choose his words at leisure, to rewrite as much as he wants; but he has no feedback from the reader at all. The task of the writer, then, is to compensate for his loss of feedback by anticipating the reader's reactions. This in turn demands that the writer can see his performance as the reader will see it. I believe that the writer's inability to project himself into the role of a reader is the single most important cause for the difference in levels of verbal and written performances.

Transformational grammar offers some suggestion why this role reversal is so difficult for the writer. All grammatical theories agree, at least in general, that the communication process involves a message, a language of some sort, a vehicle to carry the language, a sender and a receiver. There is also a general agreement about the sender's part of the communication process. The sender encodes the message into language and then encodes the language onto some physical vehicle—usually either sound waves or marks on paper. This is a model of behavior; the actual process, of course, is almost totally unconscious.

There is no general agreement on the model for the process that the receiver uses to decode the message. Structural linguistics committed itself to a model that predicates a sequential decoding. That is, the receiver completely decoded the language from the vehicle before decoding the message from the language. Transformational grammarians have gone to a great deal of effort to prove that this inductive model cannot be literally true. Chomsky, it seems to me, has demonstrated beyond doubt that the vehicle does not contain enough information to allow the receiver to abstract the language from the vehicle inductively.

The transformationalist's model is that the receiver continually operates both inductively in stripping the language from the vehicle and deductviely in generating the language from what the receiver predicts the message to be. Thus there is a kind of matching process in operation at the level of language: the receiver fits together the information from the vehicle and the information from the supposed message. When the fit is poor, the receiver must readjust either his understanding of the vehicle or his projection of the message, or both. This model is important for the composition teacher because it casts the reader into a very active role; he must continually match expectation against perception. As Kant said, "Ideas without content are empty, observations without concepts are blind."

The pedagogical corollary of this theory is that when the sender and receiver are one and the same, the matching process is completely short-circuited; he does not need to perceive the words because he already knows the meaning. This is why it is almost impossible for a writer to see his essay the same way any other reader will. For the writer, the transitions are not abrupt, the pronoun references are perfectly clear, the organization is transparent, and there is no unintended ambiguity because he knows perfectly well what the sender's exact message is.

I might mention here a classroom trick that seems helpful in getting students to realize the magnitude of this problem. I present a student essay one sentence at a time. I then ask members of the class to predict what the next sentence will be about and how he is able to make that prediction. Then I show the sentence the student actually wrote. The frequent contrast between prediction and reality is a source of fruitful discussion. I hope by this means to enable the class to see each sentence as a link in a gradually unfolding chain of ideas and relations. In a good essay each sentence adds to the reader's store of information and enables him to predict even more accurately the next sentence.

To return to the original question of this paper, the study of transformational grammar in a composition class cannot be justified until it can be demonstrated that the study of grammatical competence will affect grammatical performance. I have also suggested some reasons why this demonstration may be a long time in coming. The application of transformational grammar to stylistic analysis is promising, but the exploitation of this possibility is entirely dependent upon the study of transformational grammar in high school.

The great value of transformational grammar, it seems to me, is not for the student, but for the teacher of composition. Every decision the teacher makes is a reflection of an assumption that the teacher has tacitly made about the nature of language. The more the teacher is made aware of these assumptions and of their consequences the better he can assess their validity. Without this assessment, the teacher is condemned to a treadmill existence: forever changing texts and techniques, but never getting anywhere.

SECOND LANGUAGE TEACHING

LEONARD NEWMARK

Grammatical Theory and the Teaching of English as a Foreign Language

INTRODUCTION

Newmark begins by drawing a distinction between two different ways of language teaching. In one way, the teaching material is organized and taught on the basis of the structure of the language. The other way, the "natural" or "direct" way, subordinates linguistic concerns to teaching "natural utterances that living people would use to say what they actually might want to say."

We tend to think of traditional language teaching as belonging to the first way and the linguistic approach to language teaching as belonging to the second. Newmark points out that as time has past, the language materials produced by structural linguists have become more and more concerned with structural habits and less and less concerned with language in context. The result, according to Newmark, is that

> both traditional and structural textbooks select and organize material in the interests of a particular view of the principles governing linguistic form, and both isolate linguistic forms from natural contexts.

Reprinted with permission of the author from *The 1963 Conference Papers of the English Language Section of the National Association for Foreign Affairs*, ed. by David P. Harris, pp. 5–8.

With the advent of transformational grammar, language teachers have a powerful new view of the structure of English, and are tempted to employ this new view in their textbooks. Newmark suggests three ways in which transformational grammar tempts the language teacher.

1. Transformational grammar, at least in some areas, offers a description of English which is a genuine explanation rather than a display of data, and consequently the language teacher is tempted to include these areas in his teaching. Also, since transformational grammar is able to deal with more than just surface structures, it has a great advantage in constructing contrastive grammars to explain the differences and similarities between the first and second languages.

2. It is a temptation for the structure of a transformational grammar to be used as a model for the organization of the language course. For example, the sequence of material taught might follow the order of the rules in the grammar. Specifically, the language course might (a) teach kernel sentences first, and then the ways that kernels can be expanded; (b) teach new vocabulary only in the kernel sentence, since that is the entry point for lexical items in the grammar; and (c) delay teaching phonology, the last stage in the cycle of rules in a transformational grammar, until a relatively late point in the language program.

3. The language teacher is tempted to use transformational grammar because its psychological and pedagogical implications seem desirable. Newmark gives three instances: (a) transformational drills are easy to write and easy to use in the classroom; (b) transformational grammar does not place such great emphasis on the sound system per se. In particular, this allows the language teacher to de-emphasize the role of suprasegmental features; and (c) the transformational grammarian is interested in the same thing that the language teacher is—"the intuitive ability of the speakers of a language to generate new sentences." Furthermore, the rules of a transformational grammar are "dynamic and prescriptive, in a sense acceptable to language teachers."

Newmark concludes the article by returning to his original point: the duty of a language teacher is to teach the student to use the language in a natural way, not to teach linguistic forms in a synthetic way. Consequently, Newmark warns the language teacher against the temptation of misusing transformational grammar the way structural linguistics was misused. Newmark says that "the whole question of the utility of grammatical analysis for language teaching needs to be reopened." He concludes with three facts that support his position: (1) systematic attention to grammatical form is neither necessary nor sufficient for successful language learning; (2) teaching language in meaningful and usable contexts is both sufficient

and necessary for successful language learning; and (3) the formal properties of sentences do not reflect "relationships of meaningful use," and consequently, teaching formal relations is "incompatible with the only necessary
and sufficient method we know has succeeded for every speaker of a
language."

*

A great contribution of linguists to the teaching of foreign language
was made by the "liberal" nineteenth- and twentieth-century grammarians like Otto Jespersen who taught us to view natural languages
freshly as worthy objects of teaching: the liberal grammarians freed
us from a tradition of teaching artificial sentences constructed and
studied as illustrations of rules of formal grammar, and they urged
that we teach natural utterances that living people would use to say
what they actually might want to say. Various "natural" or "direct"
methods had grown and continued to grow out of such discontent with
traditional language teaching. When structural linguists first faced the
problem of developing methods to teach exotic languages, and later
languages like English, they maintained this "natural" emphasis on
teaching concrete uses of language.

But as structuralists grew more and more confident about the "scientific" analysis of language, they modified their teaching programs more
and more to reflect these analyses: phonemic drills and structural pattern drills were increasingly elevated from the minor role they played
in the early Army language courses to the major role they play in, say,
the Michigan English Language Institute textbooks or in recent FSI
books. This increase in pattern drill is an index of the return from
"natural" material to grammatical-illustration material.* In the traditional textbook the examples seem to be given largely for the sake of
an intellectual understanding of the formulated rules, while in the
newer structural textbook the examples are practiced on to instill
implicit "habits" whose formulation in rules may not even be presented
explicitly; but both traditional and structural textbooks select and

---

* I am, of course, aware of the vast differences between the older tradition and
the newer structural tradition in the number and selection of the illustrative
examples, the use to which these examples are put, and the underlying grammar
which the examples are selected to illustrate. Nevertheless, I see an important
similarity in the kind of systematicness which both orthodoxies take as being the
guiding principle of language teaching: whether given the name "structural
habits" or "rules of grammar," the systematicness is primarily one of formal construction rather than appropriateness of use.

organize material in the interests of a particular view of the principles governing linguistic form, and both isolate linguistic forms from natural contexts.

Now that we have a new view—that presented by transformational grammars—of the principles (or, if you like, the habits or rules) governing the formal properties of English sentences,[†] there are great temptations to write new language textbooks to reflect this view. The temptations tempt in several ways:[‡]

First, on the premise that the best description of a language affords the best base upon which to build a language-teaching program, the transformational grammar of English should appeal to authors of TEFL materials. In an important sense transformational grammar is the most promising response we have to our common desire for descriptions that explain rather than merely display language data. For example, the transformationalist's derivation of imperative sentences from underlying strings with *you* as subject and *will* as the modal auxiliary makes possible an explanation of many things—from the traditional intuition about the understood *you* in imperatives to the fact (unexplained by orthodox structural linguists) that the "interrogative tags" on the imperative are *won't you* or *will you*. In general, the transformationist's analysis of verb phrase constructions, beginning with Chomsky's simple C(M) (have + en) (be + ing) V formula, brings startling simplicity and clarity to our understanding of the

---

[†] What I have to say bears most clearly on English, since that is the language for which the most detailed set of generative rules has been formulated, but I see no particular characteristics of other languages that would militate against the validity of the position I take in the following discussion.

[‡] The most recent statement of the attractions of transformational grammar as a base for teaching foreign languages has been made by Karl V. Teeter in his review of Elinor C. Horne's *Beginning Javanese* in *Language* 39.146–151 (1963). Other tentative suggestions about the bearing of transformational grammar on the learning of languages have been offered by Yehoshua Bar-Hillel, "Third Lecture: Language and Speech; Theory vs. Observation in Linguistics," in *Four Lectures on Algebraic Linguistics and Machine Translation* (an unpublished series of lectures given in July 1962, before a NATO Advanced Summer Institute on Automatic Translation of Languages in Venice, Italy), Noam Chomsky, "Explanatory Models in Linguistics," *Logic, Methodology and Philosophy of Science: Proceedings of the* 1960 *International Congress*, edited by E. Nagel, P. Suppes, and A. Tarski, 1962, pp. 529–531, Richard Gunter, "A Problem in Transformational Teaching," *Language Learning* XI. 119–124 (1961), Mary S. Temperley, "Transformations in *English Sentence Patterns*," *Language Learning* XI. 125–134 (1961), to mention only a few. Textbooks in the teaching of English as a foreign language have been written and used by B. Kirk Rankin, III, and John J. Kane, Jr., *Review Exercises in English Grammar*, Washington, D. C., 1962, and Paul Roberts (reported in *The Linguistic Reporter* IV, No. 6, December 1962). I have not had the opportunity to examine the latter, but the former makes the application I allude to below.

grammatical structure of a number of discontinuous and elliptical verb constructions; transformational grammar seems to offer suggestions neatly and precisely for what a program for teaching English verb structure would have to include.

If contrastive grammars of native language with target language are assumed to be required for optimal planning of EFL materials, then it should seem obvious that the explicitness of generative grammars for each language is necessary for making explicit comparisons between two languages. A generative grammar has the advantage of showing not only the direct and superficial, physically manifest similarities and differences between two languages, but also the more profound differences and similarities between languages that appear when the rules of sentence formation are required to be explicitly formulated.

The second temptation I want to talk about derives from the fact that the grammar of English contains an *ordering* of rules. It seems to follow naturally that a teaching program follow the order of the rules, so that a student would learn grammatically prior rules (or habits) before grammatically later ones. Thus, he might learn the rules that generate sentences with noun objects (e.g. *I like her cake*) before he learns rules that generate sentences with nominalizations as objects (e.g. *I like her singing*); or he might learn in a general way that verbs may have objects before he learns the rules which permit him to distinguish which classes of verbs may have which classes of objects.

On a grander scale, we might even suggest specifically that an elementary EFL course limit itself to teaching only kernel sentences and that only in intermediate and advanced courses would sentences involving optional transformations be introduced. The pedagogical rationale here would be that teaching should proceed from grammatically simpler to more complex, inasmuch as this can be expected to agree with the psychological direction of less difficult to more difficult; few educators would disagree that progression from easy to difficult is important to gain efficiency in learning and to reduce the frustration of failure. That grammatical simplicity might be an index of psychological easiness has been suggested by a number of respectable linguists and psychologists.[§]

§ See Bar-Hillel, *op. cit.*, "Second Lecture: Syntactic Complexity"; Noam Chomsky and George Miller, "Finitary Models of Language Users," *Handbook of Mathematical Psychology* (in press), cited in Bar-Hillel lecture above; and Teeter, *op. cit.* and references cited in these articles for discussion of the suggestion.

Such a precise non-arbitrary notion of what constitutes simplicity in language would afford an attractive alternative to the superficial kind of grading of teaching materials that we have seen so often in textbooks. The ordering of rules and sets of rules that characterize a transformational grammar seems to offer for the first time a grammatically motivated principle for ordering the presentation of sentences.‖

Three particular ordering characteristics of present transformational grammars have especial appeal for English language teachers:

a. The position of transformational rules after phrase-structure rules in the grammar suggests the possibility of teaching a finite manageable set of elementary constructions first, then teaching the ways in which modification and combination of these elementary constructions can add the infinite set of possible sentences that any speaker of a language has at his disposal.

b. Since lexical vocabulary is introduced in a transformational grammar by phrase-structure rules only, an apparent theoretical justification seems to be offered for teaching new vocabulary in simple kernel sentences, without complicating the teaching of vocabularly by teaching new sentence patterns at the same time, and vice versa. The grammatical and semantic properties (e.g. mass vs. count nouns) of vocabulary, then, might be introduced economically at one time, and only for the simplest constructions.

c. The fact that the detailed phonological rules# come late in the grammar suggests that attention to the details of pronunciation might be left until relatively late in a foreign language teaching program. Note that such delay in teaching "a good accent" is at sharp variance with the attitudes of most applied linguists today, but is in good agreement with our common sense feeling that it is more important to be able to speak a language fluently and to say a lot of things in it than to have marvelous pronunciation but not know what to say. The relative lateness of phonological rules in a transformational grammar helps account for the fact that we can often understand a foreign speaker even when he lacks most of the phonological habits of English; if we

---

‖ The grading referred to in such techniques as those summarized in Anne Cochran, *Modern Methods of Teaching English as a Foreign Language,* Washing-D.C., 1952, Chapter 5, has largely been based on frequency counts, and those mostly of vocabulary. Frequency counts, if they have any application at all to language teaching, reflect degree of usefulness rather than degree of difficulty. For example, notice that students have very little difficulty learning taboo words in a language, in spite of their low frequency of use.

Not the morpheme-structure rules, however, which may precede the transformational rules. See M. Halle, "Questions of Linguistics," *Nuovo Cimento* XIII 494–517, (1959), and N. Chomsky, "Explanatory Models in Linguistics."

attempt to follow the order of grammatical rules in teaching simple before complex sentences, by the same token we should teach meaningful sentences before we worry much about teaching their proper pronunciation.

The third set of reasons for finding transformational grammar attractive for language teaching are psychological and pedagogical.

a. Most obvious, transformational drills are easy to construct and easy to operate in class. The fact that the transformational grammar of English calls for the derivation of, for example, interrogatives from underlying statements seems to justify the conversion practices that have been with us since traditional days.

b. In the treatment of phonological facts, transformational grammars have a strong appeal to the practical language teacher, in a way that orthodox structural grammars could not match. For one thing, the psychological reality of phonemes has been more convincingly demonstrated for phonemes thought of in the Sapir-Chomsky sense than in the Twaddell-Bloch sense; language teachers will appreciate that somehow the phonemes that represent sentences may be present in a student's rendition even when their proper allophones are not, and this seems more in accord with a theory that presents phonemes as indices of higher grammatical strings rather than as classes of physical phenomena. Language teachers will probably also welcome the transformational deemphasis of suprasegmental features which Trager-Smith structuralists have considered so basic for syntactic analysis and for teaching languages.

c. Less obvious, the goals of generative grammar themselves seem to offer more to the language teacher than those of orthodox structuralism do. Language teachers will be particularly sympathetic to the desire of the generative grammarian to explain the intuitive ability of the speakers of a language to generate new sentences. The generative grammarian tries to state explicitly what constitutes the *Sprachgefühl* of the native speaker; what is "ungrammatical" about utterances to a generative grammarian is roughly equivalent to what is "foreign" to a language teacher.

His interest in the generation of new sentences leads the generative grammarian to present his description of a language as a set of rules for the composition of sentences. The attention paid to *sentences* rather than to *words* is much welcomed by the language teacher, who has known for a long time about the practical necessity to teach the language in units of usable size, but who has had to use grammars whose descriptive strength all lay in their morphology and phonology, rather than syntax, sections. And the presentation of a grammar as an ordered set of rules is a welcome relief from the collections of inventories that constitute an orthodox structural grammar; the rules of generative grammar seem dynamic and prescriptive, in a sense acceptable to language teachers, rather than statically descriptive, as the taxonomic schemes of orthodox structural grammars are.

Since my purpose here was to sketch the appeals of transformational theory, I have not and will not go into a long excursus on why I think all these appeals are deceptive, all wrong, for the language teacher, but I must say at least a few words here on the matter. If the assumptions that underlie the application of grammatical description of languages to the teaching of those languages are granted—and they have never even been stated in a testable form—then I think some of the characteristics I have alluded to above afford legitimate reasons for preferring transformational over orthodox structural grammars.** But I would maintain that those assumptions should not be granted, and that the whole question of the utility of grammatical analysis for language teaching needs to be reopened. I want only to suggest here how I expect the question to be answered.

From the largest body of empirical evidence we can imagine—take all native learners vs. all "taught" learners—we can induce three evident facts.

1. Systematic attention to the grammatical form of utterances is neither a necessary condition nor a sufficient one for successful language learning. That it is not necessary is demonstrated by the native learner's success without it. That it is not sufficient is demonstrated by the typical classroom student's lack of success with it.

2. Teaching particular utterances in contexts which provide meaning and usability to learners is both sufficient (witness the native learner) and necessary (witness the classroom learner). Until meaning is associated with the utterance, the learner cannot use what he has learned. And when he has meaningful control over particular utterances, he will extend that control to new utterances without benefit of much practice.

3. Systematic teaching of formal relations (e.g. question-underlying statement [rather than question-answer] or active-passive) does not

---

** Even if we were to grant those assumptions we should suspect the kinds of direct application of grammatical theory to language teaching that were implied in my preceding discussion. For example, the ordering of rules in a generative grammar does not correspond in any obvious way to the production of speech. In fact we would find it silly indeed to delay teaching a student to produce an actual sentence until we had taught him the very great number of rules (including the final phonological rules) that a transformational grammar would claim to underlie that sentence.

reflect relationships of meaningful use. Thus, planning of lessons that is based on formal properties of sentences is incompatible with the only necessary and sufficient method we know has succeeded for every speaker of a language.

Transformational grammar offers the best account to date of the formal properties of sentences. When we make statements about those formal properties of English I think we are well-advised to make use of the insights offered by transformational grammar. But as TEFL's we should not allow *any* analysis of the formal properties of language to take priority over our duty to teach our students to use a language. Like the liberal grammarians before us, we should liberate language teaching from grammatical theory, and should teach the natural use of language rather than the synthetic composition of sentences.

LEONARD NEWMARK

How Not to Interfere
with Language Learning

INTRODUCTION

The main theme of the article is that much language teaching emphasizes
the mastery of linguistic form at the expense of the purpose of learning a
foreign language in the first place: the ability of the learner to say what
he wants in the second language. According to Newmark, modern foreign
language teaching has been dominated by two sets of ideas: (1) structural
linguistics and (2) reinforcement theory psychology. Applied linguistics
has made much of the importance of language interference. In this view,
the linguistic habits the speaker has learned for his first language will
interfere with his establishing the new habits necessary for speaking a
second language. As Newmark puts it

> linguists . . . consider the task of learning a new language as if it were
> essentially a task of fighting off an old set of structures in order to
> clear the way for a new set.

Reinforcement theory psychology has led

Reprinted with permission of the author from the *International Journal of American Linguistics,* Vol. 32, No. 1, Part II (January), 1966, pp. 77–83.

to programmed instruction, step-by-step instruction based in practice on the identification of what are taken to be the components of the terminal verbal behavior.

Newmark describes modern language teaching as

the marriage of linguistics and psychology in the programmed instruction of foreign languages, with linguistics providing the "systematic specification of terminal behaviors" and psychology providing "the techniques of the laboratory analysis and control of those behaviors."

In reply to the linguist's concern with language interference, Newmark argues that first language interference or a "foreign accent" is the natural result of the speaker's lack of knowledge about English. The learner is being asked to perform before he is able to control English, and consequently he pads his performance with material "from what he already knows, that is, his own language." Newmark concludes the argument on this point by saying,

seen in this light, the cure for interference is simply the cure for ignorance: learning. There is no particular need to combat the intrusion of the learner's native language—the explicit or implicit justification for the contrastive analysis that applied linguists have been claiming to be necessary for planning language-teaching courses.

In reference to the views of reinforcement-theory psychology, Newmark says that the consequence of this position is that English is taught as if it were "additive and linear," that is, each item is taught one at a time in contrastive drills, proceeding from the simplest to the complex, and each connected to a specified stimuli. Newmark argues that if this were really an accurate picture of the way we learn, "the child learner would be old before he could say a single appropriate thing and the adult learner would be dead." Furthermore, such teaching ignores the need of the user to speak correctly, but with understanding.

. . . we want the learner to be able to use the language we teach him, and we want him to be able to extend his ability to new cases, to create new utterances that are appropriate to his needs as a language user.

Newmark argues that language acquisition is not simply "additive and linear"; language is learned in whole chunks in a real context. He says that

we have always known how to teach other human beings to use a language: use it ourselves and let them imitate us as best they can at the time . . . language is learned a whole act at a time rather than learned as an assemblage of constituent skills.

Newmark then shows what a program based on the principles would look like. One way to put language into a real context is to create a dramatic situation in the classroom. The teacher can introduce variation into the situation. The variation will cause the situation to be re-enacted, for instance, a student could play the role of being a dissatisfied customer rather than a satisfied one.

$$*$$

In the applied linguistics of the past twenty years much has been made of the notion of first-language interference with second-language learning. Our dominant conception of languages as structures and our growing sophistication in the complex analysis of these structures have made it increasingly attractive to linguists to consider the task of learning a new language as if it were essentially a task of fighting off an old set of structures in order to clear the way for a new set. The focal emphasis of language teaching by applied linguists has more and more been placed on structural drills based on the linguist's contrastive analysis of the structures of the learner's language and his target language: the weight given to teaching various things is determined not by their importance to the user of the language, but by their degree of difference from what the analyst takes to be corresponding features of the native language.

A different analysis of verbal behavior has been motivated in psychology by reinforcement theory; the application of this analysis has led, of course, to programmed instruction, step-by-step instruction based in practice on the identification of what are taken to be the components of the terminal verbal behavior. What could be more natural than the marriage of linguistics and psychology in the programmed instruction of foreign languages, with linguistics providing the "systematic specification of terminal behaviors" and psychology providing "the techniques of the laboratory analysis and control" of those behaviors.*

If the task of learning to speak English were additive and linear, as present linguistic and psychological discussions suggest it is, it is difficult to see how anyone could learn English. If each phonological and syntactic rule, each complex of lexical features, each semantic value and stylistic nuance—in short, if each item which the linguist's analysis leads him to identify had to be acquired one at a time, pro-

* Harlan Lane, "Programmed Learning of a Second Language," IRAL 2. 250, 1964.

ceeding from simplest to most complex, and then each had to be connected to specified stimuli or stimulus sets, the child learner would be old before he could say a single appropriate thing and the adult learner would be dead. If each frame of a self-instructional program could teach only one item (or even two or three) at a time, programmed language instruction would never enable the students to use the language significantly. The item-by-item contrastive drills proposed by most modern applied linguists and the requirement by programmers that the behaviors to be taught must be specified seem to rest on this essentially hopeless notion of the language learning process.

When linguists and programmers talk about planning their textbooks, they approach the problem as if they had to decide what structural features each lesson should be trying to teach. The whole program will teach the sum of its parts: the student will know this structure and that one and another and another. . . . If the question is put to him directly, the linguist will undoubtedly admit that the sum of the structures he can describe is not equal to the capability a person needs in order to use the language, but the question is rarely put to him directly. If it is, he may evade the uncomfortable answer by appealing to the intelligence of the user to apply the structures he knows to an endless variety of situations. But the evasion fails, I think, against the inescapable fact that a person, even an intelligent one, who knows perfectly the structures that the linguist teaches, cannot know that the way to get his cigarette lit by a stranger when he has no matches is to walk up to him and say one of the utterances "Do you have a light?" or "Got a match?" (Not one of the equally well-formed questions, "Do you have fire?" or "Do you have illumination?" or "Are you a match's owner?").

In natural foreign language learning—the kind used, for example, by children to become native speakers in a foreign country within a length of time that amazes their parents—acquisition cannot be simply additive; complex bits of language are learned a whole chunk at a time. Perhaps by some process of stimulus sampling[†] the parts of the chunks are compared and become available for use in new chunks. The possible number of "things known" in the language exponentiates as the number of chunks increases additively, since every complex chunk makes available a further analysis of old chunks into new elements, each still attached to the original context upon which its appropriateness depends.

† I take the term and notion from W. K. Estes, "Learning Theory," *Annual Review of Psychology* 13. 110, 1962.

It is not that linguists and psychologists are unaware of the possibility of learning language in complex chunks or of the importance of learning items in contexts. Indeed it would be difficult to find a serious discussion of new language teaching methods that did not claim to reform old language teaching methods in part through the use of "natural" contexts. It is rather that consideration of the details supplied by linguistic and psychological analysis has taken attention away from the exponential power available in learning in natural chunks. In present psychologically oriented programs the requirement that one specify the individual behaviors to be reinforced leads (apparently inevitably) to an artificial isolation of parts from wholes; in structurally oriented textbooks and courses, contrastive analysis leads to structural drills designed to teach a set of specific "habits" for the well-formation of utterances, abstracted from normal social context.

Our very knowledge of the fine structure of language constitutes a threat to our ability to maintain perspective in teaching languages. Inspection of language textbooks designed by linguists reveals an increasing emphasis in recent years on structural drills in which pieces of language are isolated from the linguistic and social contexts which make them meaningful and useful to the learner. The more we know about a language, the more such drills we have been tempted to make. If one compares, say, the Spoken Language textbooks devised by linguists during the Second World War with some of the recent textbooks devised by linguists,‡ he is struck by the shift in emphasis from connected situational dialogue to disconnected structural exercise.

The argument of this paper is that such isolation and abstraction of the learner from the contexts in which that language is used constitutes serious interference with the language learning process. Because it requires the learner to attach new responses to old stimuli, this kind of interference may in fact increase the interference that applied linguists like to talk about—the kind in which a learner's previous language structures are said to exert deleterious force on the structures being acquired.

Consider the problem of teaching someone to say something. What is it we are most concerned that he learn? Certainly not the mere mouthing of the utterance, the mere ability to pronounce the words. Certainly not the mere demonstration of ability to understand the utterance by, say, translation into the learner's own language. Even the combination of the two goals is not what we are after: it is not

‡ For example, see Dwight L. Bolinger et al., *Modern Spanish*, Harcourt, Brace & Co., 1960; L. B. Swift et al., *Igbo: Basic Course*, Foreign Service Institute, 1962; John J. Gumperz and June Rumery, *Conversational Hindi-Urdu*, n.p., 1962.

saying *and* understanding that we want but saying *with* understanding. That is, we want the learner to be able to use the language we teach him, and we want him to be able to extend his ability to new cases, to create new utterances that are appropriate to his needs as a language user.

Recent linguistic theory has offered a detailed abstract characterization of language competence; learning a finite set of rules and a finite lexicon enables the learner to produce and interpret an infinite number of new well-formed sentences. Plausible detailed accounts also abound in the psychological and philosophical literature to explain how formal repertoires might be linked referentially to the real world. But the kinds of linguistic rules that have been characterized so far (syntactic, phonological, and semantic) bear on the question of well-formedness of sentences, not on the question of appropriateness of utterances. And the stimulus-response or associational- or operant-conditioning accounts that help explain how *milk* comes to mean "milk" are of little help in explaining my ability to make up a particular something appropriate to say about milk—such as *I prefer milk*—in a discussion of what one likes in his coffee, and even less my ability to ignore the mention of milk when it is staring me in the face. An important test of our success as language teachers, it seems reasonable to assert, is the ability of our students to choose to say what they want. It has been difficult for linguists and psychologists to attach any significance to the expression "saying what you want to say"; our inability to be precise about the matter may well have been an important reason for our neglect of it in language teaching. But importance of a matter is not measured by our ability at a given moment to give a precise description of it: we can be precise about the allophones of voiceless stops in English after initial /s/, but it seems absurd to claim that it is basically as important—some textbooks imply *more* important—to teach students to make these allophones properly as it is to teach them, for example, how to get someone to repeat something he has just said.

The odd thing is that despite our ignorance as experts, as human beings we have always known how to teach other human beings to use a language: use it ourselves and let them imitate us as best they can at the time. Of course, this method has had more obvious success with children than with adult learners, but we have no compelling reason to believe with either children or adults that the method is not both necessary and sufficient to teach a language.

If we adopt the position I have been maintaining—that language is learned a whole act at a time rather than learned as an assemblage of constituent skills—what would a program for teaching students to speak a foreign language look like?[§]

For the classroom, the simple formulation that the students learn by imitating someone else using the language needs careful development. Since the actual classroom is only one small piece of the world in which we expect the learner to use the language, artificial means must be used to transform it into a variety of other pieces: the obvious means for performing this transformation is drama—imaginative play has always been a powerful educational device both for children and adults. By creating a dramatic situation in a classroom—in part simply by acting out dialogues, but also in part by relabeling objects and people in the room (supplemented by realia if desired) to prepare for imaginative role-playing—the teacher can expand the classroom indefinitely and provide imaginatively natural contexts for the language being used.

The idea of using models as teachers is hardly new in applied linguistics; and nothing could be more commonplace than the admonition that the model be encouraged to dramatize and the student to imitate the dramatization of the situation appropriate to the particular bit of language being taught. The sad fact is, however, that the drill material the model has been given to model has intrinsic features that draw the attention of the student away from the situation and focus it on the form of the utterance. Instead of devising techniques that induce the model to act out roles for the student to imitate, the applied linguist has devised techniques of structural drill that put barriers in the way of dramatic behavior and a premium on the personality-less manipulation of a formal repertoire of verbal behavior.

If what the learner observes is such that he cannot absorb it completely within his short-term memory, he will make up for his deficiency if he is called on to perform before he has learned the new behavior by padding with material from what he already knows, that is, his own language. This padding—supplying what is known to make up for what is not known—is the major source of "interference," the major reason for "foreign accents." Seen in this light, the cure for interference is simply the cure for ignorance: learning. There is no particular need to combat the intrusion of the learner's native language—the explicit or implicit justification for the contrastive analysis

§ I shall restrict myself here to the question of teaching a spoken foreign language. How one teaches people to read and write a foreign language depends on their literacy in another language and on their mastery of the spoken language in which they are learning to be literate. The problems involved would take me too far afield of the subject I am discussing here.

that applied linguists have been claiming to be necessary for planning language-teaching courses. But there is need for controlling the size of the chunks displayed for imitation. In general if you want the learner's imitation to be more accurate, make the chunks smaller; increase the size of the chunks as the learner progresses in his skill in imitation. We do not need to impose arbitrary, artificial criteria for successful behavior on the part of the learner. If we limit our demand for immediate high quality of production, we may well find that his behavior is adequately shaped by the same *ad hoc* forces that lead a child from being a clumsy performer capable of using his language only with a terribly inaccurate accent, and in a limited number of social situations, to becoming a skillful native speaker capable of playing a wide variety of social roles with the appropriate language for each.

To satisfy our requirement that the student learn to extend to new cases the ability he gains in acting out one role, a limited kind of structural drill can be used: keeping in mind that the learning must be embedded in a meaningful context, the drill may be constructed by introducing small variations into the situation being acted out (e.g., ordering orange juice instead of tomato juice, being a dissatisfied customer rather than a satisfied one, changing the time at which the the action takes place) which call for partial innovation in the previously learned role. In each case the situation should be restaged, reenacted, played as meaning something to the student.

The student's craving for explicit formulization of generalizations can usually be met better by textbooks and grammars that he reads outside class than by discussion in class. If discussion of grammar is made into a kind of dramatic event, however, such discussion might be used as the situation being learned—with the students learning to play the role of students in a class on grammar. The important point is that the study of grammar as such is neither necessary nor sufficient for learning to use a language.

So far, I have been talking about the use of live models in language classrooms. How can such techniques be adapted for self-instruction? The cheapness and simplicity of operation of the new videotape recorders already make possible a large portion of the acquisition of a language without the presence of a model; it has been shown convincingly that under the proper conditions it is possible for human students to learn—in the sense of acquiring competence—certain very complex behaviors by mere observation of that behavior in use.‖

‖ For an excellent discussion of the roles of imitation and reinforcement in the acquisition and performance of complex behavior, see Albert Bandura and Richard H. Walters, *Social Learning and Personality Development*, Holt, Rinehart and Winston, 1963.

Acquiring the willingness to perform—learning in a second sense—seems to depend to a greater extent on reinforcement of the student's own behavior and is thus not quite so amenable to instruction without human feedback at the present time. However, extension of techniques (originally developed to establish phonological competence in step-by-step programmed instruction)# for self-monitoring to cover whole utterances with their appropriate kinetic accompaniment may suffice in the future to make the second kind of learning as independent of live teachers as the first and thus make complete self-instruction in the use of a language possible.

For example, the techniques used in Stanley Sapon's *Spanish A*, in the TEMAC series for Encyclopedia Britannica Films, 1961.

LEONARD NEWMARK
DAVID A. REIBEL

Necessity and Sufficiency in Language Learning

INTRODUCTION

This article is divided into two sections. In Section I the authors take the position that the adult learner of a second language acquires the second language in much the same way that he acquired his first language. In Section II the authors present and discuss four possible arguments against their position.

Section I begins with the assertion that linguists have shifted the emphasis in language teaching "from mastery of language use to mastery of language structure." Consequently, the linguist has assumed that learning takes place because of the contribution of the structuring of the material. The authors take the view that the learner's contribution to his own learning has been neglected. They feel that the preoccupation with control of structure has

> distracted the theorists from considering the role of the learner as anything but a generator of interference; and preoccupation with linguistic structure has distracted them from considering that learning a language means learning to use it.

Reprinted with permission of the authors and publisher from the *International Review of Applied Linguistics in Language Teaching*, Vol. VI, No. 2, 1968, pp. 145–164.

In the next paragraph the authors present what they consider to be both the necessary and sufficient conditions in language acquisition:

> a language will be learned by a normal human being if and only if *particular, whole instances of language use are modeled for him and if his own particular acts using the language are selectively reinforced.* The critical point here is that *unless* a learner has learned instances of language in use, he has not learned them as language, and that if he has learned enough such instances, he will not need to have analysis and generalization about those wholes made *for* him.

The authors take as a case in point the most successful instance of language learning—the child's acquisition of his first language. Since the child is not instructed in his language and yet in a short period of time is able to produce "intelligent, appropriate speech" we must conclude that

> the child proceeds in an incredibly short time to induce a grammar of the language far more complex than any yet formulated by any linguist. We must, therefore, assume that the child is somehow capable of making an enormous contribution of his own. We may call this contribution his *language learning capability.*

The authors argue that this capability must organize and store the structurally diverse data of the language in such a way that it will be available for future use. Since language exists, not for the sake of form or structure, but for the sake of use, the organization of the sentences of his language must be "in terms of the situation they share (that is, their functional *use*) rather than the form they share."

The authors point out that teaching material is organized on exactly the opposite principle: control of linguistic form at the expense of situation or use. The authors stress that "the example of the child indicates that situational rather than grammatical cohesion is what is necessary and sufficient for language learning to take place."

The main argument in Section I rests on the assumption that the process of second language acquisition is essentially the same as first language acquisition. In Section II the authors defend this assumption against four possible counter arguments:

1. "The child's brain is different from the adult's. The adult has lost the neurological ability to infer general linguistic laws from particular instances." The authors grant that the adult does not usually acquire the second language as perfectly as a child acquires his first, but they argue that the difference in degree of skill is no argument for the adult and child being "qualitatively different *kinds* of learners."

2. "The child has much more time to learn the language." The authors reply that it is difficult to say how much time the child actually spends in language learning. They insist that it is not the time spent that gives a child an advantage over the adult learner, but his

opportunity to put his knowledge to practical use, while on the other hand, "the classroom student's 'knowledge' of the language may allow him to do everything with the language except use it."

3. "The child is much more strongly motivated to learn his first language than the adult is to learn a foreign language." The authors point out that there are several possible interpretations of what the term "motivation" means. Nevertheless, they think that in any strict psychological interpretation of "motivation," the adult is as well motivated and rewarded as the child, perhaps even more so.

4. "The child offers a *tabula rasa* for language learning. The adult's native language will interfere with his acquisition of a foreign language." The authors grant that there is such a thing as second language interference, but deny that this is of any significant importance to the process of learning. The interference results from the student's inability to produce correct forms in the second language. When the learner outstrips his knowledge of the second language, if he is to talk at all, he must fall back on what he does know, namely, his first language. Thus, first-language interference is not a hindrance to be overcome by contrast analysis, rather it is a negative thing to be overcome by more knowledge of the second language.

In a strict psychological sense, "interference" means that learning one set of responses to a set of stimuli may interfere with learning a new set of responses to the same stimuli. The authors suggest that the danger of interference in this sense may be minimized if the learning situations are clearly separated. They also point out that if this model were really true, the learning of the new set of "habits" for the second language should have a corresponding weakening effect on the habits of the first language. Obviously, however, learning a second language does not necessarily in itself reduce our ability to use our native language. The authors conclude with the observation that adults do acquire "new abilities that could never have been taught them by mere summation of the formal exercises to which they may have been exposed."

ABSTRACT

In present-day "linguistically-oriented" language teaching literature the underlying principles and pedagogical recommendations drawn from them seem either supererogatory or logically and empirically inadequate to provide a plausible foundation for the teaching programs they claim to justify.

From a consideration of successful vs. unsuccessful cases of language learning, we assert three propositions:

1. Systematic organization of the grammatical form of the language material exposed to the learner is neither necessary nor sufficient for his mastery of the language.

2. Presentation of particular instances of language in contexts which exemplify their meaning and use is both sufficient and necessary.

3. Systematic teaching of structure (as in structural drills) imposes formal rather than useful organization of language material. To plan teaching programs on the basis of formal properties of sentences is thus incompatible with the only necessary and sufficient method known for learning a language.

SECTION I

In his zeal to teach language students to produce well-formed sentences, the language teacher is in great danger of underestimating the importance of teaching students to use the language. This is as true in the 20th century with its linguistically enlightened methods as it was in the 19th century for methods that men like Gouin, Sweet, and Jespersen were reacting against.[*] The growing emphasis during the past twenty years on the improvement and expansion of techniques of structural drill represents a corresponding de-emphasis on techniques of teaching language use. In constructing language textbooks and language teaching programs, linguists have—for good professional reasons but bad pedagogical ones—increasingly shifted from a reliance on the simple, direct technique of teaching language use by presenting for imitation instances of the language in use to a reliance on the complex, indirect technique of preparing the learner for language use by means of structural drills based on the linguist's expert contrastive analysis of the native and target languages.[†] With this shift in emphasis from

[*] François Gouin, *The Art of Teaching and Studying Languages* (London, 1892) (English translation by Howard Swan and Victor Bétis of Gouin's *L'Art d'enseigner et d'étudier les langues,* Paris, 1880); Henry Sweet, *The Practical Study of Languages* (London, 1899); Otto Jespersen, *How to Teach a Foreign Language* (London, 1904).

[†] A whole conference, for example, was devoted to this topic; see Francis W. Gravit and Albert Valdman, eds., *Structural Drill and the Language Laboratory,* IJAL XXIX, No. 2 (April, 1963), Part III (=IURCAFL Publication 27).

The importance that linguists ascribe to contrastive analysis is typified by the following from the "General Introductions," by Charles F. Ferguson, General Editor, to the monographs in the *Contrastive Structure Series* (Chicago, University of Chicago Press, 1962):

"The Center for Applied Linguistics, in undertaking this series of studies, has

mastery of language use to mastery of language structure, language pedagogy has gradually lost much of the value contributed to the design of language teaching materials by American linguists during the Second World War.‡

An examination of the literature on second language teaching written either by linguists or by teachers who claim a linguistic orientation will reveal a certain typical uniformity in the structure of the theoretical statements that seek to justify their choice of method and selection of material. In some cases, the theoretical discussion may be as short as two or three paragraphs, e.g. in an article in *Language Learning* or *IRAL*, or as long as whole chapters of books. In other cases, of course, the argument will not be explicitly formulated, but will be implied at various critical points in the discussion. Whatever the format selected for the presentation of the theoretical background, whether explicit or implicit, its structure can be resolved into two parts.

The underlying principles which form the first part are presented as propositions alleged to form part of linguistic science. These propositions are taken either as fundamental assumptions of linguistic science itself or as findings of linguistic science, although in just what sense they can be taken to be one or the other is not usually spelled out. A statement such as "Language is structured" may in one set of underlying principles figure as an assumption while in another discussion it seems to be claimed as one of the findings of linguistics.§

---

acted on the conviction held by many linguists and specialists in language teaching that one of the major problems in the learning of a second language is the interference caused by the structural differences between the native language of the learner and the second language. A natural consequence of this conviction is the belief that a careful contrastive analysis of the two languages offers an excellent basis for the preparation of instructional materials, the planning of courses, and the development of actual classroom techniques."

‡ For the nature of this contribution, see William G. Moulton, "Linguistics and Language Teaching in the United States 1940–1960," in Mohrmann, Sommerfelt and Whatmough, eds., *Trends in European and American Linguistics*, 1930–1960 (Utrecht, 1961), pp. 82–109 (also IRAL I (1963), pp. 21–41); but note especially pp. 86–90 (IRAL, pp. 24–27), where he particularly mentions the role of drill, and pp. 97–98 (IRAL, pp. 32–33) where he quotes C. C. Fries about the contributions of linguists to language teaching programs. See also Mary R. Haas, "The Application of Linguistics to Language Teaching," in A. L. Kroeber, ed., *Anthropology Today* (Chicago, 1953), pp. 807–818.

§ Not at all unrepresentative is the following from Jeris E. Strain, "Teaching a Pronunciation Problem," *Language Learning*, XII (1962), pp. 231–240.

"Our task is to teach the sound system of a foreign language. To do so we attempt to bring as much linguistic knowledge as possible to bear on the 'what' of our task and complement it with the best 'how' ideas that are known to us.

The second part of the theoretical discussion typically consists of statements concerning principles or details of pedagogical practice, alleged to be the logical consequences of the underlying principles. A number of these pedagogical recommendations and the teaching programs they claim to justify seem to us logically and empirically faulty. We can put our objections succinctly:

1. The pedagogical recommendations do not follow logically from the underlying principles upon which they are claimed to be based.

2. The recommended pedagogical procedures themselves can be shown to be neither necessary nor sufficient for the learning of a language.

For example, we may find as an underlying principle a statement like:

1. "Linguistic theory tells us that the ability to speak a language is fundamentally a vast system of habits—of patterns and structures used quite out of awareness."||

"In defining our task, we take certain propositions for granted, propositions based on conclusions [N.B.] reached in the scientific study of language; namely:

  a. that the sound system of a language is made up of a certain rather small set of elements which function significantly as carriers of the message (usually called phonemes).

  b. That the sound systems of two languages are never the same.

  c. that pronunciation problems can be predicted at least in part by comparing the native-language sound system with that of the target language.

  d. that skill in pronunciation consists of a set of automatic habits involving the hearing organs and the speech organs, plus the ability not only to recognize significant sounds in a stream of speech but also to react to them in an acceptable manner.

  e. that a prerequisite to developing the ability to produce significant sounds is development of the ability to recognize the significant sounds.

  f. that learning to speak a language should precede learning to read and write it."

Or the following from Albert Valdman, "Breaking the Lockstep," in F. W. Gravit and A. Valdman, *op. cit.*, p. 147:

"Scarcely anyone in this audience would quarrel fundamentally with the basic assumptions [N.B.] of the New Key:

  (1) Language is primarily speech and writing is its secondary derivative; (2) Foreign language instruction should progress in the sequence listening, speaking, reading, and writing; (3) Language consists of a complex set of habits learned through practice and analogy; (4) The acquisition of foreign language habits is considerably accelerated by structuring the subject matter and ordering it in a series of graduated minimal steps; (5) Practice is more effective if reinforced by rewarding desired terminal responses; (6) Foreign language learning will be substantially increased if positive motivational factors are present in the teaching situation."

|| William G. Moulton, "What is Structural Drill?," in F. W. Gravit and A. Valdman, *op. cit.*, p. 5.

And its putative pedagogical consequence:

1a. Structural drill is an important component of any efficient foreign language teaching program.[#]

Or the principle:

2. An important cause of difficulty in second language learning is the set of structural non-congruencies between the learner's native language and the target language.[**]

Followed by the claim that:

2a. Only materials based on a contrastive analysis can most efficiently overcome the interference in the foreign language behavior caused by the native language speech habits.[††]

The logical flaw arises in such instances when the linguist attempts to draw simple and direct conclusions about the manner of acquisition of language from his knowledge of the abstract structure of language, and claims that the success or failure of language teaching programs depends to a large extent on the degree to which the language course

---

[#] Cf. Nelson Brooks, *Language and Language Learning* (Second Edition) (New York, 1964), p. 146:

"Pattern Practice is a cardinal point in the methodology proposed in this book. Pattern practice (or structure drill, as it is sometimes called), contrary to dialogue, makes no pretense of being communication. It is to communication what playing scales and arpeggios is to music: exercise in structural dexterity undertaken solely for the sake of practice, in order that performance may become habitual and automatic. . . ."

[**] Cf. for example the following from Robert L. Politzer and Charles N. Staubach, *Teaching Spanish, A Linguistic Orientation* (Revised Edition) (New York, 1965), p. 22:

"Our appraisal of second language learning must take into account three important facts which inevitably determine much of the learning process:

1. Language is an elaborate system, full of analogical forms and patterns.
2. Language is habit, or a complex of habits.
3. The native language (an established complex of habits) interferes with the acquisition of the habits of the new language."

Subsequent pages (23–32) develop these notions in terms of drill designed to prevent, avoid, or mitigate various kinds of interference (transfer) from native language patterns or imperfectly learned second language patterns.

[††] *Ibid.*, p. 32: "For the time being, intensive drill at the points of interference remains our most practical tool in overcoming the obstacles created by the native language habits of the mature speaker."

Cf. also the following from Emma Marie Birkmaier, "Extending the Audio-Lingual Approach: Some Psychological Aspects," in Edward W. Najam, ed., *Language Learning: The Individual and the Process, IJAL XXXII, No. 1* (January, 1966), Part II (=IURCAFL Publication 40), p. 130:

"There is an automatic transfer in the learning of a second language of which the teacher must be aware, namely, the interference of the speech patterns of one's native language. Interference can be negligible in a bilingual who learns his language during childhood. This fact speaks for the introduction of foreign languages at an early age level, since the adolescent and adult will find this interference a considerable handicap.

"The teacher must constantly be aware of and give special emphasis to the

writer or language teacher orders his pedagogical material to reflect a theoretically sound description of the native and target languages.‡‡ The excessive preoccupation with the contribution of the teacher has then distracted the theorists from considering the role of the learner as anything but a generator of interference; and preoccupation with linguistic structure has distracted them from considering that learning a language means learning to use it.

Our contention is that to be effective language teachers, we need not wait for the development of a theory of language acquisition based on a theory of the structure of language. We believe that the necessary and sufficient conditions for a human being to learn a language are already known: a language will be learned by a normal human being

---

points of interference. *The automatic transfer of the learner's native speech habits must be drilled out of him.* This is really the foreign language teacher's chief job." (Emphasis added.)

The modern ancestor of such formulations is evidently the following oft-quoted summary statement by C. C. Fries, *Teaching and Learning English as a Foreign Language* (Ann Arbor, 1945), p. 9: "The most efficient materials are those that are based upon a scientific description of the language to be learned, carefully compared with a parallel description of the language of the learner."

‡‡ Fries, *op. cit.*, p. 5: "But the person who is untrained in the methods and techniques of language description is not likely to arrive at sound conclusions concerning the actual practices of the native speakers he observes. He will certainly not do so economically and efficiently. And the native speaker of the language, unless he has been specially trained to analyze his own languages processes, will be more likely to mislead than to help a foreigner when he tries to make comments about his own language. On the other hand, the modern scientific study of language has within the last twenty years developed special techniques of descriptive analysis by which a trained linguist can efficiently and accurately arrive at the fundamentally significant matters of structure and sound system amid the bewildering mass of details which constitute the actual rumble of speech. If an adult is to gain a satisfactory proficiency in a foreign language most quickly and easily he must have satisfactory materials upon which to work— i.e. he must have the really important items of the language selected and arranged in a properly related sequence with special emphasis upon the chief trouble spots. . . The techniques of scientific descriptive analysis . . . can provide a thorough and consistent check of the language material itself and thus furnish the basis for the selection of the most efficient materials to guide the efforts of the learner."

Further, p. 7: "it is the practical use of the linguistic scientist's technique of language description in the choice and sequence of materials and the principles of the method that grow out of these materials that is at the heart of the so-called 'new approach' to language learning."

Statements with the import of those just quoted from Fries are repeated almost ritualistically in foreign language methodology textbooks and articles that adopt his point of view. Our objection to this point of view stems from its uncritical equation of "the really important items" with "the chief trouble spots." W. F. Mackey's book *Language Teaching Analysis* (London, 1965) is a good example of the attempt to define the components of the language teaching program in terms of an analysis of the components of language structure. See also M. A. K. Halliday and Peter Strevens, *Linguistics and Language Teaching* (London, 1965).

if and only if *particular, whole instances of language use are modeled
for him and if his own particular acts using the language are selectively
reinforced.*§§ The critical point here is that *unless* a learner has learned
instances of language in use, he has not learned them as language, and
that if he has learned enough such instances, he will not need to have
analysis and generalization about those wholes made *for* him. If our
contention is correct, there is a heavy—and we think impossible—
burden of proof on anyone who insists (1) that language is most
efficiently taught if structure is taught separately from use (as implied
by structural drills) or (2) that the organization of language material
for the student should follow a scheme dictated by the comparative
structures of the language to be learned and the language of the
learner.

Let us consider the obvious fact that in just that case where the
most successful language learning takes place—namely, in the child—
the linguistic material displayed to the learner is not selected in the
interest of presenting discrete grammatical skills in an orderly fashion.
On the contrary, the child is exposed to an extensive variety and range
of utterances selected for their situational appropriateness at the
moment, rather than to illustrate a particular grammatical principle.
The child proceeds in an incredibly short time to induce a grammar
of the language far more complex than any yet formulated by any
linguist. We must, therefore, assume that the child is somehow
capable of making an enormous contribution of his own.‖ ‖ We may

---

§§ Cf. the following from Albert Bandura and Richard H. Walters, *Social Learning and Personality Development* (New York, 1965), p. 106:
"Relevant research demonstrates that when a model is provided, patterns of
behavior are typically acquired in large segments or in their entirety rather than
through a slow, gradual process based on differential reinforcement. Following
demonstrations by a model, or (though to a lesser extent) following verbal
descriptions of desired behavior, the learner gradually reproduces more or less the
entire response pattern, even though he may perform no overt response, and
consequently receive no reinforcement, throughout the demonstration period.
Under such circumstances, the acquisition process is quite clearly not as piece-
meal as is customarily depicted in modern behavior systems."
Note their finding that the acquisition of behavior need not be accompanied
by any overt response by the subject whatsoever, something which they demonstrate in a large number of varied learning situations. "While immediate or
inferred response consequences to the model have an important influence on the
observer's [i.e. learner's] *performance* of imitative responses, the *acquisition* of
these responses appears to result primarily from contiguous sensory stimulation
[i.e. observation]." (p. 107) (Authors' emphasis.) All this strikes hard at the
psychological base of the linguist who adopts an analytic, stimulus-response model
for language teaching, with its consequent emphasis on the accumulation of a
repertory of language behavior bit by bit via structural drill.
‖ ‖ Cf. N. Chomsky, *Aspects of the Theory of Syntax* (Cambridge, Mass., 1965),
p. 25:
"Clearly, a child who has learned a language has developed an internal repre-

call this contribution his *language learning capability,* by which we mean simply whatever it is that makes it possible for a child to observe a number of particular acts of speech in context and then to perform new acts of speech that will seem to the observer to imply that the child has formed general rules for producing intelligent, appropriate speech. It is still unknown what neurological mechanisms account for his linguistic accomplishment; but the fact that the child can produce new intelligent speech after observing only particular language acts of varied linguistic structure in contextual wholes seems indisputable.## This capability, among other things, accomplishes what it is assumed the course writer tries to accomplish for the adult learner: it organizes and stores a wealth of structurally diverse input language data in such a way as to be available for future language use in thinking, speaking, hearing, reading and writing.

Since any successful language learning program must ultimately

---

sentation of a system of rules that determine how sentences are to be formed, used, and understood. Using the term 'grammar' with a systematic ambiguity (to refer, first, to the native speaker's internally represented 'theory of his language' and, second, to the linguist's account of this), we can say that the child has developed and internally represented a generative grammar, in the sense described. He has done this on the basis of observation of what we may call primary linguistic data. This must include examples of linguistic performance that are taken to be well-formed sentences, and may include also examples designated as non-sentences, and no doubt much other information of the sort that is required for language learning, whatever this may be. . . . On the basis of such data, the child constructs a grammar—that is, a theory of the language of which the well-formed sentences of the primary linguistic data constitute a small sample. To learn a language, then, the child must have a method for devising an appropriate grammar, given primary linguistic data."

On the nature of the child's accomplishment vis-à-vis that of the linguist, cf. the following from H. E. Palmer, *The Principles of Language Study* (new edition: London, 1964), pp. 4–5:

"In English we have a tone-system so complicated that no one has so far discovered its laws, but little English children observe each nicety of tone with marvelous precision; a learned specialist in 'tonetics' (or whatever the science of tones will come to be called) may make an error, but the little child will not. . . .

"When, therefore, we find that a person has become expert in a difficult and complex subject, the theory of which has not yet been worked out, nor yet been discovered, it is manifest that his expertness has been acquired otherwise than by study of the theory."

Cf. C. F. Hockett, "Linguistic Ontogeny," *A Course in Modern Linguistics* (New York, 1958), pp. 356–357:

"In the communicative economy of the child at the earliest speech stage, his vocal signals are not words in this sense, but the indivisible and uncompoundable signals of a closed repertory: each utterance from the child consists wholly of one or another of these signals. Each signal has been learned as a whole, in direct or indirect imitation of some utterance of adult language. For a while the repertory is increased only by the holistic imitation of further adult utterances. This does not 'open' the closed system, but merely enlarges it.

"In time, the child's repertory includes some signals which are partially similar in sound and meaning. Suppose, for example, that the child already uses prelin-

teach the *use* of sentences, if the adult learner can, like the child, contribute a knowledge of the *form* of sentences from his knowledge of the form of previously learned sentences, a presentation of sentences organized in terms of the situation they share rather than the form they share would seem clearly the more efficient one.

In discussions of modern language teaching methodology, it has been argued that structural randomness in teaching materials makes language learning excessively difficult; a sufficient demonstration of the invalidity of this contention as a general principle for language teaching is the fact of the child's easy success in learning a language— whether it is his first or second one—from just such materials. Furthermore, in practice the design of teaching material to minimize *grammatical* randomness seems to maximize situational randomness. A set of successive items in a typical structural drill normally have in common *only* their shared grammatical properties—not their relatedness to a given situation. On the other hand, the successive utterances in a normal discourse, say in a dialogue or piece of connected text, rarely share the same grammatical structure, but nevertheless exhibit a highly structured situational or contextual cohesion. And the example of the child indicates that situational rather than grammatical cohesion is what is necessary and sufficient for language learning to take place.

We are saying that a chunk of language is most efficiently learned as a *unit* of form and use. This has an important implication on language pedagogy: structural drills, in which the student practices switching quickly from an utterance appropriate for one situation to another utterance appropriate for quite another situation, are ineffective in principle. They force the student to produce utterances whose use is made difficult to grasp, unless he has the rare skill (there may be a small number of learners who apparently can learn to use a language from structural drill alone) of imagining a whole fresh situation for every utterance, while keeping up with the mechanical requirements of the exercise.

How can the evident success of the child's language learning method be realized for foreign language teaching to adults?*** The proponents

---

guistic equivalents of adult /^{3}mám$\ni^1$ $\downarrow$ / and /^{3}mámɔ^2 $\uparrow$ /, and of /^{3}dǽdij^1 $\downarrow$ /, but not, it so happens, of /^{3}dǽdij^2 $\uparrow$ /. The adult forms are structured: each consists of a recurrent word plus a recurrent intonation. The child's analogs, at the moment, are unitary signals. But then comes the most crucial event in the child's acquisition of language: he analogizes, in some appropriate situation, to produce an utterance matching adult /^{3}dǽdij^2 $\uparrow$ /, which he has never heard nor said before."

*** Arguments concerning language learning abilities in the adult on the analogy of those of the child are used explicitly—albeit inconsistently—in works like the

of the various "direct methods" have developed numerous techniques that attempt to do this; and linguists have done even better than the more physicalistic of the direct methodists, by utilizing the powerful tool of dialogue memorization, which at its best provides less limiting and more realistic contexts for learning than can be provided if the strictures (e.g., no translation, structurally limited lessons) of the more rigid of the direct methodists are adhered to.

The pedagogical implication of our position is that we abandon the notion of structural grading and structural ordering of exercise material in favor of situational ordering. That is, we need to devise no more structural drills like that illustrated in Appendix I. Through the materials we would propose instead (see Appendix II for an example of one kind), the student would learn situational variants rather than structural alternants independent of a contextual base. The principal motivation for providing contextual and psychological reality for dialogues in a believable manner is not, as is so often objected, to provide the learner with something to say for a particular, necessarily limited situation. Rather, it is to present instances of meaningful use of language which the learner himself stores, segments, and eventually recombines in synthesizing new utterances appropriate for use in new situations.†††

In our language teaching research we need to pay more attention to improving and making more effective our presentations of language

ones cited in Note * above. Cf. for example the following from H. E. Palmer, *op. cit.*, p. 7: "We may well ask ourselves whether the forces which were operative in the case of [the acquisition of] our first language are available for the acquisition of a second, third, or fourth language." After a detailed discussion and analysis of the relevant possible differences, he concludes, p. 11: "No reasonable doubt remains: we are all endowed by nature with certain capacities which enable each of us, without exercise of our powers of study, to assimilate and to use the spoken form of any colloquial language, whether native or foreign. We may avail ourselves of these powers by training ourselves deliberately to utilize them, or, having more confidence in our studial efforts, or for some reason of special expediency, we may choose to leave our spontaneous capacities in their latent state and make no use of them. We cannot, however, afford to ignore them, and it would be foolish to deny their existence."

††† Our use of the terms segment, store, recombine, etc., should not be taken to mean that we have in mind some particular taxonomic or stimulus-response model of grammatical structure or language use. Modern grammatical theory makes it clear that such models could not in themselves be adequate representations of the nature of the language learning process. Cf. N. Chomsky, *op. cit.*, pp. 47–59, especially p. 57; also T. G. Bever, J. A. Fodor and W. Weksel, "On the Acquisition of Syntax," *Psychological Review* LXXII (1965), pp. 467–482. What is important is our claim that, whatever the nature of this process, it is carried out by the learner rather than being performed vicariously for him by the teacher.

For further discussions of these topics, see the following: Leonard Newmark,

in use. For example, we need careful studies to tell us what dosage of conversational material will maximize the ratio of amount retained to amount of time spent in acquisition;‡‡‡ we need to devise and employ exercises that will extend the applicability of material already learned to new situations—for instance, we may give students practice in substituting new items in previously learned dialogues, corresponding to slight changes they wish to introduce into the situation, as in Appendix II; and we need to learn to manipulate the relationship between model and observer in such a way as to increase the likelihood that the student will imitate the language behavior of his teacher.

SECTION II

Now, against the assertion that first language learning provides instructive insights for planning second language teaching programs, it is easy and usual to object that the adult is not a child and that the process of second language learning must therefore be different from that of first language learning (and then to construct teaching programs which will guarantee that the adult is *made to be* a different kind of learner from the child). It is denied that an adult can effectively be taught by grammatically unordered materials, which seem so sufficient for the child's learning (we repeat, the *only* learning process which we know for certain will produce mastery of the language at a native level).

Several serious arguments for treating the adult as a different kind of learner from the child have been advanced. We may take four to be representative:

Jerome Mintz and Jan Ann Lawson, *Using American English* (New York, 1964), Introduction, pp. 3–18, by Leonard Newmark; David A. Reibel, "The Contextually-Patterned Use of English: An Experiment in Dialogue Writing," *English Language Teaching* XIX (1964), pp. 62–71; Leonard Newmark, "How Not to Interfere with Language Learning," E. W. Najam, *op. cit.*, pp. 77–83.

‡‡‡ For example, we know that it would be easy to learn a two-word dialogue very well in an hour—"Hello." "Hello."—but little would be gained for the hour's work; on the other hand, a great deal of language might be exposed in a forty-line dialogue, but the effort to memorize the dialogue would not be worth the gain, and little of it would be retained and reemployed by the student. How long should a dialogue be in order to gain maximal retention per unit of time spent in learning? Experience in language teaching suggests that a dialogue of perhaps four to six lines—two or three short utterances per participant—for each learning dose may be optimal. This length sharply contrasts with the length of dialogues in many "linguistically oriented" textbooks.

Argument 1: The child's brain is different from the adult's. The adult
has lost the neurological ability to infer general linguistic laws from particular instances.§§§

While we recognize the psychological and neuro-pathological evidence for positing differences between child and adult brains, we
cannot consider this evidence to be decisive on the question of whether
the adult is capable of linguistic inference. Healthy adult brains do
enable adults to make various other kinds of generalizations from
particular instances—e.g., adults can gain the general skill of driving,
and can use that skill in new instances, on unfamiliar roads, in a new
car, etc. We are unaware of any empirical evidence for saying that it
is exactly the ability to make new applications of linguistic material
to new instances that is lost in adulthood.‖ ‖ ‖

---

§§§ This is the implication, for example, of this statement by Karl Teeter in his
review of E. C. Horne, *Beginning Javanese*, *Language* XXXIX (1963), p. 147;
"First of all, it needs to be clearly recognized that adults learn languages differently from children. They have lost, at least in large part, the ability to make that
remarkable induction that all children, independently of intelligence, make with
such speed when they learn a language."

‖ ‖ ‖ W. Penfield and L. Roberts, *Speech and Brain-Mechanisms* (Princeton,
1959)—see also Lenneberg's review in *Language* XXXVI (1960), pp. 97–112—
offer physiological evidence for cortical specialization during childhood development, with resulting inability later in adult life to recreate lost speech mechanisms
in new areas of the brain after trauma.

The fact that the speech mechanism must be developed in childhood if the
individual is to speak at all does not *a priori* preclude the possibility that, once
developed, it can be applied later in adult life to the learning of new languages.
Cf. especially Penfield and Roberts, *op. cit.*, pp. 251–254, where they discuss the
case of the bilingual child learning through the "direct" or "mother's" method,
or the adult learning through the "indirect" or "secondary" method. Penfield
discusses Joseph Conrad's success in learning English as an instance of the
application of the direct method to adult language learning (*op. cit.*, pp. 241–
242), but he fails to draw the proper general pedagogical conclusions from the
case. Thus the possibility is left open that, despite the loss of certain kinds of
plasticity in the brain of the adult as the combined result of maturation and
learning, new learning in later life is still possible, provided that the basic mechanisms are laid down in early life. The allegation that language learning capability
has been lost in the adult—on the grounds of the neurological evidence—fails to
recognize the possibility that so long as the *mechanism* for learning language
exists, language learning may proceed as with the child. For example, Penfield
elsewhere suggests that bilingual experience in childhood, where two languages
(or dialects) are learned under different conditions of use, provides the child with
a learning strategy that he can apply later in life either in reactivating and extending his now dormant secondary childhood language, or in acquiring additional
languages:

"I suspect that the basic units of second languages are hidden away in the
brain during the childhood of those who grow up in lands where many languages
echo in playground or home. This it is, perhaps, that makes the Pole and the
Swiss and the Hollander better language students. I suspect, further, that the
child who has the basic units of French and English hidden away in his brain

The difficulty with a statement such as Penfield's:

> When new languages are taken up for the first time in the second decade of life, it is difficult, though not impossible, to achieve a good result. It is difficult because it is unphysiological.###

is that it seems to contain a self contradiction: if it is "unphysiological" for an adult brain to learn a new language, how are we to account for the fact that it is possible at all? What could an "unphysiological" mechanism be that would explain language learning in adults? In fact, many adult learners do learn new languages very well. What is usually taken as evidence against their ability to learn as a child learns is the fact that they speak the new language with an accent. But our point is that they do learn to speak it and that the amount of skill they often acquire far exceeds in amount and importance the amount of skill they seem not to acquire. The neurophysiological evidence may be used to argue that adults are quantitatively inferior to children as language learners; it cannot be used to argue that they are qualitatively different *kinds* of learners. We submit that the same language learning capability exists in both child and adult, quite possibly in different degrees, and that the extraordinary efficiency of the "method"**** by which children learn can and should be taken advantage of in teaching adults.

Argument 2: The child has much more time to learn the language.††††

---

finds it easier in later life to take up a third language, for example, German, even by the indirect method. He has a double number of basic units to call on. And they are similar, at least in part, to those needed." "Learning a Second Language," *The Second Career* (Boston, 1963), p. 135.

Speech and Brain-Mechanisms, p. 255. Penfield does not seem here to be exercising the same caution as when he says (p. 249):

"Returning to the act of speaking: We control voice and mouth by following the verbal motor units formed and fixed by early practice. It is difficult to make any certain statement on the question of accents by reference to physiological evidence alone. One may say that children have a greater capacity for imitation than adults. That seems to be a fact, but it is not an explanation of what happens in later life."

**** *Op. cit.*, p. 254.

†††† Cf. William G. Moulton, *A Linguistic Guide to Language Learning* (Modern Language Association of America, 1966), p. 2: "One of the most striking aspects of a child's language learning is the fact that he spends so much time at it. He talks with his parents, he talks with his brothers and sisters, he talks with his playmates; if no one else is around, he even talks himself. It is a little sad to realize that the child practices so much, because this is something which no adult language learner can ever hope to match—he has too much else to do."

The argument has been made earlier: "The learning of vernacular sounds by imitation is a slow and difficult task, but the conditions of beginning in infancy, *having nothing else to do*, and, above all of the mind being unhampered by conflicting associations with the sounds of other languages, are so favorable, and the

This argument is difficult to evaluate, since we do not have reliable information about how much time the child actually does spend in learning a language. From casual observation, however, it does not appear that the young child spends as much time in language contact as would be required to explain the vast differences between the language-using abilities of native four-year-old children and those of college students after two years of language courses. The small child is busy with many things—including sleeping and solitary playing—other than language, and it is the rare mother who can bear to keep a one-way conversation going without long breaks during her periods of contact with the child.‡‡‡‡ There is also some question whether the adult might not gain as much from his ability to focus his attention over a period of time as the child gains from longer, but less concentrated contact with the language.

More important, there is a striking difference between the *kind* of linguistic proficiency children have immediately and that of classroom students (including those under the tutelage of a linguist), a difference that has nothing to do with the amount of time spent in contact: what the child knows of the language he can use (perhaps only in listening and comprehending, perhaps also in his own speech), while the classroom student's knowledge seems all too often to be unavailable for his own immediate use. To put it in other terms, the child is fluent in his language very early, increasing his fluency in direct proportion to his knowledge of the language, while the classroom student's "knowledge" of the language may allow him to do everything with the language except use it.§§§§ And notice that the classroom student does not need

---

inducements to learn are so strong, that the initiation is in most cases practically perfect." (Emphasis added.) Henry Sweet, *The History of Language* (London, 1900), p. 19. Incidentally, note also Sweet's modern-sounding references to interference ("conflicting associations") and motivation ("inducements").

‡‡‡‡ Cf. the following observation of Otto Jespersen's relevant to the passage from Sweet quoted in Note ††††: "Sweet ([*History of Language*] 19) says among other things that the conditions of learning vernacular sounds are so favourable because the child has nothing else to do at the time. On the contrary, one may say that the child has an enormous deal to do while it is learning language; it is at that time active beyond belief: in a short time it subdues wider tracts than it ever does later in a much longer time. The more wonderful is it that along with those tasks it finds strength to learn its mother-tongue and its many refinements and crooked turns." *Language, Its Nature, Development and Origin* (London, 1922), p. 141.

§§§§ Cf. also the following from Jespersen, *op. cit.*, p. 142–143: "The child has another priceless advantage: he hears the language in all possible situations and under such conditions that language and situation ever correspond exactly with one another. Gesture and facial expression harmonize with the words uttered and keep the child to a right understanding. Here there is nothing unnatural, such as is often the case in a language-lesson in later years, when one talks about

an inordinate amount of time to learn things he sees immediate use for; e.g., he quickly learns to say and respond to short greetings or to utter curses and dirty words in the new language, though from the linguistic analyst's point of view, these may be quite complex structurally. Psychological factors seem to be at least as crucial as structural ones in determining how much time is needed to learn utterances.

> Argument 3: The child is much more strongly motivated to learn his first language than the adult is to learn a foreign language.

If we take "motivation" here to imply something like "need" or "deprivation," it is not at all clear that the child does so poorly without language. In our culture, as in many others, a crying, inarticulate baby has his needs rather well taken care of: it is not until he develops language, as a matter of fact, that he seems to need what he can get only through language. And it is not clear that motivation in this sense has much to do with adult learning of language: there are cases galore of immigrants whose very livelihood depends on their mastering a language which nevertheless largely eludes them, and not a few cases of good language learners whose general reward will be no greater than one more A in a language course.

If on the other hand we take "motivation" to mean something like "effective reward," there is no theoretical, and little practical difficulty in constructing teaching programs for adults which are at least as efficient in their selective reinforcement as that which most native learners receive for their linguistic efforts. Indeed, any imputation of some general, motivational differences between first and second language learning will fail to account for the observable success of children becoming bilingual in learning a second language.

There is another equivocation often concealed in the use of the term motivation. Suppose we replace motivation with the expression "wanting to." Then saying that someone "wants to" learn a language can be taken to mean either that he wants to be in possession of the skill, or that he "wants to" do the things that will lead him to acquire it. Clearly the former should, but does not automatically, imply the latter. Thus we can explain the paradox of the person who says he "wants to" be able to play the oboe, but never learns, because he doesn't like to practice.

---

ice and snow in June or excessive heat in January. And what the child hears is just what immediately concerns and interests him, and again and again his own attempts at speech lead to the fulfillment of his dearest wishes, so that his command of language has great practical advantages for him."

In arguing for the relevance of motivation in accounting for observably different degrees of success in language learning, we seem to be led ultimately to the circularity—apparently inescapable outside of controlled laboratory conditions—of positing motivation in exactly those cases where successful learning has taken place and denying its presence in unsuccessful cases.

> Argument 4: The child offers a *tabula rasa* for language learning. The adult's native language will interfere with his acquisition of a foreign language.‖ ‖ ‖ ‖

No one can doubt the reality of the phenomena that are referred to by the term *interference*, but the metaphor implied by the term is unfortunate and misleading in discussions of language learning. It is true, indeed obvious by now, that learners will speak a foreign language with many errors which the observer can identify with characteristics in the learner's own language. But it seems to us that the pedagogical implications drawn by linguists have depended on an inadequate analysis of the term interference as applied to those phenomena.

The term "interference" is appropriately used to describe a phenomenon observable in psychological experiments in which different sets of responses are to be learned to the same set of stimuli or, more generally, when one set of behaviors is supposed to *replace* another set. In that case (when the stimulus set is held constant) the previous

---

‖ ‖ ‖ ‖ Cf. Robert L. Politzer, Foreign Language Learning, A Linguistic Introduction (Preliminary Edition) (Englewood Cliffs, N. J., 1965). p. 8:

"But the most essential difference between learning the native language and a foreign language lies in the simple fact that when you learn the foreign language you have already learned (consciously or subconsciously) a set of rules— namely the set that governs the system of the native language. If you learn a foreign language while you are still young, at an age at which the patterns and rules of your native language are still comparatively new to you, the interference that comes from the rules of the native language is likely to be small. But the older you become, the more practice you have had in speaking the native language, the more the rules and system of the native language are likely to interfere with learning the system of the foreign language. Once you are in your teens it is no longer possible to learn the foreign language in exactly the same way in which you learned your native language. The mere fact that you already have a native language that will interfere with the foreign language makes second language learning and first language learning quite different processes."

We would argue that if it were in fact true that "the mere fact that you already have a native language . . . makes second language learning and first language learning quite different processes," then bilingualism would be impossible for the child as well as for the adult, something that runs contrary to the observation that children can acquire one or more second languages with comparative ease and little or no interference.

learning of a certain set of responses may have a detrimental effect on
the learning of a new set. The problem of interference in language
study arises genuinely under conditions in which two different sets of
responses are to be learned to the *same* set of stimuli, or more generally, in the same stimulus field. Such conditions are met in certain
traditional translation-grammar procedures, but they are also met in
courses devised by linguists in which the student's attention is called
explicitly or implicitly to a contrast between the native and target
language.#### What linguists (in common with traditional teachers)
have typically *not* done consistently in planning language courses is
to minimize the conditions that lead to interference by doing for the
adult learner what is typically done for the child who is learning a
second language: namely, using one language in a set of circumstances
consistently distinguished from the set of circumstances in which the
other language is used. The example of bilingual children who learn
and use one language at home and another at school—without suffering enormous difficulties of interference—should induce language

---

Cf. the following very cogent remarks by Roger L. Hadlich, "Lexical Con-
trastive Analysis," *Modern Language Journal* XLIX (1965), pp. 426–429:

"Thus, paradoxically, when pairs of words which are known traditionally and
shown analytically to be a problem are placed in juxtaposition, explained, contrasted and drilled, students tend to continue confusing them; when they are
presented as if no problem existed students have little or no difficulty." (p. 426)

"The point is that 'problem pairs' [such as Spanish *salir* and *dejar*] are non-
native. The relation between the members of each pair is extraneous to the language being studied and is thus an artificial and perhaps unnecessary constriction,
imposed on the foreign language from without." (p. 427)

"In [contrastive] drill of this type [i.e. on pairs such as *salir* and *dejar*], even
if students are somehow prevented from making associations based on the
implicit English language criteria, they are nevertheless being taught that *salir*
and *dejar* are easily confused in Spanish and must be used with care. Awareness
of the possibility of erroneous substitution fosters in itself the substitution it is
designed to forestall and so defeats its own purpose. Thus contrastive drill is
a self-fulfilling prophesy, and problem pair confusions are the result." (p. 427)

"If we ignore all problem pairs and treat the words separately, in the terms
of the foreign language, general lexical interference will be reduced and confusion
avoided." (p. 429)

Applying these considerations in developing materials for teaching Spanish
(*A Structural Course in Spanish*, New York, 1963), Hadlich and his colleagues
D. L. Wolfe and J. G. Inman concluded:

"No effort was made, in the elaboration of the materials, to apply the contrastive analysis techniques on the vocabulary level. . . . Our students' control of the
pairs was markedly better than that of the usual first year Spanish students. No
confusions were made; the students we questioned were not aware of any problem; they were even surprised to find later that, in translating sentences containing
these words, two different words in Spanish were represented by only one in
English." (p. 426)

Equally important here as their informal finding is the clear formulation of the
possible and actual effect of contrastive drill on the student's performance.

teaching planners to spend their ingenuity in devising language teaching situations that differ grossly from situations in which the native language is used, rather than devising means of calling students' attention to fine distinctions between the native and foreign language.*****

But how can we understand the phenomenon of foreign accent without resorting to the notion of interference? Our account is something like this: A person knows how to speak one language, say his native one. Now he tries to speak another one; but in his early stages of learning the new one, there are many things he has not yet learned to do; that is, he is grossly undertrained in the new one. But he is induced to perform ("perform" may mean understand, speak, read, or write) in that new one by an external teacher or by his internal desire to say something. What can he do other than use what he already knows to make up for what he does not know? To an observer who knows the target language, the learner will seem to be stubbornly substituting the native habits for target habits. But from the learner's point of view, all he is doing is the best he can: to fill in his gaps of training he refers for help to what he already knows. The problem of "interference" viewed thus reduces to the problem of ignorance, and the solution to the problem is simply more and better training in the target language, rather than systematic drill at the points of contrast between the two languages in order to combat interference.

The child is developing his intellect simultaneously with his language and can "want to say" only what he is learning to say. The adult, on the other hand, can want to say what he does not yet know how to say, and he uses whatever means he has at his disposal. It is easy to see how the phenomenon of interference can result from his attempts to do more than he has yet learned to do in the new language. This seems to us sufficient explanation of how interference comes about, without the unnecessary hypostacization of competing linguistic systems, getting in each other's way or taking pot shots at one another.

There is much evidence to support our view. For example, if already learned habits exerted force against learning a new language (as implied by active metaphorical extension of the term "interference") we would expect the strongest habits to exert the greatest force: specifically, if a person knows imperfectly another foreign language in addition to the one he is trying to learn, we should expect his second

***** Cf. Penfield's observation (*Speech and Brain-Mechanisms*, p. 251–255) that no interference phenomena ("confusion" is his term) are noticeable in the speech of multi-lingual children who have learned several languages by either the "direct" or "mother's" method, different languages being learned under different circumstances.

language to be unable to compete with the native one in interfering with the third one. But in fact, it is commonly observed that the two imperfectly learned languages may infect each other to a greater degree than the native language will infect either one.

Again, if learning a new language followed the psychological laboratory model of learning a new set of "habits," we should expect interference in both directions: any reduction of interference (which in the view we oppose is held to be proportional to the increase in skill in the new language) should be accompanied by a weakening of the habits in the native language. But in fact we observe no direct, necessary ill effects on native habits as a result of increased learning of a second language.†††††

Finally, if every individual point of difference between native and new language had to be taught to adults through carefully constructed drills devoted to that point, it would be as impossible to learn a new language as it would be to learn one's native language one bit at a time. The observable fact is that adults do learn new languages—acquiring new abilities that could never have been taught them by mere summation of the formal exercises to which they may have been exposed. And they do learn remarkably well—remarkably, if the doctrine of the mature "frozen brain" were accepted. Linguists have been so eager to display their expertise in pointing to the minor ways in which foreign accent distorts performance in the new language that they have underestimated the enormous amount of mastery of language structure that the foreign speaker is exhibiting when he is using long utterances to say something. If the mistakes are to be scored against the learner's brain, then the successes must be scored for it; on balance, the adult must be appreciated to be a potentially magnificent learner of language.

To sum up, a minimal viable theory of foreign language learning assumes a language learning capability qualitatively the same—though perhaps quantitatively different—in the adult and in the child. This capability enables the learner to acquire the general use of a foreign language by observation and exercise of particular instances of the language in use. Such observation and exercise is necessary, because without it, language cannot be learned as language; sufficient, because the learner can do the analysis for himself. The main control the

---

††††† There may be indirect ones. If as a person learns a second language he abandons the situations in which he speaks his native one, he may actually forget the latter. But such loss of native habits is like any other loss of skills which are not exercised: the proper learning of new skills—in contexts sharply set off from those appropriate for the old ones—does not interfere with the old ones.

teacher needs to exert over the materials to be studied is that they be graspable as usable items by the learner. The language learning capability of the student will gradually take care of the rest.

APPENDIX I

(To review the use of ME, TO ME, FOR ME, etc.) Listen to the words and the statements. Include the words in the statements. For example:

Me   She talked about music.
         SHE TALKED ABOUT MUSIC TO ME.
Them   He asked some questions.
         HE ASKED THEM SOME QUESTIONS.
John   The teacher pronounced the word.
         THE TEACHER PRONOUNCED THE WORD FOR JOHN.

1. Us. He talked about Ann Arbor.
2. Me. He visited in Miami.
3. Them. They waited.
4. Me. He told a story.
5. John. She made a cake.
6. Her. He explained the program.
7. Him. I asked for a cigarette.
8. Mary. John pronounced the sentence.
9. Him. We bought a present.
10. Me. John did the work.
11. Bill. Mary introduced us.
12. Them. He got some pencils.
13. His mother. He wrote a letter.
14. The class. He is going to speak about language.
15. Her. He always says a kind thing.‡‡‡‡‡

APPENDIX II

PRÉTEXTES

Galathée et son amie sont au restaurant universitaire et Galathée voit Hector qui la cherche. Elle est en colère contre lui, et ne veut pas lui parler.

‡‡‡‡‡ Robert Lado and Charles C. Fries, *English Sentence Patterns* (Ann Arbor, 1957), p. 94.

1.

Galathée (à voix basse):	Fais semblant de ne pas voir!
L'amie (étonnée):	Pourquoi? Je ne vois personne.
Galathée (insistante):	Il y a Hector qui me cherche et je ne veux pas lui parler.
L'amie:	De toute façon je ne crois pas qu'il nous aperçoive.

2. Même que 1.

Galathée (chuchotant):	Fais semblant de ne pas entendre.
L'amie (étonnée):	Pourquoi? Je n'entends rien!
Galathée (avec urgence):	Il y a Hector qui m'appelle et je ne veux pas le voir.
L'amie:	De toute façon je crois qu'il nous aperçoit.

3. En classe. Galathée n'écoute pas et le professeur la regarde d'un mauvais oeil. Hector essaie de la rappeler à l'ordre.

Hector (sans en avoir l'air):	Fais semblant d'écouter.
Galathée (baillant):	Pourquoi? Je suis trop fatiguée.
Hector (avec urgence):	Il y a le professeur qui te regarde et il voit bien que tu ne sais pas.
Galathée (indifférente):	De toute façon il ne croit pas que je sois très intelligente.

4. A la bibliothèque. Hector et son copain voient Galathée qui vient dans leur direction. Le copain d'Hector ne peut pas sentir Galathée et veut l'éviter.

Le copain (avec urgence):	Vite, fais semblant d'étudier.
Hector (étonné):	Pourquoi? C'est bien ce que je fais.
Le copain (avec insistance):	Il y a Galathée qui approche et je ne veux pas qu'elle vienne ici.
Hector:	De toute façon je ne crois pas qu'il y ait de place libre.

PRETEXTS

Galathea and her friend are at the cafeteria and Galathea sees Hector looking for her. She is mad at him and doesn't want to speak to him.

1.

Galathea: (in a low voice)	Pretend that you don't see anyone.
Friend: (surprised)	Why? I don't see anyone.
Galathea: (impatiently)	Hector's looking for me, and I don't want to talk to him.
Friend:	Well, anyway, I don't think he will notice us.

2. Same as 1.

Galathea: (whispers)	Pretend that you don't hear anything.
Friend: (surprised)	Why? I don't hear anything!
Galathea: (urgently)	Hector's calling me and I don't want to see him.
Friend:	In any case, I think that he's noticed us.

3. During class, Galathea is not listening and the teacher is glaring at her. Hector tries to get her to pay attention.

Hector: (out of the side of his mouth)	Hey, pretend to be listening.
Galathea: (yawning)	Why? I'm too tired.
Hector: (urging)	The teacher is looking at you and he can see you are not paying attention.
Galathea: (indifferent)	Well, anyway, he doesn't think I'm very intelligent.

4. At the library. Hector and his buddy see Galathea coming in their direction. Hector's buddy can't stand Galathea and wants to avoid her.

Buddy: (urgently)	Quick, pretend that you're studying.
Hector: (surprised)	Why? That's what I am doing.
Buddy: (insisting)	Galathea is coming this way and I don't want to talk to her.
Hector:	Well, anyway, I don't think there's any room.

After his performance of the dialogue-variants has become fluent and natural, the learner is encouraged to make new uses and new combinations of the language he has acquired, as in conversations like the following. The indirect cues mitigate the compulsion to translate from English into the foreign language. The learner supplies some of the language needed to perform the conversations from previously learned dialogues. Short conversations allow the situation to be comprehended quickly and without effort.§§§§§

CONVERSATION 1

You are on the bus with a friend and spot Jules to whom you owe some money. Your friend is about to call over to Jules.

You . . . . . . Tell your friend to pretend that he is looking out of the window.

He . . . . . . Asks you why, he's about to call over to Jules.

You . . . . . . Tell him that Jules is looking for you, that you owe him money.

He . . . . . . Says O.K., but not to worry, Jules has probably not noticed you.

CONVERSATION 2

You and your boy friend are at a night club, and you spot your ex-fiancé across the room.

You . . . . . . Tell your boy friend to pretend to be talking to you.

He . . . . . . Says that that is exactly what he's doing.

You . . . . . . Say that an old friend of yours is sitting across the room, and you don't want him to notice you.

He . . . . . . Says not to worry, in any case it is too dark here to see anything.

§§§§§ An explicit use of this device is also to be found in the exercises called "Conversation" in the old *Spoken Language Series* (ca. 1945) now published by Holt, Rinehart and Winston, Inc., New York. Cf. the following from Jeannette Dearden and Karin Stig-Nielsen, *Spoken Danish* (Book One) (New York, 1945), p. v.:

"The Conversation Practice represents the central aim of the course. Situations will be outlined which will give you the setting for your conversations. Here you will be able to use all the material that you have learned up to this point."

LEON JAKOBOVITS

Implications of Recent Psycholinguistic Developments for the Teaching of a Second Language

INTRODUCTION

This paper is divided into two large sections. The first is concerned with the child's acquisition of his first language. The second section deals with second language learning. Jakobovits differentiates between learning theory and the new view originated by Chomsky in terms of the explanation of how a child acquires his first language. He characterizes the two positions in terms of the relation of *surface* and *base*:

> (in learning theory) the process of acquisition was from surface to base; that is, the knowledge represented by language learning at all levels—phonological, semantic, syntactic—was entirely based on the relations contained in the overt speech of the parents. The new approach . . . can be characterized by saying that it reverses this order; that is, the burden of acquisition is now placed on the child with relatively minor importance attached to the environment as a *reinforcing* agency. Furthermore, it minimizes the relations contained in the surface of language, attributing the significant information to be acquired to the underlying structure of language which is not contained in the surface input.

Reprinted with permission of the author from *Language Learning*, Vol. XVIII, Nos. 1 and 2 (June), 1968, pp. 89–109.

Jakobovits then points out and discusses three specific inadequacies of the older view: (1) "The acquisition of phonology," (2) "The acquisition of meaning," and (3) "The acquisition of syntax." In the view of learning theory, the child learns the identity of the sound elements of the adult language by the process of association. Jakobovits argues that the structure of the sound system of the adult language is not just a series of elements: "the 'cracking' of the phonological code of a natural language involves a process of pattern recognition and equation, not simply learning the identity of constituent elements."

From the standpoint of learning theory, the meaning of words is learned by association. This in turn leads to the view that "words tag things." Jakobovits points out that this conception of meaning is inadequate to explain our capacity to extend the meanings of words, as, for instance, the *eye* in *the eye of the needle* because learning theory can only specify the nature of the extension after it has happened, that is, it has no predictive power. As the author puts it, "the creative and novel use of words which is so characteristic of language remains completely beyond its explanatory range."

The learning theory view of syntax was that a sentence is composed of a sequence of words learned in terms of the sequential probabilities of the items. Jakobovits rejects this view on the grounds that sentences, in fact, are much more complex than that. He demonstrates this by citing several sets of sentences whose relationships with the other sentences within their set could not be accounted for by simply viewing a sentence as a sequence of items in a certain fixed pattern.

Since, according to Jakobovits, the traditional view of first language acquisition seems inadequate, "it is necessary to start anew right from the beginning." The author turns his attention to the study of how children first begin to combine words into two-word sequences (beginning at about 1½ years). The two-word combinations are neither random groupings nor the result of direct imitation of adult sentences. The two-word combinations have their own special structure consisting of what is called a "pivot" class and an "open" class of words. As the child matures, the pivot class gradually subdivides into further classes. The important point here is that children do not discover word classes by rearranging the elements they hear in adult speech in some trial-and-error way, as learning theory would suggest. Instead, the child seems predisposed to "look for" certain kinds of relationships. Thus the child's ability to discover these grammatical capacities must be based on "linguistic universals that are part of the child's innate endowment" (quoting McNeill). A second kind of grammatical capacity, also innate, is transformational rules. However, as the author points out, "the early stages of child language competence does not apparently include the ability to perform transformations."

In the second section, the author examines "the implications for language teaching of the views outlined earlier on the language acquisition process." The author discusses these three topics in reference to second language teaching: (1) "The role of practice and imitation," (2) "The distinction between competence and performance," and (3) "The nature of skills involved in foreign language acquisition."

1. "The role of practice and imitation." In the view of the Behavioral school, practice and imitation were essential steps in the learning process. It is only through practice that a novel form becomes "stamped in." In reply, Jakobovits argues that children do not readily mimick a form that they do not already possess, and in fact regularize the forms of the adult language to fit their own generalizations. As Jakobovits says, "concept attainment and hypothesis testing are more likely paradigms in language development than response strength through rote memory and repetition."

2. "The distinction between competence and performance." If one basic language competence underlies all language performance, why does "one type of performance, understanding, appear to develop before another type of performance, speaking"? After discussing a possible solution that McNeill proposes, Jakobovits advances the theory that understanding and speaking employ different kinds of capabilities or processes: understanding is essentially analytic while speaking is synthetic. "It may be that for humans, analytic processes are easier than synthetic ones. One might say that it is easier to learn the art critic's job than the artist's."

3. "The nature of skills involved in foreign language acquisition." Jakobovits points out some differences between first language learning and second language learning: (1) an adult's cognitive development is more advanced than a child's, and (2) the fact that the adult already knows one language will facilitate the learning of the second through transfer of skills and concepts acquired in the first language. In reference to the first point, Jakobovits points out that language acquisition is an innate endowment, and consequently it is not clear that advanced age and cognitive development will help. In reference to the second point, Jakobovits argues that while in some areas at least it is possible to make predictions about what features of English a learner of English will have special difficulty with, this gives us no insight into how he will eventually overcome the difficulty. For instance, the fact that we can predict that a Japanese will have trouble with /l/ and /r/ does not suggest how we should teach him to make the distinction.

Jakobovits closes the article with a discussion of four specific topics in the teaching of a second language. (1) "Teaching the knowledge of structure." Since knowing a language means knowing sets of relations "rather than constituent elements, the usefulness of efforts to teach the latter is in doubt." (2) "Teaching successful strategies of acquisition." Following Carroll, it is possible to identify strategies that successful language learners employ. It is possible that these strategies may be teachable. (3) "Teaching habit integration and automaticity." Here Jakobovits proposes teaching exercises based on meaning (for example, families of transformational rules and vocabulary organized in semantic clusters) rather than on surface forms and patterns. (4) "On semi-grammatical sentences." In fluent speech semi-grammatical sentences are as common, and perhaps even more common, than well-formed sentences. Children seem able to use semi-grammatical sentences as the base for acquiring the rules governing the creation of well-formed sentences. "The logical implication of this would be that no language teacher should ever force his pupils to use only well-formed sentences in practice conversations."

This paper attempts to summarize some recently developed notions about the language acquisition process and makes some preliminary suggestions about the implications of these ideas for the problem of teaching a second language.* The original impetus in demonstrating the shortcomings of traditional psychological and linguistic theories in the understanding of the processes of language structure and language acquisition must be credited to Chomsky (1957; 1959) who also developed new theories to cope with the problem. Subsequent writers have elaborated upon this new outlook pointing out the various specific inadequacies of the earlier notions and making concrete suggestions for new approaches (see Miller, 1965; Katz, 1966; McNeill, 1966; Lenneberg, 1967; Slobin, 1966; and several others; see the contributions in Bellugi and Brown, 1964). To appreciate fully these new developments it is necessary to consider briefly the nature of the inadequacy of the earlier notions on the language acquisition process.

FROM SURFACE TO BASE

The traditional psychological approach to the language acquisition process was to view it within the framework of learning theory. The acquisition of phonology was viewed as a process of shaping the elementary sounds produced by the infant through reinforcement of successive approximations to the adult pattern. Imitation of adult speech patterns was thought to be a source of reward to the babbling

---

* This is an invited address to the 1968 convention of TESOL (Teachers of English to Speakers of Other Languages) delivered in San Antonio, Texas, March 9, 1968. The two sources to which I am most indebted in the preparation of this paper are McNeill (1966) and Lenneberg (1967) whose stimulating ideas it is a pleasure to acknowledge.

infant and repeated practice on these novel motor habits was thought to serve the function of "stamping in" and automatizing them.

From these elementary phonological habits the words of the language were thought to emerge through parental reinforcement. It was said that the child could better control his environment by uttering words to which the parents responded by giving the child what it wanted. The child learned the meaning of words through a conditioning process whereby the referents which the word signalled appeared in contiguity with the symbol thus establishing an association. The acquisition of grammar was conceptualized as learning the proper order of words in sentences. Generalization carried a heavy theoretical burden in attempts to explain novel uses of words and novel arrangements of sentences. Perceptual similarity of physical objects and relations, and functional equivalence of responses was thought to serve as the basis for generalizing the meaning of previously learned words. Similarly, generalization of the grammatical function of words was thought to account for the understanding and production of novel sentences.

Two aspects of this approach are noteworthy. One is that the burden of language acquisition was placed on the environment: the parents were the source of input, and reinforcement was the necessary condition for establishing the "habits." The child was merely a passive organism responsive to the reinforcement conditions arranged by agencies in the environment. The second aspect to be noted was the relatively simplistic conception of the knowledge to be acquired: sentences were conceived as an ordering of words, arranged in sequential probabilities that could be learned then generalized to novel combinations. A general characterization of this overall approach would be to say that the process of acquisition was from surface to base; that is, the knowledge represented by language learning at all levels— phonological, semantic, syntactic—was entirely based on the relations contained in the overt speech of the parents. The new approach to be discussed below can be characterized by saying that it reverses this order; that is, the burden of acquisition is now placed on the child with relatively minor importance attached to the environment as a *reinforcing* agency. Furthermore, it minimizes the relations contained in the surface of language, attributing the significant information to be acquired to the underlying structure of language which is not contained in the surface input. However, before taking up this new approach, it is necessary to point out the specific inadequacies of the earlier approach.

The acquisition of phonology. The notion that the child first learns the constituent elements of the adult phonemic structure and then produces speech by associating these elements appears to be contrary to fact. In the first place, it is doubtful that speech is made up of a concatenation of physically unique sound elements. A sound typewriter which would convert each physically different sound into a different orthographic type would not produce a very readable record (Lenneberg, 1967). The reason for this is that speech recognition is not simply a process of identifying physical differences in sounds. In fact, it requires overlooking certain acoustic differences as unimportant and paying attention to certain other features in relation to the acoustic context in which the sound is imbedded. In other words, the "cracking" of the phonological code of a natural language involves a process of pattern recognition and equation, not simply learning the identity of constituent elements. The first recognizable words of a child are not composed of acoustically invariant speech sounds (see Lenneberg, 1967). Therefore, a description of phonological acquisition in terms of learning individual speech sounds which are then combined into words, must be false. Furthermore, it is not clear how a notion of shaping by successive approximation can ever account for the acquisition of sound pattern recognition and the discovery by the child of phonological structure of a hierarchical nature.

The acquisition of meaning. It is an indication of the simplistic character of previous behavioristic views of language that they have concerned themselves with the problem of reference to the almost total exclusion of the semantic interpretation of utterances. Reference deals with the relation between words and objects or aspects of the environment. Psychological theories of meaning (or reference) were based on a philosophical system of conceptualization which now appears to be false; namely the notion that "words tag things" in the physical environment. The adoption of such a view led to elementary descriptions whereby a particular combination of sounds (a word) was conditioned to an object or set of objects. When a new object having certain physical similarities to the one previously conditioned was encountered, the learned verbal response was said to have generalized to this new instance. More elaborate versions of this form of theorizing were developed to account for the obvious fact that familiar words would be used in connection with objects or situations which had no physical similarity to the originally conditioned object. However, due to the requirements imposed by viewing meaning as a conditioned response to a stimulus, these later elaborations merely pushed back the locus of the similarity from the external physical object to an internal (even though functional) representation of that object. Thus an individual's capacity to understand the extension of the word *eye* in *the eye of the needle* was thought of as arising from the fact that the internal conditioned responses elicited by the word *eye* in the above phrase are similar in some (unspecified) manner to the responses originally conditioned to the word *eye* in such instances as *this is your eye, these are my eyes, this is the doggy's eye,* etc. The total inadequacy of this kind of approach as an explanatory device is this: it leaves obscure the specific nature of the similarity of the conditioned response from the original to the extension, it is incapable of specifying the nature of the extension and cannot predict it until after it has occurred. Thus the view of reference as a conditioning process has the same shortcomings for semantics as the view of conditioning of sequential probabilities of parts of speech has for syntax. That is, the creative and novel use of words which is so characteristic of language remains completely beyond its explanatory range.

The difficulties attached to these behavioristic explanations of meaning can be resolved by abandoning the notion that "words tag things" in favor of the view that "words tag the processes by which the species deals cognitively with its environment" (Lenneberg, 1967, p. 334). This view reverses the order between the object-stimulus and its conditioned response-process. That is, rather than saying that the concept-meaning involved in the use of the word *eye* is a conditioned process (external, internal, or cortical) developed as a result of tagging various objects having certain characteristics and experiences relating to them, this view says that the word *eye* tags a class of cognitive processes developed through a categorization and differentiation process which is independent of verbal labeling. When a child (or adult for that matter) is confronted with a new word it acquires meaning only in the sense that it comes to refer to a class of cognitive processes already possessed by the individual. Novel uses of words, such as metaphoric extensions are understandable to others by virtue of the fact that human categorization and differentiation processes are similar across the species, the word merely serving as a convenient tag whereby these processes can be labeled. The language of stimulus-response theory does not seem to offer any particular advantages when conceptualizing the problem in this fashion.

A conception of meaning such as the one just outlined, has certain implications for a theory of semantics which it might be important to state explicitly. Meaning becomes a purely cognitive concept (as linguists of a generation ago used to believe) and semantics represents the linguistic expression of these cognitive operations. The problem of the development of meaning becomes the problem of cognitive development, which is to say that the dimensions of meaning—how the human species categorizes and differentiates the universe—*ante-date* the dimensions of semantics—how cognitive categories and relations find expression in linguistic terms. An adequate theory of meaning must be able to characterize the nature of this relation, namely the mapping of cognitive to linguistic processes. Note that this includes not only lexical (vocabulary) items, but also the morphophemic and inflectional system of language, since the latter contain cognitive differentiations such as present vs. past, animate vs. inanimate, definite vs. indefinite, mass vs. count, male vs. female, plural vs. singular, and so on. It follows that an adequate theory of semantics must concern itself not only with the vocabulary of a language and the relation between words and things (reference) but also with the manner in which the syntactic component of a language allows the expression of cognitive relations (meaning). While the first aspect may be conceptualized as a closed system such as that represented by a dictionary of a language, the second aspect is an open system that cannot be described by a taxonomy of properties or relations. In other words, while it is possible to make an inventory of all the words in a language, it is impossible to make an inventory of all the possible usages of any single word (with the exception perhaps of most function words). An adequate semantic theory must therefore contain at least the following two things: (a) a model of human cognition specifying a finite set of dimensions or features, probably in the form of a generic hierarchy of increasing inclusiveness as we move up the tree, and (b) a set of finite rules (or transformations) specifying the possibilities of manipulations of the elements in the tree. The description of (a) must be a general psychological theory and is made up of "psychological or cognitive universals" as defined by the biological capacity of the human species. The description of (b) must be a cultural and individual psychological theory as defined by individual differences in general intelligence and in personal experiences.

The acquisition of syntax. The failure of behavior theory to account in any significant manner for the problem of the acquisition of syntax can be interpreted as stemming from a failure to recognize the complexity of the syntax of language. As long as sentences are viewed as a sequential ordering of words or categories of words and the phenomenon to be explained as a problem in the learning of sequential probabilities of items or classes of items, no meaningful progress can be made. The relations among the following eight sentences taken from Lenneberg (1967, p. 273–275) illustrate the complexities of the problem to be dealt with:

1. colorless green ideas sleep furiously
2. furiously sleep ideas green colorless
3. occasionally call warfare useless
4. useless warfare call occasionally
5. friendly young dogs seem harmless
6. the fox chases the dog
7. the dog chases the fox
8. the dog is chased by the fox

If one compares sentence (1) and (2) it is evident that (1) is grammatical while (2) is not. The difference cannot be entirely in their meaning for, although sentence (1) is more likely to have some meaning than sentence (2), nevertheless sentence (1) will be judged more grammatical than sentence (2) even by the most prosaically inclined person. Nor can it be said that the reason sentence (1) is more grammatical than sentence (2) is that it is more familiar, since both sentences had a frequency of zero until linguists began to use it a short while ago to make the kind of point that is being made here. The ungrammatical string (4) has the same order of parts of speech as the grammatical string (1), namely (adjective + noun + verb + adverb). Similarly, the grammatical and semantically interpretable sentence (3)† has the same order of parts of speech as the ungrammatical and semantically uninterpretable string (2), namely (adverb + verb + noun + adjective). This shows that the transitional probability of parts of speech in a sentence cannot account for either their grammaticality or their susceptibility to semantic interpretation. The same is true for the order of morphemes in the sentence as shown by the fact that sentence (5) which is both grammatical and meaningful uses the same order of bound morphemes (-ly, -s, -ly) as sentence (2) which is neither grammatical nor meaningful. Sentences (6) and (7) demonstrate that the particular words used offer no clue to the meaning of the sentence. Sentence (8) can be recognized as having the same meaning as sentence (6) even though the order of subject and object is the same as that of sentence (7) showing that directional associations between the ordered elements are irrelevant to the understanding of the sentence.

These various examples should suffice to convince one that the process of acquiring language must involve a much more complex analysis procedure than that offered by such surface relations of sentences as order of elements and word-associations. As if this were not

---

† Sentence (3) might occur, as Lenneberg points out, "in an instruction booklet on pacifist rhetoric" (1967, p. 274).

enough, we are confronted with the added complication that the child is continuously exposed to both well-formed and semi-grammatical sentences in the ordinary speech of adult speakers. Out of this confused input, it has to be able to separate out the false clues from the correct ones, yet it demonstrates this ability and succeeds in the relatively short period of 24 months (roughly from age one-and-a-half to three-and-a-half). Let us now turn to these newer formulations of child language acquisition.

FROM BASE TO SURFACE

If we discard earlier theories of language acquisition as unproductive, it is necessary to start anew right from the beginning. The study of the acquisition of grammar usually begins when the child is at about a-year-and-a-half, the time when he begins to use two word combinations. Prior to that it is difficult to study the child's grammatical competence since he uses single words, and techniques have not as yet been developed to study the child's grammatical comprehension at that early age. Speech records of a child over successive periods offer a picture of a changing grammar which the psycholinguist attempts to characterize in formal terms by giving a description of its structure at each period. This approach is necessarily limited since an inference of grammatical competence must be made from the child's speech performance, the latter being affected by a number of variables that are not directly relevant to grammatical competence (e.g. memory span, temporal integration, inattention, etc.). Given this limitation, we can nevertheless inquire as to the kind of developmental picture that emerges.

Differentiation of generic classes. Children's earliest utterances of two words (or more) exhibit non-random combinations of some words. Some examples from the speech of three children reported in the literature are the following (McNeill, 1966, Table 1): *big boy, allgone shoe, two boot, that baby, here pretty.* Distributional analysis of these two-word combinations reveals that the words the child uses at this earliest stage fall into two categories in terms of their privileges of occurrence. One of the two classes contains a small number of words each having a relatively high frequency of occurrence. Examples of this class include *allgone, big, my, see* in one child's speech, *my, two, a, green,* in a second child's speech, and in a third, *this, a, here.* The second class contains a larger number of words and additions of new words to this class occur at a higher rate (some examples are: *boat, Mommy, tinkertoy, come, doed).* Words in this second class occur by themselves or in combination with words from the first class, while words in the first class never occur by themselves. For these reasons, the first class was named the "pivot" class (P) while the second class was named the "open" class (O). A shorthand expression of these facts can be represented by the following notation:

$$S \longrightarrow (P) + O$$

This notation implies that the child's competence includes a rule which says that a sentence, S, can be produced by combining any two words from class P and class O (in that order) or, alternately, by using any single word from class O. The rule excludes such sentences made up of two words from the same class, or a sentence made up of a single word from the P class.

It is to be noted that the rule[‡] for constructing this earliest sentence cannot have been developed as a result of direct mimicking of adult sentences. Many of the two-word combinations that this rule generates are in the wrong order from the point of view of adult speech (e.g. *allgone shoe* vs. the likely adult model of the *shoe is allgone*). In addition, it permits combinations that are unlikely to occur in adult speech at all (e.g. *big milk*). Such novel (and non-adult) combinations and the ready substitutability of words within each category are convincing arguments that these word combinations could not be memorized imitations of adult speech.

Distributional analysis of successive speech records of the children that have been studied shows that the words in the original pivot class begin to subdivide into progressively more differentiated categories in a hierarchical manner that can be represented as follows (based on McNeill, 1966, Fig. 1):

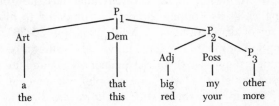

This representation shows that the original pivot class (P_1) subdivided into three classes of words: Articles, Demonstrative Pronouns, and all

[‡] The concept of a grammatical "rule" as used in generative transformational linguistics in no way implies that the individual is consciously aware of what he is doing. "Rule" is to be understood in its formal (mathematical) sense as an expression that generates a set of operations of defined elements.

the rest (P_2). Subsequently, P_2 subdivided into three further classes: Adjectives, Possessive Pronouns, and all the rest (P_3).

The implications of this picture are extremely important. Note that there is no logical necessity for the development of grammatical distinctions to assume this particular form of development. The child could have made up categories of words on a trial and error basis, continually rearranging them on the basis of evidence contained in adult speech. He could thus isolate a category of words that correspond to adjectives, or articles, or possessives, until he gradually homes in on the full fledged adult pattern. However, instead of making, as it were, a distributional analysis of adult speech, he seems to have come up with a progressive differentiation strategy that has the peculiar property of being made up of a *generic* class at each point: that is, the original pivot class must already honor in a generic form all the future distinctions at level 2; the undifferentiated pivot class at level 2 (P_2) must contain in a generic form all the future distinctions at level 3, and so on. In other words, the child seems to honor grammatical distinctions in advance of the time they actually develop. How is this possible?

McNeill's conclusion is as bold as it is inevitable: the hierarchy of progressive differentiation of grammatical categories "represents linguistic universals that are part of the child's innate endowment. The role of a universal hierarchy of categories would be to direct the child's discovery of the classes of English. It is as if he were equipped with a set of 'templates' against which he can compare the speech he happens to hear from his parents. . . . We can imagine, then, that a child classifies the random specimens of adult speech he encounters according to universal categories that the speech exemplifies. Since these distinctions are at the top of a hierarchy that has the grammatical classes of English at its bottom, the child is prepared to discover the appropriate set of distinctions" (McNeill, 1966, pp. 35–36).

The assumption of innate language universals is sure to be unacceptable to current behaviorist theories. Someone is bound to point out that one doesn't explain the "why" of a complex phenomenon by saying it is innate. The fact of the matter is, however, that the complex behavior system of any organism is bound to be dependent upon the structural and functional properties of its nervous system. Language is a product of man's cognition, and as Lenneberg (1967, p. 334) points out, "man's cognition functions within biologically given limits." Granting the innateness of language universals, the task of explaining the "how" of language acquisition is still ahead of us. The scientific investigation of language, both from the linguist's and the psycholinguist's point of view, is to give an adequate characterization of the structure of the child's innately endowed "language acquisition device," the nature of its universal categories and their interrelations.

The development of transformations. The ability to manipulate transformations constitutes an essential part of linguistic competence according to the generative linguistics developed by Chomsky, and Lenneberg (1967) argues convincingly that transformations are an essential aspect of categorization processes of all biological organisms. An insight into the nature of linguistic transformations can be gained by considering the manner by which the following two sentences are understood by an adult speaker (based on Lenneberg, 1967, pp. 286–292):

1. they are boring students
2. the shooting of the hunters was terrible

Both sentences are semantically ambiguous. The ambiguity in sentence (1) can be resolved by a process of "bracketing" which reveals that its constituent elements can be broken up into two different "phrase markers,"§ as follows:

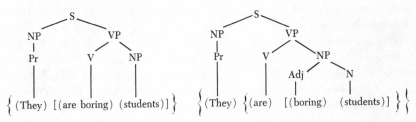

This phrase marker shows that the ambiguity of the sentence lies in the fact that the word *boring* functions in one case as an inflected verb-form, and in the other case, as an adjective modifying the word *students.* Now consider sentence (2): it is ambiguous in at least two ways (one could say that either the hunters need more practice or they need a funeral!). Only one phrase marker description is possible for this sentence, so we need some other process to explain its ambiguity. One interpretation is related to the sentence *hunters shoot inaccurately,* the other, to the sentence *hunters are shot.* The reason we understand the ambiguity of sentence (2) may thus be

§ A phrase marker is simply a graphic representation of the constituents of a sentence. "Bracketing" shown at the bottom of this figure is an alternative method of accomplishing the same thing.

attributed to the fact that we are able to recognize the relation between it and two other sentences each of which has its own distinct phrase marker. This is the essence of transformations: they are laws that control the relations between sentences that have "grammatical affinity."

The early stages of child language competence does not apparently include the ability to perform transformations, according to McNeill (1966) who relates the impetus for acquiring transformations to the cumbersomeness of having to manipulate the elementary forms of sentences in the underlying structure of language ("base strings"). (More extensive discussion on the development of transformations is not possible here. The reader is referred to McNeill, 1966, pp. 53–65).

IMPLICATIONS FOR SECOND LANGUAGE TEACHING

The view on language acquisition that has been outlined may at first appear frustrating to those whose inclination and business it is to teach language. The claim that a child has achieved linguistic competence by age three-and-a-half is likely to be scoffed at by the elementary school teacher in composition. At the claim that grammatical rules are discovered by the child through linguistic universals, the foreign language teacher is likely to wonder what happened to this marvelous capacity in the foreign language laboratory. In this section, I would like to examine the implications for language teaching of the views outlined earlier on the language acquisition process. I shall discuss a number of topics including the role of practice and imitation, the distinction between competence and performance, and the nature of skills involved in foreign language acquisition.

The role of practice and imitation. The assumption that practice plays a crucial role in language acquisition has been central to earlier speculations. To Behaviorists it is almost an axiom not to be questioned. This view rests on the basic assertion that there exists a fundamental continuity between language acquisition and the forms of learning studied in the psychological laboratory. Chomsky (1959), Miller (1965), Lenneberg (1967), and others have questioned this view on general grounds and McNeill (1966) questions it on more specific and reduced grounds. Granting the language acquisition process is guided by the child's innate knowledge of language universals, does practice theory explain how children go about finding out the locally appropriate expression of the linguistic universals?

Practice theory leads to two possible hypotheses about language acquisition: one is that when the child is exposed to a novel grammatical form, he imitates it; the other is that by practicing this novel form it becomes "stamped in." The evidence available indicates that both hypotheses are false. A direct test of children's tendency (or ability) to imitate adult forms of speech shows that children almost never repeat the adult sentence as it is presented. A child does not readily "mimic" a grammatical form that is not already in his repertoire as evidenced by his own spontaneous utterances. Direct attempts at imitation of adult sentences end up being recoded by the child, as the following examples taken from Lenneberg (1967, p. 316) illustrate:

Model Sentence	Child's Repetition
Johnny is a good boy.	Johnny is good boy.
He takes them for a walk.	He take them to the walk.
Lassie does not like the water.	He no like the water.
Does Johnny want a cat?	Johnny wants a cat?

It has been estimated that only about ten percent of a child's "imitations" of adult speech are "grammatically progressive" (that is, embodying a form novel to the child).

Whatever the means by which novel forms enter the child's speech, does practice strengthen these responses? The evolution of the child's command of the past tense of verbs provides negative evidence to this question. In the child's early language, the past tense of the irregular strong verbs in English (*came, went, sat*) appear with high frequency relative to the regularized /d/ and /t/ forms of the weak verbs. Thus, we would expect that these much practiced irregular forms would be highly stable, more so than the regular forms. Yet evidence shows that they are in fact less stable than the less practiced regular form, as indicated by the fact that at a certain point in the child's development he suddenly abandons the irregular form in favor of the regularized form and produces *comed, goed, sitted*. This kind of discontinuity shows that the practice model is not applicable here; rules that the child discovers are more important and carry greater weight than practice. Concept attainment and hypothesis testing are more likely paradigms in language development than response strength through rote memory and repetition.

This realization ought not to lead to pessimism about the potential usefulness of language *teaching*. There is strong evidence that the attainment of grammatical rules can be facilitated by proper presentation of speech materials. Observation of children's speech during play interaction with an adult (usually the mother) shows that up to half of their imitations of adult "expansions" of children's speech are grammatically progressive (McNeill citing data by Slobin, 1966, p. 75). An expansion is an adult's "correction" of the child's utterance. The advantage expansions seem to hold over other samples of adult speech may be attributable to the fact that expansions exemplify a locally appropriate expression of a linguistic universal at a time when the child is most ready to notice such a distinction. For example, if the child says *Adam cry,* and the mother expands this by saying *Yes, Adam cried* (or *Yes, Adam is crying*—depending on her understanding of what the child intends), the child is thereby given the opportunity of discovering the specific manner in which the past tense form (or progressive form) is expressed in English at a time when this distinction is maximally salient to him. The faster development of language in children of middle-class educated parents may be attributable to a tendency on the part of these mothers to expand to a greater extent than other parents. However, this hypothesis needs further investigation.

On the distinction between competence and performance. This distinction has been recognized by all psychological theories, including behavioristic ones (see Hull's, 1943, distinction between $_sE_R$ and $_s\bar{E}_R$). A confusion that may arise in language behavior comes from the fact that *understanding* is usually (if not always) superior to *speaking* and one might want to equate understanding with competence and speaking with performance. However, this cannot be the case. Both understanding and speaking must be viewed as performance variables since the non-linguistic variables that affect speaking (e.g. memory span, temporal integration, inattention, etc.) are equally likely to affect understanding. We are thus confronted with the fact that one type of performance, understanding, appears to develop before another type of performance, speaking. What may be responsible for this?

McNeill (1966) examines the specific claim that every grammatical feature appears first in understanding and second in speaking and is led to the conclusion that the overall parameters of conversion from competence to performance are simpler, less complex, easier in the case of understanding. In order to account for this fact, he postulates three kinds of memory span of different size or length, in the following order of decreasing magnitude: phonological production, grammatical comprehension, and grammatical production. This is intended to account for some data by Fraser, Bellugi, and Brown (1963) showing that a child can repeat a longer sentence than it can either understand or produce spontaneously, and also that it can understand a longer sentence than it can produce spontaneously. The difficulty with McNeill's hypothesis is that it equates sentence length with sentence complexity. It would seem that it is easier to understand a long but simple

sentence than a short but involved one. It would also appear that one
can understand a sentence too long to be repeated. Children show
evidence of having understood sentences they cannot (or will not)
repeat (see Lenneberg, 1967, p. 316). The problem may be conceptualized in a different way, as illustrated by the following diagram:

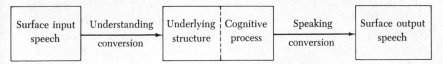

The asymmetry between the capacity to perform the understanding
conversion as opposed to the speaking conversion may be related
to the fact that the former requires an analytic approach while
the latter demands a synthetic capability. It may be that for humans,
analytic processes are easier than synthetic ones. One might say that
it is easier to learn the art critic's job than the artist's.

The acquisition of foreign language skills. Let us raise the question of the specific relevance of our discussion on first language acquisition for an understanding of second language learning and teaching.
What are the parallels to be considered? First, let us look at the argument for the differences. Assuming second language acquisition which
takes place after the age of four, one may point out the following:
(i) the individual's cognitive development is at a later and more
advanced stage; (ii) he is already in possession of the grammatical
structure of a language which may serve to facilitate the acquisition
of a second one through transfer; (iii) he already possesses concepts
and meanings, the problem now being one of expressing them through
a new vocabulary.

The importance of the first argument would seem to depend on the
relevance of cognitive development for the acquisition of language.
The view outlined in this paper is that the necessary knowledge for
language acquisition cannot be gained from experience with the outside world, that language acquisition is dependent on an innate endowment which constitutes the knowledge of language universals. Hence,
the imputed advantage of advanced age and cognitive development is
a dubious proposition. The two other arguments are based on the
assumption of the operation of transfer in grammatical structure and
in reference (vocabulary). What is the evidence in support of this
assumption? It is necessary to distinguish between two claims about
transfer theory. One refers to the general expectation that new forms
of learning do not go on independently of what the organism has

learned before. The truth of this statement would seem fairly obvious and need not concern us further. The second and specific claim expresses the expectation that the learning of certain specific and identifiable elements in Task B are facilitated (or hindered) by the previous learning of certain specific and identifiable elements in Task A. The status of this strong claim for any type of complex learning outside the laboratory is unknown. A serious test of it in second language acquisition would require the prior analysis of the two languages in a form which would identify the specific elements to be transferred at the grammatical and lexical levels. On *a priori* grounds we would expect negative transfer as much as positive transfer, assuming that transfer is relevant to the problem. Carroll (1966b) claims that the Modern Language Aptitude Test designed for English speakers predicts success in a foreign language equally well irrespective of the particular language involved. This is difficult to explain if transfer has any overall relevance to the language acquisition process. Nevertheless, some phonological studies on contrastive analysis reviewed by Carroll (1966a) would seem to indicate the operation of negative transfer effects. He cites Suppes *et al.* (1962) who "claim to be able to predict quite precisely from mathematical learning theory what [phoneme] discrimination problems will arise" (Carroll, 1966a, p. 16).

The problem is complicated still further by the possibility that transfer effects might effect performance and competence factors in different ways. Or, the various performance factors themselves (understanding, speaking, reading, writing) may be affected to different degrees. The same comment might be made for different levels of performance, that is phonology, vocabulary, and syntax. A further aspect to this problem is the consideration of whether transfer effects are necessary processes or whether the extent of their operation is dependent on the strategy with which the learner attacks the new task. An individual who tries to "fit in" the dimensions of the new task into the old structure may encounter different problems from the individual who inhibits the interaction of the two tasks, assuming that the latter strategy is possible. Finally, the fact that it is possible to predict errors of confusion, as in contrastive analysis of phonology, is not necessarily an indication that transfer effects will operate in the acquisition of the new task. Thus, the fact that the /l/ and /r/ sounds are predictable areas of confusion for a Japanese learning English says nothing about the way in which he will eventually learn the distinction. It is unlikely that this distinction is learned in isolation. Instead, it is more likely that the confusion will disappear when the overall structure of English phonology is internalized.

The above considerations lead to a number of implications for the teaching of a second language which I shall now take up.

1. *Teaching the knowledge of structure*: since it is clear that knowledge of language at all levels consists of knowing patterns of relations rather than constituent elements, the usefulness of efforts to teach the latter is in doubt. Examples of such efforts include teaching specific sound discriminations, "shaping" of phonological production, vocabulary acquisition through association of translation equivalents, and practice of specific morphological and inflectional examples. Pointing to individuals who successfully acquired a foreign language in a course using these methods has no force of argument, for it is quite possible that their success occurred despite these methods rather than because of them.

2. *Teaching successful strategies of acquisition*: Carroll (1962) has isolated a number of factors which are predictive of success in a foreign language. These may offer clues about the strategies that a successful learner uses with the possibility that such strategies may be taught to those who normally make no use of them. One of the abilities Carroll has identified deals with verbalization of grammatical relations in sentences. The successful foreign language learner is apparently capable of the following task: given a word underlined in one sentence (e.g. "The man went into the *house*") he can identify that word in another sentence which has the same grammatical function (e.g. picking one of the underlined words of the following sentence: "The *church* next to the *bowling alley* will be built in a new *location* next *year*"). We know of course that the individual is capable of recognizing the grammatical relations in the second sentence (otherwise he could not give it a semantic interpretation), so the ability must be one of explicit verbalization of implicitly known rules and relations.‖ Using, perhaps, linguistic theories of transformational grammar the teaching of such verbalizations therefore ought to facilitate foreign language acquisition.

Another variable identified by Carroll "is the ability to 'code' auditory phonetic material in such a way that this material can be recognized, identified and remembered over something longer than a few seconds" (1962, p. 128). We do not know at present the specific strategy that may be employed in facilitating this kind of coding. Whatever it may be, it seems unlikely that the superior person in this task derives

‖ Verbalizing a grammatical relation can take two forms; one refers to the type of statement that can be found in a grammar book that includes technical terms (relative clause, head noun, modifier, predicate phrase, etc.); the second refers to a statement of equivalence or relation expressed in any convenient way using whatever terms are available to the individual, whether technically correct or not.

his advantage from a special innate capacity. In the first place, it is not related to the ability to perceive phonetic distinctions, and second, given the biological foundations of language capacity (see Lenneberg, 1967) it would seem unlikely to expect innate differences in the general capacity of coding phonological material.

Contrastive analysis of grammatical structure would not seem to offer particular advantages beyond those provided by verbalization of grammatical relations and drawing attention to a grammatical distinction at a time of saliency (see the effects of *expansion,* discussed above). The expectation that the advantage of contrastive analysis lies in making the *contrast per se* is based on the assumption of transfer for which the evidence is lacking. At any rate, the pointing up of the *contrast* may just as well lead to negative transfer by facilitating the assimilation (or "fitting in") strategy. I know of no evidence that emphasizing distinctions of incompatible responses, especially those that are automatized, leads to a decrease in incompatibility.

3. Teaching habit integration and automaticity: temporal integration of phonological skills, whether at the understanding or production side, is a problem independent of the knowledge of the phonological structure and transformations of a language. It would seem likely that sensory and motor integrations of this type can be automatized through practice and repetition. The more interesting problem would relate to the time at which automaticity practice is likely to be valuable and the form it is to take. Reading represents a different aspect of phonological production skill than speaking, as is well known, and practice on reading does not represent a sufficient or necessary condition for achieving automaticity of phonological production in speaking.

The factors that enter into the problem of automatizing grammatical habits are not very clear. Tests of speech comprehension under conditions of noise (see for example Spolsky *et al.,* 1966) seem to be quite sensitive to the level of automaticity and degree of integration achieved by a foreign language speaker. They show that the problem of integration goes deeper than high proficiency in understanding and speaking demonstrated under ordinary conditions. At the moment we do not have available a psychological theory of sentence understanding or production. The relevance to this problem of recent experiments on latency of various grammatical manipulations still remains to be shown. Many language teachers seem to be convinced that pattern drills serve to automatize grammatical habits. However, it is difficult to justify this expectation on theoretical grounds. As was discussed earlier in this paper the semantic interpretation of a sentence cannot be viewed as a process of sequential analysis of categories of words. Thus, pattern drills, at best, can only serve to automatize phonological production skills, and for this latter purpose, other methods may prove equally, if not more effective. At any rate, if the pattern drill argument is taken literally, namely that the structure is automatized through practice of the specific pattern that is being repeated, then the learner could never achieve automatized speech. This follows since in ordinary speech we use an infinite variety of patterns, and therefore since the second language learner couldn't possibly be drilled on an infinite variety of patterns he could never develop automatized speech. Hence pattern drill cannot possibly do what it is supposed to be doing.

From a theoretical point of view, development of grammatical competence should be facilitated by getting the learner to perform a set of transformations on families of sentences (e.g. "I cannot pay my rent because I am broke"; "If I weren't broke I could pay my rent"; "Given the fact that I have no money, I cannot pay my rent"; "How do you think I could possibly pay my rent if I am broke"; "Since I am broke, the rent cannot be paid"; "To pay the rent is impossible given the fact that I have no money"; etc.).# The distinction between this, which we may refer to as perhaps "transformation exercises" and "pattern drill" is that the first deals with the competence involved in deep structure while the second focuses on surface structure. As Rutherford** has shown in his paper earlier at this meeting, surface structure similarities are completely unenlightening as to the semantic interpretation of sentences.

The notion of transformation exercises is equally applicable to phonology and vocabulary. DeCamp has given us some examples of practice exercises in phonological transformations in his paper read earlier at this Convention.†† Exercises in vocabulary transformations are more difficult to specify at this stage of our knowledge, but from our discussion on meaning earlier we can perhaps anticipate giving the student a task of this kind: "Change the following list of words using the sex transformation: boy, father, bull, sun"—which might yield: "girl, mother, cow, moon." Or, to give another example: "Change the following list of verbs by effecting a perfective transformation: to drown, to love, to switch on the light, to talk"—which yields: "to eat, to play

---

One of the films shown at the Convention had a demonstration of just this idea. It was made by the Ontario Citizenship Branch. The instructor, Ray Santon, referred to this technique as "structure drill" (in opposition to "pattern drill").

** "Deep and surface structure and the language drill," a paper delivered by William Rutherford of the University of California at Los Angeles.

†† "The current discrepancy between theoretical and applied linguistics" by David DeCamp of the University of Texas.

chess, to sleep, to read."‡‡ Semantic relations of this kind may be responsible for the well-known psychological fact that in memory words are organized in clusters (see, for example, Deese, 1965).

4. *On semi-grammatical sentences*: the fluent speech of most native speakers does not consist totally (or even in the majority of instances) of well-formed sentences. One would imagine that the imposition of a requirement to utter exclusively well-formed sentences would seriously hinder the fluency of most native speakers. The logical implication of this would be that no language teacher should ever force his pupils to use only well-formed sentences in practice conversation whether it be in the classroom, laboratory or outside. This conclusion is not as odd as it might seem on first account. After all children seem to acquire the competence of well-formed sentences despite the semi-grammaticality of the adult speech to which they are continually exposed. It is important to note that semi-grammaticality does not mean randomness. The reason that in most instances we are able to give a semantic interpretation of semi-grammatical sentences lies in the fact that we have the capacity of relating these semi-sentences to their well-formed equivalents. There must therefore exist lawful transformations between semi-sentences and well-formed ones. This is also the reason why we are able to understand the speech of children: the grammar of their utterances is generic of the later grammar of well-formed sentences. If this were not the case, we would not be able to expand (hence, understand) their utterances.

An important question poses itself at this juncture, and it is this: should second language teaching take specific account of the developmental stages that are likely to mark the acquisition of a language? By "specific account" is meant at least the following two things. First, to recognize and allow the production of semi-sentences on the part of the learner. Second, to expose the learner to utterances that are grammatically progressive at each stage but short of having the full complexity of well-formed sentences. The first proposition may already be the policy in some modern and intensive audio-lingual methods which encourage active speech production "at any *cost*" (sic). The second proposition is sure to be resisted by most teachers, yet the fact of the matter is that all "natural" language acquisition situations expose the learner to semi-grammatical sentences more often than not. We do not know whether this is a facilitative or retarding situation. Some parents tend to talk to their children by attempting to imitate their speech and

‡‡ The "perfective" aspect of verbs can be determined by placing the verb in a frame such as this: "If I have _____ but was interrupted, have I _____?" If the answer is "Yes" (e.g. *to talk*), the verb in question has the perfective aspect.

it is sometimes said that this kind of "baby talk" retards acquisition. The evidence on this is simply lacking. It may be, of course, that the fastest method of acquiring a second language need not be one that replicates the conditions existing under "natural" language acquisition. In fact various claims for highly intensive language courses followed by individuals with high foreign language aptitude put the time requirement for the acquisition of a foreign language between 250 and 500 hours of study (Carroll, 1966a, b). Compare to this figure a minimum estimate of 3,000 hours for first language acquisition.[§§] Of course, the two situations are not directly comparable and the level of competence achieved may be different (especially by measures of automaticity and background noise, see Spolsky, *et al.*, 1966), nevertheless the comparison highlights the fact that the "natural" rate of language acquisition process can be greatly accelerated. It is important to note that although the language acquisition capacity *per se* must be viewed as an innate capability shared by all members of the species, the *rate* at which language is acquired, especially a second language, and the effectiveness with which language is used as a *communicative process* are performance factors that are affected by individual differences within the species (variations in general intelligence, in experiences, in physical health, in motivation, etc.). It is here that the concept of *teaching* may assume its full importance.

REFERENCES

Bellugi, Ursula and Brown, Roger (Eds.). The acquisition of language. *Monographs of the Society for Research in Child Development*, 29, 1964.

Carroll, J. B. Research in foreign language teaching: The last five years. In R. G. Mead, Jr., Editor, *Language teaching: Broader contexts, Northeast Conference on the teaching of foreign languages; Reports of the Working Committees*. New York: MLA Materials Center, 1966a.

————. Individual differences in foreign language learning. Paper presented at the Thirty-Second Annual Foreign Language Conference, New York University School of Education, November 5, 1966b.

————. The prediction of success in intensive foreign language training. In Robert Glazer (Ed.), *Training research and education*. Pittsburgh: University of Pittsburgh Press, 1962.

Chomsky, Noam. Review of Skinner's "Verbal Behavior." *Language*, 35, 26–58, 1959.

————. *Syntactic structures*. The Hague: Mouton, 1957.

Deese, James. *The structure of associations in language and thought*. Baltimore: The Johns Hopkins Press, 1965.

[§§] This rough figure is arrived at by estimating the total waking hours of a child up to age three-and-a-half and taking thirty percent of that as an estimate of the amount of exposure to language.

Fraser, C., Bellugi, Ursula and Brown, R. Control of grammar in imitation, comprehension, and production. *Journal of Verbal Learning and Verbal Behavior*, 2, 121–135, 1963.

Hull, C. L. *Principles of behavior*. New York: Appleton-Century-Crofts, 1943.

Katz, J. J. *The philosophy of language*. New York: Harper, 1966.

Lenneberg, E. H. *Biological foundations of language*. New York: John Wiley & Sons, 1967.

McNeill, David. Developmental psycholinguistics. In Frank Smith and G. A. Miller (Eds.), *The genesis of language: A psycholinguistic approach*. Cambridge, Mass.: The M.I.T. Press, 1966.

Miller, G. A. Some preliminaries to psycholinguistics. *American Psychologist*, 20, 15–20, 1965.

Slobin, D. I. The acquisition of Russian as a native language. In Smith and Miller (1966).

Spolsky, B., Sigurd, B., Sato, M., Walker, E. and Arterburn, Catharine. Preliminary studies in the development of techniques for testing overall second language proficiency. Indiana Language Program, Indiana University, Bloomington, Indiana, 1966 (mimeo.).

Suppes, P., Crothers, E., Weir, Ruth, and Trager, Edith. Some quantitative studies of Russian consonant phoneme discrimination. Stanford, Calif.: Institute for Mathematical Studies in the Social Sciences, Technical Report No. 49, 1962.

BERNARD SPOLSKY

Linguistics and Language Pedagogy
—Applications or Implications?

The terms *applications* and *implications* from the subtitle of Spolsky's article suggest two views of the relationship of linguistics to language pedagogy. One view is that linguistic theory and the description of specific languages are applied directly to language pedagogy in a one-way relationship (this is the "application" view). The other view, which Spolsky argues for, is that language pedagogy needs a two-way relationship with both linguistics (linguistic theory and language description) and learning theory. In this relationship (the "implication" view) language pedagogy seeks out the implications from linguistics and learning theory that are relevant to its own interests and attempts to construct a consistent theory of language pedagogy from them. In turn, language pedagogy provides both a meeting place and a testing ground for linguistics and learning theory.

Reprinted from Monograph on Languages and Linguistics No. 22, *Report of the 20th Annual Round Table Meeting*, by James E. Alatis, Editor. Copyright 1970, Georgetown University Press, Washington, D. C., pp. 143–155. Reprinted by permission of the author and the Georgetown University Press.

Spolsky believes that language pedagogy can draw implications from three fields of linguistics: (1) linguistic theory, (2) psycholinguistics, and (3) sociolinguistics. He sets forth seventeen implications: from linguistic theory he derives eight specific implications (numbers 1–8). From psycholinguistics he derives three specific implications (numbers 9–11). From sociolinguistics he derives six specific implications (numbers 12–17). These implications constitute a hypothesis for a theory of second-language pedagogy, which must be tested against actual language teaching.

Spolsky closes the article with a discussion of the relevance of the methods of second-language teaching to work with standard dialect teaching. He argues that a theory of language pedagogy does not itself dictate a method; rather, it provides implications for the development of a method for a particular teaching task. What methods of second-language teaching would be appropriate to teaching standard dialect is an open question. Before a decision can be made, we need to know how the standard dialect differs from the child's dialect. An even larger question is whether the standard dialect should be taught at all. He argues that linguists, because they have a special knowledge, must become involved in such policy questions as "whether it is better to change the language of the lower status groups or the attitudes of society to that language."

∗

ABSTRACT

Much of the disagreement over the relevance of linguistics to language teaching has been caused by a failure to distinguish between the application of linguistics and its implications. On the one hand, linguistics and its related fields especially psycholinguistics and sociolinguistics help lay down the basis for a theory of second-language acquisition; on the other, linguistics (especially that part of it concerned with language description) may be applied in the preparation of teaching material. But the applications and the implications are distinct.

In his luncheon address to last year's Round Table, Kenneth Mildenberger (1968) called for restraint in the public debate over linguistic matters. He asked linguists not to enlarge the credibility gap that he feared was growing between them and language teachers. He urged calm discussion rather than the intemperance that might frighten teachers back to the bad old ways. With full recognition of this, I shall do my best to avoid exacerbating any controversy. But of course I cannot avoid stating what I have come to believe. One of my own teachers always pointed out, when he was attacked for the "complexity" of modern linguistics and its consequent unsuitability for pedagogy, that it would be easier to teach that there are four elements, earth, air, fire, and water, than to get involved in the intricacies of the periodic table. But get involved we must: whatever simplifications are to be made in the interest of ease of teaching, they must surely be based on our best knowledge of the truth. And the truth is seldom simple.

When you look carefully, you find, in fact, that if there is one thing that the applied linguist has been successful at, it has been in his publicity campaign. No publisher today will risk a book in the field of language teaching without linguistics or a linguist on the title page. And the recent study conducted by Hayes and his colleagues has shown that whatever effect NDEA money has had on teacher qualifications and teaching quality, it has certainly been successful in setting up the ALM gospel as the popular wisdom. In under thirty years, then, the "applied linguists" have won their public debate with the "traditionalists," and even more importantly have captured the sources of power—textbook purchasing and federal funding. For most of that time, the attacks on them came from the right wing: from old-fashioned teachers who argued to be left alone with their translation and their reading. But just as the battle seemed won, a new assault came from within, as other linguists started to say "your linguistics is wrong" and even "It's got nothing to do with language teaching anyway."

While there had been earlier statements of the new position, the clearest and most disturbing publicity for it came in Noam Chomsky's address to the 1966 Northeastern Conference on Language Teaching. Here he shocked the applied linguists in his audience, and obviously confused many of the language teachers, by stating that neither the linguist nor the psychologist yet knew enough about the process of language acquisition to tell the language teacher what to do. Shocking and confusing, because for the last twenty years, people had been standing up and saying "These are the linguistic principles of language teaching." Where can we go now, if we are left without principles? Who will tell us what to do if the linguists won't?

The picture I have painted so far is oversimplified, of course, because the actual effects in classroom practice have never been as strong as the theorists have wanted. Many a teacher believes firmly in the principles laid down for audio–lingual teaching, but in his classroom, stops to explain at length the rules of the tense system, or writes on a blackboard, or gives vocabulary lists to memorize . . . methods, however, detailed, must be interpreted and implemented by teachers, and as long as we use human teachers, each sets up his own criteria for what he will accept and what he will modify. But up till now, he has done this guiltily, fearing criticism for his incorrect method or approach. One of the most important results of the present controversy is to make possible what del Olmo (1968) refers to as the "intellectual independence of the foreign language teacher."

In this paper, I shall consider the meaning of this independence, arguing that there is a field of language pedagogy, a field that derives its theory from other "pure" fields, one of which is linguistics. For language pedagogy to develop freely, it must be free to draw its assumptions from all relevant disciplines—linguistics, psychology, and pedagogy are the most important—and to test the assumptions for consistency and applicability. Language pedagogy is limited and sterile all the time it is considered to be a field in which the assumptions, methods, and findings of a single discipline are to be applied. A good deal of difficulty has been caused by the use of the term "applied linguistics" as a free synonym for "language pedagogy." The term "applied linguistics" is not a particularly happy one: in one way, it is too broad, failing to suggest what linguistics is applied to; in another, it suggests a level of practicality that lacks the dignity of "pure linguistics." The term itself is grammatically derived from an underlying "Someone applies linguistics to something." The "someone" is an "applied linguist," the "something" is a field outside linguistics—language teaching usually, but sometimes translation, lexicography, computer work, etc.

When one admits to the profession of linguist, one is usually forced to point out that this does not mean that one spends all one's time learning languages, but that it involves a scientific study of language in general and specific languages in particular. Once this hurdle has been surmounted, the next question one faces is, "What's the use of linguistics?" One possible answer to this might be, it makes it possible to describe languages. Such an answer leads to a second question, asked probably in a more hectoring tone: "And what's the use of that?" Well, we say, these descriptions can be used in language teaching, translation, making dictionaries and grammars.

The approach implicit in these answers suggests a model that looks like Figure 1.

Figure 1

Language theory and description

Applied linguistics
Language teaching, translation, lexicography, etc.

That is to say, the findings of language theory and descriptions of languages are taken over as they stand, and applied directly to translation, language teaching, and any other relevant field.

But it is clear that in spite of the many claims that have been made, a description of a language is not in itself a set of directions as to how to learn or teach the language. If it were so, we would only need to give our students a grammar book and wait for them to start talking the foreign language. In the same way, it is clear that a grammar book does not tell us how to go about teaching the material. It specifies the material to be taught, but not the way to present it. To this description, then, there must be added a set of specifications as to how teaching should be done. Let us for the moment suggest that this will be the function of another discipline called Education, which itself is an applied field drawing on the findings of a pure science concerned with a theory of learning and teaching. Our model then needs to be revised (see Figure 2).

Figure 2

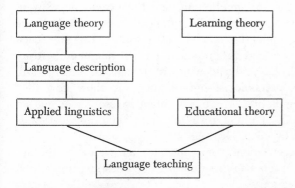

Now, we may ask, is there really any place in this model for applied linguistics? If it draws all its knowledge from language descriptions, what does it have to offer? In other words, what is the difference between the work of the descriptive linguist and the applied linguist?

It might be argued that there is a real difference between the sort of description provided by the descriptive linguist and that passed on by the applied linguist. This difference, it can be claimed, resides in the fact that the descriptive linguist is simply describing the language, while the applied linguist is adding to the description a comparison with the learner's native language, a contrastive analysis. He is adding, then, some sort of prediction of difficulties and suggestion as to hierarchy of difficulties.

At this point, it is only fair to ask in what way a contrastive analysis differs from a normal description. If it is simply in the fact that it sets out the two descriptions side by side, then we have defined the applied linguist's function as providing an indexing system. If, on the other hand, in order to achieve the contrast, he is forced to change one or both descriptions so that they are now in comparable terms, isn't he really being a descriptive linguist? The general issue raised here was discussed in some detail in last year's Round Table (Alatis 1968); the point I am making here is clearly expressed in Professor Hamp's paper.

Look at the second model again. Note that on the top line we have two theories, one of language and one of learning. Any linguistic description must be in terms of a theory of language. And there must be consistency between the theory of language and the theory of learning if the outcome of the teaching is to be successful. Indeed, one must go further: a valid theory of learning must include a theory of language learning, and a theory of language must face the problem of how language is learned. There is one case in which the two theories have seemed to be consistent: the Skinnerian view that learning is the result of operant conditioning, and the taxonomic view of linguistics (this consistency admittedly depends on a sympathetic interpretation of the Skinnerian model). A result of this has been much of the current work in programmed foreign language instruction, where a generally accepted idea has been that the linguist will specify units and the psychologist–programmer will show how they may be established as habits. There are only two problems: neither theory is valid, and the method resulting from their application is not successfull (Spolsky 1966, Ornstein 1968).

So far, then, we haven't done very much for the claims of the applied linguist. But let's go back to our original question, and see if we might find a better answer.

"What's the use of linguistics?"

"To understand more about man, through a clearer insight into his competence in language, which seems to be one of the main things that distinguishes him from the animals."

"What are the practical applications of this understanding?"

"To various forms of human engineering, such as language teaching ..."

Now a clear result of this set of answers is to put more emphasis on the "theory" of language than on the "description": to give the theory a place not just in linguistics, but in a unified theory of man (I avoid the term "human behavior" advisedly, for I often feel like being a mentalist). From these answers, we can construct a model that is very different from the earlier ones (see Figure 3).

Figure 3

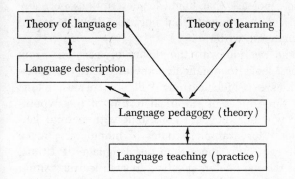

In this model, all boxes are connected with bidirectional arrows. The theory of language and the theory of learning must be consistent. The language description must be based on a theory of language; the theory must remain consistent with the data found in describing languages, and language pedagogy has clear relations with each of the other parts.

Let us consider these in turn. First, the relation with language description. As was suggested earlier, language pedagogy makes certain specific demands on descriptive linguistics for the provision of what is best called a pedagogical grammar, a grammar that may be readily adapted to the varying demands of the teaching situation. It offers to descriptive linguistics a method of checking the completeness of such a grammar. For example, language pedagogy demands of the language description that it include the basis for contrastive analysis: it might thus suggest the need for a number of different transfer grammars, and call for a description of a language in terms that permit of contrast. The textbook writer will often come to the descriptive linguist and ask him to give a specification of an area that might not normally be treated. And he will constantly be evaluating the descriptions against his own criteria: completeness, clarity, and ability to suggest a hierarchy of difficulty, the basis for an order of teaching. That he will usually be asking for rules does not necessarily mean that he will want to present these rules to his students, but rather that he will want to be able to organize the materials he teaches according to these rules. Of the descriptive linguist he will ask what can be called a "pedagogical grammar for the teacher," namely a collection of statements about the language that specifies the linguistic behaviors involved in knowing the language; at the same time, he will probably need to be ready to prepare himself a "pedagogical grammar for the learner," namely a consistent and simple set of rules about the language that may actually be given to the student. Thus, language pedagogy does not ask that linguistic descriptions be ready to be put in the hands of the students, but only that they be useful for the teacher and material writer.

Consider secondly the relation with the theory of learning. From this, language pedagogy looks to obtain hypotheses about the specification of the conditions in which learning will take place, and its activities will provide three types of empirical testing of the hypotheses. First, it will see whether they are consistent with natural language learning situations; for example, studies of bilingualism make clear that it is possible to acquire more than one language at a time, and give some ideas of the parameters involved in such learning situations. Second, laboratory tests will be carried out, setting up experiments in which as many of the variables as possible are controlled. Third, language pedagogy can test the hypotheses in normal classroom situations, realizing the general crudity of experimental design involved, but claiming the greater immediate relevance of its findings. Language pedagogy then will influence theories of learning in three ways: it will demand of them that their applicability to language teaching be clear, it will test their hypotheses, and it will provide an added connection between theories of language and of learning.

In just the same way, language pedagogy asks of the theory of language that it explain what language is in such a way as to imply how it might be taught. This demand must not be overstated: a theory of language cannot be expected initially to establish a model of production, but whatever model it does set up should have implications for language learning. Chomsky's work for instance raises the fundamental question of whether grammar is learned or innate. If the answer should be "innate," we may be faced with the need to revise our teaching approach completely, perhaps even falling back on the much-maligned "sunburn model" where it was assumed that exposure to a language was enough. But at the same time, the framework of transformational-generative grammar offers us a possible way of handling such previously nebulous concepts as analogy and imitation. It is not unreasonable to characterize the task of theoretical linguistics as the building of a machine (or model) capable of simulating the competence of the speaker of a language; but even when this is done, the task will remain of determining how this ideal model differs from the performance of human beings. The acquisition of a second language is an excellent laboratory for studying this problem. Language pedagogy then, must continually draw on language theory for implications concerning the acquisition of control of a second language, not expecting the answer, but looking for insights into the properties of language that may be taken into account in teaching. At the same time, it will make available to theorists the results of its experience, asking how the data it collects can be integrated with and accounted for by the theory.

Against this background, we may now consider the relevance of linguistics to language pedagogy. We have seen that a theory of second-language pedagogy will draw its assumptions not just from theories of language, but also from theories of learning: it will need to take into account the work of the psychologist and of the pedagogical theorist as well. It is thus not reasonable for anyone to assert that language teaching methods be based on linguistics alone, nor is it fitting for a linguist to claim sole authority on how to teach language. This must be kept clear all the time: as a linguist, I recognize that my qualifications are limited; as one concerned with language pedagogy, I realize I must go outside my own field for a full picture.

When we ask what linguistics has to offer to language pedagogy, it is useful to distinguish between applications and implications. There are certain aspects of linguistics that may be applied directly in teaching. The most important one is the description of the language being taught. There is no question but that teaching needs to be based on the best possible description of the language being taught. And the better, the fuller, the more accurate the description is, the more chance the teacher will have to assist the learner in his growing mastery of the structure of the new language. Without such knowledge there will be no possibility of satisfactory sequencing of material, no chance of distinguishing "mistakes" from the systematic errors that, as Corder (1967) has suggested, are the best evidence that language learning is taking place; no chance of useful explanation; no chance, in brief, of any meaningful control of the course of instruction.

But of course how this knowledge is to be applied is not a function of the language description. That a linguist describes a language in a given way, in a given order, or proposing a given sequence of rules, is not directly applicable; for it says nothing at all about the type of sequencing that might be used (Mackey 1965) or indeed whether linguistic sequencing is needed at all (Reibel 1968). That a linguist explains a phenomenon in a specific way does not tell a teacher how much he should use explanation in his class, or how this explanation should be given. These are questions to which language pedagogy must develop its own answers whether on the basis of linguistic theory, or from other sources.

A sound theory of language pedogogy will need to take into account the implications of three fields of linguistic activity. First is theoretical linguistics, whose task it is to explain the nature of language as a system. And modern linguistics is starting to do this, not yet conclusively, but suggesting a number of assumptions that should be taken into account. These assumptions may be summarized by saying that:

(1) Language use is essentially creative; thus, the notion of language as habit is not possible.

(2) The best explanation of this aspect of language is to say that the speaker of a language has available a system of rules to be used to produce and understand new sentences.

(3) The rules concerned are both intricate and abstract.

(4) The underlying intellectual organization required to acquire rules of this type suggests that there are universal properties of grammar.

With this in mind, let us consider a number of implications of current work in linguistics for language pedagogy. Take first the area of theoretical linguistics. Recent linguistic work has concentrated on the notion that language is creative. To explain this, it is necessary to propose an elaborate system of abstract rules that any speaker of a language develops as he acquires the language. From this, one may derive:

> Implication 1. It is not enough to teach a language learner to respond automatically to predetermined stimuli: language instruction must lead to creative language use in new situations.

The acquisition of language has been shown to depend on two things: a human learner, and exposure to a language. Every normal human being acquires a language, the one he is exposed to. The kind of exposure doesn't seem to make too much difference. Operant conditioning can be used with animals, but they don't learn to speak.

> Implication 2. Language can be acquired by active listening (listening and doing) even better than by listening and repeating.

> Implication 3. Programmed language instruction will have limited results in language teaching.

The description of language has turned out to be an even more difficult and complex task than was believed before the problems of deep structure and semantics were recognized. No one has yet succeeded in describing any language with anything remotely approaching completeness.

> Implication 4. The teacher or textbook writer will not be able to find a complete grammar of the language he is teaching. He will need to be able to draw on all available materials and to prepare his own.

Studies of semantics emphasize the close relation of semantics and syntax; and such studies as have been made of semantic systems of different languages show that different languages have a different organization and labeling of the outside world.

> Implication 5. When you learn a language, you have to learn its semantic system too: accepting word-by-word translation obscures this.

Syntax, the central component of a grammar, relates the content to the expression. There are a number of basic relationships common to all languages: function, transformation, agreement, and replacement. Syntax is realized on the surface level by a number of structural devices: function words, word endings, word order, and intonation; but there are more fundamental processes involved: ordering, substitution, deletion, and expansion.

> Implication 6. The learning of fundamental syntactic relations and processes will not be accomplished by drill based on analysis of surface structure alone.

Phonology is now conceived to be a matter of rules relating the underlying representation of sentences to their surface phonetic shape. The importance of grammatical and semantic information in understanding speech has become clearer.

> Implication 7. A language learner will need to be able to recognize the phonological distinctions made by speakers of the language and to produce recognizable distinction. The more he masters the language, the less important phonology will be in this recognition.

Much work has been done in comparing descriptions of different languages. Such comparisons have been shown to be valuable in explaining mistakes speakers of the one language make in learning the other, or in suggesting tactics that might be tried in presenting problem areas.

> Implication 8. Knowledge of the structure of the learner's native language will help the teacher.

Turning now from theoretical linguistics, we can look at some recent work in psycholinguistics. Studies of how children acquire their first language have provided support for the hypothesis that such acquisition is a matter of developing rules rather than forming habits and generalizing.

> Implication 9. Systematic errors (saying *I goed* instead of *I went*) are useful evidence to the teacher that the student is learning major rules.

> Implication 10. Presentation of material should encourage formation of rules rather than memorization of items.

Studies of language and cognition have been inconclusive in establishing any causal direction, but it is clear that different languages classify and label the outside world in different ways.

> Implication 11. When you learn a second language, you are also learning a second way of organizing your perceptions.

The third field to be considered is sociolinguistics. Studies of multilingual societies are showing the complexities in the way languages can have a different status, a different function, and a different proportion of bilingual and monolingual speakers.

> Implication 12. The functional aim of a language course must be stated specifically.

> Implication 13. It is not enough to learn a language: one also needs to learn how to use it.

> Implication 14. Language use is closely tied to political, historical, religious, cultural, and economic factors.

An individual's language use is just as complex. Even a monolingual has several styles to choose from. Learning a language is significantly affected by the learner's attitude to speakers of the language.

Implication 15. People are more likely to learn a language of high status than one of low status.

Implication 16. To learn a second language perfectly usually requires that one switch one's allegiance to the group represented by the language.

Implication 17. It is possible to learn enough of a language to use in a restricted domain.

These implications, I must make clear, are derived from work in linguistics. They need to be further refined, checked for internal consistency and for consistency with implications derivable from psychology and general pedagogical theory. They can then serve as a set of hypotheses for a theory of second-language pedagogy, to be tested by empirical study of actual language teaching.

At this point, I should like to consider, in the light of the views of language pedagogy I have postulated, the possible relevance of second-language pedagogy to work with standard dialect teaching. There is no reason to make the fuss that some do about the question of whether TESOD (if you will pardon the expression) and TESOL belong together. Matters of organizational jurisdiction are irrelevant to a scientific discussion. A brief glance at the vast differences involved in various language teaching tasks—differences of goal, learners, language, opportunity for teaching—makes it clear that there is no more difference between teaching a second language and teaching a standard dialect than there is between teaching Ewe to the Peace Corps and teaching French in a New York elementary school. Basic principles will be identical; actual methods will vary according to these priciples. A sound theory of language pedagogy does not produce a method; it suggests implications that must be taken into account in developing such a method.

Given this, we can see how foolish it is to speak of taking over foreign language methods for teaching the standard dialect until there has been a new study, in terms of a sound theory of language pedagogy, of which methods are appropriate. The first task is clearly to have a reasonably clear view of how the standard dialect being taught differs from the actual dialect of the child. Without this, one runs the risk of running into the unfortunate position of such educators as Bereiter and Engelmann (1966) who start off with the rather surprising notion that disadvantaged children do not have a language at all.

The question is complicated by two factors: the urgency of the task on the one hand, and the difficulties linguists are having getting the question of language as opposed to language use straight. It is in this area that sociolinguistics is making its most significant contributions.

But this very controversy makes clear one of the basic limitations, not just of linguistics, but of language pedagogy itself. For while language pedagogy can make clear how teaching aims are to be described, and hopefully, even, how they might be obtained, it is, like most other social sciences, irresponsible in that it cannot decide which aims are best for society. We can describe bilingualism, for instance, or the standard language. We can study the effects of speaking two languages or speaking a nonstandard dialect. But our theories are unable to help us answer some of the most important questions: should we all be bilingual? Should all Mexican-Americans learn English? Should all disadvantaged children learn and speak standard English? In this area, we must be careful not to fall into the old trap, and say: "A linguist does not make value judgments," and then go on to make a value judgment: "All languages and dialects are equally good." For one of the most important things sociolinguistics is helping us to define is the sociological values of specific languages and dialects. Luckily, for those of us who believe in cultural pluralism, no one has yet shown conclusively that any language or dialect has clear cognitive advantages or disadvantages, but the social effects are quite clear. It is not as linguists that we decide whether it is better to change the language of the lower status groups or the attitudes of society to that language; but as responsible members of a society, we must be prepared to make such a choice. And as linguists, we should insist that such choice take into account what we know of language and its use.

Linguistics and its hyphenated fields have a great deal to offer to language teachers, but the fullest benefit can only come when their implications are integrated and formed into a sound theory of language pedagogy. Because linguistics is only indirectly applicable to language teaching, changes in linguistic theory or arguments among linguists should not disturb language teachers; in the same way, the growing evidence of the inadequacy of the pure ALM or the incorrectness of many of its assumptions does not threaten linguistics. Within this framework, and with language pedagogy independent of any one discipline and even more of any one school of thought within a discipline, we can get on with the theoretical study, the discussion, the experimentation, and the development that the language teachers ask of us.

REFERENCES

Alatis, James E. (Editor). 1968. *Report of the Nineteenth Annual Round Table Meeting on Linguistics and Language Studies.* Monograph 21, Georgetown University Monograph Series on Languages and Linguistics. Washington, D. C.: Georgetown University Press.

Asher, James J. 1969. "The total physical approach to second language learning." *Modern Language Journal* 53: 3–17.

Bereiter, Carl, and Siegfried Engelmann. 1966. *Teaching Disadvantaged Children in the Preschool.* Englewood, N. J.: Prentice-Hall.

Chomsky, Noam. 1965. *Aspects of the Theory of Syntax.* Cambridge Mass.: MIT Press.

———. 1966. "*Linguistic Theory.*" *Reports of the Working Committees, Northeast Conference on the Teaching of Foreign Languages.* 43–9.

Chomsky, Noam, and Morris Halle. 1968. *The Sound Pattern of English.* New York: Harper & Row.

Corder, S. P. 1967. "The significance of learners' errors." *International Review of Applied Linguistics* 5: 161–70.

del Olmo, Guillermo. 1968. "Professional and pragmatic perspectives on the audiolingual approach: Introduction and review." *FL Annals* 2: 19–29.

Hamp, Eric P. 1968. "*What a Contrastive Grammar Is, if It Is Not.*" *Monographic 21,* 137–47, Georgetown University Monograph Series on Languages and Linguistics. Washington, D. C.: Georgetown University Press.

Hayes, Alfred S., Wallace E. Lambert, and G. Richard Tucker. 1967. "Evaluation of foreign language teaching." *FL Annals* 1: 22–45.

Hodge, Carleton T. 1968. "BC = PS + AP." *Language Science* 3: 17–20.

Mackey, William. 1965. *Language Teaching Analysis.* Bloomington and London: Indiana University Press.

Mildenberger, Kenneth W. 1968. "*Confusing Signposts—the Relevance of Applied Linguistics.*" *Monograph 21,* 205–13, Georgetown University Monograph Series on Languages and Linguistics. Washington, D. C.: Georgetown University Press.

Ornstein, Jacob. 1968. "Programmed instruction and educational technology in the language field: Boon or failure." *Modern Language Journal* 52: 401–10.

Reibel, David A. 1968. "Language learning analysis." Ms.

Spolsky, Bernard. 1966. "A psycholinguistic critique of programmed foreign language instruction." *International Review of Applied Linguistics:* 4.

———. 1968. "What does it mean to know a language, or how do you get someone to perform his competence?" Paper presented at the second conference on Problems in Foreign Language Testing.

ROBIN LAKOFF

Transformational Grammar and Language Teaching[1]

In this article the author calls for the development of a new orientation in second-language materials. She feels that previous material based on transformational grammar, like materials based on older grammatical theories, has concentrated on the form of language to the exclusion of such important factors as the speaker's intention and the situation. These factors not only govern what will be said, but also influence the correctness of the forms themselves. Finally, the attention paid to forms does not encourage the learner to explore the limits on the *use* of the form—for example, why the use of a form is good or bad in a particular situation. In place of such materials, she proposes the development of materials based on the student's ability to reason about language and his ability to understand the real-world use of language.

Lakoff begins her article by distinguishing between two traditions in

Reprinted with permission of the author from *Language Learning*, Vol. 19, Nos. 1 and 2, pp. 117–140.

[1] This is the revised version of a paper read at the Michigan Conference on Applied Linguistics: "Aspects of Language," held in Ann Arbor on January 18, 1969. I would like to express my gratitude to Ronald Wardhaugh, whose comments and advice have improved this paper in every way.

284

language teaching. The first, called *rote-memorization*, includes "traditional" rote-memorization material and the more recent material based on behaviorist psychology and structural linguistics, as well as materials developed by some transformational grammarians. The second tradition, called *rational*, assumes that man's unique ability to speak is based on his equally unique ability to reason. From the rational point of view, the language learner must be allowed to employ his ability to reason. Consequently, the teacher must provide not only data but also explanations and reasons for what can and cannot be said. The modern theory of transformational grammar has much in common with the rational tradition and has revitalized the development of materials based on this tradition.

In transformational grammar there are two levels of structure, called *deep* and *surface*, and a set of transformational rules that converts deep structure into surface structure. Apparently there are constraints on which surface forms the transformational rules can produce. For example, Lakoff points out that a constraint on the process of pronominalization would prohibit sentences like this in any language:

*He$_i$ said that John$_i$ was here.

where *he* and *John* refer to the same person. Since this constraint applies to all languages, it is said to be *universal*. In a sense the universal constraints correspond to the basic universal logical structures that the rational tradition assumed all languages shared in common. Since all languages are governed by these universal constraints, we need to teach students only those rules that are specific to the language being learned.

Lakoff feels that the best way to teach these language-specific rules is through "a process depending on reasoning rather than on memorization." In other words, we rely on "the learner's ability to reason, compare data, and generalize." Lakoff gives two situations in which conscious memorization plays a valid role in language learning. In the first situation some linguistic phenomena behave in an unpredictable way; sometimes the easiest way to deal with exceptions is to memorize them. In the second situation the rule itself can be profitably memorized, for example, the rule governing the formation of plurals.

Lakoff gives a third situation in which neither memorization nor the student's ability to reason about linguistic form will enable him to produce correct sentences. This is the common situation in which the correctness of a sentence depends on "the speaker's unstated belief about the world." In other words, along with the forms of a language, the learner must acquire a knowledge about the presuppositions that go with their use. Lakoff shows, by several examples from English and other languages, that a knowledge of presuppositions is critical for correct language use. One of her examples is the pair of sentences

John spoke with a warmth that was surprising.
*John spoke with a warmth that was usual.

The second sentence is wrong, not because it violates any formal rule of English grammar, but because it violates our presuppositions about what is usual and unusual.

It is here that Lakoff's approach is most clearly differentiated from earlier transformational grammarians. She feels that previous attempts to use transformational grammar as the basis for language materials have concentrated on the formal mechanisms of transformational rules to the exclusion of any consideration of the use and presuppositions involved in the rules. Lakoff illustrates this point by a sample analysis of the passive and the way that it might be taught to Japanese. Her approach minimizes the formal machinery of transformational grammar. In its place, she concentrates on the use of the passive in English and compares and contrasts its use with the use of a somewhat similar construction in Japanese. She states that her task is to

> help him [the Japanese student] understand *why* a speaker of Japanese will form a passive sentence rather than an active: what he presupposes when he does so, the circumstances under which he must, may, or must not apply the rule; then to show him the corresponding facts for English, and talk about where they differ, giving many examples.

Lakoff closes the article with a discussion of the question "Are we attempting to recapitulate first-language learning?" Her answer is yes and no. It is "no" because she feels that adult speakers have lost some of their earlier ability to make certain types of linguistic generalizations. For example, apparently children have a greater capacity for seeking the simplest rule that would cover the data given. In this sense, no second-language program can hope to fully recapitulate first-language learning. On the other hand, she feels that her approach resembles the process of first-language learning in that it appeals to the learner's general ability to "reason, compare data, and generalize."

ABSTRACT

There are two major theories of language learning: one, based on behavioral psychology, emphasizes pattern-practice and memorization; the other, the rationalist approach, attempts to give students the reasons for grammatical phenomena, relating facts about the second language to facts about the student's native language. Of these, the first has been much used recently, both in structuralist texts and those that are supposedly "transformational." While memorization and pattern-practice drills are sometimes useful, often they are not, because the choice between forms is based on the speaker's awareness of factors outside of the immediate syntactic environment: the definite or indefinite article, *some* or *any*, past or perfect tense are a few examples in English. To incorporate such insights in a text the writer must use his knowledge of transformational grammar indirectly, to enable him to formulate and verify his intuitions; but he will not use any "transformational rules" in the text itself. The text will be rationalistically oriented—it will encourage students to ask themselves why sentences are good and bad—and in this sense will be truly "transformational" in accordance with the beliefs held by transformational grammarians about the nature and acquisition of language.

As language teachers we have behind us two powerful traditions in language teaching. The first we can call *rote-memorization*, either the nineteenth-century and earlier variety which entailed memorizing lists of words and statements of rules, or the later behaviorist-psychology and structuralist linguistics pattern-practice variety that is common still today. The second is the intuitive-generalizing style of teaching. This tradition has been less popular: first, because it is harder to understand and needs a good teacher and good presentation to work, and second, because until recently it was considered heretical to suggest that people were in any interesting way different from rats. It was assumed that people learned languages, both native and second, as they and rats learned everything else: by repetition, by exercise, and by fitting new things into an old pattern already learned. The more you repeated something, the better it was learned.[2] It was

[2] A particularly clear exposition of the behavioral-structural position can be found in Morton (1966), which takes the point of view that it is not only possible but desirable to teach second-language learners to respond automatically to stimuli they are not supposed to understand. Thus, he says (p. 178) that the frames of his audio-lingual program for Spanish:

Permit the student-subject:
1. to "answer," with 95% accuracy, all questions asked within Task III *without aid of lexical meaning.*
2. to formulate "questions," with 90% accuracy, in response to the hearing of "statements," . . . *without the aid of lexical meaning.*
3. to manipulate . . . a finite and pre-specified number of syntactical and morphological structures *without the aid of lexical meaning.*

(all italics are mine.) It is not clear just what it is the students trained by this project have been taught to do: certainly they have not learned to use a language in anything like the way a language is naturally used, by native or non-native speakers.

also assumed to be dangerous to let people think about sentences they were learning because they would not form a pattern correctly, since they would not establish a direct stimulus (heard sentence or situation)-response relationship. It was assumed that language was just another kind of stimulus-response: the speaker heard a sentence or felt some sensation, and this triggered, without the intervention of any kind of reflection, a response, also verbal. He was just like the rat pushing a switch for food. However, if the speaker thought about a sentence, or wondered why it was grammatical before he said it, or were concerned about its relationship to other sentences, he would break this stimulus-response link and would not be using language as a native speaker does. The same learning model was assumed for first-language learning too: the child learned the pattern by repeating the sentences he heard from his parents.[3] When he had repeated all the sentences that had been said in the first five years, and had memorized those, he had acquired the grammar of his parents and was a native speaker. Second-language learning was viewed as the same sort of process as first-language learning. It was important, too, to present to the second-language learner only correct sentences. Otherwise, like a rat presented with contradictory stimuli, he might not know which response was correct.

The second type of teaching was found, for example, in the *Nouvelles Methodes* of the Port-Royal school in France in the seventeenth century,[4] and here and there since that time in "rational" grammars. Never as popular as the other type and recently held in great disrepute, this type of teaching was based on the notion that human beings were quite different from rats and other animals in that they could reason. This distinguishing attribute was what allowed men to speak in the first place. Speech was the product of man's rationality: for someone to learn to speak a language correctly, he had to make use of his reasoning ability. Therefore, the teacher had to tell him why one said the things one said in the way one said them—and,

[3] That such a notion of first-language learning is untenable is evident to anyone reading a book like Weir (1963). In this book, the author presents and discusses tapes of her infant's speech in its crib, where there was no stimulus to provoke the child's response, yet it spoke a great deal to itself. Much of this speech involves experimenting with words, "practicing" vocabulary, rehearsing grammatical paradigms, and the like—anything but an imitation of adult's sentences!

[4] The Port-Royal grammars, written principally by Claude Lancelot (who collaborated with Antoine Arnauld to produce the recently much-discussed *Grammaire Generale et Raisonnee*), employed the linguistic theory of medieval grammarians like Sanctus, who held that language was a product of man's reasoning faculty, to produce grammars of various European languages, namely Greek, Latin, Spanish, Italian, and Portuguese.

therefore, he also had to explain that some things could not be said, and give the reasons for that: he had to provide the learner with both grammatical and ungrammatical sentences. There was an assumption that all men reasoned in the same way. However, there were also rules that took this basic universal logical structure and changed it into language-particular, illogical structures, in which things were "understood"—that is, not overtly present—and word-order, sometimes, was changed.

If the writer explained the universal logic, said the rational grammarians, and provided the rules that related it to the superficial illogical structures in which people spoke, learners would work out the relationships between their own language and the one they were learning. They would thus do a quicker and more thorough job of learning the second language, learning it less artificially and more idiomatically. They would, in fact, learn it as a native speaker does. The teacher's job, however, was harder because he had to discover what the underlying logic was, and this was not invariably obvious—in fact, it generally was not obvious at all. The behaviorists criticized this theory as mentalistic and unscientific, and ignored it along with all other theories that said that language was any more than a system of automatic responses to stimuli.

In the last ten years a new linguistic theory, transformational grammar, has arisen, in direct opposition to the behavioral-structuralist theories within which so many language texts have been written. As far as language and language learning are concerned, it has much in common with the beliefs of the rational grammarians. One very significant added element in the modern theory, of course, is the existence of transformational rules, the form of which and the sphere of applicability of which are strictly controlled by the theory itself, avoiding the fuzziness, arbitrariness and the *ad hoc* treatments of data that characterize the work of the "intuitive" rationalist school. In nontransformational intuitive grammar,[5] sentences are related to one another on no grounds except the intuition of the writer. Sometimes the relationships postulated would be considered correct by modern analyses; sometimes they were absurd. The theory provided no automatic way of distinguishing truth from fiction: there was no formal definition of a possible underlying structure or a possible rule. Moreover, though the theory assumed an underlying universal logical structure, there were no constraints on the form of this structure, or on the permissible types of rules changing it to the superficial structure. Virtually anything could be treated as an underlying

[5] The works of Otto Jespersen are good examples of grammars of this type.

structure, and—in theory at least—virtually any operation could be performed on it. One sentence might have many possible analyses, with no means of discriminating among them as to which was right, and with no assumption made that there must be only one underlying structure for a nonambiguous superficial sentence. Transformational theory, as exemplified most fully perhaps in Chomsky's *Aspects of the Theory of Syntax,* formalized these intuitive concepts so that they could be checked, constrained, and tested.

In this work, Chomsky assumed two levels of grammar and a set of transformational rules mediating between them. At the level of deep structure, everything is present that enables one to know what the sentence means: identical words, later deleted, abstract elements of various sorts that leave syntactic markings elsewhere in the sentence, and so forth. Transformational rules delete these under various conditions, producing surface structures. Therefore, the transformational analysis of a sentence like (1):

(1) I saw a boy that hates ice cream.

assumes a deep structure in which the noun phrase *a boy* occurs twice: once where it will occur in the surface structure, as the object of the main clause, and once where *that* occurs in the superficial structure. These two nouns are co-referential; both refer to the same boy necessarily or else the sentence would be meaningless, or rather, nonsensical, because infinitely ambiguous: without a principle of recoverability of deletion—allowing only identical elements to be deleted—one would never know what *that* referred to, and the sentence could be interpreted in infinite ways. But since all languages contain this principle, it is inconceivable that *that* could have replaced any noun but *a boy,* identical in reference to the subject, which is still present superficially. It is evident that *that* refers to *boy,* an animate human masculine singular noun, because of constraints on what can occur in the relative clause. If *that* were really just an infinitely ambiguous form not going back to a deep-structure noun *boy,* the ungrammaticality of (2)–(4) would be unrelated to that of sentences like (5)–(7) below—a patently absurd situation, since the speaker of English knows the same thing is wrong with both sets of sentences:

(2) °I saw a boy that elapsed yesterday.
(3) °I saw a boy that was pregnant.
(4) °I saw a boy that laughed at themselves.

But if we assume that the noun *boy* underlies *that* at some level of the grammar, we can immediately tell why all these sentences are ungrammatical, without having new special rules in the grammar to explain them: (2)–(4) are ungrammatical for the same reasons as (5)–(7) are (and the translations of both sets, in any natural language, also are):

    (5) *The boy elapsed yesterday.
    (6) *The boy was pregnant.
    (7) *The boy laughed at themselves.

These are some of the reasons for proposing a theory with deep structures and transformational rules to change them into the superficial structures.

In addition, transformational grammar assumes that most sentences in a language are formed by combining two or more smaller sentences: sentence (1) is produced by combining (8) and (9):

    (8) I saw a boy.
    (9) A boy hates ice cream.

There will be constraints on what kinds of sentences can be combined if the transformational rule yielding relative sentences is to apply properly. Another obvious fact these sentences illustrate is that it is not possible to construct "the longest sentence" of any language: one could always, for instance, add a new relative clause, or a conjunction, or a complement sentence as in (10), where *that . . . stupid* is a complement embedded in the larger sentence:

    (10) I told the boy *that he was stupid.*

The result is that there is no "longest sentence" of any language. Moreover, it follows that one could not expect to learn a language, native or foreign, by merely memorizing a list of sentences, however long. So the behaviorist theory of language learning is incompatible with this evidence. Moreover, a child at age five is already able to tell whether a given sentence of his language is grammatical or not—though he has never heard that sentence before. As Chomsky points out, on the basis of facts such as these, language-learning must be viewed as a process depending on reasoning rather than on memorization.

I should perhaps not have made such a categorical statement. Some linguistic phenomena are, of course, not based on logic: they are accidental. If we watch a child learning to speak his own language, or—even more clearly—an adult successfully learning a second language, we note that he often has recourse to his memory. The child learns vocabulary by memorization: though he quickly learns how to generalize—to find the rules—for constructing new sentences, he soon learns that if he constructs new words by a rule he devises, he will often not be understood, logical as his formulations may be. He learns a set of endings on words—plurals, tenses, diminutives, etc.— as a list that he must memorize. There are no "reasons" why the plural has an ending and the singular has not. (He does, of course, learn that this is a rule—if he learns ten cases where the plural is formed with -s, he will try out an eleventh case he has never heard before, and generally be correct.) He also must learn that sentence (10) is good, but sentence (11) which has roughly the same "logical" structure is not, nor is (12). These facts—which "complementizers," as they are called, go with which verbs—must be memorized, just as vocabulary items are.

> (11) *I ordered the boy that he gives me his book.
> (12) *I said the boy to be stupid.

And similarly, there are in every language exceptions to rules, and these must be memorized. There is no conceivable "rule" to tell one why (13) is a good sentence of English, and (14) not. There are languages where the translation of both are good. If there is a difference of that sort in languages, it is generally the case that we are dealing with something "illogical"—something that requires some amount of rote-memorization: it is not universal.

> (13)   John is likely to leave.
> (14) *John is probable to leave.

There are also cases where rules can be given to the learner, where all he will need to know to tell whether to apply the rule in a given case is what other words are present in the sentence, and what they mean: these are purely superficial phenomena. So, for instance, in sentence (1), a restrictive relative clause, the pronoun *that* is grammatical. But in sentence (15), *who* cannot be replaced with *that*: (15) is a nonrestrictive relative sentence.

> (15) I saw the boy, who was running fast.

Facts like these can be stated in rules, and generalizations learned. In this way they are different from the sorts of facts given earlier, which are idiosyncratic and must be memorized individually. But in both cases, rote learning is possible either of the list of forms or of the rule that generates a set of possible forms. The teacher can give a rule like "*That* is never used in nonrestrictive relative clauses" and have the students memorize it; and, assuming that the teacher has fully and accurately explained the distinction between restrictive and nonrestrictive relative clauses, there will be no mistakes. Pattern-practice drills are of value in these cases. There is nothing wrong with constructing drills to facilitate the memorization of facts about pluralization, complementizer-selection (as in (13)), subject-raising (as in (14)), or restrictive vs. nonrestrictive relative pronouns.

In all these cases, the speaker or learner or teacher need only know the superficial form of the sentence in question. He need not worry about contextual factors outside the scope of rules: what has been said earlier, what the speaker knows about the topic of conversation, what is common knowledge, or knowledge of the world. But there are cases where such factors are irrelevant. Sometimes— more frequently than has been assumed—to judge whether a sentence is correct in its context, one must know something about the speaker's unstated belief about the world. In these cases, often, any of several variants of a sentence, out of context, will be completely grammatical—but in the specific context only one is correct. No rule can be given to the learner to enable him to make the correct distinctions; in these situations, a rule, to be of use, must provide the environment in which it applies—and in these cases, the relevant environment generally is implicit, rather than overtly present in another part of the sentence. Nor, of course, will memorization be of use here. Distinctions of this sort—I will discuss some examples below— are probably the hardest things to learn in the syntax of another language. Misusing them does not really create chaos, as failure to learn the memorizable rules may; it merely creates in the mind of the native speaker hearing the sentence a certain confusion, a sense that the other speaker is not using the language right or does not know something everyone else in the world knows, or something the speaker has already said he knows.

Numerous cases can be cited where rote learning and the listing of rules to memorize will be of little avail. In English, there are, for example, the articles, the past tense/perfect distinction, and the distinction between *some* and *any*. In Japanese there is the example of the use of honorific prefixes and suffixes and in Spanish, there are certain types of conjunctives. Of course, there are countless other examples too.

Consider the use of the articles in English. In any given sentence, either a definite or indefinite is generally possible. (I overlook special cases, like that of proper or mass nouns.) So, judging merely from the immediate environment, both (16) and (17) are grammatical:

(16) The boy is over there.
(17) A boy is over there.

That is, it is impossible to state a rule using as the environment the superficial form of the sentence alone to predict whether (16) or (17) will be correct in a given sentence. The problem is even worse in complex sentences. Sentence (18) is good, but (19), with only an adjective changed, is not:

(18)   John spoke with a warmth that was surprising.
(19) °John spoke with a warmth that was usual.

and in (20) and (21), only a definite article is good if the adjective is one of the same class as *usual* in (19):

(20)   John spoke with the enthusiasm that was expected.
(21) °John spoke with an enthusiasm that was expected.

To return to the earlier examples, in ordinary conversation, a speaker may say, "I'm looking for a boy who was asking for money yesterday." The conversation may then take a completely different turn, and deal for some time with different topics entirely. But if after a while, the second speaker in the conversation wants to refer again to the boy in question, he can use sentence (16), but not (17) to call attention to that fact, even though the boy may not have been the topic of conversation for some time and even though the first speaker himself used the indefinite article. In the sentences of (18)–(21), it is the meaning of the adjective that conditions the choice of article. The meaning has to do with how likely the speaker feels the warmth, or enthusiasm, was: whether he anticipated it or not. This fact, too, cannot be expressed as an invariable rule, or learned by memorizing sentences that follow the pattern. One must know what is in the speaker's mind, the hearer's mind, and in the previous conversation before one can judge the grammaticality of such sentences. Consider too sentences like (22) and (23):

(22) Albert is a doctor in my neighborhood.
(23) Albert is the doctor in my neighborhood.

The difference between these sentences cannot be found in any context that can be located by a rule. Either could perfectly well begin a conversation between two people one of whom didn't know Albert. The distinction lies in whether the speaker feels that it is normal, or necessary, for every neighborhood to have a doctor, or whether this is merely incidental, and Albert is a doctor who happens to live or work in the speaker's neighborhood. The choice of article thus depends on the speaker's feelings or beliefs about the world and how he sees its organization. No rule can give the learner this information. One can give general rules for article choice: use the definite article for something that is already known, or mentioned; otherwise use the indefinite. But that will not be of much help in a case like this, without additional information such as what presuppositions the speaker is making about the topics of the sentence. A native speaker can always match up his presupposition with the correct choice of article. The non-native speaker, unless he has learned the language extremely well, or has as his native language one in which there is an article system similar to that of English, will make mistakes, some more frequently than others. The task of the serious teacher, then, is to teach the non-native speaker what presuppositions go with what uses of the articles. He must do this by identifying, in the learner's native language, where similar presuppositions have overt counterparts, and matching these language-specific superficial structures with those of the learned language. In practice, of course, it is extremely difficult to do this; frequently, as seems to be the case with Japanese, the presuppositions underlying the use of the English articles do not show up overtly at all in the Japanese nominal system. Then the teacher must simply give various situations in which one article would be used rather than another, or none, and explain as well as possible *why* the choice must be this way: the teacher must give the learner a boost to making his own generalizations, to learning how the native speaker understands and intuitively uses these sentences. This necessarily implies that it is essential to give the learner ungrammatical sentences, so that he can study these along with the grammatical ones to decide for himself what the difference is, so that when he is on his own and has to make a decision for himself, he can rely on his own new generalizing ability in this sphere to make the right generalization. With rote pattern-practice alone, he would either be helpless presented with a situation that fell outside of the patterns he had studied (which would, of course, be extremely frequent) or he would overgeneralize, applying a pattern where it did not fit, since he would not know the reason why that pattern took that form. This is often true, as anyone who has taught English to speakers of Japanese knows. Either the article is omitted entirely where it should appear, or the wrong one is used, since the speaker has no idea which, if any, article is correct in the given environment.

A second case from English involves the distinction between the past and perfect tenses. This distinction is very difficult for anyone whose tense-system is not as complex as that of English, or where the meanings of the tenses are differently divided. Compare, for example, sentences (24) and (25), pointed out by Jespersen.[6] Both are grammatical, but they are used in different situations:

(24) The patient has gradually grown weaker.
(25) The patient gradually grew weaker.

or (26) and (27):

(26) I saw John every day for twenty years.
(27) I have seen John every day for twenty years.

If (24) is used, the assumption must be that the patient is still alive. If (25) is used, there is no such assumption. That is, to tell which of two tenses to use in referring to something that happened in the past, the speaker must have access to information about what is true in the present, information that is nowhere overtly stated. No list could be used to predict accurately which of these sentences could be used in a given conversation. The use of (24) instead of (25), though not overtly carrying information that the patient was alive, could mislead a hearer. Similarly in (26) and (27) if there is a gap in time between the years in which the speaker saw John every day, and the time at which he is speaking, only (26) is possible. The use of (27) for (26) creates confusion if the speaker has not seen John for some time. The sentence is not ungrammatical, as *I saw the boy that elapsed, or *I said John to be a fool, are; but its use in the wrong context stamps one as a non-native speaker of English, just as certainly as the others would. But no rule can be given for the learner to follow in any situation.

Consider one last case from English. It is frequently stated that if in a positive sentence *some* can occur, in the corresponding negative,

[6] *A Modern English Grammar*, IV, p. 67.

interrogative, or conditional sentence *any* is found instead. As that statement stands, it sounds as though the *some-any* distinction would be a very good candidate for rote learning and pattern practice. But the following sentences are not amenable to any imaginable form of pattern-practice drill:

(28) Does someone want these beans?
(29) Does anyone want these beans?
(30) If he eats some candy, let me know.
(31) If he eats any candy, let me know.

All these sentences are grammatical. Each pair is identical superficially except for the presence of *some* or *any*. If the rule above is correct, the pair of sentences should be synonymous. But it is clear that there are situations where (28) is appropriate, but not (29), and (30) but not (31), or vice versa. For example, (28) might be used if the speaker expected someone to ask for the beans and (29) if he really didn't think anyone would want them. The speaker might use (30) if he secretly hoped the person addressed would eat the candy but (31) if he hoped he wouldn't. Thus, we can explain the strangeness of (32) and (33), where these presuppositions are combined with overt statements that directly contradict them:

(32) ?If he eats some candy, I'll punish him severely.
(33) ?If he eats any candy, I'll give him ten dollars as a reward.

(In all these cases, the *any* is unstressed, not the stressed *any* [*at all*]). The oddness of these sentences cannot be acribed to anything present overtly in the sentences themselves, nor even necessarily to anything in the speaker's or the hearer's knowledge of the world. The presence of *some* or *any* can be predicted only if you know what is going on in the speaker's mind—that is, if you are the speaker. Hence, one cannot give a rule for the distribution of *some* and *any* in sentences of this type: rather, the learner must be informed as to which to use according to his state of mind, or his beliefs about things.

These presuppositions that I have been discussing are not confined exclusively to English. Far from it: no doubt if we analyze many of the constructions speakers of English find it difficult to master in other languages, we shall find they involve unstated presuppositions; the teacher's task is to help the student match up presupposition with superficial form. The Japanese use of honorifics is one such example. An honorific such as *o-* or *-san* carries with it the notion that the person or thing to which it is applied is in some sense important to the speaker—that it is necessary for his comfort or existence. Once one makes this assumption, it is easy to see, for instance, why food names like those for rice, tea, or soy sauce, but not for less basic foods, commonly receive the honorific. One can also understand how this is related to the use of honorifics for people or toilets. Unless the learner understands that the use is based on a presupposition, he will try to find a rule the applicability of which is decided within the sentence itself. He will, of course, fail and he will think the whole system is ridiculous. That is why it is customary for westerners to giggle when they see, for instance, *o-shoyu* translated as "honorable soy sauce," and *o-teárai* as "honorable toilet." And well they may, for these translations are ludicrous. The essential point to understand is that if a person is important or essential to someone else, he is held in honor and is exalted. But if a thing is important, a different kind of importance is involved, for example being essential for life. Thus, a better translation of *o-shoyu* might be something like "useful, beneficial soy sauce," as opposed to *John-san,* "the exalted John." One must know the feelings of the speaker toward the person or thing. These attitudes may be conventional in a culture or may be universal. Here, then, too, presupposition is a factor in grammaticality, and misinterpretation of presupposition will result in ludicrous—even if intelligible—sentences.

Finally, I should like to take a case from Spanish to illustrate this point once more. In Spanish, one finds sentences like (34) and (35). (34) contains *vive* in the indicative and (35) contains *viva,* a subjunctive:

(34) Busco a un hombre que vive en Madrid.
(35) Busco a un hombre que viva en Madrid.

These sentences assume different things about the relationship between speaker and *hombre.* In (34) we can attempt to paraphrase the thoughts unconsciously present in the speaker's mind (I say *"unconsciously"* because these presuppositions are very seldom conscious, that is why these distinctions are so hard to teach) in this way: "I know that this man exists and lives in Madrid. You know who I mean. It's a specific person I have in mind—though I may not know his name."

(35) is quite different in the presuppositions it assumes: "For some reason, I need a man who lives in Madrid. Maybe no person of that description exists, but that is the sort of thing I am looking for." For instance, if someone has asked, *"Que busca Ud.?"* "What are

you looking for?" the answer can only be (35). And, normally, "*A quien busca Ud.*" "Who are you looking for?" will be answerable only by (34). (34) can also be followed by a sentence identifying the *hombre: Se llama Juan Valdez.* But it would be absurd to follow (35) with such a statement: the speaker doesn't even know whether someone answering that description exists, let alone what his name is. No conceivable rule could clarify these facts for the non-native speaker, no pattern-practice could enable him to memorize the correct uses of subjunctive and indicative. He must know what the presuppositions are.

These examples provide ample evidence that there are many important facts about English and other languages that cannot be taught by behaviorist-structuralist methods. Then do I advocate the use of the techniques of transformational-rationalist grammar? Obviously I do; but I want to make very clear that I am not a partisan of much that has, faddishly, been produced recently as applications of transformational grammar.[7] While many things about these treatments are admirable, and the attempt to bring rationalism to the teaching of language should of course be applauded and encouraged, I do not feel that these attempts have succeeded. These authors are not really using transformational grammar; they are using only its hollow shell of formalism; they are not employing rationalism at all, but resorting to new forms of the same old mumbo-jumbo; they have substituted one kind of rote learning for another, and the new kind is harder than the old. Their treatments do not allow scope for presenting the sorts of facts I have been talking about any more than did the structuralists' treatments allow them to do so, and for much the same reasons. Rather than teaching students to reason, they seem to me to be teaching students to use new formulas. Instead of filling in patterns of sentences—surface structures—students now have to learn patterns of abstractions—the rules themselves. And these rules are, without exception, fakes. Little is known about the exact form of most transformational rules. Among the most mysterious are the favorites of writers and textbooks, like passivization and relativization, about which practically nothing positive is known. Hence the formulations are either wrong or grossly oversimplified, to the extent that the relevant generalizations—the point of introducing transformational concepts in the first place—cannot be stated. The result is that the student does not get any idea why people have gone to so much trouble to make learning the language so much harder. The writer fails to

---

[7] For example, of a number of recent works dealing with the teaching of English as a first or second language: Jacobs and Rosenbaum (1968), Roberts (1966), and Thomas (1966).

bring home the essential points: that sentences are related to other sentences both within a language and across languages; that sentences often are related that do not look anything like each other; and that often sentences that look alike are not related at all at a deep level. They have no reasons for their rules. Where Rosenbaum and Jacobs, for example, give motivations, they tend to be false and hard to understand as well. And, since they do not talk about deep structures and universal facts about language, they must omit the very sorts of facts I have mentioned above that cannot be treated in the kinds of transformational rules that are known at present. These facts can be dealt with only very informally. In the work that we are doing we try to do this,[8] and though it may not look as impressive, we feel that it will teach more. Previous writers have failed to utilize one of the most crucial assumptions of transformational theory—the logical nature of man and language—because they do not make use of the student's ability to generalize and form intuitions about the sentences he hears and says. They merely teach another language at the same time as they teach the one the student is trying to learn. They teach both badly: the transformational grammar because it is oversimplified and misunderstood; the language itself because it is lost in the tangles of formal statements.

As an illustration of the way we are trying to use transformational grammar, as opposed to the way others have, I would like to look at the treatment of passives in English. Passivization is a rather touchy subject now among most transformational grammarians who are aware of recent thought in the field. It is embarrassing because, until a few years ago, it was one of the best-understood rules in the grammar. Everyone who had read *Aspects* knew that the passive transformation took an active sentence, that met the structural description of (36):

$$(36) \quad NP_1 - Aux - V - X - NP_2 - Y - by + passive - Z \Rightarrow$$
$$\qquad\quad 1 \qquad 2 \quad\; 3 \quad 4 \quad\; 5 \qquad 6 \qquad\quad 7 \qquad\qquad\; 8$$

and transformed it into (37):

$$(37) \quad 5 - 2 + be + en - 3 - 4 - 7 + 1 - 6 - \phi - 8$$

[8] "We" refers here as elsewhere, to the Language Research Foundation of Cambridge, Mass. The grammar to which I am specifically referring is a teacher's manual now being written by myself as an aid in the teaching of English to speakers of Japanese; though, since it is based on universal principles, it would also be of use as a reference in the teaching of English to speakers of other languages. A text for the student's use is being written concurrently under the direction of Bruce Fraser, based on the teacher's manual. These materials will be published by the TEC Company of Tokyo, Japan.

Now it is fairly evident that this rule is not very convincing: it has many more terms than a normal transformational rule, the assignment of constituents is quite *ad hoc*; item 7, *by* + *passive* is a strange constituent; and the fact that it is a rewriting of the node *Manner Adverb* is even stranger. It can be shown that this transformation will wrongly predict the assignment of constituent structure in the surface structure. Besides, it doesn't tell anything that we know about the relation between active and passive sentences. So, for instance, it gives no reason, in itself, why reflexive sentences can't passivize: that is, why (38) is not a good sentence:

(38) *John was washed by himself.

But no formulation that has yet been proposed has given either a satisfactory deep structure underlying passive sentences or the transformational rule that produces the superficial forms. Thus it is oversimplification, to present, as is done in some of these books, a rule like (39) and call it "passivization": note that it is an oversimplification of the already ludicrously oversimplified (36)–(37):

(39) $NP_1 - Aux - V - NP_2 \Rightarrow NP_2 - Aux - Be + en - V - NP_1$

Partisans of this approach may object that, after all, this formulation describes accurately what is going on, insofar as that it shows the learner how, given an active sentence, it can form the corresponding passive. After all, what does it matter to him that theorists rack their minds over the rule?

In fact, it doesn't really matter that the theorists have problems. What does matter is that the reason theorists have troubles with the passive, and have discarded this formulation of passivization, is, simply, that it doesn't express the generalizations about the passive that the correct rule, coupled with the right deep structure, would. Therefore, it is of no use as a pedagogical device: it does not enable students to reason better, nor does it make clearer generalizations that they need to know to use the passive as a native speaker does. This rule does not tell the student that verbs like *want, have,* and *suit* are exceptions to passivizaton: no formulation can tell them this; the list simply must be learned. It does not enable them to recognize environments in which passivization is not found—which would be the only justification for this transformational treatment. In short, it does not do any more than the classical statement in English: "To form the passive, exchange the subject and direct-object noun phrases of a transitive verb, insert the verb *to be* after the auxiliary if there is one, and put any verb following *be* in its past participle form." This is simple and concise, it avoids the difficulty of first explaining the terminology NP₁ ➤, +, and so on, and makes things much less mysterious. If you like, you can give rule (39), treating it as a formula, but I think it is wrong to call it a transformation: it isn't a transformation in any modern sense. It is just a mnemonic device, and I'm not so sure it's all that mnemonic.

There must be a better way to talk about the formation of passives in English. Transformational grammar has enabled researchers who do work in the field to precisely and accurately make observations about passive sentences, and their relationship to actives, with respect to form and meaning. These observations remain valid and useful regardless of whether we know what the deep structure or the transformational rule looks like. The job of the textbook writer is to take these observations, including the presuppositions that one needs to be aware of in order to use the English passive correctly, and put them into understandable form. So, dealing with speakers of Japanese, we must also bear in mind that Japanese contains a construction which, in some of its uses, approximates that of the English passive. It exchanges the functions of subject and object and adds an ending on the verb, and serves to create a new focus, or topic, of the sentence. But one of the big pitfalls for speakers of Japanese is that it does other things as well: it seems to carry with it, sometimes at least, the presupposition: "the act affects the subject in a bad way." (Compare, in English, the construction *something happened to someone*, which involves a similar presupposition.) The Japanese passive therefore can be used with intransitive verbs if their action affects the subject unfavorably. But the English construction called the passive does not have the same deep structure as this use of the Japanese passive: the meaning is different. Apparently, in Japanese, two deep structures have merged transformationally so that they share the same surface structure and only one of the Japanese "passives" is really the equivalent of the English. Whatever the theoretical interpretation of the nonoverlapping of Japanese and English passives, the fact is that the speaker of Japanese must be taught not to say, "The accident was occurred on June 29," or "Bill was died last night." These mistakes are frequent, because the Japanese construction is identified in books so closely with the English passive. Our task, in explaining the difference between the English passive and the Japanese passive, does not lie in making the Japanese student of English memorize Rule (39): this will not help him at all. Our task, rather, is to help him understand *why* a speaker of Japanese will form a passive sentence rather than an active: what he presupposes when he does so, the circumstances under which he must, may, or must not apply the rule; then to show him the corresponding facts for English, and talk about where they differ, giving many examples. We will want to explain that *John was shot by Harry* is *not* a paraphrase, in English, of *Harry shot John, to my discomfiture*, as the translations of these sentences would be in Japanese. We must talk, particularly, about environment: in English, there are situations where the passive cannot be used without sounding odd, due to discourse phenomena, where the similarly named construction might at times be quite acceptable in Japanese. We might give as an example the fragment of discourse in (40):

(40) Charlie is really terrible. He never forgives an insult.

We are talking here about Charlie: he is the topic of the paragraph, or the conversation. It is normal, when one continues to talk about the same general topic, to want to keep the topic in focus—to keep indicating that this is the crux of the matter, the thing the speaker is interested in talking about. But it might also be that a sentence will come up where someone else does something to Charlie: for example, the speaker, in giving an example of how Charlie never forgets an insult, might want to talk about something someone did to annoy Charlie. He can say (41), of course:

(41) Once someone bit Charlie on the arm, and Charlie never forgave him.

This is perfectly grammatical, and perfectly understandable. But it creates an abrupt break with the rest of the sentence which is stylistically odd. Here, a speaker may choose to use the passive, since it puts *Charlie* back in subject position, where the topic of a sentence usually is in English, as in (42):

(42) Once he was bitten on the arm by someone, and he never forgave him.

To explain to the non-native speaker this sort of delicate discrimination, we must refer to notions like a "topic," "focus," and "discourse," which neither the sort of transformational treatment which stops at formal mechanisms, nor the very similar behavioral-structural approach can capture.

It should be noted that the ungrammaticality of *John was washed by himself* is universal. It follows from universal constraints noticed by Postal (1968) to the effect that in a wide variety of environments nouns cannot cross over nouns that are co-referential to them. Since this is universal, and has to be on the basis of the nature of the constraint, we know that we need not mention it in a grammar of English for speakers of Japanese. This is helpful in case the writer of the textbook is not thoroughly familiar with the native language of the users of the textbook—a circumstance that is necessarily and unfortunately frequent.

It isn't that we avoid stating rules. In discussing the passive, what we have done is to provide a nonformal explanation in English words, of what is done to an active sentence to produce the corresponding passive. It is, basically, a description in words of the oversimplified transformational rule, but its virtue is first that it is immediately accessible and second that it makes no claims to being the explanation for these facts, but merely a description. We use transformational grammar, of course: the rules themselves, wherever they appear to exist or can be guessed at as a model for our nonformal descriptions; and, more importantly, our own knowledge of transformational theory and practice keeps us from doing irresponsible things, and gives us a means of testing our findings, as well as a heuristic device that makes the deep structures more accessible to our investigation.

The theory of transformational grammar has built into it various self-policing mechanisms in the form of principles by which the linguist can judge whether an analysis is rigorous or *ad hoc*; whether it is a complete analysis, or only scratches the surface of the problem, whether a formulation is precise or vague. These principles will enable the linguist to know, for instance, whether to posit an analysis in which two superficially different sentences are identical at a deeper level; whether two superficially identical sentences are different at a deeper level. One, the principle of recoverability of deletion mentioned already allows deletion to take place only in case there is an element identical to the element to be deleted, which will remain in the surface structure so that its meaning can be recovered, or there is an abstract element that has left behind it syntactic markers from which its original presence can be deduced. We allow two sentences to be derived from the same deep structure only in case the selectional restrictions in one are the same as those in the other: the same kinds of nouns can be subjects or objects, the same classes of verbs occur. We assume two superficially identical sentences are not really identical if it can be shown that, by substituting one word for another, one of the meanings is made impossible. Tests of this kind allow us to propose deep structures in a responsible way, and relate these deep structures to the proper surface structures. This is of use in language teaching in a number of ways, none direct in the sense that writing transformational rules is direct. First, we ourselves become more sensitive to language through applying these tests and demanding proof of every claim. This enables us, hopefully, to see better than someone who has not been trained the relationships among sentences in English, and their relationship to universal facts and language-particular rules of the learner's native language. Then, when we say that a sentence of a certain type in English is related to, or obeys some of the constrants of, a sentence of maybe a quite-different looking type in the learner's language, we have a reasonable idea that we are basing our conclusions on more than personal caprice. The danger of the latter is that, if the relationship is not real, or is only partial, the speaker may wrongly generalize. So, for instance, let us say that we have taught the speaker sentence (43):

(43) John couldn't lift 500 lbs.

and we point out to him that it is ambiguous because it can be paraphrased either by (44) or (45):

(44) John was physically unable to lift 500 lbs.
(45) It is impossible that John lifted 500 lbs.

Now if we look only this far into the language, and don't do any testing, we may give the speaker a rule saying: *can* can have either of these two meanings. And, if, as is frequent, there are in the learner's language two verbs translatable as *can*, one with one sense and one with another, if we're not careful we may say that *can* will translate either of these, freely, and that the synonymy is total.

But now let us look at sentence (46). Here something surprising happens. Only the second interpretation, that of "is possible that," is found:

(46) John couldn't be as stupid as Harry!

The reason is that the verb following the modal in (43) is active, or voluntary, while that of (46) is stative, or involuntary. Physical inability is not a factor in the meaning of stative verbs. If we know this fact, we are better able to explain the use of the modal *can* to non-native speakers, and, having tested and looked at various facts, we can avoid overgeneralizations, such as assuming (since when there are two identical verbs conjoined in a sentence conjunction reduction is possible) that, if the verbs *can* underlying (43)'s two meanings are identical, we could get sentences like (47):

(47) John couldn't lift 500 lbs. or be as stupid as Harry.

with the interpretation of the first *can* as "be physically able." Knowing there is a distinction and pointing it out avoids this danger.

We can also use transformational analyses when two sentences that look quite different share similar deep structures. This can be shown to be true for (48) and (49):

(48) Bill cut the salami with a knife.
(49) Bill used a knife to slice the salami.

It would take too long to go through the proofs that these sentences do, in fact, come from similar or identical deep structures.[9] But if we can make that assumption, we can show that this similarity of underlying structure can be put to use in teaching English as a foreign language. Suppose we are dealing with a language in which either the analogue of (48) or of (49) did not occur, or where one or both looked quite different from either (48) or (49), and we wanted to teach how both were used. We could point out that they shared a common meaning; and, further, that just as the ungrammaticality of (50) can be expressed in terms of selectional restrictions between a verb and its subject (*use* selects an animate subject) the analogous sentence with *with*, (51), is ungrammatical in the same way. If one of these constructions exists in the learner's language, he can make the generalization and know at once which sentences will be grammatical, which will not, though no rule can be stated (since *with* occurs with other meanings and restrictions) in English.

(50) *The book used a knife to cut the salami.
(51) *The book cut the salami with a knife.

Using insights such as these, made possible by a knowledge of transformational grammar, but not its formal devices, we can, we hope, teach languages better.

This leads to the final question, with which I want to deal briefly.

[9] Evidence for this view is given in Lakoff (1968).

I said earlier that the structuralists resorted to rote learning and pattern practice in the belief that they would thus recapitulate in second-language learning the processes of first-language learning as seen by behavioral psychologists. I said that we were trying to teach students to use their reasoning ability to generalize, and that giving them ungrammatical sentences and detailed contexts enables them to do so. I also said that first-language learning clearly involved rule-formation, or generalization from raw data. Are we then trying to reproduce the process of first-language learning in second-language teaching? It should be noted that in the other transformational approaches, the answer would have to be "no." It is never assumed that the child memorizes rules such as have been given.

Despite numerous psycholinguistic experiments, which show the order in which rules are learned, and mistakes made in learning a few isolated syntactic phenomena, mostly in English, practically nothing is known about first-language learning. No one knows how the child sifts out the rules from the huge mass of data, how he decides what is grammatical from the semigrammatical and ungrammatical strings he hears along with the fully grammatical ones. Also unknown is how he tells what rules are universal, what are not. It is not likely that we will know the answers to these questions for a long time. The question of the nature of first-language acquisition is just as dark, in fact, as second-language acquisition.

We can say a little, and that little enables us to give the answer to our question: are we attempting to recapitulate first-language learning? The answer is both yes and no. No, first, because certain abilities the child has are lost, and we cannot hope to use them again after he is ten years old or so. We do not even know what these abilities are. We know the child can, given raw data, derive the rules with no help from anyone. He can learn and memorize astounding amounts of vocabulary, including lists of exceptions. And he does all this, or most of it, unconsciously. You never hear him muttering, "Let's see—is there a variable in that relative-clause formation rule or not?" or "Hmmm . . . I wonder if equi-NP-deletion is governed, and what the exceptions to it are?" But somehow he knows. We have tried to enable the second-language learner to recapture some of his old ability by providing him with lists of things to be memorized (as is usual) and with the generalizations that the child would make himself. We have not yet tested our grammar: it is not even written. We would hope that, provided artificially with what the child has naturally, the second-language learner would go about learning his second language rather in the way he learned his first. But we must remember that artificial devices are seldom as good as the real thing. Probably too the fact that the generalizations must be consciously articulated will make a difference in how they are learned. But the similarity lies in appealing to the learner's ability to reason, compare data, and generalize. In this way our second-language teaching is like process of first-language learning as transformational theory views it.

Some interesting similarities and differences have been noticed between the two types of learning. First, some work of Carol Chomsky's seems to indicate, if we can give this interpretation to her findings, as she did not, that universals are learned in a different way and at a different time from language-particular facts, in first-language learning.[10] According to a universal constraint on pronominalization, in no language is it possible to say sentences like (52):

(52) *He$_i$ said that John$_i$ was here.

where *he* and *John* refer to the same person. But some pronominalization related facts are dialectal, or at least not universal. Thus, for instance, in a sentence like (53):

(53) John asked Bill when to leave.

in most dialects of English, the understood subject of *leave* is John. But dialects have been found where it can also be *Bill*. So this is not universal. It has been found that, with facts that are universal, like those in sentence (52), a child learns not to make mistakes in them very quickly, over a short time. But with cases like (53), he goes through a period of fluctuation—from one interpretation to the other, it takes a good deal longer for him to master the rule completely, and he makes many more mistakes. This is of interest in teaching second languages, because, as I noted above, it gives us a bit of a clue as to how to integrate universals in our texts. We now have, perhaps, some evidence from transformational grammar, that universals are kept apart from language-specific facts by the child in learning a first language. Moreover, he keeps them apart: one never hears a question in a language class as to the grammaticality of (52), while one might get questions on the meaning of sentences like (53). Therefore, we can assume the speaker is probably unconsciously aware that the universals are universal, and we need not talk about them, unless they are of use in explaining language-specific facts.

[10] Unpublished doctoral dissertation, Harvard, 1968.

And, lastly, there seems to be a difference in the way a rule is learned by first- and second-language learners. There is some evidence that a child, given data, will try to extract from it the simplest possible rule: the simplest in terms of structural description, structural change, and exceptions if any. He will do this sometimes even if it means speaking sentences quite different from the sentences he actually hears. (This, again, could not be explained by behaviorists.) Thus, children are frequently faced with sentences involving the rules of negative-attachment and negative-incorporation, as when they hear (54) and (55):

    (54) Nobody ever did that to anyone.
    (55) I didn't see anybody.

In the first of these sentences, there is one negative word in the deep structure, and three indefinites, one of which happens to be the subject of the sentence. In (55), there is also one negative, and one nonsubject indefinite. In the first case, the negative is obligatorily attached to the indefinite subject. In the second, it has not been attached to anything. The rule in standard English is that, once the negative is written out once, whether by attachment or not, it is not repeated anywhere. This is, of course, not true in many languages, including nonstandard English dialects, where multiple negation is the rule. It can also be shown that a rule allowing multiple negation is simpler in formulation than one allowing only single negation. But standard English has the more complicated formulation. It has been observed[11] that children frequently will learn the rule as though it allowed multiple negation—the simpler way—even though they may never have heard such sentences. But in second-language learning, there seems to be no mislearning of this sort. Speakers of English do not learn the negation rules of Spanish particularly readily, or more easily than speakers of Spanish learn the corresponding rules of English. This shows that we cannot assume that second-language learners still have at their disposal the means to invent rules, no matter how much information they are given: if they did have these means, they would probably search for the simplest formulation. Instead, the only mistake they make with rule-learning is that they apply the rules of their own language in learning the other language—a sure sign they have not learned the new rule. So, the evidence, scanty as it is, from psycholinguistics shows that we cannot expect to recapitulate first-language learning. We are doing something different, something that

[11] This is discussed by Kiparsky (1968).

utilizes the unique capacities of human beings to a fuller extent than other methods, which we hope will give learners more insight into other languages and enable them to use them more like native speakers. We do not know whether we will succeed, or whether our premises are even valid. But it seems like an interesting and promising experiment, and we have great hopes for it.

REFERENCES

Chomsky, N. (1965). *Aspects of the Theory of Syntax*. Cambridge, Mass.: M.I.T. Press.

Jacobs, R., and P. S. Rosenbaum. (1968). *English Transformational Grammar*. Boston: Ginn–Blaisdell.

Kiparsky, P. (1968). "Universals of Change," in *Universals of Linguistic Theory*, edited by E. Bach and R. Harms. New York: Holt, Rinehart and Winston.

Lakoff, G. (1968). "Instrumental Adverbs and the Concept of Deep Structure," *Foundations of Language*, Vol. 4, No. 1, pp. 4–29.

Morton, F. R. (1966). "The Behavioral Analysis of Spanish Syntax: Toward an Acoustic Grammar," *International Journal of American Linguistics*, Vol. 32, No. 1 (Publication 40), pp. 170–184.

Postal, P. (1968). "The Cross-Over Principle." Ditto, Thomas J. Watson Research Center, Yorktown Heights, N. Y.

Roberts, P. (1966). *The Roberts English Series: A Linguistics Program*. New York: Harcourt, Brace & World.

Thomas, O. (1966). *Transformational Grammar and the Teacher of English*. New York: Holt, Rinehart and Winston.

Weir, R. H. (1963). *Language in the Crib*. The Hague: Mouton & Co.

READING

CAROL CHOMSKY

Reading, Writing, and Phonology

It has often been stated that English has a very unsystematic spelling system. This statement usually implies that an ideal spelling system would have a consistent spelling for each sound in the language (Chomsky calls this "phonetic" spelling). However, another definition of an ideal spelling system would be that a word is always spelled the same way, no matter how it is pronounced (Chomsky calls this "lexical" spelling). In this article the author argues that the English spelling system is basically a lexical system, and that this view of the spelling system has definite implications for teaching reading and spelling.

Carol Chomsky's concept of lexical spelling is borrowed from Noam Chomsky and Morris Halle's book *The Sound Pattern of English*. Noam Chomsky and Halle argue that speakers of a language possess an intuitive ability to recognize the similarity between variant forms of the same word.

From the *Harvard Educational Review*, Vol. 40, No. 2 (May 1970), pp. 287–309. Copyright © 1970 by President and Fellows of Harvard College. Reprinted by permission of the author and the *Review*.

311

In their theory they attempt to capture this similarity by providing an abstract level of representation that would write all variant forms of the same word in the same way; this, of course, is the lexical spelling system mentioned above. The lexical spelling represents a word family. The actual pronunciation of any individual member of this family is derived from a rich set of phonological rules. Noam Chomsky and Halle's book deals with two questions: (1) What are the abstract, underlying phonological forms? (2) What are the rules that embody these abstractions into phonetic reality? They feel that the conventional orthography of English provides a near optimal way of writing the underlying forms. In other words, they claim that the English spelling system is basically a lexical rather than a phonetic system.

Carol Chomsky gives two kinds of evidence to support this position. Her first point is that there are numerous cases in English in which words have an incorrect phonetic spelling but a perfectly consistent lexical spelling. The examples here are pairs of related words that have systematically different pronunciations, for example, an alternation between long and short vowels (the *a* in *nation–national*) or the alternation in the pronunciation of a consonant symbol (the *c* in *medicate–medicine*). She points out that in the words *kill* and *sill* the change from [k] to [s] creates a new and unrelated word, but in *medicate* and *medicine* the change from [k] to [s] does not; the latter is only a phonetic change, not a lexical one, and therefore is not reflected in the spelling system.

Her second argument that English orthography is lexical rather than phonetic is that it does not provide the information about stress placement and vowel reduction that would be necessary to indicate actual pronunciation of written words, and is therefore not a phonetic system. Here she gives the classic example from *The Sound Pattern of English* of the three different pronunciations of *telegraph* in the words *telegraph*, *telegraphic*, and *telegraphy*. The point is that since the change in pronunciation is completely predictable, given a knowledge of the phonological rules of English, the operation of these rules are not reflected in the orthographic system. The English spelling system represents words before the predictable phonological changes are made. The spelling thus underlies and is systematically related to all of the actual pronounced forms. This, of course, is exactly what a lexical spelling system is supposed to accomplish. A phonetic spelling system, on the other hand, would give each of the three pronunciations of *telegraph* a different spelling.

If we accept the view that English spelling is basically lexical, then we have a new model for how the reading process works:

> What the mature reader seeks and recognizes when he reads is not what are commonly called grapheme-phoneme correspondences, but rather the correspondence of written symbol to the abstract lexical spelling of words. Letters represent segments in lexical spelling, not sounds.

The beginning reader, however, probably operates much closer to the phonetic level. As the reader gains in skill and as his own grasp of the phonological rules mature, he will begin to read on a lexical rather than a phonetic level. Some poor readers, though, may have difficulty in moving beyond the phonetic level. For these children, Chomsky suggests that "At some point emphasis ought to be shifted away from the phonetic aspects of spelling to a consideration of the underlying lexical properties of the orthographic system." She suggests that one way of doing this would be to discuss "word families" to see how the same root changes its pronunciation according to which endings are added. Since the words that typically demonstrate predictable shifts in pronunciation are Latinate, discussion of these forms may actually help the child to acquire a mature phonological system.

A second specific area of application of the lexical view of English spelling is in teaching spelling. Chomsky suggests that good spellers have a picture of the underlying form of a word independent of its actual various pronunciations. When good spellers attack a hard word, they know that related forms of the word, though pronounced differently, may provide a clue to the correct spelling. For example, the second syllable in *industry* has a reduced vowel, and so pronunciation is no guide to spelling; however, in the related form *industrial*, the stress has shifted to the syllable in question and we know that the vowel should be a *u*. Chomsky closes her article with several sample "spelling lessons" that illustrate the advantage of approaching English orthography as a lexical system.

✳

ABSTRACT

The author discusses the relation of conventional English orthography to the sound structure of the language, showing that this relation is much closer than is ordinarily assumed. She points out that many of the non-phonetic aspects of English spelling are motivated rather than arbitrary, in that they correspond to a level of representation within the phonological system of the language which is deeper than the phonetic level. Finally she considers the implications of this view of the orthography for reading and spelling.

The inconsistencies of English spelling are often a source of regret to the reading teacher and to those concerned with reading in general. Because English spelling is frequently not phonetic, because of the large number of words which are lacking in grapheme-phoneme correspondence, it is often concluded that the orthography is irregular and a relatively poor system for representing the spoken language. While it is true that English spelling in many instances is deficient as a phonetic transcription of the spoken language, it does not necessarily follow that it is therefore a poor system of representation. This paper discusses a far more positive view of English orthography which has emerged from recent work in phonological theory within the framework of transformational grammar.

In the *Sound Pattern of English*[1] Chomsky and Halle demonstrate a variety of ways in which the relation of conventional English orthography to the sound structure of the language is much closer than is ordinarily assumed. Simply stated, the conventional spelling of words corresponds more closely to an underlying abstract level of representation within the sound system of the language, than it does to the surface phonetic form that the words assume in the spoken language. Phonological theory, as presented in *The Sound Pattern of English*, incorporates such an abstract level of representation of words and describes the general rules by which these abstract underlying forms are converted into particular phonetic realizations. English spelling corresponds fairly well to these abstract underlying forms rather than to their phonetic realizations. When viewed in its correspondence to this underlying form, English spelling does not appear as arbitrary or irregular as purely phonetic criteria might indicate. Indeed, from this viewpoint, conventional orthography is seen in its essentials as a "near optimal system for representing the spoken language."[2] In this paper I will attempt to clarify this notion of abstract underlying form, to show its place and function within a grammar of English, and to explain its relation to the spoken language. I will also speculate briefly on the possible relevance of this view of the orthography to reading, the teaching of reading, and the teaching of spelling.

The motivation for postulating an abstract form of words which underlies their phonetic form is roughly as follows. One aspect of writing a grammar for a language is deciding how words are to be represented in the grammar's dictionary, or lexicon. This essentially means deciding on a spelling for each word, what I will call "lexical spelling." One way, obviously, would be to proceed according to pronunciation and use a phonetic transcription, or the type of broad phonetic transcription that is often termed a phonemic transcription. (Those who regret the frequent lack of grapheme-phoneme corre-

---

[1] N. Chomsky and M. Halle, *The Sound Pattern of English* (New York: Harper & Row, 1968).

[2] N. Chomsky, "Phonology and Reading," in *Basic Studies in Reading*, edited by Levin and Williams (New York: Harper & Row, 1970).

spondence in English spelling seem to be looking for just this in the orthography.)

At first glance, this phonetic approach would seem to be the simplest and certainly the most direct way of proceeding. However, the attempt to incorporate into the grammar a spelling system so closely tied to the pronunciation of English immediately runs into trouble. There are numerous reasons why. Let me give one example here. In English, words undergo pronunciation shifts when suffixes are added to them: e.g., the [ɛy]—[æ] alternation in *nation–national*, *nature–natural*, *sane–sanity*. These pairs of words, because of the vowel alternation, would have to receive two spellings each in a "phonemic" lexicon, each member of the pair constituting a separate lexical item. That is, one spelling would be needed with [ɛy] for the word in isolation: *nation*, and another with [æ] for the stem to which certain suffixes are added: *nation, -al, -ality, -alistic*, etc.

Now these [ɛy]—[æ] alternations, as it happens, are not isolated cases or irregular occurrences. This type of vowel alternation is very common in English and takes place under specifiable conditions of great generality and wide applicability. It is in fact an integral feature of the phonological system of the language which speakers of English have internalized and which they use automatically in producing and understanding utterances. For we find that the same principles which govern the [ɛy]–[æ] alternation cited govern also other vowel alternations, such as the [ɪy]—[ɛ] alternation in *extreme* —*extremity*, *convene–convention*, the [ay]—[ɪ] alternation in *expedite–expeditious*, *wide–width*, and the [o]—[ɑ] alternation in *phone–phonic*, *compose–composite*.

Word pairs such as these, though phonetically different, are recognized by speakers of the language as variant forms of the same word. It is revealing, therefore, when designing the grammar's lexicon, to postulate just one lexical spelling for the vowel, and then to state the general principles which apply to this one shared vowel to produce the two different vowels actually present in the pronunciations of the words. The lexical spelling thus acquires the character of an abstract representation, from which the actual phonetic realizations are predictable according to general rules of pronunciation.

This dual feature, of abstract spelling and rules for converting to pronunciation, is a highly desirable feature of a grammar. Among other things, it retains in the lexical spelling similarities which are real in the language. *Nation* and *national* are not different words in the sense that *nation* and *notion* are different words. They are different forms of the same word. For the lexical spelling to capture this sameness, in spite of surface phonetic differences, is highly desirable. Of course this sameness is exactly what is captured by conventional English orthography in the examples above, where the alternations presented are the familiar long–short vowel alternations. From this viewpoint, this divergence of the conventional orthography from phonetic transcription appears well motivated. It offers the advantage of expressing an underlying reality of the language which is masked by surface phonetic features.

In order to clarify the role of the lexical spelling of words within a transformational grammar, let me indicate what place this abstract entity occupies in the grammar. I have said that the lexical spelling is the way words are spelled in the grammar's lexicon. The other components of the grammar that concern us here are the syntactic component and the phonological component. The syntactic component consists of phrase structure rules and transformational rules. Its output is, among other things, a sentence whose syntactic structure is indicated (see diagram below), in which the words are repre-sented in their lexical spelling, just as they come from the lexicon. It is this string of words, together with information about their syntactic structure, that serves as input to the phonological component. The phonological component in its turn is a complex system of phonological rules that apply to this string and convert it into phonetic representation. This sequence may be diagrammed thus:

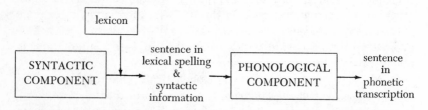

The sentence "We established telegraphic communication," for example, would assume the following forms in the above sequence of operations:

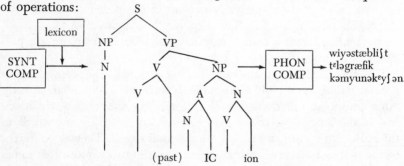

The phonological component contains rules that operate on the lexical spellings, taking into account their syntactic environments, in order to produce a phonetic representation. These are rules that place stress where it belongs, that introduce phonetic effects such as palatalization, velar softening, spirantization, voicing, diphthongization, vowel reduction, vowel shift, laxing and tensing of vowels, and so on. In short, all the rules that make up the phonological system of the language. Their role is to operate on abstract lexical representations within their syntactic context in order to produce the phonetic forms that actually occur in speech.

In producing and interpreting speech, a speaker of the language constantly operates with rules such as these. Certainly he has no conscious knowledge of them any more than he has conscious knowledge of the syntactic rules which enable him to produce and understand sentence structures in his language. In the course of acquiring his language he has internalized the rules of its phonological system, and as a mature speaker he operates in accordance with them both in speaking and in comprehending the spoken language.

Among the interesting decisions that have to be made when designing the grammar is the question of what information properly belongs in the lexical spelling and what should be introduced by the phonological rules. The necessary phonetic output could be achieved with a number of different distributions of information and operations within the grammar. In general, the principle adhered to is that phonetic variation is not indicated in the lexical spelling when it is predictable by general rule. All such predictable phonetic information is left to the phonological rules. As an example, consider the long–short vowel alternations discussed above: *nation–national*, *wide–width*, *phone–phonic*, etc. It is sufficient to use only the long vowel in the lexicon, and to leave it to the phonological rules to shorten this vowel automatically in the presence of certain suffixes. Although the vowel shift could theoretically be introduced either in the lexicon or by the phonological rules, it is preferable to introduce it by phonological rule, as mentioned, for the double reason of expressing the underlying sameness of the vowel, and generality of the feature of vowel shift within the language.

Consider also the common items of words such as *courage/courageous*, or *anxi-ous/anxi-ety*, or *photograph/photograph-y/photograph-ic*. Although the phonetic variations are considerable, they are perfectly automatic, and the lexical spellings can ignore them. They will be introduced by the phonological component. Of course, the conventional orthography ignores them as well. These are good examples of cases where the conventional orthography, by corresponding to lexical spelling rather than phonetic representation, permits immediate direct identification of the lexical item in question, without requiring the reader to abstract away from irrelevant phonetic detail. Conventional orthography has itself abstracted away from the phonetic details, and presents the lexical item directly, as it were.

Now it is a feature of English that it has a rich system of phonetic variations which function very much like the vowel alternations discussed. That is, English has many kinds of surface phonetic variations which need not, and preferably ought not, be represented in the lexical spelling of words. They are wholly predictable within the phonological system of the language, and are therefore best introduced within the grammar by means of automatic phonological rules. As with vowel alternation, these other variations obscure an underlying sameness which the lexical spelling is able to capture. And as with vowel alternations, these surface phonetic variations are not reflected in the conventional orthography.

Consider, for example, the extensive system of consonant alternations in English which are surface phonetic variations only. These phonetic variants are expressed neither in the lexical spellings of words in the grammar, nor in the conventional orthography. Such consonant alternations are surprisingly common. Some examples are:

Phonetic Variants	Sample Word Pairs
[k]—[s]	medicate—medicine
	critical—criticize
	romantic—romanticize
[g]—[dʒ]	sagacity—sage
	prodigal—prodigious
[d]—[dʒ]	grade—gradual
	mode—modular
[t]—[ʃ]	resident—residential
	expedite—expeditious
[t]—[tʃ]	fact—factual
	quest—question
	right—righteous
[z]—[ʒ]	revise—revision
[s]—[z]	sign—resign
	gymnastics—gymnasium

All of these phonetic variations are automatic and predictable within the phonological system of the language. They need not be represented in the lexical spelling of the words, and indeed, underlying similarities which are real in the language would be lost in the grammar if these differences were to be represented on the lexical level. And the same is true of the conventional orthography. By being "unphonetic" in all of these cases, by not exhibiting grapheme-phoneme correspondence, the orthography is able to reflect significant regularities which exist at a deeper level of the sound system of the language, thus making efficient reading easier.

Two other such surface phonetic variations of English, in addition to vowel alternations and consonant alternations, are the interrelated features of stress placement and vowel reduction. Again, these two features are not reflected in the lexical spelling of words because they operate predictably according to rule. The orthography also fails to record them. Surprising as it may seem, the placement of primary stress and the varying degrees of lesser stress in English works largely according to phonological rule, given the lexical spellings of words and information about the syntactic structures in which they appear. Less surprising is the fact that vowel reduction, the pronunciation of certain vowels as a neutral schwa [ə] in unstressed positions, takes place according to rule.

Take, for example, the word *télegraph*. It is stressed on the first syllable. In *telegráphic*, primary stress shifts to the third syllable, and in *telégraphy*, to the second syllable. Since this is a regular variation which many lexical items undergo, and not an unusual feature of this particular word, none of this need be expressed on a lexical level, nor is it expressed in the conventional orthography. It is left to the phonological component of the grammar to introduce these variations.

Consider also the phenomenon of vowel reduction in this same word. The above forms assume the following phonetic shapes in speech:

(a) telegraph   [té lə græf]
(b) telegraphic   [tɛ lə græf]   -ic
(c) telegraphy   [tə lé grəf]   -y

In (a) and (b) the second vowel is reduced; in (c), the first and third vowels. The predictable nature of these variations is discussed by Chomsky and Halle in the following passage from *The Sound Pattern of English*.[3]

[3] Chomsky and Halle, *op. cit.*, pp. 11–12.

> It is quite obvious . . . that this phonetic variation (of stress and vowel reduction in the three forms of *telegraph*) is not fortuitous— it is not of the same type as the variation between *I* and *we*, which depends on specific assignment of the latter to the category of plurality. Given the grammar of English, if we delete specific reference to the item *we*, there is no way to predict the phonetic form of the plural variant of *I*. On the other hand, the rules for English grammar certainly do suffice to determine the phonetic variation of *telegraph* without specific mention of this lexical item, just as they suffice to predict the regular variation between *cat* and *cats* without specifically mentioning the plural form. It is quite obvious that English grammar is complicated by the fortuitous variation between *I* and *we* but not by the totally predictable variation between *cat* and *cats*. Similarly, the grammar would be more complicated if *telegraph* did *not* undergo precisely the variation in (a)–(c); if, for example, it had one phonetic form in all contexts, or if it had the form (a) in the context -ic, (b) in the context -y, and (c) in isolation.

Once again, surface phonetic variations which are automatic and which obscure similarities in lexical items are not represented at the lexical level (or in the orthography), but are introduced by the phonological component of the grammar.

I have referred several times to the abstract nature of the lexical spellings in the grammar. Now that a number of examples have been given, this abstract character of the lexical level becomes clearer. In the lexical spelling, many predictable phonetic features of the spoken language are suppressed, e.g., vowel alternations, consonant alternations, schwa, stress, and others that I have not gone into. The lexical spelling, and the conventional orthography which corresponds so closely to it, abstract away from these variations in pronunciation and represent deeper similarities that have a semantic function in the language. The lexical items are, after all, the meaning–bearing items in the language. Lexical spellings represent the meaning–bearing items directly, without introducing phonetic detail irrelevant to their identification. Thus on the lexical level and in the orthography, words that *are* the same *look* the same. In phonetic transcription they look different. In reading, one is very likely aided by this feature of the conventional orthography. It permits reading to occur with more efficiency. That is, the spelling system leads the reader directly to the meaning–bearing items that he needs to identify, without requiring that he abstract away from superficial and irrelevant phonetic detail. In speech, on the other hand, one operates on both the abstract levels, with the phonological rules mediating between the two.

It seems also that this abstract lexical level is highly resistant to historical change, and remains the same over long periods of time.

Pronunciation shifts that occur as a language changes over time appear to be the result of changes in phonological rules rather than changes in the lexical spellings themselves. For this reason a stable orthography remains effective over time in spite of changes in the way a language is pronounced. And it appears that a wide range of dialect differences also stem from adjustments of phonological rules rather than differences in lexical spellings. This would explain why conventional English orthography is a reasonably adequate system of representation for both British and American English, and the vast range of English dialects that exist within each country and around the world.

Given that lexical spellings differ from phonetic representations in the numerous ways just illustrated, the question naturally arises what implications this may have for speakers of the language and their internal organization of its sound system. Are these abstract lexical representations that are postulated by the linguist merely convenient fictions that the linguist manufactures for the purposes of his grammar, or do they have a psychological reality for the language user? In other words, is the claim that the orthography corresponds to something real in the linguistic knowledge of the reader based on anything that the reader can honestly be said to know?

It seems to me that in a very real sense the lexical level of representation and the corresponding aspects of English orthography do have a psychological reality for the language user. I realize that this assertion will be troublesome to many readers, so let me be very specific about what I mean. I spoke above of the "common item" of words such as *anxi-ous/anxi-ety*, and *courage/courage-ous*. Pairs such as *critic-al/critic-ize*, *revis-e/revis-ion*, *illustrat-e/illustrat-ive* also contain common items. There is little question that speakers recognize these words as related. But clearly what is common to these pairs is not their *surface* form, their phonetic representation, for they are pronounced differently:

anxi-ous : [ǽŋkʃ]
anxi-ety : [æŋgzáy]
courage : [kʌ́rədʒ]
courage-ous : [kəréydʒ]
critic-al : [krítɪk]
critic-ize : [krítɪs]
revis-e : [riváyz]
revis-ion : [rivíʒ]
illustrat-e : [íləstrɛyt]
illustrat-ive : [ɪlʌ́strət]

What is common to them, as was shown earlier, is their *underlying* form, their lexical spelling, which the orthography corresponds to quite closely. To say that this form has psychological reality is to say only that this common item is recognized by the language user *as a common item*, and that its different phonetic realizations are regular within the sound system of the language. The variations in the pairs listed above are not idiosyncratic within the grammar, as is for example the variation between *woman* and *women*, but take place according to general phonological rule. These variations are automatic and do not complicate the grammar in any way. Indeed they would complicate the grammar if they did *not* occur precisely the way they do.

To look at it another way, one might consider, for example, the status of the [k]-[s] alternation in *kill/sill* as compared to *medicate/ medicine*. The difference in status can readily become clear to one who knows the language. In *kill/sill* the phonetic change from [k] to [s] creates a new lexical item. It is both a phonetic and a lexical change. But in *medicate/medicine* it is a phonetic change only. The lexical item remains the same, as does the lexical spelling and the orthography. A speaker who is not aware of this differing status of the two [k]-[s] alternations can have the difference brought to the level of awareness without difficulty, because it reflects a fact about his language that he uses continually, and that is far more general than this one example. In order to become aware of this fact he does not need to be taught it, as a foreigner learning English would, but merely to have it brought to his attention.

The implications of this view of English orthography with regard to reading are several. First, it implies that what the mature reader seeks and recognizes when he reads is not what are commonly called grapheme-phoneme correspondences, but rather the correspondence of written symbol to the abstract lexical spelling of words. Letters represent segments in lexical spelling, not sounds. It is the phonological rule system of the language, which the reader commands, that relates the lexical segments to sounds in a systematic fashion.

Stated somewhat differently, the mature reader does not proceed on the assumption that the orthography is phonetically valid, but rather interprets the written symbols according to lexical spellings. His task is facilitated by the fact that the orthography closely corresponds to this lexical representation. He does not need to abstract away from unnecessary phonetic detail to reconstruct this lexical representation as would be required if the English spelling system were phonetically based. What he needs to identify are the lexical items, the meaning–bearing items, and these are quite readily accessible to him from the lexically based orthography.

It is highly likely that the child, however, in the beginning stages of reading, does assume that the orthography is in some sense "regular" with respect to pronunciation. In order to progress to more complex stages of reading, the child must abandon this early hypothesis, and come eventually to interpret written symbols as corresponding to more abstract lexical spellings. Normally he is able to make this transition unaided as he matures and gains experience both with the sound structure of his language and with reading. It may be, however, that the difficulty encountered by some poor readers is related to the fact that they have not made this crucial transition. This question should be amenable to study. If it appears that this is indeed a factor for some poor readers, then a second related question can be raised, namely how to encourage this progress in children who have not achieved it on their own.

Most methods of teaching reading have little or nothing to offer with respect to this shift in emphasis from a phonetic to a lexical interpretation of the spelling system. Beginning reading instruction that deals analytically with letters and sounds, whether it is based on phonics, the linguistic method, or any other method, tends to treat phonetically accurate spellings as regular in the language, and phonetic inaccuracies as irregular. Children translate spellings into sounds by means of letter–sound correspondences or spelling patterns without ever being expected to apply their knowledge of the phonological system of English to the task. They learn to decode written English much as a foreigner would who knows nothing of English phonology. The child thus gains the impression that spelling is meant to be a direct representation of the pronounced form of words. No provision is made at any point for having him revise this notion in favor of a more realistic view of spelling regularity based on word relationships and underlying lexical similarities. It would seem wise to take this view of regularity into a account in dealing with reading beyond the introductory stages. At some point emphasis ought to be shifted away from the phonetic aspects of spelling to a consideration of the underlying lexical properties of the orthographic system. Crucial to this shift in emphasis is the expectation that the child will rely more and more heavily on phonological processing as he learns to decode written English more efficiently.

In practice, this could take the form of discussing "word families" with children, and bringing out the variety of pronunciations associated in a regular way with individual spellings. As soon as the children's vocabulary permits, they could take up words like *major–majority*, *history–historical–historian*, *nature–natural*, etc., to see how one and the same root changes its pronunciation as different endings are added to it. They might even profitably be introduced to the idea of the abstractness of spelling by considering that the root alone doesn't really have a specific pronunciation until you know what ending goes with it. For example, *natur-* and *histor-* are recognizable roots, but they need to have endings before you can tell which pronunciation is intended.

In this connection it might be helpful if the teacher of reading were aware that words whose spelling is phonetically accurate do not constitute a distinct and meaningful category in the language. They are not the only systematically spelled words in the language, as is often believed. All words whose conventional spelling is close to their abstract lexical spelling are spelled systematically, and this is the more meaningful category. Within this larger category are words whose spelling is close to pronunciation, and many whose spelling is more distant from pronunciation. The former are phonetically spelled words such as *mat* and *pin*, and the latter are words such as *explanation*, *courage*, and *resign* which require more extensive phonological processing. The important point is that they are all spelled systematically, given the sound structure of English. Exceptions are words which fall outside the system, i.e., whose conventional spelling displays aspects which bear little relation to their abstract lexical spelling and which appear unmotivated and arbitrary from a phonological point of view. These are words such as *freight, sword, guard,* and the like.

It is of interest to realize that the child, when he learns to read, is not being introduced to a system of representation that is inconsistent with the language that he speaks. It is simply that the orthography bears an *indirect* rather than a direct relation to his pronunciation. The direct correlation is to lexical spelling, a level of linguistic processing that is beneath the surface, related to pronunciation by regular phonological rules that are part of the child's normal linguistic equipment. This correspondence can be diagrammed as follows:

$$\text{LETTERS} = \overset{}{\underset{\text{lexical spelling}}{\text{segments in}}} \overset{\text{phonological rules}}{\longleftarrow - - - - - - - - \longrightarrow} \text{PRONUNCIATION}$$

Letters correspond to segments in lexical spelling, which in turn are related to pronunciation through the medium of the phonological rules. The correspondence is to something real in the child's linguistic system that he is equipped to handle. It is because it is one step removed from his pronunciation that it is not superficially apparent.

To make this point clearer, consider the role that knowing the language plays for an adult in reading English aloud. The written form *photograph*, for example, is convertible into a particular phonetic configuration, with primary stress on the first syllable, lesser stress on the third syllable, second syllable unstressed, reduced second vowel, and full vowel quality expressed by the first and third vowel. The adult speaker of English is able to utilize elementary letter–sound correspondences to recognize the basic morphological components of the word, *foto-græf*, and then to superimpose all the above phonetic information on these components *because he knows the language* and can apply its phonological rule system. Add the written suffix -*y* to this form: *photography*, and the phonetic information which he super-imposes is radically different: primary stress on second syllable, first and third syllables unstressed, reduced first and third vowels, full vowel quality of second vowel. He converts to different phonetic configurations in the two cases *because of phonological knowledge which he brings to the reading situation, not because of anything that is explicit in the orthography.* He does not have to be told how to apply stress and change vowel quality in these forms because he already knows.

On the other hand, a foreigner who knows no English but has learned the elementary letter-sound correspondences of the English alphabet will be unable to do this. Knowing nothing of the language, such a foreigner finds himself in a very different position when he tries to pronounce these two words. Lacking the necessary information about English phonology, he will read phonetically, and pro-nounce *photograph* alike in both contexts. What the foreigner lacks is just what the child already possesses, a knowledge of the phono-logical rules of English that relate underlying representations to sound. To be sure the child (or adult) has no awareness of this knowl-edge, and would be hard pressed to bring it to the level of awareness. But of course there is no need to do so. It works automatically and enables English speakers to manage well with an orthography that in a sense tells them what they need to know and leaves the rest to them.

The ability of the child to interpret the orthography directly at the lexical level should increase naturally as his phonological competence increases and as he becomes more familiar with the relations ex-pressed by the spellings of words. The full phonological system of English depends heavily on a learned stratum of vocabulary including

Latinate forms and a network of affixes which account for a large
portion of surface phonetic variations. As the maturing child comes to
control these forms in the spoken language he internalizes both their
underlying representations and the phonological rules which relate
the latter to pronunciations. This process of internalization depends
in part on recognizing the relevant similarities in words which are
pronounced differently. It is no doubt facilitated in many cases by
an awareness of how words are spelled. Thus the underlying system
which the child has constructed from evidence provided by the
spoken language and which contributes to his ability to interpret
the written language may itself be improved by his increased familiarity with the written language.

Another aspect of progress in reading relates to the freedom that
the reader has, given the lexical nature of the orthography, to avoid
phonological processing as he reads. Earlier I pointed out an advantage of the lexically based orthography: the reader does not have to
abstract away from unnecessary phonetic detail to reconstruct the
lexical representation of words. It is also true that he does not have
to carry out the inverse activity. He does not have to construct phonetic forms from the underlying lexical forms presented by the
orthography. Silent reading may take place primarily at the lexical
level, without requiring the experienced reader to convert to the surface phonetic level. If he wishes to convert to phonetic representation,
as for example in reading aloud, he does so through the automatic
application of the phonological rules of the language. But this phonological processing may be minimal in rapid silent reading. Indeed,
it may be that part of learning to read rapidly and well is learning to
dispense with the application of phonological rules. Experienced
readers probably engage in varying degrees of phonological processing depending on the type of material they are reading and the reading speed they employ at any given time. But they have learned how
to dispense with a good deal of the phonological processing when
they wish to. Less skilled readers may not have acquired this ability.
Children probably do pronounce to themselves while they are still
inexperienced at reading, and only later begin to be able to relinquish
this phonological processing. It is likely that with increasing experience they gradually come to exploit the lexical nature of the orthography more and more effectively. Certainly there would seem to be
no need to deal with words at the surface phonetic level, given an
orthography that directly represents the underlying form of words.
Children's reading, therefore, ought to improve as the amount of
phonological processing that they engage in decreases.

From this point of view, reading aloud would seem to be of questionable value in improving silent reading. In the very early stages of reading, when the child reads primarily phonetically, there is probably little difference between the two, and oral reading is useful as a check on what the child is actually doing. But as the child progresses to the point where he begins to interpret lexical representations directly from the orthography, he ought to be encouraged to give up converting these lexical representations to phonetic ones. Phonological processing at this point would be a hindrance rather than a help. Skilled silent reading, as pointed out above, can bypass the phonological rules to some extent or even entirely. By the nature of the orthography it never needs to bring them into play. But reading aloud does require their full application. Reading aloud burdens the experienced reader doubly. It is not only that he has to engage in the motor activity of pronouncing what he has read. In order to pronounce it, he must first engage in the mental activity of determining the full phonetic characteristics of what he has read. That is, instead of performing a minimum of phonological processing as in silent reading, he must perform the maximum when reading aloud. Since phonological processing is essentially extraneous to the mature reading process, it would seem ill-advised to focus children's attention on it when they are finally beginning to read "lexically." The teacher may wish to develop oral reading for its own sake, of course, independent of silent reading. But she should keep in mind the possibility that practice in oral reading may have little positive effect on the child's abilities in silent reading, and may even encourage him to persist in aspects of unskilled silent reading that he ought to be leaving behind.

An interesting and important question which is raised by this view of sound structure and reading concerns the age at which the child achieves a mature command of the phonological structure of his language. It is quite possible, perhaps most likely, that full knowledge of the sound system that corresponds to the orthography is not yet possessed by the child of six or seven, and may indeed be acquired fairly late. Chomsky puts it this way:[4]

> The conventional orthography corresponds closely to a level of representation that seems to be optimal for the sound system of a fairly rich version of . . . spoken English. Much of the evidence that determines, for the phonologist, the exact form of this underlying system is based on considerations of learned words and complex derivational patterns. It is by no means obvious that a child of six has

[4] Chomsky, N., *op. cit.*

mastered this phonological system in full. He may not yet have been presented with the evidence that determines the general structure of this system. . . . It would not be surprising to discover that the child's intuitive organization of the sound system continues to develop and deepen as his vocabulary is enriched and as his use of language extends to wider intellectual domains and more complex functions. Hence the sound system that corresponds to the orthography may itself be a late intellectual product.

A serious possibility, following from these hypotheses, is that one of the important ways to improve reading might be to enrich the child's vocabulary so as to enable him to construct for himself the underlying representations of sound that correspond so closely to the written form. As far-fetched as this possibility may seem at first, it ought to be given serious consideration in light of the close tie that exists between English phonology and English orthography. The orthography assumes a fairly sophisticated degree of internal organization of the sound system of the language. Extending the child's vocabulary to include Latinate forms and polysyllabic derived forms is one of the best ways to provide him with the means of constructing the phonological system of his language more fully as he matures. He ought to become familiar with word groups such as *industry–industrial, major–majority, history–historical–historian, wide–width, sign–signature*, etc., and have their relationships made explicit for him. In general, connections should be brought out among words that he already knows but may not yet have classified together, and new words should be introduced for the purpose of establishing new connections. His awareness of these relationships and the variant phonetic forms that words assume in different contexts will facilitate and accelerate his internalization of the phonology of his language.

Literacy acquisition from this point of view may well extend over a much longer period of time than ordinarily assumed, and be closely interrelated with these other aspects of the child's linguistic development. Although little is known at the present time about the child's acquisition of these deeper aspects of the sound structure of English, it is certainly likely that it continues well into the school years. It would be interesting to try to assess the child's implicit knowledge of this phonological system at various stages of his development. An attempt might also be made to determine the degree to which advances in reading ability form part of this same process of development. It would not be at all surprising, perhaps for adults as well as children, if those who control the sound system of English better also exploit its orthography more effectively.

Spelling is another area of interesting practical application of this view of the orthography. In the case of spelling it seems to me that the major contribution might be to the teacher's own assumptions about the orthography. If she works on the assumption that spelling corresponds to something real, *that it makes sense,* she will encourage the child to recognize and exploit the regularities that do exist. If she is familiar with some of the more obvious regularities it will help, but basically she and the children can work together to characterize regularities, armed primarily with their joint knowledge of the language as native speakers, and the recognition that the conventional spelling system does in fact have a great deal to recommend it.

To start, there are quite specific things that can be pointed out to children who need help, so that they may approach the stage that good spellers seem to reach on their own. Good spellers, children and adults alike, recognize that related words are spelled alike even though they are pronounced differently. They seem to rely on an underlying picture of the word that is independent of its varying pronunciations. And when encountering a troublesome word, they are in the habit of automatically putting to use the idea that related words may vary a good deal in their pronunciation, but that the spelling by and large remains the same. When they are not sure how to spell a particular word, the first thing that they do is bring to mind other related words in the hope of finding one that contains the solution. If it is a reduced vowel that is causing the trouble, a differently stressed variant of the word will often provide the answer. For example, there is no way to guess the second vowel of *industry* from the pronunciation of the word, but thinking of *industrial* solves the problem. And this is often the case with reduced vowels.

After all, how *do* we know that the second vowel of *declaration, inspiration* and *adoration* are written differently, when they are pronounced exactly alike? Obviously because of *declare, inspire,* and *adore.* We do not have to memorize the spellings of *declaration, inspiration,* and *adoration,* but merely be able to make the connection in each case to the related verb. Once the connection is clear, the correct spelling is automatic.

If the child developes the habit of seeking such connections, of thinking of related words that settle his spelling uncertainties for him, he not only spells better, but in the long run he familiarizes himself with the general underlying regularities of the orthography. Instead of memorizing individual words one after the other, he equips himself with the systematic means of dealing with large segments of vocabulary.

The examples which follow suggest several types of "spelling lessons" that can be constructed to bring out a number of these features of the spelling system. These samples are intended primarily to indicate a general approach. In practice, of course, vocabulary would have to be adapted to the abilities of individual classes.

Children could be asked, for example, to fill in the missing reduced vowel in a list such as column (1), and then to justify their choices by thinking of related words which retain vowel quality. They would then produce something like column (2).

(1)	(2)
dem_cratic	democracy
pres_dent	preside
prec_dent	precede
comp_rable	compare, comparison
comp_sition	composer, compose
hist_ry	historical, historian
janit_r	janitorial
manag_r	managerial
maj_r	majority
ill_strate	illustrative
ind_stry	industrial
imm_grate	migrate
cons_lation	console
ab_lition	abolish
comp_tent	compete

Or, simply given column (2), they could be asked to think up other forms of the words, and to characterize the specific ways in which the vowel sounds shift around. Anything that focuses their attention on related words and concomitant pronunciation shifts ought to be good practice for finding specific related words when they need them.

This approach works not only for recovering the full form of reduced vowels, but often for selecting the correct consonant from a choice of two when pronunciation is ambiguous. For example, in column (1), the italicized consonant could, given its pronunciation, be written using either of the letters in parentheses. The related word in column (2) narrows the choice to just one of these.

(1)		(2)
criti*c*ize	(*c, s*)	critical
medi*c*ine	(*c, s*)	medical

nation	(t, sh)	native
gradual	(d, j)	grade
righteous	(t, ch)	right
racial	(t, c, sh)	race

Another helpful exercise involves consonants which are silent in some words but pronounced in others. For example:

(1)	(2)
muscle	muscular
sign, (design)	signature, signal (designate)
bomb	bombard
condemn	condemnation
malign	malignant
soften	soft

Children could be given column (2) and asked to think of related words in which the underlined consonant becomes silent. Or, conversely, they could be given column (1) and asked to think of related words in which the silent consonant is recovered phonetically. Or they could be given the words in column (1) orally and asked to name the silent consonant. For those who can't do it, the column (2) word can be elicited or, if necessary, pointed out as helpful evidence.

The need for practice in this sort of thinking seems to be quite strong for some children. This was brought home to me recently by a conversation that I had about some of these silent consonants with a seventh-grade girl, a child of average intelligence but a poor speller. The conversation went like this:

What letter is silent in the word "muscle"?
   E.
Ok, you're right. But how about a *consonant* that's silent?
   I don't know. There isn't any.
Well, how do you spell "muscle"?
   M-u-s-l-e
There's something left out. What do you call a man who has a lot of muscles?
   Strong.
Yes, but what do you call him that's related to the word "muscle"?
   I don't know.
Did you ever hear the word "muscular"?
   Yeah, I guess so.

Well, how do you spell "muscular"?
   M-u-s-c- . . .
That's all you need. So how do you spell "muscle"?
   M-u-c- . . .
Wait. How does "muscular" begin?
   M-u-s-c- . . .
Ok. Now "muscle."
   M-u-s-c-l-e.

It was a struggle, but she got there. The next try showed how little understanding she had of the idea that words are actually connected to each other in meaning and form, even words that she was perfectly familiar with.

How do you spell "sign"?
   S-i-g-h-n
What do you call it when you sign your name?
   Your signature.
How do you spell "signature"?
   S-i-g-n . . .
Ok. So how do you spell "sign"?
   S-i-g-h-n
But you just told me that "signature" begins with *S-I-G-N* . . !
   So what's one got to do with the other?

This is the sort of thing that needs attention if a child is to improve his spelling. Better spelling is not a matter of individual words (S-i-g-h-n on the analogy of *sigh* is actually a pretty good try as an isolated word.), but will come about as an outgrowth of an understanding and awareness of the relationships between words.

Still another type of exercise involves consonant alternations which occur not only in the pronunciation of words, but are reflected in the orthography as well. For example, the letter *t* and *c* alternate in many word pairs:

(1)	(2)
coinciden*t*al	coinciden*c*e
pira*t*e	pira*c*y
presiden*t*	presiden*c*y
presen*t*	presen*c*e
residen*t*	residen*c*e
luna*t*ic	luna*c*y
democra*t*ic	democra*c*y

It helps to recognize the general pattern, for it resolves the question of how to spell the pronounced [s] of column (2). *Presidency* is spelled with *c* and not *s* because it is related to *president, presence* is related to *present*, and so on. The *t-c* alternation is general enough so that being aware of it can be useful.

It is interesting to note that this *t-c* orthographic alternation, which is phonetically a [t]-[s] alternation, is a phonologically predictable alternation. It requires only one underlying lexical spelling, with *t*. I.e., the *t* of the underlying form of *pirate* automatically becomes phonetic [s] in the context -y, so that instead of [payrətiy], the phonological rules produce [payrəsiy]. By the same rules *president* + y becomes [prɛ zə dən siy], and so on. The orthography chooses to reflect this phonetic change in the case of [t] ⇒ [s] whereas it ignores many other such automatic phonetic changes, as we have seen. For example, it does not reflect the phonetic change [k] ⇒ [s] as in *medical–medicine*. When the orthography reflects a phonetic change such as [t] ⇒ [s] in *pirate–piracy* it corresponds to an internal level of representation which is not as abstract as the lexical level. Some phonological processing has already been applied to the lexical spelling to produce the phonetic variants indicated by the orthography.

Exercises such as these are to be construed as samples of a particular approach which can be extended as the need arises. However, it is perhaps much more to the point for the teacher to develop a way of dealing with spelling errors that the children produce day by day than to equip herself with preselected word lists. Most important is that she transmit to the child the notion that spelling very often is not arbitrary, but rather corresponds to something real that he already knows and can exploit. A good way to handle misspellings that come up in class is to search with the child for a systematic reason why the word should be spelled the way it is, if indeed one can be found. In many cases, such a reason can be found. Often this will mean simply bringing a relation between two familiar words to the child's attention. To use some examples drawn from the spontaneous writing of a group of 3rd and 4th graders, the child who misspells *president* as *presedent* needs to have pointed out that it is related to *preside*. The child who misspells *really* as *relly* needs to think of *reality* to get it right. *Apon* is more likely to be written *upon* if the child realizes that it is a combination of *up* and *on*. *Immagrate* will become *immigrate* if it is connected with *migrate*. *Medisin* will lose the *s* and acquire a *c* if it is connected to *medical*.

Sometimes a related word that could help settle the difficulty for the child is a word that he doesn't know. *Illustrative,* for example, may not be part of the vocabulary of the child who writes *illastrate* for *illustrate.* In such cases, it may make better sense to introduce the new word than to have him memorize a seemingly arbitrary spelling for his familiar word.

Exploiting opportunities that come up naturally in class is certainly one of the most dynamic ways of fitting words into context and developing the idea of word relationships. This can be exciting and can really increase children's language sense if undertaken by a teacher who enjoys etymologies and who is sensitive to language herself. Herbert Kohl's excellent description of just such a beginning and where it can lead in *36 Children*[5] is one of the best examples I have seen recently of how meaningfully this can be done. Starting with one child's use of the word "psyches" as an insult (the children visualized this word as s-i-k-e-s.), he led the class into a discussion of etymologies, Greek myth, word meanings, and word relationships. It caught on. Over a period of time the undertaking was extended to include word origins more generally, the question of how words acquire their meanings, and even a consideration of historical change and the notion of "right" and "wrong" in language in a descriptive vs. prescriptive framework.

The general conclusion to be derived from the view of the orthography presented here is that spelling, far more often than it seems from a purely phonetic standpoint, does make sense. Many spelling errors could be avoided if the writer developed the habit of looking for regularities that underlie related words when in doubt. This is part of the strategy used by good spellers as a matter of course. For the child who spells poorly it is far more productive to learn how to look for these regularities than simply to memorize the spellings of words as isolated examples. Providing him with a strategy based on the realities of the language is clearly the best way to equip him to deal with new examples on his own.

It would be less than realistic to close this discussion of the regularities of English spelling without a glance at the other side of the coin. English spelling does after all have its less consistent aspects. To restore a sense of balance I offer the following passage in conclusion.

[5] Herbert Kohl, *36 Children* (New York: The New American Library, 1967), pp. 23–29.

Hints on Pronunciation for Foreigners[6]

I take it you already know
Of tough and bough and cough and dough?
Others may stumble but not you,
On hiccough, thorough, laugh and through.
Well done! And now you wish, perhaps,
To learn of less familiar traps?

Beware of heard, a dreadful word
That looks like beard and sounds like bird,
And dead: it's said like bed, not bead—
For goodness' sake don't call it "deed"!
Watch out for meat and great and threat
(They rhyme with suite and straight and debt.)

A moth is not a moth in mother
Nor both in bother, broth in brother,
And here is not a match for there
Nor dear and fear for bear and pear,
And then there's dose and rose and lose—
Just look them up—and goose and choose,
And cork and work and card and ward,
And font and front and word and sword,
And do and go and thwart and cart—
Come, come, I've hardly made a start!
A dreadful language? Man alive.
I'd mastered it when I was five.

T. S. W.
(only initials of writer known)

[6] From a letter published in the *London Sunday Times* (January 3, 1965), from J. Bland. Cited by Mackay and Thompson, "The Initial Teaching of Reading and Writing," *Programme in Linguistics and English Teaching*, Paper no. 3, University College, London, and Longmans Green and Co., Ltd., London and Harlow, 1968, p. 45.

RONALD WARDHAUGH

Linguistic Insights into
the Reading Process

In this essay, Wardhaugh reviews the work of five linguists who have been concerned with the reading process and the more theoretical question of the relationship of writing to sound and meaning. He begins by stating that the topic of linguistics and reading is of great interest to applied linguistics for three reasons: (1) it forces linguists to discuss some of the difficulties in applying theoretical research to the solution of practical problems (like teaching children to read); (2) it makes linguists aware of the limitations of their field of knowledge; and (3) it shows how linguistics itself changes in its concerns, techniques, and rhetoric.

Wardhaugh discusses first the work of Leonard Bloomfield and Charles Fries, who together are credited with being the originators of the "linguistic" method of teaching reading in North America. Bloomfield rejected the then current phonics approach to teaching reading because he felt that it had confused speech with writing. In its place he proposed an approach based on the linguistic study of sound-symbol correspondences

Reprinted with permission of the author from *Language Learning*, Vol. 18, Nos. 3 and 4, pp. 235–252.

(or to use the linguistic terms, phoneme-grapheme correspondences). In his approach, the child is gradually and systematically introduced to the ways in which English orthography represents speech sounds. For Bloomfield, learning to read is a matter of understanding the spelling system of English, not of learning what words and sentences mean.

Bloomfield's ideas were developed and given wider prominence by the works of Charles Fries. One of the few differences between Fries and Bloomfield is Fries' emphasis on the student's ability to recognize the contrast between whole words, in addition to his ability to sound out the letters of single words. For both men, and for the "linguistic" approach as a whole, a child is assumed to already know his own language, including the relation of sound to meaning. Alphabetic writing is a way of representing the sounds of a language. Thus, learning to read is nothing more than unlocking a coded way for presenting something one already knows. As Wardhaugh puts it, "Reading comprehension is, therefore, a specific instance of general linguistic comprehension."

The third linguist whose work Wardhaugh discusses is Richard Venezky. Venezky, like Bloomfield and Fries, is concerned with the relationship between letters and sounds. However, Venezky sees that relationship as being much more complex than Bloomfield and Fries did. Venezky argues that it is first necessary for the reader to convert the spelling of the word into an idealized form of the word, which he calls the morphophonemic representation. The morphophonemic representation is then converted into pronunciation (more accurately, into a phonemic representation of the word's pronunciation) by a set of rules. Venezky is trying to make explicit the kind of intuitive knowledge that a speaker must have in order to pronounce English words. As Wardhaugh puts it, Venezky is' giving a set of rules that convert writing to speech, whereas Bloomfield and Fries present a much less explicit set of rules that merely associate writing and speech. Readers who are interested in Venezky's approach should consult his recent book *The Structure of English Orthography*, published by Mouton in 1972.

The final work that Wardhaugh discusses is Noam Chomsky and Morris Halle's book *The Sound Pattern of English*. Readers can get an idea of some of the themes and implications of this major and difficult work from Carol Chomsky's article in this anthology. Chomsky and Halle are interested in the relation of sound and meaning. The intermediary between the two, in their theory, is an abstract phonological unit that can be directly related to words with their meaning and grammar on the one hand and to actual pronunciation on the other. For them the conventional orthography of English provides a near optimal way of writing this intermediary. Thus the relationship between letters and sounds is more complex for them than for Venezky because they feel that spelling indicates abstract information about the word as well as its pronunciation.

Wardhaugh makes two observations about Chomsky and Halle's proposals: (1) He wonders "how much of such a rich system of phonology as that postulated in *The Sound Pattern of English* can we ascribe to a six-year-old"? Much of their description is valid only for the abilities of an adult, and a highly literate one at that. However, even a six-year-old is capable of a good many complex phonological operations. Wardhaugh concludes that the child has a more limited command of the sets of rules and phonological abstractions than the sets described by Chomsky and Halle. (2) Wardhaugh emphasizes the importance of the direction of the relationship between meaning and sound in Chomsky and Halle's system. For Chomsky and Halle, in order to pronounce a word, one must know the meaning and grammatical organization of the entire sentence as well as the meaning and grammar of the individual word. Wardhaugh gives as an example the phrase *American history teacher*. This phrase has two meanings. Each meaning has its own grammatical analysis and pronunciation. Chomsky and Halle themselves raise the question as to whether young children have either the knowledge or the ability to deal with such abstract relations. Wardhaugh suggests that the child's limited abilities and knowledge may lend support to the less sophisticated approaches taken by Bloomfield and Fries.

Wardhaugh concludes that in order to learn to read, a child needs to develop a strategy for associating written symbols with superficial phonological units. He feels that the phonics approach is on the right track, but calls for greater incorporation of linguistic insights into phonics instruction as well as for closer cooperation among linguists, psychologists, and educators.

The reader might be interested in Wardhaugh's own excellent book on reading, *Reading: A Linguistic Perspective*, Harcourt, Brace and World, 1969.

ABSTRACT

Various linguists have put forward proposals for studying the reading process and for teaching reading. Bloomfield and Fries tried to use linguistic knowledge to devise a method of teaching reading based on a belief that children had to learn sound–symbol relationships in order to read. Venezky has proposed a model of the reading process which is something of a bridge between their work and that of Chomsky and Halle. The latter have proposed that present English orthography is an optimal system for the language and that the phonemes of so much interest to Bloomfield and Fries are no more than methodological artifacts. However, they acknowledge that their phonological model might not be an appropriate one for children. If this is the case, then certain insights from Bloomfield and Fries may still be relevant. The possible applications of linguistics to reading are still uncertain in the absence of empirical evidence to support any of the present hypotheses.

Within applied linguistics the topic of linguistics and reading is of great interest for several reasons which should be stated at the outset.[1] First of all, it forces us to discuss some of the difficulties involved in attempts to use insights from research in theoretical linguistics in the solution of a practical problem, in this case the problem being one of teaching children to read and of understanding the reading process. In other cases the problem may be one of teaching a foreign language, of translating a text, or of choosing a national language. The same difficulties arise in each case: just what linguistic knowledge is relevant to solving the problem and how may knowledge which is considered relevant be used? The teaching of reading is a very real problem almost everywhere in the world and often a controversial one. Those linguists who have looked at it have adopted a variety of different approaches because they have viewed the nature of the problem differently and because they have also held different views about the proper nature of linguistic inquiry. In this paper, therefore, I will try to indicate some of the different views of the reading process held by different linguists and some of the solutions that they have proposed.

The second reason which makes this topic interesting is that it allows us to observe some of the limitations of linguistic knowledge in solving a practical problem. In the course of the paper, some indication will be given of specific areas in which the limits of linguistic knowledge are reached and in which other kinds of knowledge are called for. It is apparent that certain linguists have confused nonlinguistic matters with linguistic ones, possibly to the extent of overreaching themselves. Such overreaching is not unique to linguists: experts from many disciplines are accustomed to speaking on topics outside their field of competence with the same air of authority they assume within that field!

The third reason is no less important than the first two: it is to show how linguistics itself is changing in its concerns, its techniques, and its rhetoric. This last statement should become clearer when the approaches to the reading process taken by Bloomfield and Fries are compared with those taken by Chomsky and Halle. There is a vast difference in both the content and the style of their discussions of the problem; however, there is some reason to say that the conclusions

[1] This is a revised version of a paper presented at the Autumn Meeting of The British Association for Applied Linguistics, in Edinburgh on September 28, 1968.

of Bloomfield and Fries on the one hand and those of Chomsky and Halle on the other may not actually be so very far apart.

The earliest proposals to use modern linguistic knowledge in the teaching of reading apparently came from Leonard Bloomfield, who was disturbed by certain aspects of school instruction, particularly the instruction given in language and in reading. For example, in a statement published in the very first volume of *Language* in 1925 explaining in part why the Linguistic Society of America had been founded, he wrote as follows:

> Our schools are conducted by persons who, from professors of education down to teachers in the classroom, know nothing of the results of linguistic science, not even the relation of writing to speech or of standard language to dialect. In short, they do not know what language is, and yet must teach it, and in consequence waste years of every child's life and reach a poor result.[2]

Bloomfield felt that the methods being used to teach his son to read were unenlightened and revealed a lack of knowledge about language. Consequently, he devised his own method of teaching his son to read and shared his opinions, methods, and materials with those of his friends who had like interests. These later became known as the Bloomfield system for teaching reading when they found their way into *Let's Read*.[3]

Bloomfield rejected the "code-breaking" approach known as phonics as a way of teaching reading, claiming that the proponents of phonics confused statements about speech with those about writing to the point that they often appeared to be teaching children to speak, whereas all they were really doing was teaching them to associate written symbols with already known words. He objected to practices such as breaking up words into smaller parts corresponding to letters, crediting individual letters with having sounds; sounding out words

(e.g., *cat* as [kᵊ æ tᵊ]), and blending sounds in an attempt to decode written words. Not only did Bloomfield reject a "code-breaking" or phonics approach, but he also rejected the competing "whole word" approach, claiming that it ignored the alphabetic nature of the English writing system in that it treated English as though it were Chinese.

Bloomfield believed that children learning to read should first be

---

[2] Leonard Bloomfield, "Why a Linguistic Society?" *Language*, I (1925), p. 5.

[3] Leonard Bloomfield and Clarence L. Barnhart, *Let's Read* (Detroit: Wayne State University Press, 1961).

trained in visual discrimination and then be taught to associate visually discriminated objects (letter and word shapes) to already known sounds and meanings. The story line (the meaning of the reading materials) was, he believed, far less important than the regularity of the connection between sounds and symbols, the phoneme–grapheme correspondences. In order therefore to guarantee that children should easily acquire a mastery of these correspondences, Bloomfield insisted that they be trained to discriminate in a left-to-right direction and also to name the letters of the alphabet without error. He believed that requiring children to name the letters in new words from left to right guaranteed both visual discrimination and correct word attack. Just as linguists, and presumably children (intuitively in their case), could segment an utterance into phonemes, beginning readers had to learn to segment words into graphemes, and the teacher systematically had to teach children to relate the two discrimination abilities. The Bloomfield approach is, therefore, one which is based on the introduction of regular sound–symbol, or phoneme–grapheme, correspondences so that children can acquire the fundamental understanding they must acquire in order to read, the understanding that writing is a representation of speech, and, on the whole, quite a systematic one.

Bloomfield was also concerned with the notion of contrast, seeing a need to teach whole written words such as *can, van,* and *fan* in contrast with each other and to introduce all the contrastive details of the English writing system gradually and systematically, so that the child learning to read would realize, as Bloomfield wrote, that *"printed letter = speech sound to be spoken."*[4] It is not surprising therefore that the resulting lists, exercises, and testing materials look something like the old "word family" lists in many of the old-fashioned nineteenth century readers. Here is an example of some testing materials from *Let's Read*:

> ban, can, Dan, fan, gan, . . .
> bat, cat, fat, gat, hat, . . .
> bad, cad, dad, fad, gad, . . .
> bap, cap, dap, gap, Hap, . . .
> bag, cag, dag, fag, gag, . . .[5]

According to Bloomfield, the basic task the child learning to read had to master was that of understanding the spelling system of English not that of understanding the meanings of English words and

[4] Bloomfield and Barnhart, p. 36.
[5] Bloomfield and Barnhart, p. 101.

sentences. Therefore, it was quite possible for teachers to use nonsense syllables and nonsense words in order to allow their students to achieve such mastery. He wrote as follows on this point:

> Tell the child that the nonsense syllables are parts of real words which he will find in the books that he reads. For example, the child will know *han* in *handle* and *jan* in *January* and *mag* in *magnet* or *magpie*. The acquisition of nonsense syllables is an important part of the task of mastering the reading process.[6]

Later, Robert Hall, gave very much the same kind of advice, claiming that the "ultimate test of any method of teaching reading is whether the learners can deal with nonsense syllables. . . ."[7] Both Bloomfield and Hall are really advocating an emphasis on a "code-breaking" approach, but not the particular "code-breaking" approach known as phonics. In his work, Bloomfield was concerned almost exclusively with monosyllabic words and polysyllabic words received very little attention. In defense of this emphasis, he claimed that his son found no difficulty in transferring to polysyllabic words once he had achieved a mastery of the monosyllabic patterns. This observation is a very interesting observation to which I shall have further occasion to refer in connection with the work of contemporary linguists.

Believing that the major task the beginning reader must master is one wholly concerned with the interpretation of words and not one concerned with guessing at the meanings of words by using accompanying illustrations, Bloomfield rejected the use of illustrations in reading materials on the grounds that they are either irrelevant or misleading. Some of the materials for teaching reading that Fries and his followers were to develop following Bloomfield's example likewise do not contain pictures so that children may be left free to focus their attention on the words themselves rather than on the illustrations accompanying the words. The results of applying Bloomfield's theories to reading are reading materials like the following:

A rap. A gap.

Dad had a map.
Pat had a bat.
Tad had a tan cap.
Nan had a tan hat.

---

[6] Bloomfield and Barnhart, pp. 41–42.

[7] Robert A. Hall, Jr., *Introductory Linguistics* (Philadelphia: Chilton Company, 1964), p. 432.

Nan had a fat cat.
A fat cat ran at a bad rat.[8]

There is much that is admirable in Bloomfield's ideas on reading. First of all, his work on English phoneme–grapheme correspondences was based on a good knowledge of the important surface phonological contrasts in English. Bloomfield also stressed the fact that the English writing system is basically an alphabetical one and that it is not as inconsistent as it is often made out to be, particularly when it is approached from the viewpoint of *how sounds are represented in writing* and not from that of how letters are pronounced, or, even worse, *should* be pronounced. Then, too, there is in his work on reading a welcome insistence that the proper context of reading and the basic insights necessary to understand the reading process are to be found in linguistic rather than in social and psychological factors. However, the Bloomfield method has much more to say about the linguistic *content* of reading materials than about an actual *method* of teaching reading. What comments on methodology there are in Bloomfield's writings seem to be based on an extrapolation of some procedures, such as contrast, which linguists have found useful in their work as linguists, and not on procedures derived from teaching reading. This type of extrapolation is characteristic of much work in applied linguistics in general. It is certainly not unique to the problem of using linguistic insights in understanding the reading process or in the teaching of reading!

A more recent proposal than Bloomfield's to use linguistic insights in reading was made by Charles Fries in *Linguistics and Reading*,[9] undoubtedly the most influential book on linguistics and reading published to date. Like Bloomfield, Fries took the position that reading experts are quite unfamiliar with linguistics and in general exhibit little knowledge of language at all; consequently, he set out to correct this defect and to offer an outline of a method for teaching reading that drew heavily on linguistic insights in a manner reminiscent of the approach behind his well-known book on second-language teaching, *Teaching and Learning English as a Foreign Language*.[10]

One important distinction that Fries insisted on is in the use of the terms *phonics*, *phonemics*, and *phonetics*, and a whole chapter in his

---

[8] Leonard Bloomfield and Clarence L. Barnhart, *Let's Read*, Part I (Experimental Edition) (Bronxville, N. Y.: C. L. Barnhart, Inc., 1963), p. 37.

[9] Charles C. Fries, *Linguistics and Reading* (New York: Holt, Rinehart and Winston, Inc., 1963).

[10] Charles C. Fries, *Teaching and Learning English as a Foreign Language* (Ann Arbor: University of Michigan Press, 1945).

book is devoted to the problem of clarifying the differences among these terms and setting the record straight. The chapter contains example after example of the confused use of the three terms in the literature on reading and is a telling indictment of most writing on the subject of phonics, that is most writing on the "code-breaking" view of reading. Like Bloomfield before him, Fries emphasized that written English is alphabetic in nature and that English spelling is not inconsistent if statements about speech and statements about writing are clearly distinguished and if letters (graphemes) are regarded as representations of significant speech sounds (phonemes). Fries pointed out the regular spelling patterns in English and said that it was the reading teacher's task to teach these to beginning readers by presenting them in carefully arranged sequences and by giving beginning readers considerable practice in recognizing them in contrasting words.

Fries considered that in learning to read, children had to master a new visual task, in which they had to associate quite automatically visual responses with previously discriminated auditory responses. He believed that this process, which he regarded as a transfer process, required visual training, for example training in left-to-right eye movements and in the discrimination of the important features of letters and words. For this reason Fries rejected the concurrent introduction of both upper- and lower-case letters in beginning texts in favor of the exclusive use of upper-case letters so as to reduce the burden of discrimination for the child who was learning to read. He apparently rejected the argument that the elimination of ascenders and descenders and the resultant uniform "block" shapes of written words might result in the loss of many useful visual clues and would reduce the amount of visual information available to the child. Instead, Fries believed that children would find written words composed out of twenty-six uniform letters easier to perceive than the corresponding words composed out of twice that number of letters. Later he modified this view.

Fries also insisted on the use of contrastive word patterns since for him the principle of contrast was basic to both linguistic structure and visual perception. He rejected the spelling out of words that Bloomfield recommended, insisting instead that the critically important skill for children to acquire is one of being able to make visual discriminations between whole words and between whole patterns or units of meaning. He sought, therefore, to minimize any factor which would tend to require children to focus on units smaller than whole words. Although Fries recognized that written English is alphabetic and the alphabet is a contrastive system, he claimed that the more important system of contrasts was the one associated with words and meanings; consequently, his method was essentially a "whole-word" method rather than a "phonics" method of the traditional kind. Fries also stressed the importance of oral reading in the belief that the written message is but a representation of the oral message; however, his goal was still most definitely silent reading in the later stages of the program. The following is an example of a page from one of the Fries readers, as these were later developed from his ideas.

The Cat on the Van.

Dan is on the van.
Nat is on the van.
The pan is on the van.

The cat can bat the pan.
Dan can pat the cat.
The man ran the van.[11]

Like Bloomfield, Fries had very little to say about comprehension: both apparently regarded comprehension as a basically passive activity which is highly dependent on oral language skills. Children must learn to react instantly to the contrasts between *mat* and *mate* and between *bit* and *beat*. They already react to the differences between these words when they are spoken. What they must do in learning to read is to associate a visual pattern which they have learned to discriminate from other visual patterns to a speech pattern which they already know and can discriminate from other speech patterns. A child who is learning to read is already subconsciously aware of the different kinds of meanings and patterns in his language or he could not communicate in that language. What he needs to have unlocked for him is the code that is writing, so that he can have access to these different kinds of meanings and patterns through the medium of print. Fries went so far as to claim that this code can be unlocked for the beginning reader within a year of his learning to "talk satisfactorily," an age which he put at four or five. Needless to say, this claim has appeared to be rather extravagant to many who actually teach reading. Fries, therefore, did not regard the problem of teaching reading comprehension as a serious one. He obviously took issue with wide-ranging definitions of the reading process which

[11] Charles C. Fries, Agnes C. Fries, Rosemary G. Wilson, and Mildred K. Rudolph, *Merrill Linguistic Readers, Reader I* (Columbus: Charles E. Merrill Books, Inc., 1966), p. 36.

relate that process to social, psychological, and physiological factors in favor of a view of the reading process as a kind of high-speed visual recognition of meanings that are already familiar to the reader. Reading comprehension is, therefore, a specific instance of general linguistic comprehension.

In both the Bloomfield and Fries approaches there is a strong insistence that a particular kind of linguistic knowledge is of paramount importance in gaining insight into the reading process and in determining the content of a reading series. There is also an assumption that principles of linguistic analysis, such as patterning and contrast, can by extrapolation become useful principles in reading pedagogy. Henry Lee Smith has pointed out[12] that there are certain valid pedagogical points which linguists have tended to ignore when they have talked about reading. In listing a number of these, he specifies such matters as typography, choice of illustrations, some repetition of patterns and words, and attention to both story line and characters. Smith cautions that it would be unwise for linguists who take an interest in reading to assume that reading teachers have learned nothing about teaching reading from their experiences, either individually or collectively. His words have been heeded to some extent in recent writings on linguistics and reading. They were obviously motivated in part by the hostility which characterized some of the original linguistics–reading discussions. That such hostility, particularly on the part of the reading experts, should have been aroused is not surprising when one reads some of the statements made by linguists about reading. For example, the statements by Bloomfield and Hall that there should be no illustrations in reading texts and the one by Fries that reading is a passive activity run counter to what most authorities on reading consider to be pedagogically sound observations. It must be emphasized that linguistics as a discipline has nothing at all to contribute to the discussion of whether or not there should be illustrations in a reading text: the inclusion or exclusion of illustrations is entirely a pedagogical decision. Likewise, any definition of reading which makes it out to be a passive activity indicates a certain lack of awareness of the many problems inherent in the teaching of reading.

It would not be unfair to say that what has become known as the linguistic method of teaching reading in North America is one which relies heavily on the work of Bloomfield and Fries. In essence, the method entails little more than the presentation of regular phoneme-

---

[12] Henry Lee Smith, "Review of *Let's Read*," *Language*, 39 (1963), pp. 67–78.

grapheme, or sound–spelling, relationships in beginning reading texts, in many ways a kind of neo–phonics. The materials developed by the followers of Bloomfield and Fries reflect this concern: there is almost no indication in these materials that the possible linguistic contribution to reading involves anything more than the systematic introduction of the regularities and irregularities of English spelling. There is, in fact, scarcely more than an occasional passing reference to any other than this one solitary point that linguists have made about English.

The concern for phoneme–grapheme correspondences and for the importance of these in teaching reading has led to many studies, some quite sophisticated, of the relationships of various phonological segments to various graphological segments. These studies vary in quality and purpose. One of the best studies has come from Richard Venezky, particularly because he has attempted to relate his correspondence studies to a model of the reading process.[13] Venezky has done more than count phonemes and graphemes, compute frequencies of correspondence, and attempt to program a logical sequence of correspondences. Rather, he has attempted to construct a set of rules for translating orthographic symbols into speech sounds, because he considers it useful to characterize the reading process in those terms. His work is, therefore, an attempt to construct a model of the reading process which recognizes the distributions of phonemes and graphemes, the frequencies of occurrence, and the patterns of correspondences. Central to the model is a set of rules which relates all of these. Venezky writes of the process of learning to read as follows:

> Learning to read . . . requires primarily the translation from written symbols to sound, a procedure which is the basis of the reading process and is probably the only language skill unique to reading.
> . . . .
> The patterns summarized here represent an ideal system for translating from spelling to sound. . . .[14]

He describes how the model works as follows:

> As examples of how this model organizes spelling-to-sound rules, the processes for predicting the pronunciation of *social* and *signing* are shown below.

[13] Richard L. Venezky, "English Orthography: Its Graphical Structure and its Relation to Sound," *Reading Research Quarterly*, 2:3 (1967), pp. 75–105.
[14] Venezky, p. 102.

social would be mapped into //sosɪæl// by the grapheme–to–morphophoneme rules for the separate units *s, o, c, i, a, l.* On the first morphophonemic level, the main word stress would be placed on the first syllable, resulting in //sósɪæl//. Then, through vowel reduction, //ɪæl// would become //jəl// and the resulting //sj// would be palatalized to //š//. The form //sóšəl// would then be mapped onto the phonemic level, giving /sóšəl/.

signing would first be broken into *sign* and *ing* and then each of these graphemic allomorphs would be mapped onto the morphophonemic level, yielding //sɪgn// and //ɪng//. Upon combination of the two forms and the application of stress and certain phonotactical rules, the form //sɪgnɪŋg// would result. By rules for leveling consonant clusters, final //ŋg// would become //ɲ// and //gn// would become //n// with compensatory alternation of //ɪ// to //aɪ//. These operations yield //sáɪnɪŋ// which is automatically mapped into /sáɪnɪŋ/.[15]

There are some very interesting differences between such an approach and that of Bloomfield and Fries. First of all, there is a concern with a level of representation called *morphophonemic*, a representation which looks very like the standard orthography. Then there is a set of ordered rules which, for example, assign stress and convert morphophonemes sometimes into morphophonemes but always eventually into phonemes. This last phonemic level is important in Venezky's work. He makes no attempt to eliminate it. Nor are the conversion rules necessarily made to conform to the demands of the kind of evaluation measure that the generative–transformationalists insist on in their work. In the *signing* example, the morphophoneme //ɪ// become the phonemes /ai/ (through an intermediate morphophonemic stage) in apparently idiosyncratic way that a computer can handle which is apparently unrelated to the way in which certain other morphophonemes are given their phonemic realizations. However, Venezky's work does recognize some important patterns of English orthography as, for example, in the following comment on the *a* grapheme and on the possible pedagogical consequences. Venezky points out that the letter *a* has two primary pronunciations in stressed position, /æ/ and /e/, and he notes the orthographic and phonological relationships of pairs of words like *annal* and *anal*, *rat* and *rate*, and *sane* and *sanity*. He adds this comment:

[15] Venezky, pp. 94–95.

The Bloomfieldian sequencing begins with the /æ/ pronunciation for *a*, introducing the /e/ pronunciation at a later time with no special emphasis on the relation between /æ/ and /e/ when derived from *a*. An alternative to this approach is to present both pronunciations at once, working with such pairs as *rat:rate*, *mat:mate*, *fat:fate*, *hat:hate*, and *man:mane*. Both the associations of *a* to /æ/ and *a* to /e/ and the discrimination of the graphemic environments would be emphasized. Whether or not a child first learning to read can handle this task probably depends upon the pedagogy employed. The potential generalization derived from the differentiation approach, however, certainly is greater than that from the simple-sequence method.[16]

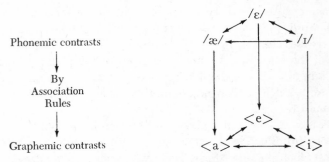

Phonemic contrasts

By Association Rules

Graphemic contrasts

Diagram I (Bloomfield and Fries)

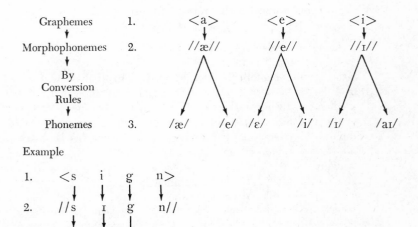

Graphemes   1.

Morphophonemes   2.

By Conversion Rules

Phonemes   3.

Example

1.
2.
3.

Diagram II (Venezky)

Venezky has added a further dimension to understanding the reading process beyond that of the contributions of Bloomfield and Fries. As is indicated in Diagram I, Bloomfield and Fries were concerned with a model of the process in which the beginning reader was required to establish a set of visual contrasts and then to associate this set of visual contrasts to a set of already known phonemic contrasts. Venezky is less concerned with such simple sets of contrasts and associations. As indicated in Diagram II, he favors drawing up a set of conversion rules rather than a set of association rules. Moreover, he is very much concerned with proceeding from writing to speech rather than in the opposite direction.

In addition to postulating such a model of the process, Venezky also point out the way in which pairs of lax and tense, or, in his terms, "checked" and "free," vowels relate to each other in English, in such words pairs as *fat:fate*, *met:mete*, *sit:site*, *rob:robe*, and *run:rune*. He stresses the fact that English orthographic conventions require the use of the same vowel letter in certain orthographic patterns, as with the *a* in *sane:sanity*, the *e* in *concede:concession*, and the *i* in *collide:collision*, but he makes no attempt to account for the patterning synchronically.

As is well known the phonemic level of representation of so much interest to Bloomfield, Fries, and Venezky, holds no attraction to Noam Chomsky and Morris Halle who regard it as no more than the methodological artifact of a particular kind of linguistic inquiry which they have attacked repeatedly. Chomsky and Halle favor a level of representation which they call *systematic phonemic*, a level which they claim the standard orthography captures quite well. They write as follows on this point in *The Sound Pattern of English:*

> There is, incidentally, nothing particularly surprising about the fact that conventional orthography is . . . a near optimal system for the lexical representation of English words. The fundamental principle of orthography is that phonetic variation is not indicated where it is predictable by general rule. Thus, stress placement and regular vowel or consonant alternations are generally not reflected. Orthography is a system designed for readers who know the language, who understand sentences and therefore know the surface structure of sentences. Such readers can produce the correct phonetic forms, given the orthographic representation and the surface structure, by means of the rules that they employ in producing and interpreting speech. It would be quite pointless for the orthography to indicate these predictable variants. Except for unpredictable variants (e.g., *man–men*, *buy–bought*), an optimal orthography would have one representation for each lexical entry. Up to ambiguity, then, such a

system would maintain a close correspondence between semantic units and orthographic representations.[17]

According to this claim, therefore, English orthography is a good orthography for a speaker who "knows" the language. Chomsky and Halle proceed to describe the reading process in the following terms. Diagram III attempts to model what they say.

> [The] process of reading aloud . . . might . . . be described in the following way. We assume a reader who has internalized a grammar *G* of the language that he speaks natively. The reader is presented with a linear stretch *W* of written symbols, in a conventional orthography. He produces as an internal representation of this linear stretch *W* a string *S* of abstract symbols of the sort that we have been considering. Utilizing the syntactic and semantic information available to him, from a preliminary analysis of *S*, as well as much extra-linguistic information regarding the writer and the context, the reader understands the utterance, and, in particular, assigns to *S* a surface structure Σ. With Σ available, he can then produce the phonetic representation of *S* and, finally, the physical signal corresponding to the visual input *W*. Clearly, reading will be facilitated to the extent that the orthography used for *W* corresponds to the underlying representations provided by the grammar *G*. To the extent that these correspond, the reader can rely on the familiar phonological processes to relate the visual input *W* to an acoustic signal. Thus one would expect that conventional orthography should by and large, be superior to phonemic transcription, which is in general quite remote from underlying lexical or phonological representation and not related to it by any linguistically significant set of rules. . . . [Conventional orthography] can be read only when the surface structure (including the internal structure of words) is known, that is, when the utterance is to some degree understood.[18]

[17] Noam Chomsky and Morris Halle, *The Sound Pattern of English* (New York: Harper & Row, 1968), p. 49.
[18] Chomsky and Halle, pp. 49–50.

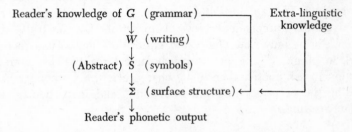

Diagram III (Chomsky and Halle)

The Sound Pattern of English is primarily concerned with two problems. The first is the search for the optimal set of abstract phonological units to represent meaning units, that is for the best set of underlying lexical representations for English. The second is the search for the optimal set of rules to realize these lexical representations as phonetic output in order to convert a level of systematic phonemics into one of systematic phonetics. The result of the first search is the postulation of a set of systematic phonemes which look remarkably like the set of phonemes one needs to postulate for Early Modern English. For example, the set of systematic vowel phonemes contains only monophthongal representations and uses both tense and lax and round and unround as distinctive features. The symbolization used by Chomsky and Halle looks very much the same as that of standard English orthography and neatly draws together both phonetically quite different vowels, such as those in *deduce* and *deduction, Canada* and *Canadian,* and *divine* and *divinity,* and variant pronunciations such as the well-known variant pronunciations of *ration, level, sinecure,* and *progress.* The result of the search for the optimal set of phonological units or systematic phonemes is an extremely elegant and attractive system. The result of the second search for generative phonological rules is the postulation of a set of such rules which resemble, even in their clothing in distinctive features and a generative phonology, that set of rules more traditionally-minded linguists must postulate to account for such phenomena as the Great Vowel Shift and other well-known sound changes. *The Sound Pattern of English* is a rather convincing demonstration that it is possible to describe a vast amount of English phonology within the system the authors postulate. The demonstration of the importance of two types of cluster, strong and weak, in determining stress placement, the generality of the transformational rules, and the importance of ordering and cycling in the application of the rules are undoubtedly important contributions to linguistic theory. However, there are many *ad hoc* decisions and exceptions and certainly the main vocabulary discussed in *The Sound Pattern of English* is of Romance origin. Moreover, the authors make few claims either for the truth of the system, stating only that *The Sound Pattern of English* is a report on "work in progress,"[19] or for its psychological reality. The interesting question to ask oneself then is of what use is the system for understanding the processes involved in reading, and in particular in beginning reading.

[19] Chomsky and Halle, p. vii.

It is possible to make some observations about the proposals put forward by Chomsky and Halle. The first one is that this type of theoretical work may really be of little or no use for gaining any insights at all into the reading process. One might observe that since Chomsky and Halle are largely concerned with vocabulary of Romance origin, what they have to say about such vocabulary adds little to any understanding of the processes involved in beginning reading. A beginning reader neither knows nor needs to know this vocabulary, and he certainly should not be taught it as part of the task of learning to read. His reading materials should be filled with vocabulary of Germanic origin, possibly of a simple monosyllabic variety. Certainly, it should not be words like *policy, politic, politicize, politico–economic, polyandrous, polyandry, polygamous, polygamy, polyhedral, polyhedrous, pond, Pontiac, pontificate,* and so on, which is one randomly selected sequence from the World Index to *The Sound Pattern of English.*[20] It is an interesting fact that most of us can pronounce these words correctly without even knowing what some of them mean, but they are, except for *pond,* not the words we would expect a six-year-old to know or want him to read. Rather they are just the words we expect him to be able to read later when, as a result of learning to read, he is in the position of being able to read in order to learn. Much of Comsky and Halle's description is valid only for a particular kind of person, a highly literate one. The crucial question is how much of such a rich system of phonology as that postulated in *The Sound Pattern of English* can we ascribe to a six-year-old. Undoubtedly we must ascribe a great deal, for certainly a six-year-old can assign stress correctly, does reduce vowels automatically, and does make the majority of surface phonetic contrasts without difficulty. A six-year-old undoubtedly possesses much of the basic phonological competence he will have as an adult. At the same time though, it is likely that the sets of transformational rules that he uses and of lexical representations that he has at his disposal are more limited than the sets discussed in *The Sound Pattern of English.*

A second observation about the system concerns what may be called its direction. The system put forward in *The Sound Pattern of English* is one which appears to focus on how meaning is encoded into sound, in spite of the claims to neutrality between speaker and hearer which Chomsky has made repeatedly. For example, Chomsky and Halle point out that an awareness of surface structure is necessary if one is to assign certain stress patterns correctly and to make

[20] Chomsky and Halle, p. 458.

the rules operate properly in the production of sentences. However, the task which confronts a reader is one of decoding print to discover meaning. His task is one of somehow getting to meaning through print. The beginning reader must use the visual cues he has on the page to reconstruct the meaning, must somehow give a syntactic reading to a phase such as *American history teacher* ([*American history*] *teacher* or *American* [*history teacher*] before he can pronounce it correctly. The writing system does not mark surface structure except in certain gross ways such as by word spacing and punctuation marks. The beginning reader's task is apparently one of relating symbols to sounds at an age when such abilities as the ability to assign a surface structure may be quite different from those of sophisticated adults. Chomsky and Halle comment as follows on some of the problems:

> There are many interesting questions that can be raised about the development of systems of underlying representation during the period of language acquisition. It is possible that this might be fairly slow. There is, for example, some evidence that children tend to hear much more phonetically than adults. There is no reason to jump to the conclusion that this is simply a matter of training and experience; it may very well have a maturational basis. Furthermore, much of the evidence relevant to the constructure of the underlying systems of representation may not be available in early stages of language acquisition. These are open questions, and it is pointless to speculate about them any further. They deserve careful empirical study, not only because of the fundamental importance of the question of "psychological reality" of linguistic constructs, but also for practical reasons; for example, with respect to the problem of the teaching of reading.[21]

The comment is a most interesting one because if empirical evidence confirms the suspicion that Chomsky and Halle have, then it would tend to justify much of the approach taken to reading by Bloomfield and Fries. It would justify an approach which utilizes a taxonomic phonemic, or broad phonetic, level of representation and which relates such a level to orthographic patterns, an approach too which excludes work with derivational patterning in favor of work with sound–letter associations and which, by some kind of happy default, does not get itself involved with patterns of stress assignment in polysyllabic words, patterns which one can assume a six-year-old already controls to a great extent by virtue of the fact that he is a native speaker.

[21] Chomsky and Halle, p. 50.

It could well be that the basic problem a child has in learning to read is really one of learning the association between written symbols and surface rather than deep phonology. For example, he must learn that *hatter:hater, petter:Peter, dinner:diner, comma:coma,* and *supper: super* show a systematic spelling difference associated with a systematic surface phonological difference. In the terminology used by reading teachers he must learn that a double consonant indicates a "short" vowel and that a single consonant plus vowel indicates a "long" vowel. Even though the use of the letters *a, e, i, o,* and *u* in the above words is "correct" in Chomsky's and Halle's terms in spite of the very different phonetic realizations, the child's problem is one of cueing in to the visual task involved in decoding, a task which even the generative–transformationalists refer to as the problem of identifying the visual response. Likewise, with a set of words like *metal, rebel, civil, Mongol,* and *cherub,* it is important that the child have available to him a strategy for approaching these words so that he can attempt to pronounce them as *metal* or *meetal, rebel* or *reeble,* and so on. It helps him very little to be told that the spellings are the best ones for English because there are also English words like *metallic, rebellion, civilian, Mongolian,* and *cherubic.* A six-year-old is even less likely to know these derivatives than the base forms and any knowledge about the "best" spellings for the second vowel in each word is more appropriate to teaching him to spell than to read. Perhaps *The Sound Pattern of English* is a better book for those interested in teaching spelling than in teaching reading, tasks which appear to be rather different!

What the child basically needs in beginning reading is a set of strategies for decoding print. No one is really sure what strategies successful beginning readers do employ. There is reason to suspect that they do not use the strategies which teachers who believe in the various phonics approaches attempt to teach. These latter strategies, sometimes called phonic generalizations, have been severely attacked by linguists. However, a few of them seem to contain germs of truth, particularly recognizable after reading *The Sound Pattern of English,* as, for example, statements about final *e*'s making preceding vowels "long," about an *i* before *gh* having its "long" sound, about *c*'s before *e*'s or *i*'s being "soft," and so on. But then such is likely to be the case. Phonics instruction cannot be all wrong—rather it shows evidence of considerable confusion in its general orientation and the need for a transfusion of linguistic insights, not euthanasia.

This discussion of the work of Bloomfield, Fries, Venezky, Chomsky, and Halle leads to certain conclusions. The first very obvious one is that some linguists do have an interest in applying their theoretical knowledge to the solution of practical problems. However, the second is that the proposed applications vary considerably and the results are sometimes contradictory. Linguists have different ideas about linguistics and about the nature of the problems to which linguistics might contribute a solution. Some linguists are also more definite in their proposals than others. It is possible to contrast the attempt by Fries at what appears to be a definitive attack on the reading problem to the extremely tentative suggestions put forward by Chomsky and Halle. Furthermore, the reading process itself is not an easy one to understand. Linguists have different notions about what language is, about how it may be described, about what its fundamental units are, about how these are related, and about what processes may operate. All these are linguistic matters quite properly and all have some relevance to understanding the reading process and teaching reading. But there are also nonlinguistic matters which must be taken into account when one turns to problems in learning and teaching, and help must be sought from psychologists and educators as well as from linguists. The greatest need at present is for empirical work in which linguists, psychologists, and educators combine their insights in an attempt to improve our understanding of the reading process and the teaching of reading.

WILLIAM LABOV

The Logic of Nonstandard English

In this essay, Labov attacks the two theories that have been put forward
to explain the poor school performance of Negro children from ghetto
areas. The first theory, embodied in the preschool programs of Carl
Bereiter and Siegfried Engelmann, blames the poor performance on a
"cultural deficit" brought about by an impoverished environment in the
child's early years. In particular, the cultural deprivation manifests itself
in impoverished verbal ability. Such verbally deprived children are said
to be unable to speak in complete sentences, do not know the names of
common objects, and cannot form concepts or convey logical thoughts.
The second theory, put forward by Arthur Jensen, blames the Negro
ghetto child's poor performance on genetic limitations rather than cultural
deficits.

Labov's argument is arranged under six headings or sections: (1) Verbality, (2) Verbosity, (3) Grammaticality, (4) Logic, (5) What's wrong

Reprinted from Monograph No. 22, *Report of the Twentieth Annual Round Table
Meeting in Languages and Linguistics*, Georgetown University Press, Washington, D.C., 1969, pp. 1–39.

with being wrong?, and (6) The linguistic view. We will summarize the main points that Labov makes under each heading.

(1) *Verbality.* Verbality is a technical phrase meaning "verbal ability." For Bereiter, the language of Negro ghetto children is so rudimentary as to be virtually nonexistent. Bereiter, in his own words, decides to treat Negro ghetto children as if they had no language at all. His position is based on observations of the speech behavior of Negro ghetto children. The children's poor performance is taken as direct evidence of poor verbal ability, and this, in turn, is used as an explanation of their poor school performance.

Labov counters this argument by presenting samples from two other interviews. The first interview is a semiformal interrogation, while the second is something approaching a party. As Labov puts it, the child who had nothing to say about anything in the first interview changes into an active participant struggling to get a word in edgewise in the second. Labov argues that the semiformal interview that has provided Bereiter with his test data is in no way a measure of the actual verbality that these children possess. Labov concludes that Bereiter has confused social ability with verbal ability.

(2) *Verbosity.* A less extreme position than denying that Negro ghetto children have a language is to deny that they can use their language well. The assumption here is that it is impossible to be "flexible, detailed, and subtle" in the use of nonstandard English. Labov argues against this point by contrasting the speech of a nonstandard Negro English with a speaker of standard English. The nonstandard speaker turns out to be clear and concise while the standard speaker wanders in a haze of vague ideas and verbage. Labov concludes that

> When we have discovered how much middle-class style is a matter of fashion and how much actually helps us express our ideas clearly, we will have done ourselves a great service; we will then be in a position to say what standard grammatical rules must be taught to nonstandard speakers in the early grades.

(3) *Grammaticality.* Here Labov attacks the validity of the conclusions that Bereiter draws from his own data. Bereiter argued that the statements *They mine, Me got juice,* and the response *In the tree* to the question *Where is the squirrel?* revealed that the children using them lacked a sense of the grammatical and logical relations between words. Labov denies that there is anything illogical about these expressions. For example, he points out that if *They mine* is illogical, then all speakers of Russian, Hungarian, and Arabic are also illogical, because that is exactly the way that they would say this sentence.

Labov's argument about the grammaticality of these three sentences is more technical. In the first sentence, the deletion of *are* from *They are mine* is the result of an optional extra rule in nonstandard English, namely, any form that can be contracted can also be optionally deleted. For the nonstandard speaker to use this rule, he must first know the rule governing contractions (which is also part of standard English). In short, to produce this sentence, the nonstandard has to know everything that the standard speaker knows, and then some.

In the second sentence, *Me got juice*, the nonstandard feature is the use of the object form of the pronoun instead of the expected subject form. Labov cites evidence showing that children actually know the difference in meaning between the subject and object forms, but have often not incorporated the difference into their active, production grammars.

In the third sentence, *In the tree*, Bereiter's objection is something of a mystery. Labov states that this type of ellipsis (*in the tree* is a shortened or elliptic form of *the squirrels are in the tree*) is not only perfectly normal standard English but also depends on a knowledge of both the full form and of the rules that allow the full form to be shortened.

(4) *Logic*. In this section, Labov attacks the notion that nonstandard Negro English does not have the ability to express logical thought. Labov discusses in detail the nonstandard use of double negatives. He argues that the nonstandard speaker makes the same three-way contrast between statements that have a positive meaning, statements that have a negative meaning, and statements that have an intentional double negative. The only difference between standard and nonstandard English is in the way that the negative meaning is signaled.

Labov also shows that nonstandard speakers have an asymmetrical relation between standard and nonstandard English: nonstandard speakers correctly perceive both standard and nonstandard English, but they produce only nonstandard. Therefore, when they are asked to repeat standard English, they must first translate it into their nonstandard English. Finally, Labov argues that the English produced by nonstandard speakers differs from standard English only in surface detail. Labov concludes that

> There is nothing in the vernacular which will interfere with the development of logical thought, for the logic of standard English cannot be distinguished from the logic of any other dialect of English by any test that we can find.

(5) *What's wrong with being wrong?* In this section Labov points out some of the dangers of the implementation of the programs produced by Bereiter and Engelmann and others. The title of this section gives a possible defense against Labov's attacks, namely, even if the programs based on verbal and cultural deprivation are not as well founded as their authors thought, do the programs themselves actually do any real harm? Labov feels that they have serious and damaging consequences for two reasons: (1) The use of these programs biases the users toward acceptance of the verbal deprivation theory. One consequence of this is that teachers will be given "a ready-made, theoretical basis for the prejudice they already feel against the lower-class Negro child and his language." A second consequence is that there is acceptance of the position that poor verbal be-

havior can be traced to cultural deprivation. Labov argues that when failure has reached such massive proportions we cannot lay the blame on the inadequacy of individual students. Programs based on verbal and cultural deprivation assume that the child is inadequate to the demands of the school. Labov argues that it is really the other way around: "Operation Headstart is designed to repair the child, rather than the school; to the extent that it is based upon this inverted logic, it is bound to fail."

(2) The second reason the use of programs based on verbal deprivation is doing serious harm to the educational system is that the programs will fail, and this failure may produce an even more damaging reaction from those who are committed to this theory. One such reaction is to blame the failure on something even more basic than cultural deprivation: genetic inferiority. The leading proponent of this extreme view is Arthur Jensen. Jensen, like the other psychologists interested in the deficit hypothesis, assume that the problem of failure is traceable to the child, not to the expectations of the school. Labov feels that the school's expectations are largely irrelevant to the social world that the child lives in.

(6) *The linguistic view.* Labov states that all linguists would agree on the following points:

1. Nonstandard dialects are highly structured language systems in their own right; they are not merely a degenerate form of some standard language.

2. Nonstandard Negro English is a separate system closely related to standard English, but kept apart by a number of persistent and systematic differences.

3. The majority of these differences are extensions and restrictions of formal rules and different choices of redundant elements. They do not represent subtle semantic differences.

4. Therefore, linguists reject the view of the verbal deprivationists that the vernacular language can be disregarded or that it is an obstacle to learning.

Labov concludes with an examination of Jensen's claim that middle-class whites have greater "conceptual" intelligence than the working-class and Negroes. Labov shows by an analysis of the use of the word *anyone* that all speakers of English must be able to manipulate abstract constructions, which is exactly the ability that Jensen reserves for middle-class whites.

ABSTRACT

The traditional view of nonstandard English held by many public school teachers is that it is an illogical form of speech; that when children are taught the standard forms they are also being taught to think logically. Linguists have endeavored for many years to show that differences in language are matters of social convention established by historical processes which shift continually the social prestige of dialect variants.

Recent programs for teaching the "culturally disadvantaged," particularly those of Karl Bereiter and his associates, have revived the notion that nonstandard dialects are illogical, attributing poor educational performance to cognitive disabilities reflected in language.

The educational programs proposed are based upon sociological and linguistic misinterpretations of the data. The linguistic behavior reported by Bereiter is merely the product of a defensive posture which children adopt in an alien and threatening situation. Such behavior can be produced at will in any group of children and can be altered by changing the relevant sociolinguistic variables.

There are many important questions concerning the cognitive correlates of syntactic complexity which current research technique has not yet answered. At present, there is no basis for attributing poor educational performance to the grammatical and phonological characteristics of any nonstandard dialect of English.

In the past decade, a great deal of federally-sponsored research has been devoted to the educational problems of children in ghetto schools. In order to account for the poor performance of children in these schools, educational psychologists have attempted to discover what kind of disadvantage or defect they are suffering from. The viewpoint which has been widely accepted, and used as the basis for large-scale intervention programs, is that the children show a cultural deficit as a result of an impoverished environment in their early years. Considerable attention has been given to language. In this area, the deficit theory appears as the concept of "verbal deprivation": Negro children from the ghetto area receive little verbal stimulation, are said to hear very little well-formed language, and as a result are impoverished in their means of verbal expression: they cannot speak complete sentences, do not know the names of common objects, cannot form concepts or convey logical thoughts.

Unfortunately, these notions are based upon the work of educational psychologists who know very little about language and even less about Negro children. The concept of verbal deprivation has no basis in social reality: in fact, Negro children in the urban ghettos receive a great deal of verbal stimulation, hear more well-formed sentences than middle-class children, and participate fully in a highly verbal culture; they have the same basic vocabulary, possess the same capacity for conceptual learning, and use the same logic as anyone else who learns to speak and understand English.

The notion of "verbal deprivation" is a part of the modern mythology of educational psychology, typical of the unfounded notions which tend to expand rapidly in our educational system. In past decades linguists have been as guilty as others in promoting such intellectual fashions at the expense of both teachers and children. But the myth of verbal deprivation is particularly dangerous, because it diverts attention from real defects of our educational system to imaginary defects of the child; and as we shall see, it leads its sponsors inevitably to the hypothesis of the genetic inferiority of Negro children which it was originally designed to avoid.

The most useful service which linguists can perform today is to clear away the illusion of "verbal deprivation" and provide a more adequate notion of the relations between standard and nonstandard dialects. In the writings of many prominent educational psychologists, we find a very poor understanding of the nature of language. Children are treated as if they have no language of their own in the preschool programs put forward by Bereiter and Engelmann (1966). The linguistic behavior of ghetto children in test situations is the principal evidence for their genetic inferiority in the view of Arthur Jensen (1969). In this paper, I will examine critically both of these approaches to the language and intelligence of the populations labelled "verbally" and "culturally deprived."[1] I will attempt to explain how the myth of verbal deprivation has arisen, bringing to bear the methodological findings of sociolinguistic work, and some substantive facts about language which are known to all linguists. I will be particularly concerned with the relation between concept formation on the one hand, and dialect differences on the other, since it is in this area that the most dangerous misunderstandings are to be found.

1. VERBALITY

The general setting in which the deficit theory has arisen consists of a number of facts which are known to all of us: that Negro children in the central urban ghettos do badly on all school subjects, including arithmetic and reading. In reading, they average more than

[1] I am indebted to Rosalind Weiner, of the Early Childhood Education group of Operation Headstart in New York City, and to Joan Baratz, of the Educational Development Corp., Washington, D. C., for pointing out to me the scope and seriousness of the educational issues involved here, and the ways in which the cultural deprivation theory has affected federal intervention programs in recent years.

two years behind the national norm.[2] Furthermore, this lag is cumulative, so that they do worse comparatively in the fifth grade than in the first grade. Reports in the literature show that this bad performance is correlated most closely with socioeconomic status. Segregated ethnic groups, however, seem to do worse than others: in particular, Indians, Mexican-Americans, and Negro children. Our own work in New York City confirms the fact that most Negro children read very poorly; however, our studies in the speech community show that the situation is even worse than has been reported. If one separates the isolated and peripheral individuals from the members of the central peer groups, the peer group members show even worse reading records, and to all intents and purposes are not learning to read at all during the time they spend in school.[3]

In speaking of children in the urban ghetto areas, the term *lower-class* is frequently used as opposed to *middle-class*. In the several sociolinguistic studies we have carried out, and in many parallel studies, it is useful to distinguish a "lower-class" group from "working-class." Lower-class families are typically female-based or "matri-focal," with no father present to provide steady economic support, whereas for the working-class there is typically an intact nuclear family with the father holding a semiskilled or unskilled job. The educational problems of ghetto areas run across this important class distinction; there is no evidence, for example, that the father's presence or absence is closely correlated with educational achievement.[4] The peer groups we have studied in South Central Harlem,

[2] A report of average reading comprehension scores in New York City was published in the *New York Times* on December 3, 1968. The schools attended by most of the peer group members we have studied showed the following scores:

School	Grade	Reading score	National norm
J. H. S. 13	7	5.6	7.7
	9	7.6	9.7
J. H. S. 120	7	5.6	7.7
	9	7.0	9.7
I. S. 88	6	5.3	6.7
	8	7.2	8.7

The average is then more than two full years behind grade in the ninth grade.

[3] See W. Labov and C. Robins, "A Note on the Relation of Reading Failure to Peer-Group Status in Urban Ghettos" (1968).

[4] There are a number of studies reported recently which show no relation between school achievement and presence of a father in the nuclear family. Preliminary findings to this effect are cited from a study by Bernard Mackler of CUE in Thos. S. Langer and Stanley T. Michaels, *Life Stress and Mental Health* (New York: Free Press), Chapter 8. Jensen 1969 cites James Coleman's study *Equality of educational opportunity*, p. 506, and others to illustrate the same point.

representing the basic vernacular culture, include members from both family types. The attack against "cultural deprivation" in the ghetto is overtly directed at family structures typical of lower-class families, but the educational failure we have been discussing is characteristic of both working-class and lower-class children.

In the balance of this paper, I will therefore refer to children from urban ghetto areas, rather than "lower-class" children: the population we are concerned with are those who participate fully in the vernacular culture of the street and who have been alienated from the school system.[5] We are obviously dealing with the effects of the caste system of American society—essentially a "color marking" system. Everyone recognizes this. The question is, by what mechanism does the color bar prevent children from learning to read? One answer is the notion of "cultural deprivation" put forward by Martin Deutsch and others: the Negro children are said to lack the favorable factors in their home environment which enable middle-class children to do well in school. (Deutsch and assoc. 1967; Deutsch, Katz, and Jensen 1968). These factors involve the development of various cognitive skills through verbal interaction with adults, including the ability to reason abstractly, speak fluently, and focus upon long-range goals. In their publications, these psychologists also recognize broader social factors.[6] However, the deficit theory does not focus upon the interaction of the Negro child with white society so much as on his failure to interact with his mother at home. In the literature we find very little direct observation of verbal interaction in the Negro home; most typically, the investigators ask the child if he has dinner with his parents, and if he engages in dinner-table conversation with them. He is also asked whether his family takes him on trips to museums and other cultural activities. This slender thread of evidence is used to explain and interpret the large body of tests carried out in the laboratory and in the school.

The most extreme view which proceeds from this orientation—and one that is now being widely accepted—is that lower-class Negro children have no language at all. The notion is first drawn from Basil

[5] The concept of "nonstandard Negro English," and the vernacular culture in which it is embedded, is presented in detail in Labov, Cohen, Robins and Lewis 1968, sections 1.2.3 and 4.1. See Volume II, section 4.3, for the linguistic traits which distinguish speakers who participate fully in the NNE culture from marginal and isolated individuals.

[6] For example, in Deutsch, Katz and Jensen 1968 there is a section on "Social and Psychological Perspectives" which includes a chapter by Proshansky and Newton on "The Nature and Meaning of Negro Self-Identity" and one by Rosenthal and Jacobson on "Self-Fulfilling Prophecies in the Classroom."

Bernstein's writings that "much of lower-class language consists of a kind of incidental 'emotional' accompaniment to action here and now" (Jensen 1968:118). Bernstein's views are filtered through a strong bias against all forms of working-class behavior, so that middle-class language is seen as superior in every respect—as "more abstract, and necessarily somewhat more flexible, detailed and subtle." One can proceed through a range of such views until one comes to the practical program of Carl Bereiter, Siegfried Engelmann and their associates. (Bereiter et al 1966; Bereiter and Engelmann 1966). Bereiter's program for an academically oriented preschool is based upon their premise that Negro children must have a language with which they can learn, and their empirical finding that these children come to school without such a language. In his work with four-year-old Negro children from Urbana, Bereiter reports that their communication was by gestures, "single words," and "a series of badly-connected words or phrases," such as *They mine* and *Me got juice.* He reports that Negro children could not ask questions, that "without exaggerating . . . these four-year-olds could make no statements of any kind." Furthermore, when these children were asked "Where is the book?" they did not know enough to look at the table where the book was lying in order to answer. Thus Bereiter concludes that the children's speech forms are nothing more than a series of emotional cries, and he decides to treat them "as if the children had no language at all." He identifies their speech with his interpretation of Bernstein's restricted code: "the language of culturally deprived children . . . is not merely an underdeveloped version of standard English, but is a basically non-logical mode of expressive behavior" (Bereiter et al 1966:113). The basic program of his preschool is to teach them a new language devised by Englemann, which consists of a limited series of questions and answers such as *Where is the squirrel? The squirrel is in the tree.* The children will not be punished if they use their vernacular speech on the playground, but they will not be allowed to use it in the schoolroom. If they should answer the question *Where is the squirrel?* with the illogical vernacular form *In the tree* they will be reprehended by various means and made to say, *The squirrel is in the tree.*

Linguists and psycholinguists who have worked with Negro children are apt to dismiss this view of their language as utter nonsense. Yet there is no reason to reject Bereiter's observations as spurious: they were certainly not made up: on the contrary, they give us a very clear view of the behavior of student and teacher which can be duplicated in any classroom. In our own work outside of the adult-dominated environments of school and home,[7] we do not observe Negro children behaving like this, but on many occasions we have been asked to help analyze the results of research into verbal deprivation in such test situations.

Here, for example, is a complete interview with a Negro boy, one of hundreds carried out in a New York City school. The boy enters a room where there is a large, friendly white interviewer, who puts on the table in front of him a block or a fire engine, and says "Tell me everything you can about this." (The interviewer's further remarks are in parentheses.)

> [12 seconds of silence]
> (What would you say it looks like?)
> [8 seconds of silence]
> A space ship.
> (Hmmmm.)
> [13 seconds of silence]
> Like a je-et.
> [12 seconds of silence]
> Like a plane.
> [20 seconds of silence]
> (What color is it?)
> Orange. [2 seconds]. An' whi-ite. [2 seconds]. An' green.
> [6 seconds of silence]
> (An' what could you use it for?)
> [8 seconds of silence]
> A je-et.
> [6 seconds of silence]
> (If you had two of them, what would you do with them?)
> [6 seconds of silence]
> Give one to some-body.
> (Hmmm. Who do you think would like to have it?)
> [10 seconds of silence]
> Cla-rence.
> (Mm. Where do you think we could get another one of these?)
> At the store.
> (Oh ka-ay!)

---

[7] The research cited here was carried out in South Central Harlem and other ghetto areas in 1965–1968 to describe structural and functional differences between nonstandard Negro English and standard English of the classroom. It was supported by the Office of Education as Cooperative Research Projects 3091 and 3288. Detailed reports are given in Labov, Cohen and Robins 1965, Labov 1965, and Labov, Cohen, Robins and Lewis 1968.

We have here the same kind of defensive, monosyllabic behavior which is reported in Bereiter's work. What is the situation that produces it? The child is in an asymmetrical situation where anything he says can literally be held against him. He has learned a number of devices to *avoid* saying anything in this situation, and he works very hard to achieve this end. One may observe the intonation patterns of

$$\begin{array}{l} \ ^3\text{'o' }_2\text{know} \\ ^1\text{a} \\ \hline \text{ip}^3 \\ ^2\text{a space }^2\text{shi} \\ \hline \end{array}$$

which Negro children often use when they are asked a question to which the answer is obvious. The answer may be read as "Will this satisfy you?"

If one takes this interview as a measure of the verbal capacity of the child, it must be as his capacity to defend himself in a hostile and threatening situation. But unfortunately, thousands of such interviews are used as evidence of the child's total verbal capacity, or more simply his "verbality"; it is argued that this lack of verbality *explains* his poor performance in school. Operation Headstart and other intervention programs have largely been based upon the "deficit theory"— the notions that such interviews give us a measure of the child's verbal capacity and that the verbal stimulation which he has been missing can be supplied in a preschool environment.

The verbal behavior which is shown by the child in the test situation quoted above is not the result of the ineptness of the interviewer. It is rather the result of regular sociolinguistic factors operating upon adult and child in this asymmetrical situation. In our work in urban ghetto areas, we have often encountered such behavior. Ordinarily we worked with boys 10–17 years old; and whenever we extended our approach downward to 8- or 9-year olds, we began to see the need for different techniques to explore the verbal capacity of the child. At one point we began a series of interviews with younger brothers of the "Thunderbirds" in 1390 5th Avenue. Clarence Robins returned after an interview with 8-year-old Leon L., who showed the following minimal response to topics which arouse intense interest in other interviews with older boys.

> CR: What if you saw somebody kickin' somebody else on the ground, or was using a stick, what would you do if you saw that?

LEON: Mmmm.
CR.   If it was supposed to be a fair fight—
LEON: I don' know.
CR: You don' know? Would you do anything . . . huh? I can't hear you.
LEON: No.
CR: Did you ever see somebody got beat up real bad?
LEON: . . . Nope ? ? ?
CR: Well—uh—did you ever get into a fight with a guy?
LEON: Nope.
CR: That was bigger than you?
LEON: Nope.
CR: You never been in a fight?
LEON: Nope.
CR: Nobody ever pick on you?
LEON: Nope.
CR: Nobody ever hit you?
LEON: Nope.
CR: How come?
LEON: Ah 'on' know.
CR: Didn't you ever hit somebody?
LEON: Nope.
CR: [incredulous] You never hit nobody?
LEON: Mhm.
CR: Aww, ba -a-a-be, you ain't gonna tell me that.

It may be that Leon is here defending himself against accusations of wrong-doing, since Clarence knows that Leon has been in fights, that he has been taking pencils away from little boys, etc. But if we turn to a more neutral subject, we find the same pattern:

CR: You watch—you like to watch television? . . . Hey, Leon . . . you like to watch television? [Leon nods] What's your favorite program?
LEON: Uhhmmmm . . . I look at cartoons.
CR: Well, what's your favorite one? What's your favorite program?
LEON: Superman.
CR: Yeah? Did you see Superman—ah—yesterday, or day before yesterday: when's the last time you saw Superman?
LEON: Sa-aturday . . .
CR: You rem—you saw it Saturday? What was the story all about? You remember the story?
LEON: M-m.

CR: You don't remember the story of what—that you saw of
        Superman?
LEON: Nope.
CR: You don't remember what happened, huh?
LEON: Hm-m.
CR: I see—ah—what other stories do you like to watch on T.V.?
LEON: Mmmm ? ? ? . . . umm . . . [glottalization]
CR: Hmm [4 seconds]
LEON: Hh?
CR: What's th'other stories that you like to watch?
LEON: ^{2}Mi - ighty ^{2}Mouse^2 . . .
CR: And what else?
LEON: Ummmm . . . ahm . . .

This nonverbal behavior occurs in a relatively *favorable* context for
adult-child interaction; since the adult is a Negro man raised in Harlem, who knows this particular neighborhood and these boys very
well. He is a skilled interviewer who has obtained a very high level
of verbal response with techniques developed for a different age level,
and he has an extraordinary advantage over most teachers or experi-
menters in these respects. But even his skills and personality are ineffective in breaking down the social constraints that prevail here.

When we reviewed the record of this interview with Leon, we decided to use it as a test of our own knowledge of the sociolinguistic
factors which control speech. We made the following changes in the
social situation: in the next interview with Leon, Clarence

(1) brought along a supply of potato chips, changing the "interview"
    into something more in the nature of a party;

(2) brought along Leon's best friend, 8-year-old Gregory;

(3) reduced the height imbalance (when Clarence got down on the
    floor of Leon's room, he dropped from 6 ft. 2 in. to 3 ft. 6 in.);

(4) introduced taboo words and taboo topics, and proved to Leon's
    surprise that one can say anything into our microphone without
    any fear of retaliation.

The result of these changes is a striking difference in the volume and
style of speech.

CR: Is there anybody who says *your momma drink pee?*
(LEON: [rapidly and breathlessly] Yee-ah!
(GREG: Yup!
LEON: And your father eat doo–doo for breakfas'!
CR: Ohhh!! [laughs]
LEON: And they say *your father—your father eat doo–doo for din-
        ner!*

GREG: When they sound on me, I say *C. B. M.*
CR: What that mean?
{LEON: Congo booger-snatch! [laughs]
{GREG: Congo booger-snatcher! [laughs]
GREG: And sometimes I'll curse with *B. B.*
CR: What that?
GREG: Black boy! [Leon—crunching on potato chips] Oh that's a *M. B. B.*
CR: M. B. B. What's that?
GREG: 'Merican Black Boy!
CR: Ohh . . .
GREG: Anyway, 'Mericans is same like white people, right?
LEON: And they talk about Allah.
CR: Oh yeah?
GREG: Yeah.
CR: What they say about Allah?
{LEON: Allah—Allah is God.
{GREG: Allah—
CR: And what else?
LEON: I don' know the res'.
GREG: Allah i—Allah is God, Allah is the only God, Allah—
LEON: Allah is the *son* of God.
GREG: But can he make magic?
LEON: Nope.
GREG: I know who can make magic.
CR: Who can?
LEON: The God, the *real* one.
CR: Who can make magic?
GREG: The son of po'— [CR: Hm?] I'm sayin' the po'k chop God! He only a po'k chop God![8] [Leon chuckles].

The "nonverbal" Leon is now competing actively for the floor; Gregory and Leon talk to each other as much as they do to the interviewer.

One can make a more direct comparison of the two interviews by examining the section on fighting. Leon persists in denying that he fights, but he can no longer use monosyllabic answers, and Gregory cuts through his façade in a way that Clarence Robins alone was unable to do.

[8] The reference to the *pork chop God* condenses several concepts of black nationalism current in the Harlem community. A *pork chop* is a Negro who has not lost traditional subservient ideology of the South, who has no knowledge of himself in Muslim terms, and the *pork chop God* would be the traditional God of Southern Baptists. He and his followers may be pork chops, but he still holds the power in Leon and Gregory's world.

CR: Now, you said you had this fight, now, but I wanted you to tell me about the fight that you had.

LEON: I ain't had no fight.

⎧ GREG: Yes you did!   He said Barry,

⎨ CR: You said you had one! you had a fight with Butchie,

⎧ GREG: An he say Garland . . . an' Michael.

⎨ CR: an' Barry . . .

⎧ LEON: I di'n'; you said that, Gregory!

⎨ GREG: You did.

⎧ LEON: You know you said that!

⎨ GREG: You said Garland, remember that?

⎧ GREG: You said Garland!   Yes you did!

⎨ CR: You said Garland, that's right.

GREG: He said Mich—an' I say Michael.

⎧ CR: Did you have a fight with Garland?

⎨ LEON: Uh-uh.

CR: You had one, and he beat you up, too!

GREG: Yes he did!

LEON: No, I di—I never had a fight with Butch! . . .

The same pattern can be seen on other local topics, where the interviewer brings neighborhood gossip to bear on Leon and Gregory acts as a witness.

CR: . . . Hey Gregory! I heard that around here . . . and I'm 'on' tell you who said it, too . . .

LEON: Who?

⎧ CR: about you . . .

⎨ LEON: Who?

⎧ GREG: I'd say it!

⎨ CR: They said that—they say that the only person you play with is David Gilbert.

⎧ LEON: Yee-ah! yee-ah! yee-ah! . . .

⎨ GREG: That's who you play with!

LEON: I 'on' play with him no more!

⎧ GREG: Yes you do!

⎨ LEON: I 'on' play with him no more!

GREG: But remember, about me and Robbie?

LEON: So that's not—

GREG: and you went to Petey and Gilbert's house, 'member?
          Ah haaah!!

LEON: So that's—so—but I would—I had came back out, an' I ain't go to his house no more . . .

The observer must now draw a very different conclusion about the verbal capacity of Leon. The monosyllabic speaker who had nothing to say about anything and cannot remember what he did yesterday has disappeared. Instead, we have two boys who have so much to say they keep interrupting each other, who seem to have no difficulty in using the English language to express themselves. And we in turn obtain the volume of speech and the rich array of grammatical devices which we need for analyzing the structure of nonstandard Negro English (NNE): negative concord [I 'on' play with him no more], the pluperfect [had come back out], negative perfect [I ain't had], the negative preterite [I ain't go], and so on.

One can now transfer this demonstration of the sociolinguistic control of speech to other test situations—including IQ and reading tests in school. It should be immediately apparent that none of the standard tests will come anywhere near measuring Leon's verbal capacity. On these tests he will show up as very much the monosyllabic, inept, ignorant, bumbling child of our first interview. The teacher has far less ability than Clarence Robins to elicit speech from this child; Clarence knows the community, the things that Leon has been doing, and the things that Leon would like to talk about. But the power relationships in a one-to-one confrontation between adult and child are too asymmetrical. This does not mean that some Negro children will not talk a great deal when alone with an adult, or that an adult cannot get close to any child. It means that the social situation is the most powerful determinant of verbal behavior and that an adult must enter into the right social relation with a child if he wants to find out what a child can do: this is just what many teachers cannot do.

The view of the Negro speech community which we obtain from our work in the ghetto areas is precisely the opposite from that reported by Deutsch, Englemann and Bereiter. We see a child bathed in verbal stimulation from morning to night. We see many speech events which depend upon the competitive exhibition of verbal skills: sounding, singing, toasts, rifting, louding—a whole range of activities in which the individual gains status through his use of language.[9] We see the younger child trying to acquire these skills from older children—hanging around on the outskirts of the older peer groups, and imitating this behavior to the best of his ability. We see no connection between verbal skill at the speech events characteristic of the street culture and success in the schoolroom.

[9] For detailed accounts of these speech events, see Labov, Cohen, Robins and Lewis 1968, section 4.2.

2. VERBOSITY

There are undobutedly many verbal skills which children from ghetto areas must learn in order to do well in the school situation, and some of these are indeed characteristic of middle-class verbal behavior. Precision in spelling, practice in handling abstract symbols, the ability to state explicitly the meaning of words, and a richer knowledge of the Latinate vocabulary, may all be useful acquisitions. But is it true that *all* of the middle-class verbal habits are functional and desirable in the school situation? Before we impose middle-class verbal style upon children from other cultural groups, we should find out how much of this is useful for the main work of analyzing and generalizing, and how much is merely stylistic—or even dysfunctional. In high school and college middle-class children spontaneously complicate their syntax to the point that instructors despair of getting them to make their language simpler and clearer. In every learned journal one can find examples of jargon and empty elaboration—and complaints about it. Is the "elaborated code" of Bernstein really so "flexible, detailed and subtle" as some psychologists believe? (Jensen 1968:119). Isn't it also turgid, redundant, and empty? Is it not simply an elaborated *style*, rather than a superior code or system?[10]

Our work in the speech community makes it painfully obvious that in many ways working-class speakers are more effective narrators, reasoners, and debaters than many middle-class speakers who temporize, qualify, and lose their argument in a mass of irrelevant detail. Many academic writers try to rid themselves of that part of middle-class style that is empty pretension, and keep that part that is needed for precision. But the average middle-class speaker that we encounter makes no such effort; he is enmeshed in verbiage, the victim of sociolinguistic factors beyond his control.

I will not attempt to support this argument here with systematic quantitative evidence, although it is possible to develop measures which show how far middle-class speakers can wander from the point. I would like to contrast two speakers dealing with roughly the same topic—matters of belief. The first is Larry H., a 15-year-old core member of the Jets, being interviewed by John Lewis. Larry is one

---

[10] The term *code* is central in Bernstein's description of the differences between working-class and middle-class styles of speech. (1966) The restrictions and elaborations of speech observed are labelled as "codes" to indicate the principles governing selection from the range of possible English sentences. No rules or detailed description of the operation of such codes are provided as yet, so that this central concept remains to be specified.

of the loudest and roughest members of the Jets, one who gives the least recognition to the conventional rules of politeness.[11] For most readers of this paper, first contact with Larry would produce some fairly negative reactions on both sides: it is probable that you would not *like* him any more than his teachers do. Larry causes trouble in and out of school; he was put back from the eleventh grade to the ninth, and has been threatened with further action by the school authorities.

JL: What happens to you after you die? Do you know?
LARRY: Yeah, I know.
JL: What?
LARRY: After they put you in the ground, your body turns into—ah
          —bones, an' shit.
JL: What happens to your spirit?
LARRY: Your spirit—soon as you die, your spirit leaves you.
JL: And where does the spirit go?
LARRY: Well, it all depends . . .
JL: On what?
LARRY: You know, like some people say if you're good an' shit, your
          spirit goin' t'heaven . . . 'n' if you bad, your spirit goin' to
          hell. Well, bullshit! Your spirit goin' to hell anyway, good
          or bad.
JL: Why?
LARRY: Why? I'll tell you why. 'Cause, you see, doesn' nobody
          really know that it's a God, y'know, 'cause I mean I have
          seen black gods, pink gods, white gods, all color gods, and
          don't nobody know it's really a God. An' when they be
          sayin' if you good, you goin' t'heaven, tha's bullshit, 'cause
          you ain't goin' to no heaven, 'cause it ain't no heaven for
          you to go to.

Larry is a paradigmatic speaker of nonstandard Negro English (NNE) as opposed to standard English (SE). His grammar shows a high concentration of such characteristic NNE forms as negative inversion [*don't nobody know . . .*], negative concord [*you ain't goin' to no heaven . . .*], invariant *be* [*when they be sayin' . . .*], dummy *it* for SE *there* [*it ain't no heaven . . .*], optional copula deletion [*if you're good . . . if you bad . . .*], and full forms of auxiliaries [*I have*

---

[11] A direct view of Larry's verbal style in a hostile encounter is given in Labov, Cohen, Robins and Lewis 1968, Vol. II, pp. 39–43. Gray's Oral Reading Test was being given to a group of Jets on the steps of a brownstone house in Harlem, and the landlord tried unsuccessfully to make the Jets move. Larry's verbal style in this encounter matches the reports he gives of himself in a number of narratives cited in section 4.8.

seen . . .]. The only SE influence in this passage is the one case of *doesn't* instead of the invariant *don't* of NE. Larry also provides a paradigmatic example of the rhetorical style of NNE: he can sum up a complex argument in a few words, and the full force of his opinions comes through without qualification or reservation. He is eminently quotable, and his interviews give us many concise statements of the NNE point of view. One can almost say that Larry *speaks* the NNE culture.[12]

It is the logical form of this passage which is of particular interest here. Larry presents a complex set of interdependent propositions which can be explicated by setting out the SE equivalent in linear order. The basic argument is to deny the twin propositions

(A) If you are good,   (B) then your spirit will go to heaven.
(-A) If you are bad,   (C) then your spirit will go to hell.

Larry denies (B), and asserts that *if* (A) *or* (—A), *then* (C). His argument may be outlined as follows:

(1) Everyone has a different idea of what God is like.
(2) Therefore nobody really knows that God exists.
(3) If there is a heaven, it was made by God.
(4) If God doesn't exist, he couldn't have made heaven.
(5) Therefore heaven does not exist.
(6) You can't go somewhere that doesn't exist.
(-B) Therefore you can't go to heaven.
(C) Therefore you are going to hell.

The argument is presented in the order: (C), because (2) because (1), therefore (2), therefore (—B) because (5) and (6). Part of the argument is implicit: the connection (2) therefore (—B) leaves unstated the connecting links (3) and (4), and in this interval Larry strengthens the propositions from the form (2) *Nobody knows if there is . . .* to (5) *There is no . . .* Otherwise, the case is presented explicitly as well as economically. The complex argument is summed up in Larry's last sentence, which shows formally the dependence of (—B) on (5) and (6):

An' when they be sayin' if you good, you goin' t'heaven,
[The proposition, if A, then B]
Tha's bullshit,

[12] See Labov, Cohen, Robins and Lewis 1968, Volume II, p. 38, 71–73, 291–292.

[is absurd]
'cause you ain't goin' to no heaven
[because –B]
'cause it ain't no heaven for you to go to.
[because (5) and (6)].

This hypothetical argument is not carried on at a high level of seriousness. It is a game played with ideas as counters, in which oppo-
nents use a wide variety of verbal devices to win. There is no personal
commitment to any of these propositions, and no reluctance to
strengthen one's argument by bending the rules of logic as in the
(2–5) sequence. But if the opponent invokes the rules of logic, they
hold. In John Lewis's interviews, he often makes this move, and the
force of his argument is always acknowledged and countered within
the rules of logic. In this case, he pointed out the fallacy that the
argument (2–3–4–5–6) leads to (–C) as well as (–B), so it cannot
be used to support Larry's assertion (C):

> JL: Well, if there's no heaven, how could there be a hell?
> LARRY: I mean—ye–eah. Well, let me tell you, it ain't no hell,
>   'cause this is hell right here, y'know!
> JL: This is hell?
> LARRY: Yeah, this is hell right here!

Larry's answer is quick, ingenious and decisive. The application of
the (3–4–5) argument to hell is denied, since hell is here, and therefore conclusion (C) stands. These are not ready-made or precon-
ceived opinions, but new propositions devised to win the logical
argument in the game being played. The reader will note the speed
and precision of Larry's mental operations. He does not wander, or
insert meaningless verbiage. The only repetition is (2), placed before
and after (1) in his original statement. It is often said that the nonstandard vernacular is not suited for dealing with abstract or hypothetical questions, but in fact speakers from the NNE community
take great delight in exercising their wit and logic on the most improbable and problematical matters. Despite the fact that Larry H.
does not believe in God, and has just denied all knowledge of him,
John Lewis advances the following hypothetical question:

> JL: . . . But, just say that there is a God, what color is he?
>   White or black?
> LARRY: Well, if it is a God . . . I wouldn' know what color, I
>   couldn' say,—couldn' nobody say what color he is or really
>   *would* be.

JL: But now, jus' suppose there was a God—

LARRY: Unless'n they say . . .

JL: No, I was jus' sayin' jus' suppose there is a God, would he be white or black?

LARRY: . . . He'd be white, man.

JL: Why?

LARRY: Why? I'll tell you why. 'Cause the average whitey out here got everything, you dig? And the nigger ain't got shit, y'know? Y'understan'? So—um—for—in order for *that* to happen, you know it ain't no black God that's doin' that bullshit.

No one can hear Larry's answer to this question without being convinced that they are in the presence of a skilled speaker with great "verbal presence of mind," who can use the English language expertly for many purposes. Larry's answer to John Lewis is again a complex argument. The formulation is not SE, but it is clear and effective even for those not familiar with the vernacular. The nearest SE equivalent might be: "So you know that God isn't black, because if he was, he wouldn't have arranged things like this."

The reader will have noted that this analysis is being carried out in standard English, and the inevitable challenge is: why not write in NNE, then, or in your own nonstandard dialect? The fundamental reason is, of course, one of firmly fixed social conventions. All communities agree that SE is the "proper" medium for formal writing and public communication. Furthermore, it seems likely that SE has an advantage over NNE in explicit analysis of surface forms, which is what we are doing here. We will return to this opposition between explicitness and logical statement in sections 3 and 4. First, however, it will be helpful to examine SE in its primary natural setting, as the medium for informal communication of middle-class speakers.

Let us now turn to the second speaker, an upper-middle-class, college educated Negro man being interviewed by Clarence Robins in our survey of adults in Central Harlem.

CR: Do you know of anything that someone can do, to have someone who has passed on visit him in a dream?

CHAS. M.: Well, I even heard my parents say that there is such a thing as something in dreams some things like that, and sometimes dreams do come true. I have personally never had a dream come true. I've never dreamt that somebody was dying and they actually died, (Mhm) or that I was going to have ten dollars the next day and somehow I got ten dollars in my pocket. (Mhm). I don't particularly believe in that, I don't think it's true. I do feel, though, that there is such a thing as—ah—witch-craft. I do feel that in certain cultures there is such a thing as witchcraft, or some sort of *science* of witchcraft; I don't think that it's just a matter of believing hard enough that there is such a thing as witchcraft. I do believe that there is such a thing that a person can put himself in a state of *mind* (Mhm), or that—er—something could be given them to intoxicate them in a certain —to a certain frame of mind—that—that could actually be considered witchcraft.

Charles M. is obviously a "good speaker" who strikes the listener as well-educated, intelligent and sincere. He is a likeable and attractive person—the kind of person that middle-class listeners rate very high on a scale of "job suitability" and equally high as a potential friend.[13] His language is more moderate and tempered than Larry's; he makes every effort to qualify his opinions, and seems anxious to avoid any misstatements or overstatements. From these qualities emerge the primary characteristic of this passage—its *verbosity*. Words multiply, some modifying and qualifying, others repeating or padding the main argument. The first half of this extract is a response to the initial question on dreams, basically:

(1) Some people say that dreams sometimes come true.
(2) I have never had a dream come true.
(3) Therefore I don't believe (1).

Some characteristic filler phrases appear here: *such a thing as, some things like that, particularly*. Two examples of dreams given after (2) are afterthoughts that might have been given after (1). Proposition (3) is stated twice for no obvious reason. Nevertheless, this much of Charles M.'s response is well-directed to the point of the question. He then volunteers a statement of his beliefs about witchcraft which shows the difficulty of middle-class speakers who (a) want to express a belief in something but (b) want to show themselves as judicious, rational and free from superstitions. The basic proposition can be stated simply in five words:

But I believe in witchcraft.

However, the idea is enlarged to exactly 100 words, and it is difficult to see what else is being said. In the following quotations, padding

[13] See Labov, Cohen, Robins and Lewis 1968, section 4.6, for a description of subjective reaction tests which utilize these evaluative dimensions.

which can be removed without change in meaning is shown in brackets.

(1) "I [do] feel, though, that there is [such a thing as] witchcraft." *Feel* seems to be a euphemism for "believe."

(2) "[I do feel that] in certain cultures [there is such a thing as witchcraft.]" This repetition seems designed only to introduce the word *culture*, which lets us know that the speaker knows about anthropology. Does *certain cultures* mean "not in ours" or "not in all"?

(3) "[or some sort of *science* of witchcraft.]" This addition seems to have no clear meaning at all. What is a "science" of witchcraft as opposed to just plain witchcraft?[14] The main function is to introduce the word "science," though it seems to have no connection to what follows.

(4) "I don't think that it's just [a matter of] believing hard enough that [there is such a thing as] witchcraft." The speaker argues that witchcraft is not merely a belief; there is more to it.

(5) "I [do] believe that [there is such a thing that] a person can put himself in a state of *mind* . . . that [could actually be considered] witchcraft." Is witchcraft as a state of mind different from the state of belief denied in (4)?

(6) "or that something could be given them to intoxicate them [to a certain frame of mind] . . ." The third learned word, *intoxicate*, is introduced by this addition. The vacuity of this passage becomes more evident if we remove repetitions, fashionable words and stylistic decorations:

> But I believe in witchcraft.
> I don't think witchcraft is just a belief.
> A person can put himself or be put in a state of mind that is witchcraft.

Without the extra verbiage and the O.K. words like *science, culture,* and *intoxicate,* Charles M. appears as something less than a first-rate thinker. The initial impression of him as a good speaker is simply our long-conditioned reaction to middle-class verbosity: we know that people who use these stylistic devices are educated people, and we are inclined to credit them with saying something intelligent. Our reactions are accurate in one sense: Charles M. is more educated than Larry. But is he more rational, more logical, or more intelligent? Is

[14] Several middle-class readers of this passage have suggested that *science* here refers to some form of control as opposed to belief; the "science of witchcraft would then be a kind of engineering of mental states; other interpretations can of course be provided. The fact remains that no such subtleties of interpretation are needed to understand Larry's remarks.

he any better at thinking out a problem to its solution? Does he deal more easily with abstractions? There is no reason to think so. Charles M. succeeds in letting us know that he is educated, but in the end we do not know what he is trying to say, and neither does he.

In the previous section I have attempted to explain the origin of the myth that lower-class Negro children are nonverbal. The examples just given may help to account for the corresponding myth that middle-class language is in itself better suited for dealing with abstract, logically complex and hypothetical questions. These examples are intended to have a certain negative force. They are not controlled experiments: on the contrary, this and the preceding section are designed to convince the reader that the controlled experiments that have been offered in evidence are misleading. The only thing that is "controlled" is the superficial form of the stimulus: all children are asked "What do you think of capital punishment?" or "Tell me everything you can about this." But the speaker's interpretation of these requests, and the action he believes is appropriate in response is completely uncontrolled. One can view these test stimuli as requests for information, commands for action, as threats of punishment, or as meaningless sequences of words. They are probably intended as something altogether different: as requests for display;[15] but in any case the experimenter is normally unaware of the problem of interpretation. The methods of educational psychologists like Deutsch, Jensen and Bereiter follow the pattern designed for animal experiments where motivation is controlled by such simple methods as withholding food until a certain weight reduction is reached. With human subjects, it is absurd to believe that an identical "stimulus" is obtained by asking everyone the "same question." Since the crucial intervening variables of interpretation and motivation are uncontrolled, most of the literature on verbal deprivation tells us nothing about the capacities of children. They are only the trappings of science: an approach which substitutes the formal procedures of the scientific method for the activity itself. With our present limited grasp of these problems, the best we can do to understand the verbal capacities of children is to study them within the cultural context in which they were developed.

It is not only the NNE vernacular which should be studied in this way, but also the language of middle-class children. The explicitness and precision which we hope to gain from copying middle-class forms

---

[15] The concept of a "request for verbal display" is here drawn from Alan Blum's treatment of the therapeutic interview in *The Sociology of Mental Illness*, mimeographed (to appear in *For Thomas Szaz*).

are often the product of the test situation, and limited to it. For example, it was stated in the first part of this paper that working-class children hear more well-formed sentences than middle-class children This statement may seem extraordinary in the light of the current belief of many linguists that most people do not speak in well-formed sentences, and that their actual speech production or "performance" is ungrammatical.[16] But those who have worked with any body of natural speech know that this is not the case. Our own studies of the "Grammaticality of Every-day Speech" show that the great majority of utterances in all contexts are complete sentences, and most of the rest can be reduced to grammatical form by a small set of "editing rules."[17] The proportions of grammatical sentences vary with class backgrounds and styles. The highest percentage of well-formed sentences are found in casual speech, and working-class speakers use more well-formed sentences than middle-class speakers. The widespread myth that most speech is ungrammatical is no doubt based upon tapes made at learned conferences, where we obtain the maximum number of irreducibly ungrammatical sequences.

It is true that technical and scientific books are written in a style which is markedly "middle-class." But unfortunately, we often fail to achieve the explicitness and precision which we look for in such writing; and the speech of many middle-class people departs maximally from this target. All too often, "standard English" is represented by a style that is simultaneously overparticular and vague. The accumulating flow of words buries rather than strikes the target. It is this verbosity which is most easily taught and most easily learned, so that words take the place of thought, and nothing can be found behind them.

When Bernstein describes his "elaborated code" in general terms, it emerges as a subtle and sophisticated mode of planning utterances, achieving structural variety, taking the other person's knowledge into account, and so on. But when it comes to describing the actual dif-

---

[16] In a number of presentations, Chomsky has asserted that the great majority of the sentences which a child hears are ungrammatical ("95 percent"). In Chomsky 1965:58, this notion is presented as one of the arguments in his general statement of the "nativist" position: "A consideration of the character of the grammar that is acquired, *the degenerate quality and narrowly limited extent of the available data,* [my emphasis] the striking uniformity of the resulting grammars, and their independence of intelligence, motivation, and emotional state, over wide ranges of variation, leave little hope that much of the structure of the language can be learned . . ."

[17] The editing rules are presented in W. Labov, "On the the Grammaticality of Every-day Speech," paper given at the annual meeting of the Linguistic Society of America, New York City, December 1966.

ference between middle-class and working-class speakers, we are presented with a proliferation of "I think," of the passive, of modals and auxiliaries, of the first person pronoun, of uncommon words; these are the bench marks of hemming and hawing, backing and filling, that are used by Charles M., devices which often obscure whatever positive contribution education can make to our use of language. When we have discovered how much middle-class style is a matter of fashion and how much actually helps us express our ideas clearly, we will have done ourselves a great service; we will then be in a position to say what standard grammatical rules must be taught to nonstandard speakers in the early grades.

3. GRAMMATICALITY

Let us now examine Bereiter's own data on the verbal behavior of the children he dealt with. The expressions *They mine* and *Me got juice* are cited as examples of a language which lacks the means for expressing logical relations—in this case characterized as "a series of badly connected words." (Bereiter 1966:113 ff.) In the case of *They mine*, it is apparent that Bereiter confuses the notions of logic and explicitness. We know that there are many languages of the world which do not have a present copula, and which conjoin subject and predicate complement without a verb. Russian, Hungarian, and Arabic may be foreign; but they are not by that same token illogical. In the case of nonstandard Negro English we are not dealing with even this superficial grammatical difference, but rather with a low-level rule which carries contraction one step farther to delete single consonants representing the verbs *is*, *have*, or *will*. (Labov, Cohen, Robins & Lewis 1968:sect. 3.4) We have yet to find any children who do not sometimes use the full forms of *is* and *will*, even though they may frequently delete it. Our recent studies with Negro children four to seven years old indicate that they use the full form of th ecopula *is* more often than preadolescents 10 to 12 years old, or the adolescents 14 to 17 years old.[18]

Furthermore, the deletion of the *is* or *are* in nonstandard Negro English is not the result of erratic or illogical behavior: it follows the same regular rules as standard English contraction. Wherever standard English can contract, Negro children use either the con-

[18] From work on the grammars and comprehension of Negro children four to eight years old being carried out by Professor Jane Torrey of Connecticut College in extension of the research cited above in Labov, Cohen, Robins and Lewis 1968.

tracted form or (more commonly) the deleted zero form. Thus *They mine* corresponds to standard *They're mine*, not to the full form *They are mine*. On the other hand, no such deletion is possible in positions where standard English cannot contract: just as one cannot say *That's what they're* in standard English, *That's what they is* equally impossible in the vernacular we are considering. The internal constraints upon both of these rules show that we are dealing with a phonological process like contraction, sensitive to such phonetic conditions as whether or not the next word begins with a vowel or a consonant. The appropriate use of the deletion rule, like the contraction rule, requires a deep and intimate knowledge of English grammar and phonology. Such knowledge is not available for conscious inspection by native speakers: the rules we have recently worked out for standard contraction (Labov, Cohen, Robins & Lewis 1968:3.4) have never appeared in any grammar, and are certainly not a part of the conscious knowledge of any standard English speakers. Nevertheless, the adult or child who uses these rules must have formed at some level of psychological organization clear concepts of "tense marker," "verb phrase," "rule ordering," "sentence embedding," "pronoun," and many other grammatical categories which are essential parts of any logical system.

Bereiter's reaction to the sentence *Me got juice* is even more puzzling. If Bereiter believes that *Me got juice* is not a logical expression, it can only be that he interprets the use of the objective pronoun *me* as representing a difference in logical relationship to the verb: that the child in is fact saying that *the juice got him* rather than *he got the juice!* If on the other hand the child means "I got juice," then this sentence form shows only that he has not learned the formal rules for the use of the subjective form *I* and oblique form *me*. We have in fact encountered many children who do not have these formal rules in order at the ages of four, five, six, or even eight.[19] It is extremely difficult to construct a minimal pair to show that the difference between *he* and *him*, or *she* and *her*, carries cognitive meaning. In almost every case, it is the context which tells us who is the agent and who is acted upon. We must then ask: what differences in cognitive, structural orientation are signalled by the fact that the child has not learned this formal rule? In the tests carried out by Jane Torrey it is evident that the children concerned do understand the difference in meaning between *she* and *her* when another person uses the forms;

[19] From the research of Jane Torrey cited in footnote 18.

all that remains is that the children themselves do not use the two forms. Our knowledge of the cognitive correlates of grammatical differences is certainly in its infancy; for this is one of very many questions which we simply cannot answer. At the moment we do not know how to construct any kind of experiment which would lead to an answer; we do not even know what type of cognitive correlate we would be looking for.

Bereiter shows even more profound ignorance of the rules of discourse and of syntax when he rejects *In the tree* as an illogical, or badly-formed answer to *Where is the squirrel?* Such elliptical answers are of course used by everyone; they show the appropriate deletion of subject and main verb, leaving the locative which is questioned by *wh* + *there*. The reply *In the tree* demonstrates that the listener has been attentive to and apprehended the syntax of the speaker.[20] Whatever formal structure we wish to write for expressions such as *Yes* or *Home* or *In the tree*, it is obvious that they cannot be interpreted without knowing the structure of the question which preceded them, and that they presuppose an understanding of the syntax of the question. Thus if you ask me "Where is the squirrel?" it is necessary for me to understand the processes of *wh*-attachment, *wh*-attraction to the front of the sentence, and flip-flop of auxiliary and subject to produce this sentence from an underlying form which would otherwise have produced *The squirrel is there*. If the child had answered *The tree*, or *Squirrel the tree*, or *The in tree*, we would then assume that he did not understand the syntax of the full form, *The squirrel is in the tree*. Given the data that Bereiter presents, we cannot conclude that the child has no grammar, but only that the investigator does not understand the rules of grammar. It does not necessarily do any harm to use the full form *The squirrel is in the tree*, if one wants to make fully explicit the rules of grammar which the child has internalized. Much of logical analysis consists of making explicit just that kind of internalized rule. But it is hard to believe that any good can come from a program which begins with so many misconceptions about the input data. Bereiter and Engelmann believe that in teaching the child to say *The squirrel is in the tree* or *This is a box* and *This is not a box* they are teaching him an entirely new language, whereas in fact they are only teaching him to produce slightly different forms of the language he already has.

---

[20] The attention to the speaker's syntax required of the listener is analyzed in detail by Harvey Sacks in his unpublished 1968 lectures.

4. LOGIC

For many generations, American school teachers have devoted themselves to correcting a small number of nonstandard English rules to their standard equivalents, under the impression that they were teaching logic. This view has been reinforced and given theoretical justification by the claim that nonstandard Negro English lacks the means for the expression of logical thought.

Let us consider for a moment the possibility that Negro children do not operate with the same logic that middle-class adults display. This would inevitably mean that sentences of a certain grammatical form would have different truth values for the two types of speakers. One of the most obvious places to look for such a difference is in the handling of the negative; and here we encounter one of the nonstandard items which has been stigmatized as illogical by school teachers: the double negative, or as we term it, negative concord. A child who says *He don't know nothing* is often said to be making an illogical statement without knowing it. According to the teacher, the child wants to say *He knows nothing* but puts in an extra negative without realizing it, and so conveys the opposite meaning "he does not know nothing" which reduces to "he knows something." I need not emphasize that this is an absurd interpretation: if a nonstandard speakers wishes to say that "he does *not* know *nothing*," he does so by simply placing contrastive stress on both negatives as I have done here (He *don't* know *nothing*) indicating that they are derived from two underlying negatives in the deep structure. But note that the middle-class speaker does exactly the same thing when he wants to signal the existence of two underlying negatives: "He doesn't know *nothing*." In the standard form *He doesn't know anything*, the indefinite *anything* contains the same superficial reference to a preceding negative in the surface structure as the nonstandard *nothing* does. In the corresponding positive sentence, the indefinite *something* is used. The dialect difference, like most of the differences between the standard and nonstandard forms, is one of surface form, and has nothing to do with the underlying logic of the sentence.

The Anglo-Saxon authors of the Peterborough Chronicle were surely not illogical when they wrote *For ne waeren nan martyrs swa pined alse he waeron*, literally "For never weren't no martyrs so tortured as these were." The "logical" forms of current standard English are simply the accepted conventions of our present-day formal style.

We can summarize the ways in which the two dialects differ in the following table:

	SE	NNE
Positive	He knows something.	He know something.
Negative	He doesn't know anything.	He don't know nothing.
Double negative	He *doesn't* know *nothing*.	He *don't* know *nothing*.

This array makes it plain that the only difference between the two dialects is in superficial form. When a single negative is found in the deep structure, SE converts *something* to the indefinite *anything*, NNE converts it to *nothing*. When speakers want to signal the presence of two negatives, they do it in the same way. No one would have any difficulty constructing the same table of truth values for both dialects.

English is a rare language in its insistence that the negative particle be incorporated in the first indefinite only. Russian, Spanish, French and Hungarian show the same negative concord as nonstandard English, and they are surely not illogical in this. What is termed "logical" in standard English is of course the conventions which are habitual. The distribution of negative concord in English dialects can be summarized in this way:[21]

(1) In all dialects of English, the negative is attracted to a lone indefinite before the verb: *Nobody knows anything*, not **Anybody doesn't know anything*.

(2) In some nonstandard white dialects, the negative also combines optionally with all other indefinites: *Nobody knows nothing, He never took none of them*.

(3) In other white nonstandard dialects, the negative may also appear in preverbal position in the same clause: *Nobody doesn't know nothing*.

(4) In nonstandard Negro English, negative concord is obligatory to all indefinites within the clause, and it may even be added to preverbal position in following clauses: *Nobody didn't know he didn't* meaning "Nobody knew he did."

Thus all dialects of English share a categorical rule which attracts the negative to an indefinite subject, and they merely differ in the extent to which the negative particle is also distributed to other indefinites in preverbal position. It would have been impossible for us to arrive at this analysis if we did not know that Negro speakers are using the same underlying logic as everyone else.

[21] For the detailed analysis of negative concord in NNE, see Labov, Cohen, Robins and Lewis 1968, section 3.6, and W. Labov, "Negative Attraction and Negative Concord in Four English Dialects," paper given at the 1968 annual meeting of the Linguistic Society of America, New York, December 1968.

Negative concord is more firmly established in nonstandard Negro English than in other nonstandard dialects. The white nonstandard speaker shows variation in this rule, saying one time *Nobody ever goes there* and the next *Nobody never goes there;* core speakers of the NNE vernacular consistently use the latter form. In the repetition tests which we conducted with adolescent Negro boys,[22] standard forms were regularly repeated back instantly with negative concord. Here, for example, are three trials by two 13-year-old members of the "Thunderbirds":

MODEL: Nobody ever sat at any of those desks, anyhow.
BOOT–1:   Nobody never sa—No [whitey] never sat at any o' tho' dess, anyhow.
    –2:   Nobody never sat at any o' tho' dess, anyhow.
    –3:   Nobody [es'] ever sat at no desses, anyhow.

DAVID–1:   Nobody ever sat in-in-in-in- none o'—say it again?
    –2:   Nobody never sat in none o' tho' desses anyhow.
    –3:   Nobody—aww! Nobody never ex— Dawg!

It can certainly be said that Boot and David fail the test; they have not repeated the sentence back "correctly"—that is, word for word. But have they failed because they could not grasp the meaning of the sentence? The situation is in fact just the opposite: they failed because they perceived only the meaning and not the superficial form. Boot and David are typical of many speakers who do not perceive the surface details of the utterance so much as the underlying semantic structure, which they unhesitatingly translate into the vernacular form. Thus they have an asymmetrical system:

Perception:	Standard	Nonstandard
Production:	Nonstandard	

This tendency to process the semantic components directly can be seen even more dramatically in responses to sentences with embedded questions:

MODEL: I asked Alvin if he knows how to play basketball.
BOOT: I ax Alvin do he know how to play basketball.
MONEY: I ax Alvin if—do he know how to play basketball.

MODEL: I asked Alvin whether he knows how to play basketball.
LARRY F. –1:   I axt Alvin does he know how to play basketball.
    –2:   I axt Alvin does he know how to play basketball.

[22] More complete data on these Memory Tests is given in Labov, Cohen, Robins and Lewis 1968, section 3.9.

Here the difference between the words used in the model sentence and in the repetition is striking. Again, there is a failure to pass the test. But it is also true that these boys understand the standard sentence, and translate it with extraordinary speed into the NNE form—which is here the regular Southern colloquial form. This form retains the inverted order to signal the underlying meaning of the question, instead of the complementizer *if* or *whether* which standard English uses for this purpose. Thus Boot, Money, and Larry perceive the deep structure of the model sentence:

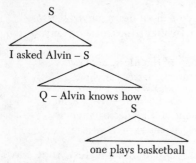

The complementizers *if* or *whether* are not required to express this underlying meaning; they are merely two of the formal options which one dialect selects to signal the embedded question. The colloquial Southern form utilizes a different device—preserving the order of the direct question. To say that this dialect lacks the means for logical expression is to confuse logic with surface detail.

To pass the repetition test, Boot and the others have to learn to listen to surface detail. They do not need a new logic; they need practice in paying attention to the explicit form of an utterance rather than its meaning. Careful attention to surface features is a temporary skill needed for language learning—and neglected thereafter by competent speakers. Nothing more than this is involved in the language training in the Bereiter and Englemann program, or in most methods of "teaching English." There is of course nothing wrong with learning to be explicit—as we have seen, that is one of the main advantages of standard English at its best—but it is important that we recognize what is actually taking place, and what teachers are in fact trying to do.

I doubt if we can teach people to be logical, though we can teach them to recognize the logic that they use. Piaget has shown us that in middle-class children logic develops much more slowly than grammar, and that we cannot expect four-year-olds to have mastered the conservation of quantity, let alone syllogistic reasoning. Whatever problems working-class children may have in handling logical operations are not to be blamed on the structure of their language. There is nothing in the vernacular which will interfere with the development of logical thought, for the logic of standard English cannot be distinguished from the logic of any other dialect of English by any test that we can find.

5. WHAT'S WRONG WITH BEING WRONG?

If there is a failure of logic involved here, it is surely in the approach of the verbal deprivation theorists, rather than in the mental abilities of the children concerned. We can isolate six distinct steps in the reasoning which has led to programs such as those of Deutsch, Bereiter and Engelmann:

(1) The lower-class child's verbal response to a formal and threatening situation is used to demonstrate his lack of verbal capacity, or verbal deficit.

(2) This verbal deficit is declared to be a major cause of the lower-class child's poor performance in school.

(3) Since middle-class children do better in school, middle-class speech habits are seen to be necessary for learning.

(4) Class and ethnic differences in grammatical form are equated with differences in the capacity for logical analysis.

(5) Teaching the child to mimic certain formal speech patterns used by middle-class teachers is seen as teaching him to think logically.

(6) Children who learn these formal speech patterns are then said to be thinking logically and it is predicted that they will do much better in reading and arithmetic in the years to follow.

In sections 1–4 of this paper, I have tried to show that these propositions are wrong, concentrating on (1), (4), and (5). Proposition (3) is the primary logical fallacy which illicitly identifies a form of speech as the *cause* of middle-class achievement in school. Proposition (6) is the one which is most easily shown to be wrong in fact, as we will note below.

However, it is not too naive to ask, "What is wrong with being wrong?" There is no competing educational theory which is being dismantled by this program; and there does not seem to be any great harm in having children repeat *This is not a box* for twenty minutes a day. We have already conceded that NNE children need help in analyzing language into its surface components, and in being more explicit. But there are serious and damaging consequences of the verbal deprivation theory which may be considered under two headings: (1) the theoretical bias, and (2) the consequences of failure.

(1) It is widely recognized that the teacher's attitude towards the child is an important factor in his success or failure. The work of Rosenthal on "self-fulfilling prophecies" shows that the progress of children in the early grades can be dramatically affected by a single random labelling of certain children as "intellectual bloomers." (Rosenthal & Jacobson 1968) When the everyday language of Negro children is stigmatized as "not a language at all" and "not possessing the means for logical thought," the effect of such a labelling is repeated many times during each day of the school year. Every time that a child uses a form of NNE without the copula or with negative concord, he will be labelling himself for the teacher's benefit as "illogical," as a "nonconceptual thinker." Bereiter and Engelmann, Deutsch and Jensen are giving teachers a ready-made, theoretical basis for the prejudice they already feel against the lower-class Negro child and his language. When they hear him say *I don't want none* or *They mine*, they will be hearing through the bias provided by the verbal deprivation theory: not an English dialect different from theirs, but the primitive mentality of the savage mind.

But what if the teacher succeeds in training the child to use the new language consistently? The verbal deprivation theory holds that this will lead to a whole chain of successes in school, and that the child will be drawn away from the vernacular culture into the middle-class world. Undoubtedly this will happen with a few isolated individuals, just as it happens in every school system today, for a few children. But we are concerned not with the few but the many, and for the majority of Negro children the distance between them and the school is bound to widen under this approach.

Proponents of the deficit theory have a strange view of social organization outside of the classroom: they see the attraction of the peer group as a "substitute" for success and gratification normally provided by the school. For example, Whiteman and Deutsch introduce their account of the deprivation hypothesis with an eye-witness account of a child who accidentally dropped his school notebook into a puddle of water and walked away without picking it up.

> A policeman who had been standing nearby walked over to the puddle and stared at the notebook with some degree of disbelief. (Whiteman and Deutsch 1968:86–7)

The child's alienation from school is explained as the result of his coming to school without the "verbal, conceptual, attentional and learning skills requisite to school success." The authors see the child as "suffering from feelings of inferiority because he is failing; . . . he withdraws or becomes hostile, finding gratification elsewhere, such as in his peer group."

To view the peer group as a mere substitute for school shows an extraordinary lack of knowledge of adolescent culture. In our studies in South Central Harlem we have seen the reverse situation: the children who are rejected by the peer group are quite likely to succeed in school. In middle-class suburban areas, many children do fail in school because of their personal deficiencies; in ghetto areas, it is the healthy, vigorous popular child with normal intelligence who cannot read and fails all along the line. It is not necessary to document here the influence of the peer group upon the behavior of youth in our society; but we may note that somewhere between the time that children first learn to talk and puberty, their language is restructured to fit the rules used by their peer group. From a linguistic viewpoint, the peer group is certainly a more powerful influence than the family.[23] Less directly, the pressures of peer group activity are also felt within the school. Many children, particularly those who are not doing well in school, show a sudden sharp down turn in the fourth and fifth grades, and children in the ghetto schools are no exception. It is at the same age, at nine or ten years old, that the influence of the vernacular peer group becomes predominant.[24] Instead of dealing with isolated individuals, the school is then dealing with children who are integrated into groups of their own, with rewards and value systems which oppose those of the school. Those who know the sociolinguistic situation cannot doubt that reaction against the Bereiter–Engelmann approach in later years will be even more violent on the part of the students involved, and that the rejection of the school system will be even more categorical.

The essential fallacy of the verbal deprivation theory lies in tracing the educational failure of the child to his personal deficiencies. At present, these deficiencies are said to be caused by his home environment. It is traditional to explain a child's failure in school by his inadequacy; but when failure reaches such massive proportions, it seems

[23] See for example, Herbert Gans on "The Peer Group Society," *The Urban Villagers* (N. Y.: Free Press, 1962).

[24] For the relationship between age and membership in peer groups, see Peter Wilmott, *Adolescent Boys of East London* (London: Routledge and Kegan Paul, 1966).

to us necessary to look at the social and cultural obstacles to learning, and the inability of the school to adjust to the social situation. Operation Headstart is designed to repair the child, rather than the school; to the extent that it is based upon this inverted logic, it is bound to fail.

(2) The second area in which the verbal deprivation theory is doing serious harm to our educational system is in the consequences of this failure, and the reaction to it. If Operation Headstart fails, the interpretations which we receive will be from the same educational psychologists who designed this program. The fault will be found not in the data, the theory, nor in the methods used, but rather in the children who have failed to respond to the opportunities offered to them. When Negro children fail to show the significant advance which the deprivation theory predicts, it will be further proof of the profound gulf which separates their mental processes from those of civilized, middle-class mankind.

A sense of the "failure" of Operation Headstart is already in the air. Some prominent figures in the program are reacting to this situation by saying that intervention did not take place early enough. Bettye M. Caldwell notes that:

> . . . the research literature of the last decade dealing with social-class differences has made abundantly clear that all parents are not qualified to provide even the basic essentials of physical and psychological care to their children. (Caldwell 1967:16)

The deficit theory now begins to focus on the "long-standing patterns of parental deficit" which fill the literature. "There is, perhaps unfortunately," writes Caldwell, "no literacy test for motherhood." Failing such eugenic measures, she has proposed "educationally oriented day care for culturally deprived children between six months and three years of age." The children are returned home each evening to "maintain primary emotional relationships with their own families," but during the day they are removed to "hopefully prevent the deceleration in rate of development which seems to occur in many deprived children around the age of two to three years." (Caldwell 1967:17)

There are others who feel that even the best of the intervention programs, such as those of Bereiter and Engelmann, will not help the Negro child no matter when they are applied—that we are faced once again with the "inevitable hypothesis" of the genetic inferiority of the Negro people. Many readers of this paper are undoubtedly familiar with the paper of Arthur Jensen in the *Harvard Educational Review* (1969) which received early and widespread publicity. Jensen begins with the following quotation from the United States Commission on Civil Rights as evidence of the failure of compensatory education.

> The fact remains, however, that none of the programs appear to have raised significantly the achievement of participating pupils, as a group, within the period evaluated by the Commission. (p. 138)

Jensen believes that the verbal deprivation theorists with whom he had been associated—Deutsch, Whiteman, Katz, Bereiter—have been given every opportunity to prove their case—and have failed. This opinion is part of the argument which leads him to the overall conclusion that "the preponderance of the evidence is . . . less consistent with a strictly environmental hypothesis than with the genetic hypothesis"; that racism, or the belief in the genetic inferiority of Negroes, is a correct view in the light of the present evidence.

Jensen argues that the middle-class white population is differentiated from the working-class white and Negro population in the ability for "cognitive or conceptual learning," which Jensen calls Level II intelligence as against mere "associative learning" or Level I intelligence:

> certain neural structures must also be available for Level II abilities to develop, and these are conceived of as being different from the neural structures underlying Level I. The genetic factors involved in each of these types of ability are presumed to have become differentially distributed in the population as a function of social class, since Level II has been most important for scholastic performance under the traditional methods of instruction.

Thus Jensen found that one group of middle-class children were helped by their concept-forming ability to recall twenty familiar objects that could be classified into four categories: animals, furniture, clothing, or foods. Lower-class Negro children did just as well as middle-class children with a miscellaneous set, but showed no improvement with objects that could be so categorized.

The research of the educational psychologists cited here is presented in formal and objective style, and is widely received as impartial scientific evidence. Jensen's paper has already been reported by

Joseph Alsop and William F. Buckley Jr. as "massive, apparently authoritative . . ." (N. Y. Post 3/20/69) It is not my intention to examine these materials in detail; but it is important to realize that we are dealing with special pleading by those who have a strong personal commitment. Jensen is concerned with class differences in cognitive style and verbal learning. His earlier papers incorporated the cultural deprivation theory which he now rejects as a basic explanation.[25] He classifies the Negro children who fail in school as "slow–learners" and "mentally–retarded," and urged that we find out how much their retardation is due to environmental factors and how much is due to "more basic biological factors." (Jensen 1968:167) His conviction that the problem must be located in the child leads him to accept and reprint some truly extraordinary data. To support the genetic hypothesis he cites the following table of Heber for the racial distribution of mental retardation.

Estimated prevalence of children with IQs below 75.

SES	White	Negro
1	0.5	3.1
2	0.8	14.5
3	2.1	22.8
4	3.1	37.8
5	7.8	42.9

This report, that almost half of lower-class Negro children are mentally retarded, could be accepted only by someone who has no knowledge of the children or the community. If he had wished to, Jensen could easily have checked this against the records of any school in any urban ghetto area. Taking IQ tests at their face value, there is no correspondence between these figures and the communities we know. For example, among 75 boys we worked with in Central Harlem who would fall into Heber's SES 4 or 5, there were only three with IQs below 75: one spoke very little English, one could barely see, and the third was emotionally disturbed. When the second was retested, he

---

[25] In Deutsch, Katz and Jensen 1968, Jensen expounds the verbal deprivation theory in considerable detail. For example: "During this 'labeling' period . . . some very important social-class differences may exert their effects on verbal learning. Lower-class parents engage in relatively little of this naming or 'labeling' play with their children . . . That words are discrete labels for things seems to be better known by the middle-class child entering first grade than by the lower-class child. Much of this knowledge is gained in the parent-child interaction, as when the parent looks at a picture book with the child . . ." (p. 119).

scored 91, and the third retested at 87.[26] There are of course hundreds of realistic reports available to Jensen: he simply selected one which would strengthen his case for the genetic inferiority of Negro children, and deliberately deleted the information that this was a study of an area selected in advance because of its high incidence of mental retardation.[27]

In so doing, Jensen was following a standing tradition among the psychologists who developed the deficit hypothesis. The core of Martin Deutsch's environmental explanation of low school performance is the Deprivation Index—a numerical scale based on six dichotomized variables. One variable is "The educational aspirational level of the parent for the child." Most people would agree that a parent who did not care if a child finished high school would be a disadvantageous factor in the child's educational career. In dichotomizing this variable Deutsch was faced with the embarrassing fact that the educational aspiration of Negro parents is in fact very high—higher than for the white population, as he shows in other papers.[28] In order to make the Deprivation Index work, he therefore set the cutting point for the deprived group as "college or less." (Whiteman and Deutsch 1968:100) Thus if a Negro child's father says that he wants his son to go all the way through college, the child will fall into the "deprived" class on this variable. In order to receive the two points given to the "less deprived" on the index, it would be necessary for the child's parents to insist on graduate school or medical school! This decision is never discussed by the author: it simply stands as a *fait accompli* in the tables. This is the type of data manipulation carried on by those who are strongly committed to a particular hypothesis; the selection and presentation of the data are heavily determined by the desire of the writers to make things come out right.

No one can doubt that the inadequacy of Operation Headstart and

[26] Heber's studies of 88 Negro mothers in Milwaukee are cited frequently throughout Jensen 1969. The estimates in this table are not given in relation to a particular Milwaukee sample, but for the general population. Heber's study was specifically designed to cover an area of Milwaukee which was known to contain a large concentration of retarded children, Negro and white, and he has stated that his findings were "grossly misinterpreted" by Jensen (*Milwaukee Sentinel*, June 11, 1969).

[27] The IQ scores given here are from group rather than individual tests and must therefore not be weighted heavily: the scores are from the Pintner-Cunningham test, usually given in the first grade in New York City schools in the 1950s.

[28] Table 15–1 in Deutsch and associates 1967:312, section C, shows that some degree of college training was desired by 96, 97 and 100 percent of Negro parents in Class Levels I, II, and III respectively. The corresponding figures for whites were 79, 95, and 97 percent.

of the verbal deprivation hypothesis has now become a crucial issue in our society.[29] The controversy which is beginning over Jensen's article will undoubtedly take as given that programs such as Bereiter and Engelmann's have tested and measured the verbal capacity of the ghetto child. The cultural sociolinguistic obstacles to this intervention program are not considered; and the argument proceeds upon the data provided by the large, friendly interviewers that we have seen at work in the extracts given above.

6. THE LINGUISTIC VIEW

Linguists are in an excellent position to demonstrate the fallacies of the verbal deprivation theory. All linguists agree that nonstandard dialects are highly structured systems; they do not see these dialects as accumulations of errors caused by the failure of their speakers to master standard English. When linguists hear Negro children saying *He crazy* or *Her my friend* they do not hear a "primitive language." Nor do they believe that the speech of working-class people is merely a form of emotional expression, incapable of expressing logical thought.

All linguists who work with nonstandard Negro English recognize that it is a separate system, closely related to standard English, but set apart from the surrounding white dialects by a number of persistent and systematic differences. Differences in analysis by various linguists in recent years are the inevitable products of differing theoretical approaches and perspectives as we explore these dialect patterns by different routes—differences which are rapidly diminishing as we exchange our findings. For example, Stewart differs with me on how deeply the invariant *be* of *She be always messin' around* is integrated into the semantics of the copula system with *am, is, are*, etc. The position and meaning of *have . . . -ed* in NNE is very unclear, and there are a variety of positions on this point. But the grammatical features involved are not the fundamental predicators of the logical

[29] The negative report of the Westinghouse Learning Corporation and Ohio University on Operation Headstart was published in the *New York Times* (on April 13, 1969). This evidence for the failure of the program is widely publicized, and it seems likely that the report's discouraging "conclusions will be used by conservative Congressmen as a weapon against any kind of expenditure for disadvantaged" children, especially Negroes. The two hypotheses mentioned to account for this failure are that the impact of Headstart is lost through poor teaching later on, and more recently, that poor children have been so badly damaged in infancy by their lower-class environment that Headstart cannot make much difference. The third "inevitable" hypothesis of Jensen is not reported here.

system. They are optional ways of contrasting, foregrounding, emphasizing, or deleting elements of the underlying sentence. There are a few semantic features of NNE grammar which may be unique to this system. But the semantic features we are talking about are items such as "habitual," "general," "intensive." These linguistic markers are essentially *points of view*—different ways of looking at the same events, and they do not determine the truth values of propositions upon which all speakers of English agree.

The great majority of the differences between NNE and SE do not even represent such subtle semantic features as these, but rather extensions and restrictions of certain formal rules, and different choices of redundant elements. For example, SE uses two signals to express the progressive: *be* and *-ing*, while NNE often drops the former. SE signals the third person in the present by the subject noun phrase and by a third singular *-s*; NNE does not have this second redundant feature. On the other hand, NNE uses redundant negative elements in negative concord, uses possessives like *mines*, uses *or either* where SE uses a simple *or*, and so on.

When linguists say that NNE is a "system," we mean that it differs from other dialects in regular and rule-governed ways, so that it has equivalent ways of expressing the same logical content. When we say that it is a "separate" subsystem, we mean that there are compensating sets of rules which combine in different ways to preserve the distinctions found in other dialects. Thus as noted above NNE does not use the *if* or *whether* complementizer in embedded questions, but the meaning is preserved by the formal device of reversing the order of subject and auxiliary.

Linguists therefore speak with a single voice in condemning Bereiter's view that the vernacular can be disregarded. I have exchanged views on this matter with all of the participants in the Round Table, and their response shows complete agreement in rejecting the verbal deprivation theory and its misapprehension of the nature of language. The other papers in this series will testify to the strength of the linguistic view in this area. It was William Stewart who first pointed out that Negro English should be studied as a coherent system; and in this all of us follow his lead. Dialectologists like Raven McDavid, Albert Marckwardt, and Roger Shuy have been working for years against the notion that vernacular dialects are inferior and illogical means of communication; and their views are well represented here. As the overwhelming testimony of this conference shows, linguists agree that teachers must know as much as possible about nonstandard Negro English as a communicative system.

The exact nature and relative importance of the structural differences between NNE and SE are not in question here. It is agreed that the teacher must approach the teaching of the standard through a knowledge of the child's own system. The methods used in "teaching English as a foreign language" are invoked, not to declare that NNE is a foreign language, but to underline the importance of studying the native dialect as a coherent system for communication. This is, in fact, the method that should be applied in any English class.

Linguists are also in an excellent position to assess Jensen's claim that the middle-class white population is superior to the working-class and Negro populations in the distribution of "Level II" or "conceptual" intelligence. The notion that large numbers of children have no capacity for conceptual thinking would inevitably mean that they speak a primitive language, for even the simplest linguistic rules we discussed above involve conceptual operations more complex than those used in the experiment cited by Jensen. Let us consider what is involved in the use of the general English rule that incorporates the negative with the first indefinite. To learn and use this rule, one must first identify the class of indefinites involved: *any, one, ever,* which are formally quite diverse. How is this done? These indefinites share a number of common properties which can be expressed as the concepts "indefinite," "hypothetical," and "nonpartitive." One might argue that these indefinites are learned as a simple list by "association" learning. But this is only one of the many syntactic rules involving indefinites— rules known to every speaker of English, which could not be learned except by an understanding of their common, abstract properties. For example, everyone "knows" unconsciously that *anyone* cannot be used with preterite verbs or progressives. One does not say, *Anyone went to the party* or *Anyone is going to the party.* The rule which operates here is sensitive to the property [+hypothetical] of the indefinites. Whenever the proposition is not inconsistent with this feature, *anyone* can be used. Everyone "knows" therefore that one can say *Anyone who was anyone went to the party,* or *If anyone went to the party* . . . or *Before anyone went to the party* . . . There is another is another property of *anyone* which is grasped unconsciously by all native speakers of English: it is [+distributive]. Thus if we need one more man for a game of bridge or basketball, and there is a crowd outside, we ask, *Do any of you want to play?* not *Do some of you want to play?* In both cases, we are considering a plurality, but with *any* we consider them one at a time, or distributively.

What are we then to make of Jensen's contention that Level I thinkers cannot make use of the concept "animal" to group together a miscellaneous set of toy animals? It is one thing to say that someone is not in the habit of using a certain skill. But to say that his failure to use it is genetically determined implies dramatic consequences for other forms of behavior, which are not found in experience; the knowledge of what people must do in order to learn language makes Jensen's theories seem more and more distant from the realities of human behavior. Like Bereiter and Engelmann, Jensen is handicapped by his ignorance of the most basic facts about human language and the people who speak it.

There is no reason to believe that any nonstandard vernacular is in itself an obstacle to learning. The chief problem is ignorance of language on the part of all concerned. Our job as linguists is to remedy this ignorance: Bereiter and Engelmann want to reinforce it and justify it. Teachers are now being told to ignore the language of Negro children as unworthy of attention and useless for learning. They are being taught to hear every natural utterance of the child as evidence of his mental inferiority. As linguists we are unanimous in condemning this view as bad observation, bad theory, and bad practice.

That educational psychology should be strongly influenced by a theory so false to the facts of language is unfortunate; but that children should be the victims of this ignorance is intolerable. It may seem that the fallacies of the verbal deprivation theory are so obvious that they are hardly worth exposing; I have tried to show that it is an important job for us to undertake. If linguists can contribute some of their available knowledge and energy towards this end, we will have done a great deal to justify the support that society has given to basic research in our field.

REFERENCES

Bereiter, Carl, et al. 1966. "An Academically Oriented Pre-School for Culturally Deprived Children." In Fred M. Hechinger (ed.), *Pre-School Education Today.* (New York, Doubleday) 105–137.

———— and Siegfried Engelmann. 1966. *Teaching Disadvantaged Children in the Preschool.* Englewood Cliffs, N. J., Prentice-Hall.

Caldwell, Bettye M. 1967. "What is the Optimal Learning Environment for the Young Child?" *American Journal of Orthopsychiatry,* Vol. XXXVII, No. 1, 8–21.

Chomsky, Noam. 1965. *Aspects of the Theory of Syntax.* Cambridge, Mass., M. I. T. Press.

Deutsch, Martin, and Associates. 1967. *The Disadvantaged Child.* New York, Basic Books.

————, Irwin Katz, and Arthur R. Jensen (eds.). 1968. *Social Class, Race, and Psychological Development.* New York, Holt.

Jensen, Arthur. 1968. "Social Class and Verbal Learning." In Deutsch, Katz, and Jensen 1968.

————. 1969. "How Much Can We Boost IQ and Scholastic Achievement?" *Harvard Educational Review*, Vol. 39, No. 1.

Labov, William. 1967. "Some Sources of Reading Problems for Negro Speakers of Non-Standard English." In A. Frazier (ed.), *New Directions in Elementary English* (Champaign, Ill., National Council of Teachers of English), 140–167. Reprinted in Joan C. Baratz and Roger W. Shuy. 1969. *Teaching Black Children to Read.* (Washington, D. C., Center for Applied Linguistics), 29–67.

————, Paul Cohen, and Clarence Robins. 1965. *A Preliminary Study of the Structure of English Used by Negro and Puerto Rican Speakers in New York City.* Final Report, Cooperative Research Project No. 3091, Office of Education, Washington, D. C.

————, Paul Cohen, Clarence Robins, and John Lewis. 1968. *A Study of the Non-Standard English of Negro and Puerto Rican Speakers in New York City.* Final Report, Cooperative Research Project No. 3288, Office of Education, Washington, D. C. Vol I and Vol. II.

————, and Clarence Robins. 1969. "A Note on the Relation of Reading Failure to Peer-Group Status in Urban Ghettos." *The Teachers College Record*, Volume 70, Number 5.

Rosenthal, Robert, and Lenore Jacobson. 1968. "Self-Fulfilling Prophecies in the Classroom: Teachers' Expectations as Unintended Determinants of Pupils' Intellectual Competence." In Deutsch, Katz, and Jensen 1968.

Whiteman, Martin, and Martin Deutsch. "Social Disadvantage as Related to Intellective and Language Development." In Deutsch, Katz, and Jensen 1968.